D1082191

2 CORINTHIANS

THE IVP NEW TESTAMENT COMMENTARY SERIES

LINDA L. BELLEVILLE

GRANT R. OSBORNE, SERIES EDITOR

D. STUART BRISCOE AND HADDON ROBINSON,
CONSULTING EDITORS

IVP Academic

An imprint of InterVarsity Press
Downers Grove, Illinois

InterVarsity Press
P.O. Box 1400, Downers Grove, IL 60515-1426
World Wide Web: www.ivpress.com
E-mail: email@ivpress.com

InterVarsity Press® is the book-publishing division of InterVarsity Christian Fellowship/USA®, a movement of students and faculty active on campus at hundreds of universities, colleges and schools of nursing in the United States of America, and a member movement of the International Fellowship of Evangelical Students. For information about local and regional activities, write Public Relations Dept., InterVarsity Christian Fellowship/USA, 6400 Schroeder Rd., P.O. Box 7895, Madison, WI 53707-7895, or visit the IVCF website at <www.intervarsity.org>.

Design: Cindy Kiple

Images: Einzug in Jerusalem—Entry into Jerusalem by Wilhelm Morgner at Museum am Ostwall, Dortmund, Germany. Erich Lessing/Art Resource, NY.

ISBN 978-0-8308-4008-3

Printed in the United States of America ∞

Library of Congress Cataloging-in-Publication Data

Belleville, Linda L.
  2 Corinthians/Linda L. Belleville.
    p. cm.—(The IVP New Tesament commentary series:8)
  Includes bibliographical references.
  ISBN 0-8308-1808-1 (cloth: alk. paper)
  1. Bible.   N.T. Corinthians, 2nd—Commentaries.   Title.
  II. Series.
  BS2675.3.B45   1995
227'.3077—dc20

                                                                      95-42910

                                                                           CIP

P	18	17	16	15	14	13	12	11	10	9	8	7	6	5	4	3	2	1
Y	26	25	24	23	22	21	20	19	18	17	16	15	14	13	12	11

In memory of my father
Joseph A. Stipek (1910-1994)

General Preface

In an age of proliferating commentary series, one might easily ask why add yet another to the seeming glut. The simplest answer is that no other series has yet achieved what we had in mind—a series to and from the church, that seeks to move from the text to its contemporary relevance and application.

No other series offers the unique combination of solid, biblical exposition and helpful explanatory notes in the same user-friendly format. No other series has tapped the unique blend of scholars and pastors who share both a passion for faithful exegesis and a deep concern for the church. Based on the New International Version of the Bible, one of the most widely used modern translations, the IVP New Testament Commentary Series builds on the NIV's reputation for clarity and accuracy. Individual commentators indicate clearly whenever they depart from the standard translation as required by their understanding of the original Greek text.

The series contributors represent a wide range of theological traditions, united by a common commitment to the authority of Scripture for Christian faith and practice. Their efforts here are directed toward applying the unchanging message of the New Testament to the ever-changing world in which we live.

Readers will find in each volume not only traditional discussions of authorship and backgrounds, but useful summaries of principal themes and approaches to contemporary application. To bridge the gap between commentaries that stress the flow of an author's argument but skip over exegetical nettles and those that simply jump from one difficulty to another, we have developed our unique format that expounds the text in uninterrupted form on the upper portion of each page while dealing with other issues underneath in verse-keyed notes. To avoid clutter we have also adopted a social studies note system that keys references to the bibliography.

We offer the series in hope that pastors, students, Bible teachers and small group leaders of all sorts will find it a valuable aid—one that stretches the mind and moves the heart to ever-growing faithfulness and obedience to our Lord Jesus Christ.

Author's Preface

I welcome the opportunity to express my appreciation to Jim Hoover at InterVarsity Press for extending an invitation to write a commentary on a Pauline letter that has played a central role in my thinking, writing and teaching since seminary days. It has been a joy and a challenge to consider the relevance of Paul's most personal and pastoral of missives for ministry in today's church and society.

A number of other acknowledgments are needed. I am deeply indebted to my tutorial assistant Bob Wood, my husband Brian and my sister-in-law Brenda Belleville for their helpful suggestions, careful reading and meticulous correcting of the first draft. I also wish to thank my students at North Park Theological Seminary for their keen interaction and personal support inside and outside the classroom—and my children Katie and Paul for their youthful encouragement. An additional word of appreciation is due to editors Grant Osborne and Stuart Briscoe, who read the manuscript with a careful eye to relevance and application. Finally, I would be remiss not to mention my colleagues at North Park, who model the grace of our Lord Jesus Christ on a daily basis.

Introduction

It has been said that conflict reveals the measure of a person. This is particularly the case for Paul as he writes 2 Corinthians. The Corinthians, like many Christians today, were slow learners and set in their ways, often making the same mistakes and constantly straining at the bit. In writing 2 Corinthians Paul cajoles, congratulates, scolds, bares his heart, confides, reasons and plays the fool in his attempt to get the church back on track and away from apostolic competitors who do not have the church's best interests at heart. The letter is a gold mine for pastors and churches alike, because in it we see a broad range of pastoral techniques applied to a diversity of theological and practical issues, including stewardship of finances, Christian suffering, church discipline, conflict management, interpersonal relationships, the nature of the gospel ministry, interchurch competition, the transforming work of the Spirit, death and mortality, life and resurrection, idolatry, commercialism, and evangelistic strategies and methods.

☐ Life Setting

Paul's relationship with the Corinthian church was for the most part stormy, marked by almost continuous challenges to his apostolic authority, ministerial credentials and personal spirituality. To begin to understand 2 Corinthians, which comes at the tail end of a long and stressful exchange, we need to grasp something about the city of Corinth, the constituency of the church and the historical developments surrounding the relationship between Paul and the Corinthian Christians—a relationship that would tax the resources, patience and stamina of even the most gifted pastors and church leaders today.

The City In 146 B.C. Corinth was virtually destroyed, the male population was exterminated, and the women and children were sold into slavery. This punishment was carried out by the Roman consul Lucius Mummius in reprisal for the city's participation in a revolt against Rome. The city was rebuilt by Julius Caesar in 46 B.C. and resettled as a Roman colony with retired soldiers and freedmen drawn primarily from the ranks of the poor (Strabo *Geography* 8.6.23). Under Emperor Augustus it was designated the capital of the province in 27 B.C., and it remained so when in A.D. 44 Achaia was granted senatorial status under the governance of a proconsul. In a moment of enthusiasm at the Isthmian Games, Emperor Nero (A.D. 54-68) declared the city free.

Corinth was one of the most strategically located cities in the Greco-Roman Empire. On a plateau overlooking the Isthmus of Corinth, which separated the northern and southern parts of the province and the western (Corinthian Gulf) and eastern (Saronic Gulf) sea straits, its geographical location allowed for the control of both north-south trade routes and east-west shipping. In the space of a few decades after its rebuilding, the city regained its former prestige and became a major center of trade and industry. Its reputation was enhanced by the presence of the temple of Aphrodite (the goddess of love, fertility and beauty), situated 1,886 feet up on the Acrocorinth, and by the sanctuary of Asclepius (god of healing). New Corinth, like ancient Corinth, became well known during Roman times as a place of commercialized pleasure (Strabo *Geography* 8.6.20; as early as Aristophanes [fifth-fourth century B.C.] "to Corinthianize" was polite Greek for practicing immorality) and as host to the Isthmian games—not unlike our Olympic Games.

Numbering some 500,000 slaves and 200,000 nonslaves at its height, Corinth's cosmopolitan population was made up of a mix of local

Greeks, Orientals (including a large number of Jews) and Italians. As a comparatively new, thriving city of the nouveaux riches, it could be compared with urban areas like San Francisco, Chicago and Boston and their "yuppie" populations.

The Social Background of the Corinthian Church "Neither the sexually immoral nor idolaters nor adulterers nor male prostitutes nor homosexual offenders . . . will inherit the kingdom of God. And that is what some of you were" (1 Cor 6:9-11). Paul's description of the Corinthian believers as having been actively involved in the idolatry and immorality of their society points to a primarily Gentile constituency. "Not many of you were wise by human standards; not many were influential; not many were of noble birth" (1 Cor 1:26) suggests that the majority lacked education, position in society or association with the moneyed families of the city. Nonetheless, there were some from the upper ranks of society. Seven members are described in language that suggests social or financial standing (Titius Justus, Acts 18:7; Crispus, Acts 18:8; Stephanas, 1 Cor 1:16; Gaius, Rom 16:23; Priscilla and Aquila, Acts 18:2, 18; Rom 16:3-5; Phoebe, Rom 16:1-2; Erastus, Rom 16:23; see Theissen 1982:69-119).

While the majority were not well endowed in a material or educational sense, they became amply endowed in a spiritual sense. "For in [Christ] you have been enriched in every way. . . . You do not lack any spiritual gift," states Paul (1 Cor 1:5-7). Yet this very enrichment resulted in an inflated self-image and a spiritual arrogance that taxed Paul's patience as a pastor (1 Cor 4:14-15; 2 Cor 6:11-13; 13:5-10) and challenged his authority as an apostle (1 Cor 4:18-21; 2 Cor 13:1-10).

The Paul-Corinthian Relationship The Paul-Corinthian relationship, spanning seven years, three personal visits and four letters, is one of the most complex topics in New Testament studies. In view of this complexity, it may be helpful to think of the relationship in terms of the following ten stages of development.

Stage One After a forced exit from Thessalonica and again from Berea (Acts 17:1-15; 1 Thess 2:17-18), Paul made his way down the Aegean coast to Athens for a short layover (Acts 17:16-34; 1 Thess 3:1-2) and then to Corinth, where he settled down for about a year and a half (A.D. 50-52; Acts 18:1-18). It is quite likely that he initially came to Corinth prior to the Isthmian Games to ply his native Cilician trade as a worker of goat's-hair cloth. (Goat's-hair cloth was used to make cloaks, curtains, tents and other fabrics intended to give protection against the damp.) At some point he received enough financial support from the Macedonian churches that he was able to drop his trade and give full attention to evangelism (Acts 18:5).

Stage Two About A.D. 52 Paul left Corinth to briefly visit Jerusalem and then Antioch, his home base and supporting church. From there he went to Ephesus and set up his base of operations in the lecture hall of a local philosopher named Tyrannus (literally "the tyrant"). Three years were spent evangelizing, as Luke reports, "all the Jews and Greeks who lived in the province of Asia" (Acts 19:10). It was during this three-year period that Paul wrote the Corinthians three letters and made his second visit to the city.

Stage Three Somewhere between A.D. 52 and 53 Paul wrote the first of four letters to Corinth, commonly called the "previous letter." He makes reference to this letter in 1 Corinthians 5:9, where he states, "I have written you in my letter not to associate with sexually immoral people." From Paul's comment we can gather that this was a letter reproving the believers for not severing their ties with the immorality so prevalent around them. While some think that the "previous letter" is to be identified with 2 Corinthians 6:14—7:1, it is likely that this first letter was not preserved (see "Critical Issues," pp. 26-30).

Stage Four In 1 Corinthians 7:1 Paul refers to a letter that the Corinthian church sent to him sometime between A.D. 53 and 54 ("Now for the matters you wrote about"). It was delivered by a three-person delegation that quite likely waited for a response (1 Cor 16:17, "I was glad when Stephanas, Fortunatus and Achaicus arrived"). The concerns raised by the church in their letter to Paul are addressed in 1 Corinthians 7—16, prefaced by the phrase *now about (peri de)*. These concerns included questions about the preferability of celibacy to marriage (7:1-40), buying meat that had been sacrificed to an idol (8:1—9:27; 10:23-32), the superiority of certain spiritual gifts over others (12:1—14:40), how to go about collecting money for the Jerusalem church relief fund (16:1-4) and when they could expect a visit from Apollos (16:12).

Stage Five In the spring of A.D. 54 (compare 1 Cor 5:7-8 and 16:8) Paul responded to the Corinthians' letter with our canonical 1 Corinthians (probably taken back to Corinth by Stephanus, Fortunatus and Achaicus, 16:17). In addition to the questions the Corinthians raised through official sources (7:1; 16:17), Paul also received news of a more disturbing nature through unofficial sources ("Chloe's household," 1:11; "I hear that," 11:18). That the church was having difficulty adjusting to a new lifestyle and a new set of values is obvious from reports of incest (5:1-12), lawsuits (6:1-11), members' continuing to engage the services of local prostitutes (6:12-20), idolatry (10:1-22) and drunkenness at the Lord's Supper (11:17-34). At the heart of the Corinthians' problems was an attitude of spiritual arrogance. "It is actually reported," Paul says, "that there is sexual immorality among you, and of a kind that does not occur even among pagans: A man has his father's wife. And you are proud!" (5:1-2).

Stage Six There is little indication that Paul's correction in 1 Corinthians had its intended effect. In fact, it appears that the relationship between Paul and the church deteriorated. Evidence that all was not well is already there in 1 Corinthians. Paul refers to "some" who "have become arrogant, as if I were not coming to you" (4:18). There was also some suspicion that he was not truly an apostle because he would not accept pay from them but instead worked to support himself (9:1-18).

News of this deteriorating situation reached Paul and resulted in what is usually called Paul's "painful visit" in the summer or fall of A.D. 54 (2 Cor 2:1; 12:14, 21; 13:1-2). It turned out to be painful because while he was there, someone in the congregation publicly insulted him and challenged his authority, demanding proof that Christ was speaking through him (13:3). The church, meanwhile, sat by and did nothing to support Paul. After issuing a strong rebuke (13:2), Paul returned to Ephesus, abandoning his plan to visit the Macedonian churches, revisit Corinth (1:16) and then go on to Jerusalem with the collection for the poor (Gal 2:10; for the opinion that the challenge occurred after Paul left Corinth and was directed at him through Timothy, his second in command, see M. J. Harris 1976:309).

Stage Seven When Paul returned to Ephesus, he wrote the church a "severe letter" by means of which he hoped to avoid another painful encounter with them (2 Cor 1:23). In it he rebuked them for not coming to his aid when publicly confronted, tested their obedience to apostolic authority and called them to show their loyalty by punishing the individual who had challenged him (2:1-11; 7:8-13). That this was a difficult letter for Paul to compose is clear from his statement that he wrote "out of great distress and anguish of heart and with many tears" (2:4). It was delivered, probably in the early part of 55, by Titus, who had the difficult job of attempting to enforce Paul's directives (7:5-16).

Do we have this letter? Earlier commentators tended to think so. It was typically identified with 1 Corinthians on the basis of an equation of "the one who did the wrong" and "the injured party" in 2 Corinthians 7:12 with the incestuous man and the man's father in 1 Corinthians 5:1-5. But Paul's statements about his personal forgiveness of the man and the severe letter's primary intent to secure the Corinthians' obedience do not square with the data of 1 Corinthians. So this theory has now been virtually abandoned. More recently it has been argued that 2 Corinthians 10—13 preserves at least a portion of the severe letter. But major discrepancies between Paul's description of the severe letter and chapters 10—13 have led most to conclude that the Corinthian church did not preserve it (see "Critical Issues," pp. 30-33).

Stage Eight In the summer of 55 Paul left Ephesus to do some evangelism in Troas (2 Cor 2:12). Along the way he and his traveling companions had a near-death experience in the province of Asia (1:8), where having received "the sentence of death," they "despaired even of life" (1:8-9). After being "delivered . . . from such a deadly peril" (1:10), Paul and company made their way to Troas. But in spite of what looked to be a promising evangelistic venture, he became too anxious about the Corinthian response to his severe letter to continue (2:12-13). Titus was apparently supposed to meet him in Troas, and when he did not come, Paul went on to Macedonia in the hopes of hearing news of him and his Corinthian mission (2:13).

Stage Nine Paul did finally meet up with Titus somewhere in Macedonia (the exact location is not identified). The news Titus brought regarding the Corinthian church was both good and bad. The good news was that the Corinthians had obeyed Paul's command to punish the "offender" (2 Cor 2:5-11; 7:6-16) and in this way demonstrated their loyalty to Paul. The bad news was twofold; criticisms were being leveled against him on two fronts. First, the Corinthians were charging him with fickleness in arranging his travel plans—saying yes to paying them a return visit only to change his mind at a later point (1:12—2:4). They also accused him of professional arrogance while he lacked appropriate credentials (3:1—4:5). Second, Paul was being attacked by a group of itinerant Jewish Christian preachers who were trying to erode his pastoral authority at Corinth by saying that he did not measure up to the standards one would expect of a genuine gospel minister (12:11-13). He did not carry letters of recommendation (3:1-3) or preach the gospel for pay, as a legitimate evangelist would (2:17; 11:7). He was also not a very effective speaker, as evidenced by his inability to reach his own people (3:12-18; 11:6) and his lack of charisma (10:10). And where was the display of the Spirit in revelations (12:1), ecstatic experiences (12:2-6) and the working of miracles (12:12)? When you came right down to it, Paul was a big talker in his letters but amounted to nothing in person (10:10). Paul responds to these charges with our canonical 2 Corinthians, written in either the fall of A.D. 55 or 56 (see p. 20).

Stage Ten In the winter of A.D. 56 Paul made a third and final visit to Corinth. The account in Acts 20:2-3 states that he "arrived in Greece, where he stayed for three months." The length of Paul's stay suggests that 2 Corinthians had been successful. Paul's statement in Romans 15:26 (written during his stay in Greece) that "Macedonia and Achaia were pleased to make a contribution for the poor among the saints in Jerusalem" implies this as well. But the success was only temporary. Forty years later, Clement, bishop of Rome, had to write the Corinthian church a letter that addressed some of the same problems (A.D. 96).

□ **The Historical Situation**

Authorship New Testament scholarship typically groups 2 Corinthians with the Pauline letters referred to as the Hauptbriefe—Romans, 1 Corinthians, 2 Corinthians and Galatians, the four major letters for which Pauline authorship is not contested. The author is clearly identified at the start ("Paul, an apostle of Christ Jesus by the will of God," 1:1), as well as at the close ("I appeal to you—I, Paul," 10:1). This accords with the external evidence. Second Corinthians is included in Marcion's Canon (c. 140) and in the Muratorian Canon (c. 170). Polycarp seems to know it (c. 110, *Letter to the Philippians* 2.6, 11), but Irenaeus is the first to quote it explicitly (c. 175, *Adversus Haereses* 4.28.3).

Date An exact date for 2 Corinthians is hard to determine. There are two likely possibilities. One is that the letter was written about one year after the writing of 1 Corinthians. In 2 Corinthians 9:2 Paul speaks of the Achaian churches' readiness since "last year" *(apo perysi)* to give to the Jerusalem relief fund. This may well refer to the Corinthians' earlier query about the mechanics of collecting money for this fund ("Now about the collection," 1 Cor 16:1). Since the Corinthians' query is commonly dated in the spring of 54, this would place the writing of 2 Corinthians in A.D. 55, or, more precisely, in the latter months of this year, to accommodate a painful visit, a severe letter, a near-death experience in Asia, a short period of evangelism in Troas and travel to Macedonia.

The difficulty with an A.D. 55 date, however, is Paul's comment in Romans 15:19 that by the time he visited Corinth for the third and final time (in the winter of 56) he had proclaimed the gospel from Jerusalem "all the way around to Illyricum." The question is where to fit a pioneer work in the western portion of the Balkan peninsula. There is little room for it from A.D. 54 to A.D. 55—and even less if, as some believe, Philippians is to be dated during this period. A ready solution is to date this evangelistic foray after Paul's trip to Macedonia in the fall of 55. If so, this would delay the writing of 2 Corinthians until the fall of 56.

Place of Composition Paul was in the province of Macedonia when he wrote 2 Corinthians. This is clear from 7:5 ("when we came into Macedonia"), 8:1 ("we want you to know about the grace that God has given the Macedonian churches") and 9:2 ("I have been boasting about it to the Macedonians"). The subscription in B^1 P K 81 104 locates Paul more specifically in Philippi ("written from Philippi"). But of this we cannot be certain. Second Corinthians was then delivered by Titus and two church representatives, who later traveled with Paul to Jerusalem with the relief funds (8:16-24; see the commentary at 8:1).

Structure Following the private letter conventions of the day, 2 Corinthians includes a letter opening ("Paul to Corinth, greetings," 1:1-2), a thanksgiving section ("Praise be to the God and Father of our Lord Jesus Christ," 1:3-7), a body opening ("We do not want you to be uninformed, brothers," 1:8-11), a body middle ("Now this is our boast," 1:12—13:9), a body closing ("This is why I write these things," 13:10-11) and a letter closing ("Greet one another with a holy kiss," 13:12-14).

Beyond this, there are four ways in which the letter departs from standard first-century conventions. First, a eulogy ("Praise be to God who . . .") replaces the usual expression of thanksgiving, signaling a more remote—if not strained—relationship between Paul and the Corinthians (Belleville 1991:112-14).

Second, there are two body-closing sections. Customarily the Hellenistic letter had one closing section, which typically included (1) a purpose for writing ("I do not say this to condemn you," 7:3; "This is why I write these things," 13:10), (2) a reference to the writer-reader relationship ("You have such a place in our hearts that we would live or die with you," 7:3), (3) the sending of an emissary ("the coming of Titus," 7:6) and (4) the announcement of a personal visit ("this will be my third visit," 13:1; Doty 1973). The first three elements occur in 7:3-13, while the first and fourth appear in chapters 10—13.

Third, Paul goes on at great length about his forthcoming visit. While the body-closing section typically amounted to a few lines or paragraphs, in 2 Corinthians Paul devotes four chapters to his upcoming visit.

And fourth, the two body-closing sections are separated by two chapters asking the Corinthians to follow through on what they have pledged for the Jerusalem collection.

What ties chapters 7—13 together is what scholars commonly call "visit-talk." Chapter 7 is about Titus's trip to Corinth with the severe letter. Chapters 8 and 9 announce the impending visit of Titus and his two companions to complete the Jerusalem collection. Chapters 10—13 are a strong word of warning that on his return visit Paul will not spare those who sinned earlier. In fact, visit-talk not only closes the letter body but also opens it. In the first half of chapter 1 Paul shares with the church news of the deadly peril that he faced while traveling from Ephesus to Troas, while in the second half of the chapter he deals with a charge of fickleness regarding his travel plans. In chapter 2 Paul continues his visit-talk by telling the Corinthians why a letter had been sent in lieu of a return visit. Indeed, the only chapters that are free from visit-talk are 3—6, and even these make reference to Paul's founding visit (3:1-3) and his missionary travels (6:3-10).

The emphasis on visit-talk in 2 Corinthians suggests that this is at the heart of a number of problems Paul was having with the church. His role was that of an absentee pastor who was trying to sustain a relationship with a congregation through the occasional visit, the use of on-site colleagues like Timothy and Titus, and the occasional letter, which was intended as a substitute for his apostolic and pastoral presence. Some at Corinth were quick to spot the failings of this approach and to exploit its weaknesses. They charged Paul with making travel plans that he never intended to keep and with writing threatening letters that he never intended to enforce in person.

Purpose Paul's main purpose in writing 2 Corinthians was to tie the congregation closer to himself by gaining their complete confidence. In so doing, he hoped to distance the church from self-acclaimed apostolic meddlers, whose intent was not to help the church but to subjugate it ("enslaves you or exploits you or takes advantage of you or pushes himself forward or slaps you in the face," 11:20). In the first seven chapters Paul tries to gain the Corinthians' trust by demonstrating the validity of his ministry. From a literary standpoint, chapters 1—7 divide into a background section, where Paul sets forth his ministerial credentials (1:8—5:21), and a request section, where he appeals to the church to give him complete loyalty (6:1—7:16) and points to continuing involvement in idolatrous activities as a major obstacle to doing this (6:14—7:1).

Paul's overall strategy for winning the church's allegiance is twofold. One, he seeks to present the Corinthians with credentials that inspire confidence in him as a minister of the gospel and serve as ammunition against the criticisms of intruders who were seeking to displace him at Corinth (5:12), and two, he attempts to show how closely intertwined their lives are, so that to reject him would be in effect to reject themselves. Paul's secondary aims in these chapters are to inform them of his near-death experience in Asia (1:8-11), to explain his change of itinerary (1:12—2:4) and to get them to reaffirm their love for the offender now that he has repented (2:5-11).

Chapters 8—9 are devoted to getting the Corinthians to fulfill what they had promised to contribute toward the Jerusalem relief fund. Paul's strategy is to motivate them by means of the example of the Macedonian churches (8:1-15), the not-so-subtle sending of Titus to see the project to completion and a forthcoming visit of representatives from other churches that have already fulfilled their pledges (8:16—9:6).

Chapters 10—13 amount to a passionate plea not to be fooled by recently come missionaries ("false apostles," 11:13-14), who have their own, and not the Corinthians', best interests at heart (11:1-4). Paul engages in what he calls "foolish boasting"—that is, boasting as the world boasts. So he argues that he is not the least bit inferior to these rival apostles that the Corinthians have come to place such great store in (12:11). He is also concerned that the Corinthians know the criteria for distinguishing true and false apostles—the true apostle's life being marked by hardship, dangers and deprivations, and not by personal acclaim, a winning personality or sensationalism (11:23—12:10). Paul's final purpose is to announce his forthcoming visit and to warn the Corinthians that he will not hesitate to discipline them if they have not cleaned up their act (12:19—13:10).

□ Critical Issues

While the authorship of 2 Corinthians has never been seriously questioned, the integrity of the letter continues to be one of the most discussed and debated critical issues today. Scholarly discussions have filtered down to the church, so it is not uncommon to find someone raising this issue in a Sunday-school class or even assuming as fact that 2 Corinthians is not a unity. In particular, the theory that 2 Corinthians is a composite of a number of letter fragments that were editorially assembled when Paul's letters were being collected is becoming increasingly popular. (See, for example, Hans Dieter Betz's commentary *2 Corinthians 8—9* in the Hermeneia series.) It is therefore important to gain some familiarity with the current issues and debates.

Four blocks of material have been the primary focus of attention: (1)

2:14—7:4, (2) 6:14—7:1, (3) chapters 8—9 and (4) chapters 10—13.

2 Corinthians 2:14—7:4

> Now when I went to Troas to preach the gospel of Christ and found that the Lord had opened a door for me, I still had no peace of mind, because I did not find my brother Titus there. So I said good-by to them and went on to Macedonia. . . . [Now] when we came into Macedonia, this body of ours had no rest, but we were harassed at every turn—conflicts on the outside, fears within. (2:12-13; 7:5)

With increasing frequency today, the integral place of 2:14—7:4 in chapters 1—7 is being called into question. Among the reasons commonly put forward for questioning it are the following:

1. Paul's travel narrative is abruptly broken off at 2:13 and not resumed until 7:5.

2. His apostolic defense in 2:14—7:4 has little if anything to do with the pre- and posttravel narratives.

3. The polemical tone of 2:14—7:4 is in conflict with the conciliatory tone of the surrounding material.

4. It is psychologically improbable that Paul would have broken off the narrative at just this point, thereby leaving the reader in suspense regarding the Corinthians' reaction to the severe letter and Paul's not finding Titus in Troas.

5. The presence at 2:14 of a conventional thanksgiving is at odds with the mood of haste and anxiety in the preceding verses.

In light of these incongruities it is suggested that a later editor of the Pauline corpus inserted 2:14—7:4 at the spot where it is now found in our canonical 2 Corinthians.

Two theories about the origin of 2:14—7:4 have gained the most support among interpolation proponents today. The first considers 2:14—7:4 (except 6:14—7:1) to be part of the first of a series of four or five letters that arose out of a situation of developing tensions between Paul and the Corinthians over the intrusion of itinerant preachers who sought to divert Corinthian support from Paul to their own cause. Günther Bornkamm made this proposal (1961-1962:258-64), and scholars like Dieter Georgi, Wolfgang Schenk, Helmut Koester and Walter Schmithals have agreed with him. The second theory regards 2:14—7:4

and chapters 10—13 as forming Paul's severe letter, written at the height of interaction with his opponents at Corinth and followed by a letter of reconciliation reflecting a resolution of the conflict in Paul's favor. Johannes Weiss set forth this hypothesis in the early decades of this century as part of a broader reconstruction effort involving both Corinthian letters (1970:348). Supporters include Rudolf Bultmann, Philipp Vielhauer, J. T. Dean, Erich Dinkler and Alfred Loisy.

Interpolation theories, however, create more problems than they solve. In the first place, there is no manuscript evidence to suggest that 2 Corinthians circulated in any form other than its present one. In addition, if it is hard to see why Paul would have broken off his travel narrative at this point, it is equally difficult to imagine why an editor would have inserted a fragment at such an unlikely spot. Also, the arguments commonly put forth lose their cumulative force on closer inspection.

First, the line of continuity between 2:12-13 and 7:5-16 is more apparent than real. Verses 12-13 deal with evangelistic ineffectiveness, while 7:5-16 has to do with divine comfort in the midst of trials. Second, there is a commonality of themes and terms in 2:12-17 and 7:3-16 that belies disunity. Chapter 2:12-17 opens and closes with a reference to preaching the gospel, and evangelistic terminology dominates throughout; in 7:3-4 Titus's news and the themes of parental pride and confidence, comfort and joy in affliction find their logical development in verses 5-16. Third, differences in tone and mood are overstated. A polemical note is already struck at 1:12 with Paul's defense of his conduct as a church planter. Nor is it accurate to say that the reader is left in suspense about the church's reaction to Paul's severe letter. The Corinthians' obedience to Paul's directive to punish the offender is already spelled out in 2:5-11.

It is the sudden shift from anxiety in 2:12-13 ("I still had no peace of mind") to thanksgiving at 2:14 ("But thanks be to God, who always leads us in triumphal procession in Christ") that needs some explanation. What is Paul up to here? Explanations include a premature reference to his relief on meeting Titus, a change of pace following a dictation pause and a last-minute introduction of themes that he failed to touch on in his opening eulogy (1:3-11). Yet a look though at the broader context of the letter shows that Paul's shift from anxiety to thanksgiving is an integral part of his repeated emphasis on the ability of God's power to triumph over human weakness. The classic statement is found in 12:9: "[God] said to me, 'My grace is sufficient for you, for my power is made perfect in weakness.' " So for Paul to present the human condition (v. 13) followed by a statement of divine initiative (v. 14) is quite characteristic (compare Rom 6:16-17; 7:24-25; 1 Cor 15:56-57).

2 Corinthians 6:14—7:1

We are not withholding our affection from you, but you are withholding yours from us. As a fair exchange—I speak as to my children—open wide your hearts also. . . . Make room for us in your hearts. We have wronged no one. (6:12-13; 7:2)

The integral place of 6:14—7:1 within chapters 6—7 has also been seriously challenged. It is commonly argued that 6:14—7:1 breaks the connection of thought between 6:13 and 7:2, which otherwise is thought to provide an excellent sequence. It is also claimed that 6:14—7:1 constitutes a literary unit that is complete in itself and that the strict ethic expressed in these verses is at odds with Paul's emphasis on Christian freedom found earlier in the letter. It is further maintained that the subject matter of these verses—the avoidance of idolatrous pagan associations—has nothing whatsoever to do with the immediate context or, for that matter, with anything else in the letter (Belleville 1991:94-95).

A common explanation of this state of affairs has been that 6:14—7:1 is a surviving fragment of the "previous letter" referred to in 1 Corinthians 5:9-11, which was misplaced within the Corinthian correspondence and inserted in its present spot by a later editor. Of late, though, equally serious doubts regarding the authenticity of these verses have been raised, particularly as recent studies have pointed up their strong affinity in concept and terminology with the Qumran Scrolls. Those impressed with the non-Pauline character of these verses have construed 6:14—7:1 as (1) Paul's quotation of an ethical homily or other piece of traditional material (e.g., Murray J. Harris), (2) an apocalyptic-paraenetic fragment inserted fortuitously (Günther Bornkamm), (3) an Essene text that Paul has reworked to reflect a Christian viewpoint (e.g., K. G. Kuhn) or even (4) an anti-Pauline fragment reflecting a viewpoint similar to that of

Paul's Galatian opponents, which the redactor of the Pauline corpus transmitted for reasons unknown to us (Hans Dieter Betz).

Several difficulties present themselves on closer examination of the arguments and the evidence. For one, there is no manuscript, versional or patristic evidence to support a theory of editorial interpolation. Indeed, it is difficult to imagine why any editor would insert a fragment warning against idolatrous associations between the commands "open wide your hearts also" and "make room for us in your hearts." The possibility of an accidental insertion or an interchange of leaves has been suggested, but the likelihood that a leaf was broken off with complete sentences at the beginning and end is slim.

Then too, the internal arguments lose their force on closer inspection. First, the connection between 6:13 and 7:2 is not as smooth as some have claimed. "Open wide your hearts" (6:13) and "Make room for us in your hearts" (7:2), while tedious and redundant if placed back to back, represent a typical Pauline repetition after a block of intervening material (compare "We do not lose heart" in 2 Cor 4:1 and 16; "We are confident" in 2 Cor 5:6 and 8). Second, the verb "give way," "withdraw" (chōrēsate) at 7:2 picks up the verbs "come out from" (exelthate) and "separate yourselves" (aphoristhēte) in 6:17—otherwise the change of verbs makes no sense at all (compare 6:13 and 7:2). Third, "I do not say this to condemn you" (7:3) refers back quite naturally to Paul's call in 6:14—7:1 to sever idolatrous associations but not readily to anything else in the broader context.

It is true, however, that the warning against idolatry and moral defilement is abruptly introduced and the subject not explicitly dealt with elsewhere in the immediate context. The range of explanations include (1) a dictation pause, which allowed Paul time to dwell either on a specific problem related to the Corinthian situation or on a theme that he had recently dealt with in his evangelistic preaching, (2) Paul's tendency to stray off the topic, (3) the need to bring up lingering problems dealt with in more substantial fashion in previous letters, (4) news just received from Titus about continuing problems, (5) the need to clarify his use of "open wide" (platynthēte), which in other contexts carries the connotation of religious permissiveness or, as in Deuteronomy 11:16, conveys a warning against worshiping other gods and (6) an attempt at structural diplomacy, by sandwiching the paraenetic warnings between statements of affection so as to cushion the blow. The vast majority of scholars, however, think that Paul is specifying the cause for the constraint mentioned in 6:12, as either compromising pagan associations or acceptance of Jewish opponents. That Paul would be giving the reason the Corinthians were withholding their affection from him and that he would put it in a sermonic form with which they were familiar seems to be a reasonable explanation of the data.

In terms of the Pauline versus non-Pauline debate, in the final analysis it must be admitted that the sample for comparison is quite small. Still, the final impression is more non-Pauline than Pauline. Second Corinthians 6:14—7:1 contains a noticeably high number of *hapax legomena* (*heterozygeō, metochē, symphōnēsis, synkatathesis, Beliar, pantokratōr* and *molysmos*). Terms found elsewhere in Paul are used differently here ("body/flesh," "share," "promises"). The rhetorical accumulation of parallel phrases in verses 14-16 and the chain of Old Testament citations are not characteristic of Paul. And the phraseology is not particularly Pauline (for example, *echontes oun* + hortatory subjunctive; pollution of the flesh and spirit; the opening and closing citation formulas), nor are some of the ideas (such as cleansing from fleshly and spiritual pollution; the perfection of holiness). The atypical language of the exhortation at 7:1 is to be particularly noted: "Let us purify ourselves from everything that contaminates body and spirit, perfecting holiness out of reverence for God." All this may indeed point to Paul's use of a homily that was especially familiar to the Corinthians. His use of preformed texts is amply documented, and he may well be using one here.

2 Corinthians 8—9

> There is no need for me to write to you about this service to the saints. (9:1)

In 1776 J. S. Semler advanced the idea that 2 Corinthians 9 is a separate letter addressed to Christian congregations in Achaian cities other than Corinth. The basis for this proposal is the fact that chapter 9 seems merely to repeat the content of chapter 8, can stand on its own as a self-contained unit and is introduced by a grammatical construction *(peri men)* that, it is claimed, typically refers to what follows without connection to what has come before. Interpolation theories since Semler have become much more complex and wide-ranging, but the key argument has remained that the Jerusalem collection is introduced in chapter 9 as if there had been no previous mention of it in chapter 8.

One of the most common interpolation theories is that 8:1-24 is a note of commendation for Titus and his two traveling companions ("brothers"), who were entrusted with the task of resuming and completing the Jerusalem collection at Corinth, while 9:1-15 is a commendatory letter to the rest of the congregations in Achaia. This is thought to be confirmed by two facts. First, there are two different target groups. In chapter 8 Paul uses the example of the Macedonians to motivate the Corinthians to complete their collection, while in chapter 9 he uses the forthcoming visit of some Macedonians to spur those "in Achaia" (v. 2) to fulfill their pledge. Second, there seem to be two different missions of the two "brothers" described. In chapter 8 their role is to guarantee that Paul's collecting efforts are above board, whereas in chapter 9 their presence is intended to encourage the Achaian churches to fulfill what they had promised.

Alternatively, it can be argued that there is much that holds these two chapters together. A recent study of *peri men gar* by Stanley K. Stowers (1990:340-48) showed that this construction is actually used in a variety of ways—one of the most common being as a warrant or explanation for what precedes. Chapter 9 would then be Paul's explanation for how the Corinthians are to show the proof of their love and the reason for Paul's pride in them (8:24). Also, the references in 9:3 and 5 to "the brothers" assume 8:6 and 16-24, where Paul spells out who these companions are. Nor does the presence of "Achaia" in chapter 9 mean much, since Paul seems to prefer using provincial titles throughout the letter ("Macedonia" in 1:16; 2:13; 7:5; 8:1; 11:9; "Achaia" in 1:1; 9:2; 11:10).

That the "brothers" would have more than one role regarding the collection reflects the two fronts that Paul must tackle in this letter. He must first safeguard against accusations that the collection is merely a smoke screen for personal funds that he is unwilling to accept overtly (8:20-21). And, second, he must deal with the flagging collection efforts in Corinth (9:3-5).

What of the fact that Paul seems to reintroduce the topic of the collection at 9:1? F. F. Bruce thinks that a short break in dictation can account for it (1971:225). Ralph P. Martin believes that this points to chapters 8 and 9 being separate compositions but written in swift succession (1986:250). Both scenarios are certainly plausible, but a more probable explanation is that Paul is merely recognizing the need to reintroduce the primary topic after a lengthy discussion in 8:16-24 of the credentials and mission of Titus and his two companions. If the article with the noun "service" is understood as referring back to the previous mention of the collection in chapter 8 (anaphoric use), then the ties between the chapters are closely drawn indeed. The NIV catches the sense of what Paul probably intended when it translates 9:1 as "there is no need for me to write to you about *this* service to the saints."

2 Corinthians 10—13

By the meekness and gentleness of Christ, I appeal to you . . . that when I come I may not have to be as bold as I expect to be toward some people who think that we live by the standards of this world. (10:1-2)

Second Corinthians 10—13 is perhaps the most challenging critical issue that the interpreter of 2 Corinthians faces. It is impossible to read Paul's stern words in 10:1-2 after the conciliatory tone of the previous chapters and the diplomatic and restrained argumentation of chapters 1—7 (not to mention the appeal for funds in chapters 8—9) and not wonder what is going on. Not only is the tone unexpected, but Paul also goes on to threaten that unless the Corinthians clean up their act, he will do it for them on his next visit (13:1-2, 5, 10). How can he threaten them in this fashion after claiming that they are a cause for joy and pride (7:4) and those in whom he can have complete confidence (7:16)? Then too, his opponents suddenly get primary attention, and Paul's language, while circumspect in chapters 1—9, becomes abruptly explicit and to the point in chapters 10—13. The "some" who peddle the word of God for profit (2:17) and carry letters of recommendation (3:1-3) are now called "false apostles, deceitful workmen" and servants of Satan (11:13-15), who are out to "enslave," "exploit" and "slap" the Corinthians (11:20).

Would this change of tone, language and approach not jeopardize the trust that Paul has worked so hard to engender in chapters 1—9? Is this not, in effect, pastoral suicide? A commonly proposed solution is to look at chapters 10—13 as a separate letter (or fragment thereof) that was inserted at this point in our canonical 2 Corinthians by a later editor of Paul's letters.

Two theories regarding the identity of such a letter are worthy of comment. The first is that chapters 10—13 are to be identified with Paul's "severe letter" written prior to chapters 1—9. This theory was first suggested by A. Hausrath in the 1870s. It is based, in part, on what are thought to be intentional allusions in chapters 1—9 to statements made in chapters 10—13. For example:

"The reason I wrote you was to see if you would . . . be obedient in everything" (2:9) refers back to "we will be ready to punish every act of disobedience" (10:6).

"It was in order to spare you that I did not return to Corinth" (1:23) refers back to "On my return I will not spare those who sinned earlier" (13:2).

"I wrote as I did so that when I came I should not be distressed by those who ought to make me rejoice" (2:3) refers back to "This is why I write these things when I am absent, that when I come I may not have to be harsh in my use of authority" (13:10).

Two letters as opposed to one are also thought to be suggested by Paul's references to Titus and his traveling companions. For in 12:18 Paul speaks of having sent "a brother" with Titus, while in chapter 7, from all appearances, he traveled alone. Supporters of Hausrath's proposal include James Moffatt, James H. Kennedy, Alfred Plummer, Kirsopp Lake, Robert H. Strachan, Floyd Filson and, most recently, Francis Watson.

At first glance this is an attractive explanation. But closer scrutiny reveals serious difficulties. For one, the key ingredient of the severe letter, namely Paul's command that the Corinthians punish the person who had publicly insulted him and challenged his authority, is missing from chapters 10—13. Instead, chapters 10—13 focus on itinerant preachers who are encroaching on Paul's missionary territory. Two, the pointed remarks and sarcastic tone of chapters 10—13 do not fit Paul's description of the severe letter as having been written out of great distress, anguish of heart and with many tears (2:4). Three, chapters 10—13 project a visit, while the severe letter replaces a promised visit (1:23—2:4). Four, "I wrote" in chapters 1—9 can easily refer back to a no longer extant letter, while the threat of punishment and not sparing the Corinthians in chapters 10—13 can pertain to continuing problems that Paul hopes will be resolved before his upcoming visit.

In light of such difficulties, the identification of chapters 10—13 with the severe letter has by and large been abandoned in favor of a second theory first proposed by Johann S. Semler in 1776: that chapters 10—13 were written after chapters 1—9 and in response to news of new developments at Corinth. Paul's threatening tone, direct challenge of the intruders and command that the Corinthians do some housecleaning can be plausibly explained, it is argued, if chapters 10—13 are a response to news of a worsening situation received after the writing of chapters 1—9. Recent proponents of this view include C. K. Barrett, Richard Batey, F. F. Bruce, Victor Furnish, Ralph P. Martin and Murray J. Harris.

One of the primary difficulties with both theories is that there is no manuscript evidence to support the notion that chapters 10—13 circulated independently of chapters 1—9 at any given point. Further, while Paul obliquely speaks of his upcoming visit in 9:4 ("if any Macedonians come with me"), it is only in chapters 10—13 that an explicit announcement is made and details are given. Indeed, it would have been a breach of epistolary etiquette for Paul to have written without formally announcing a forthcoming visit.

For these and other reasons many maintain the integral place of chapters 10—13 in 2 Corinthians. Explanations of the abrupt change of tone and language at 10:1 include (1) Paul penned these words after a bad night's sleep; (2) Paul received fresh news after a lengthy dictation pause; (3) chapters 1—9 are addressed to the Corinthian congregation, while chapters 10—13 are directed at certain "false apostles" who interposed themselves into the congregation; (4) chapters 1—9 are addressed to the majority who supported Paul (2:6) and chapters 10—13 are aimed at the minority who were still against him; (5) chapters 10—13 may reflect Paul's habit of picking up the pen from his secretary and writing the final comments and greeting in his own hand (compare 1 Cor 16:21).

This last theory offers the most promising explanation of the overall disparity between chapters 1—7 and 10—13. The change of tone at 10:1 can be plausibly accounted for if Paul picked up the pen from his scribe and penned these final chapters himself—especially if we assume a dictation pause of sufficient length to allow for the receipt of disturbing news following Titus's departure. It would not be the only time that a congregation had done an about-face after Paul's (or a deputy's) departure (compare Gal 1:6-9). In Paul's absence it would be easy for the intruding missionaries to once again gain a foothold in the congregation. This is one of the problems of pastoring at a distance. What was there to prevent the Corinthians from reverting to the original state of affairs once Paul—or his deputy—had left the scene?

☐ Special Themes

Dealing with Opposition There is a tendency in evangelicalism today to place great store in charismatic preaching, professional programming and a worship service that is glamorous and glitzy—in short, to expect a good performance rather than a good message. Paul faced serious personal challenges throughout his ministry because he rejected the performance orientation of his own culture and focused only on preaching "Jesus Christ and him crucified" (1 Cor 2:2). Unbelieving Jews stirred up trouble for him in virtually every city where he preached (Acts 13—17). Their antagonism even extended at times to pursuing him from city to city (as in Acts 14:19; 17:13). In his letters, however, some of his sternest words are reserved for Jewish Christian missionaries who preached a legalistic gospel (Gal 1:6-9; 2:15-16) and encroached on his missionary field thinking that they could do a better job (2 Cor 10:12-16).

It was at Corinth that he encountered his most formidable pastoral challenge in the form of traveling Jewish Christian preachers who not only invaded his territory but also claimed credit for his work, stressed sensationalism and challenged his credentials and his authority. They pointed disparagingly at the fact that he refused financial support from his churches (1 Cor 9:3-18; 2 Cor 12:13), did not carry letters of recommendation (2 Cor 3:1-3), was not successful in reaching his own people (3:14—4:4) and was an unimpressive speaker (10:10-11). They flaunted their achievements, claiming a superior heritage (11:21-22), greater spirituality ("visions and revelations," 12:1; "signs, wonders and miracles," 12:12), more knowledge (11:6) and better speaking ability. They also insinuated that the Jerusalem collection was merely a covert get-rich-quick scheme on Paul's part (8:18-21; 12:16-18).

Paul calls these preachers "false apostles" and "deceitful workmen" who were "masquerading as servants of righteousness" when in fact they were servants of Satan (2 Cor 11:13-15). They were preaching another Jesus, Spirit and gospel (11:4), and their intention was to lead people astray from a sincere and pure devotion to Christ (11:3; compare Gal 1:8).

The identity of these interlopers has long intrigued New Testament scholars. Some maintain that they were Palestinian Jews who, either backed by or falsely claiming the prestige of the mother church, sought to extend the Jerusalem church's authority over the Gentile churches and to enforce either adherence to Jewish practices (Acts 15:1) or the provisions of the Jerusalem decree (Acts 15:23-29; F. F Bruce, C. E. B. Cranfield, C. K. Barrett, Fred Fisher, Philip E. Hughes, Murray J. Harris, Jerome Murphy-O'Connor, Ernst Käsemann, Derk Oostendorp). Others think Paul is dealing with gnostic-pneumatic Jews who viewed Jesus as a pure vessel that received the descending Christ (Ernest Bernard Allo, Walter Schmithals, Rudolf Bultmann). An increasingly common interpretation is that the Corinthian intruders were Hellenistic Jewish missionaries who patterned themselves after the charismatic, miracleworking ecstatic of the Greco-Roman Empire (Wilhelm Lütgert, Gerhard Friedrich, Victor Furnish, Dieter Georgi). A fairly recent proposal is that Paul is dealing with ethnic and religious Jews who masqueraded as Christian leaders in an attempt to impede the gospel (Scott E. McClelland).

A number of Paul's comments in 2 Corinthians are suggestive of both the identity and the intentions of the intruders. "Are they Hebrews? . . . Are they Israelites?" (11:22) points to a Jewish heritage. The lack of references to circumcision and the Mosaic law indicates something other than a Judaizing (that is, legalistic) opponent. The additional lack of theological argumentation suggests that doctrinal differences were not the issue. Indeed, Paul's focus throughout the letter is on combating the assertion that he possesses inferior credentials, not that he preaches an inferior gospel.

Several of the credentials put forward by his opponents point to a claim of spiritual superiority proven through outward show. Signs, wonders and miracles are claimed to be "things that mark an apostle" (12:12). Visions and revelations are grounds for boasting (12:1). Eloquent speech (10:10; 11:6) and the proper heritage (11:22) are sources of pride. All this, along with the language of "super-apostles," suggests a mistaken emphasis on external show, or as Paul puts it, "looking only on the surface of things" (10:7). This fits with the picture of the intruders presented early on in 2 Corinthians as those who seek personal recognition through such things as letters of recommendation and a church's financial support (2:17—3:1). They take pride in what is seen rather than in what is in the heart (5:12).

Paul's focus on visions, revelations and the miraculous suggests that at issue was what constituted an appropriate witness to the gospel. A mistaken emphasis on the miraculous by these so-called super-apostles resulted in a misconstrual of Jesus as a wonderworker rather than a suffering servant, and a misrepresentation of the Spirit as a miracle empowerer rather than a guarantor of the gospel message. In so doing they effectively put forward "a different gospel" (11:4). For Paul, the role of the miraculous was to validate, not displace, the gospel. This is clear from the recurring thought in his letters that his preaching was one of word accompanied by power, conviction and the Spirit (1 Thess 1:5; see also Rom 15:19; 1 Cor 2:4; Gal 3:5).

Some have thought that Paul is being unduly harsh in his judgments of these rival preachers. Yet his remarks are not dissimilar to judgments made against false prophets in the Old Testament, whose intent was to lead Israel astray from its commitment to Yahweh and the covenant (as in Deut 18:20; compare Jer 28:15-17). The label "opponent" is given not to those who challenge Paul personally but to those who undermine his role as a preacher and teacher of the gospel in a particular community. These so-called apostles are "false" in Paul's opinion because their intent is not to preach the gospel and upbuild the congregation but to inflate their own ego. Financial gain (2 Cor 2:17; 11:20) and the desire for dominance ("enslave," "slap you in the face," 2 Cor 11:20) are their motivations.

In a day and age where there is a similar emphasis on spiritual achievements, financial empires, miraculous gifts and performance skills in the pulpit, we do well to heed the warning of how easy it is to end up communicating another Jesus, another Spirit and another gospel.

Christian Suffering and Divine Power

> That is why, for Christ's sake, I delight in weaknesses, in insults, in hardships, in persecutions, in difficulties. For when I am weak, then I am strong. (12:10)

The central theme of 2 Corinthians is divine power in weakness. It is a theme that the church in the West has tended to shrug off as appropriate only for Christians living under oppressive political regimes. Health, wealth and prosperity is a message often presented in the media and preached from the pulpit in the West. Not so with Paul. He defines the role of the gospel preacher in terms of the trials and hardships through which God's power is seen and appropriated. It is the same for the church, which, Paul says, must suffer "the same sufferings we suffer" before it can experience the same "comfort" we experience (1:6-7). This is in contrast to Paul's opponents at Corinth, who presented themselves as power evangelists and polished speakers, emphasizing an outward show of the Spirit in revelations, ecstatic experiences and the working of miracles.

Every chapter echoes this theme. The point of Christian hardship is so that "we might not rely on ourselves but on God, who raises the dead" (1:9). Thanksgiving is given to God because he triumphs over our evangelistic failures (2:12-14). "We always carry around in our body the death of Jesus, so that the life of Jesus may also be revealed in our body" (4:10). "We groan, longing to be clothed with our heavenly dwelling," which is "an eternal house in heaven, not built by human hands" (5:2-3). What commends someone as a servant of God are "troubles," "distresses," "hard work" and "sleepless nights" (6:4-5); "insults," "hardships" and "difficulties" (12:10).

For Paul it is when he is "weak" that he is "strong" (12:10). Like many nowadays, the Corinthians did not want to hear this message. But to preach anything else, Paul says, is to preach "a different gospel" (11:4) and to raise the question whether we truly are "in the faith" (13:5). "When I am weak, then I am strong." There are no alternative models. This is because there was no alternative for Christ, whose sufferings "flow over into our lives" (1:5). As Ralph Martin aptly puts it, "Jesus' death is rightly seen not as a mere fact of past history but as the hallmark of all that characterized his historical person and saving significance" (1986:18). It was the hallmark of Jesus. And so it is to be the hallmark of every church and believer.

The Work of the Spirit The Spirit plays a central and varied role in 2 Corinthians. In terms of the local congregation, he is responsible for its birth, unity and continuing existence. He is God's deposit *(arrabōn)*, given to the church as a guarantee of what is to come (1:22). As such, he confirms the ongoing validity of God's relationship to his people *(bebaioō)*, commissions and equips for service *(chriō)*, secures against falsificaton or tampering, and preserves the "goods" of this relationship until the day of redemption *(sphragizō, 1:21-22)*. If "the fellowship of the Holy Spirit" in 13:14 is to be understood as a subjective genitive, as appears likely from the context, then it is also the Spirit who brings about congregational unity (see the commentary).

With regard to the individual, the Spirit works to bring enlightenment (3:16-17), regeneration (3:6) and the ongoing and progressive transformation of mortality into immortal material existence (5:1-5; compare 4:10-11, 16-17). One of Paul's distinctive contributions in 2 Corinthians is to show that the Spirit not only gives assurance of our future transformation but is also working to bring this transformation about (4:12, 16; 5:5). God gives the Spirit "as a deposit" at conversion (5:5) and is now, through his Spirit, producing in us what Paul describes as "an eternal glory that far outweighs them all" (4:17).

As he seeks to commend his ministry to the church at Corinth, Paul also points to the role of the Spirit in supplying the minister's true credentials. Against traveling preachers who sought to supplant Paul's authority and position at Corinth by appealing to what they thought to be better credentials, like church support (2:17), letters of recommendation (3:1-3), a superior heritage (11:21-22), speaking ability (10:10-12), knowledge (11:6) and the working of miracles (12:12), Paul turns rather to the birth and continuing existence of the church (1:21-22; 3:1-3), his faithful witness to the gospel (11:4) and a life record of apostolic sufferings, ethical qualities and divine weaponry as the genuine, Spirit-provided credentials (6:4-7).

The Corinthian intruders, though able to work the apostolic "signs," nonetheless misrepresent the role of the Spirit as a wonderworker rather than a guarantor of the content of the gospel. Paul's linking of the Spirit in 6:6-7 with the apostolic arsenal of "truthful speech," "the power of God" and "weapons of righteousness" shows the proper role of the Spirit in confirming the message and convicting the hearer.

The Spirit plays a central role as well in the gospel ministry. He brings about understanding regarding the temporal character of the Mosaic covenant (3:13-17) and makes known the truths of the new covenant through the preaching and transformed lives of the gospel preacher (3:2, 18). It is also because of the permanent glory of the new covenant, as opposed to the transient glory of the old, that the new covenant preacher has the freedom, unlike Moses—and perhaps unlike Paul's opponents—to unveil his face. This durable glory, according to Paul, stems from the new covenant being a covenant of the life-giving Spirit versus the death-giving letter (3:6-11).

Finally, as Paul urges his readers to "open wide their hearts" as he has opened wide his own (6:11-13), he indicates that it is the Spirit who brings about this relational intimacy between pastor and congregation. For through their common possession of the Spirit their lives are drawn inseparably together. They are not only confirmed, anointed and sealed together but the Spirit is also placed in their hearts as a down payment of their common destiny in Christ (1:21-22) and their common inheritance in heaven (5:1-5).

What Paul says about the Spirit in 2 Corinthians is of critical importance to the church today—especially churches where special emphasis is placed on the sensational gifts of the Spirit. For Paul looks to the inward change of heart as the primary evidence of the Spirit's presence and not to any outward sign such as tongues, gifts of healing or miraculous powers. Although one aspect of the Spirit's role is the working of signs, wonders and miracles, it is a role that serves merely to confirm, not displace, the message that is being preached. Similarly, an effective witness is a life of self-sacrifice and self-denial, not mystical religious experiences, a flashy résumé, special speaking ability or exceptional training. Just as in Paul's day, our society looks upon credentials like "insults," "hardships" and "difficulties" (12:10) as weaknesses. But the fact is that only through such so-called weaknesses can God's power be truly evident to those around us (12:9-10).

Authority and Discipline There are very few of Paul's letters where his authority is not highlighted. This is evident already at the start of each letter, where he commonly identifies himself as "Paul, an apostle of Christ Jesus" (Rom, 1-2 Cor, Gal, Eph, Col, 1-2 Tim, Tit). But it is in 2 Corinthians, where Paul faced one of his greatest ministerial challenges, that the nature of apostolic authority is most clearly set forth. Indeed, many consider Paul's authority as an apostle and preacher of the gospel to be the pervasive, underlying theme of the letter (see Furnish 1984:34).

Paul sets out definite boundaries for the exercise of his authority in 2 Corinthians. These boundaries, which were agreed on by Paul and the "pillars" of the Jerusalem church, amounted to an ethnic division of labor. He was to preach to the Gentiles, and James, Peter and John were to go to the Jews (Gal 2:9)—a division that accords with Paul's own commissioning as apostle to the Gentiles (Rom 1:5; 15:15-16; Gal 1:16; 1 Tim 2:7). Yet there is nothing absolute about these boundaries. Paul's own evangelistic strategy involved an initial outreach in the synagogue (Acts 13:5, 14; 14:1; 17:2, 10; 18:4; 19:8). And Peter (1 Cor 1:12; 9:5) was a well-known figure at Corinth. What Paul in fact defines are predominant spheres of ministry, not exclusive ones (Belleville 1993a:56).

Not only does Paul speak of ministerial boundaries, but he also refers to territorial fields: "We, however, will not boast beyond proper limits, but will confine our boasting to the field God has assigned to us" (2 Cor 10:13). These "limits" were violated in Corinth by traveling preachers who overreached themselves and tried to displace Paul from his rightful mission field (2 Cor 10:12-15). What this rightful field amounted to is clearly spelled out in Romans 15:18-20, where Paul speaks of preaching the gospel in uncharted areas so as to not build on another apostle's foundation. The Corinthians became his field not because they were Gentiles per se but because he was the first to come to them (2 Cor 10:14). Paul also included within his field churches, like Laodicea and

Colossae, that his converts—and not he personally—established. It was his practice to focus his evangelistic efforts on large urban centers with a view to enlarging his sphere of authority *(kata ton kanona)* to surrounding areas *(ta hyperekeina)* through the evangelistic efforts of his converts (10:15-16; Col 1:3-8). The limiting of Paul's authority to Gentiles whom he or his converts were the first to reach may indeed explain why his letters are directed almost exclusively to the Gentile constituency of churches with an explicit Jew-Gentile mix (1-2 Cor, Gal, Eph, Phil, 1-2 Thess; Belleville 1993a:56).

Although Paul viewed his authority as a right that he possessed by virtue of his apostolic commission and expected his churches to accept without debate, he usually waived that right in favor of reasoned argumentation. This is the case even with the recalcitrant Corinthian church. His relationship to his churches is articulated, with rare exception, in terms of request rather than command. *Parakaleō* ("I ask")—an appeal by one who has the authority to command but the tact not to (2 Cor 2:8; 6:1; 10:1)—is Paul's usual approach. This approach arises out of his concept of authority as that which aims to build up rather than tear down (10:8). Pastoral authority is conceived in nurturing versus authoritarian terms ("not that we lord it over your faith, but we work with you," 1:24). The letter's primary images evoke the intimacy of familial relationships—the father who jealously guards his daughter's purity (11:2-3), the parent who saves up for his children (12:14).

Even so, Paul does on occasion use his authority as a kind of stick to warn his children what will happen if his requests are not heeded. When the Corinthians move beyond the request stage, Paul does not hesitate to exercise his authority. For example, in the so-called painful letter, intermediate to 1 and 2 Corinthians, he commands the church to discipline the individual who had publicly insulted him and challenged his authority (2 Cor 2:5-11; 7:9-13). He also warns the arrogant at Corinth that he will, if need be, deal harshly with them on his return in accordance with the authority given to him by the Lord (2 Cor 13:10; compare 10:8). And yet the conjoining of command and request in his second letter to the Thessalonians suggests Paul's reluctance to use a hard-line approach ("Such people we command and urge in the Lord Jesus Christ to settle down and earn the bread they eat," 2 Thess 3:12).

The church, as well, possesses authority by virtue of its being the "body" of which Christ is the "head" (Eph 1:22; 4:15-16; 5:23; Col 1:18; 2:19). The responsible exercise of corporate authority was something that Paul had great difficulty inculcating in his churches—especially a church like Corinth. It is the responsibility of the congregation to punish wrongdoing (2 Cor 2:6; 10:6), to excommunicate in the case of persistent sin (1 Cor 5:2, 10-13) and to reinstate the repentant (2 Cor 2:7-8). This authority derives from the power of the Lord Jesus that is present with believers gathered in his name (1 Cor 5:4) and from possession of the "mind of Christ" (1 Cor 2:16). The Gentile churches in particular had trouble following through with enforcing and waiving penalties for sin. For example, Paul had to rebuke the Corinthians both for not exercising discipline (2 Cor 2:9) and for going too far in not reinstating when repentance was secured (2:6). It is not much different today. Many churches have equal difficulty knowing when and how to discipline and when and how to forgive.

Pastoral Ministry

I face daily the pressure of my concern for all the churches. Who is weak, and I do not feel weak? Who is led into sin, and I do not inwardly burn? (11:28-29)

Paul's desire for his churches was that they attain to that level of maturity that can be measured by nothing less than the full stature of Christ himself (Eph 4:13). The obstacles to maturity that he faced as a pastor must have appeared at times overwhelming: legalists in Galatia, Jewish troublemakers at Thessalonica, spiritual one-upmanship, immoral life-styles and challenges to his authority at Corinth, personal disagreements at Philippi, heresy at Colossae and the infiltration of false teachers at Ephesus—to name just a few.

How then did Paul, as a pastor and role model for his congregations, deal with such problems? As an apostle of Christ, he could have merely said the word and commanded obedience (1 Thess 2:6-7). Domination, however, was not Paul's style. Instead he adopted a "let's think this through" approach to win his churches over to his way of thinking. Second Corinthians, one of the most personal and pastorally challenging of Paul's letters, superbly demonstrates the approach he used to move his most recalcitrant converts along the road toward Christlike maturity.

Pastoral Reinforcement For Paul the pastoral task always included reinforcement and encouragement. "I have great confidence in you. . . . I am glad that I can have complete confidence in you" (7:4, 16). Paul, where possible, reinforces what is going well in the lives of his converts. Sometimes this is not feasible, as with the Galatian churches, who had gotten entirely off-track (see Gal 1:6-10, "I am astonished that you are so quickly deserting . . ."). But Paul finds cause for praising even the strong-willed Corinthians. For one, they were obedient in punishing the individual who had publicly insulted him, and they thereby fulfilled his boasting to Titus about them (7:5-15). Moreover, not only were they the first to give to the Jerusalem relief fund, but their enthusiasm led Paul to brag about them to the Macedonian churches, so that other churches were encouraged to contribute as well (9:1-2).

The Pastoral Role Model "Now this is our boast: Our conscience testifies that we have conducted ourselves in the world, and especially in our relations with you, in the holiness and sincerity that are from God" (1:12). One of Paul's primary pastoral tools was his own example. Jesus, in speaking about the Pharisees, advised his disciples to do as they said, not as they did (Mt 23:2-3). Paul, by contrast, exhorts his churches to do as he does.

The role model that we find in 2 Corinthians is wide-ranging. In answering his detractors' claim that he was a deceiver and a manipulator (4:1-6; 7:2), Paul points to (1) the Christlike character that he exhibited while with them (1:12), (2) his refusal to use the common manipulative techniques of the day to get crowds' attention (4:2), (3) his carrying around the death of Jesus so that the life of Jesus might be at work in them (4:10-12), (4) the ministerial hardships and troubles he endured (6:4-10; 11:23-33), (5) how he plied a trade so as not to be a financial burden on the church (11:7-9) and (6) his expending himself over and over again for the Corinthians (11:28-29).

Pastoral Nurturing "You have such a place in our hearts that we would live or die with you" (7:3). Nowhere does Paul excel more as a pastor than in his ability to make his teaching part of the very fabric of the church's existence. He does this by sharing not only the gospel message but also himself. Those who accepted the gospel became not merely converts to be discipled but family to be nurtured.

This is clear from the strong parental language and child-rearing imagery that Paul uses. He addresses the Corinthians as his "children" (6:13; compare 1 Cor 4:14) in whom he takes great pride and about whom he boasts to others (7:4). He likens his task to that of a father protecting the purity of his virgin daughter (11:1-3). He forgoes financial support because parents are to save up for their children, not children for their parents (12:14). And he anxiously calls on them to open their hearts to him as he has to them (6:11-13).

Pastoral Correction "I [ask] you that when I come I may not have to be as bold as I expect to be toward some people who think that we live by the standards of this world" (10:2). Paul, with rare exception, tackles the job of correcting faulty thinking through reasoned argumentation and modifying wrong behavior by request rather than command. When the Corinthians are tempted to think that he does not accept support from them because he does not care about them, Paul appeals to the parental (12:14-18) and ministerial (11:7-33) sacrifices he has made on their behalf. When they fall short, he reminds them of what they had already been taught (for example, "we know that," 5:1) and warns them about the consequences of continuing misconduct (12:19—13:10).

Paul exercises discipline only as a last resort. "This is why I write these things when I am absent," he states, "that when I come I may not have to be harsh in my use of authority—the authority the Lord gave me for building you up, not for tearing you down" (13:10). But when he must use discipline, he does not hesitate to bring the full weight of his apostolic authority to bear: "I already gave you a warning when I was with you the second time. I now repeat it while absent: On my return I will not spare those who sinned earlier or any of the others" (13:2). Even then, it is not without personal cost. It meant "great distress," "anguish of heart," "many tears" (2:4), "no peace of mind" (2:13), "conflicts on the outside" and "fears within" (7:5).

Pastoral Strategy Paul uses interchurch competition to spur the Corinthians toward Christlike maturity. The example of the Macedonian churches' generosity in giving to the Jerusalem relief fund despite extreme poverty becomes for Paul a means by which he seeks to get the Corinthian church to fulfill the pledge they had made the year before

(8:1-15). He also uses their fear of losing face before other churches to motivate them to give: "I am sending the brothers in order that our boasting about you in this matter should not prove hollow" (9:3); "if any Macedonians come with me and find you unprepared, we—not to say anything about you—would be ashamed of having been so confident" (9:4).

Most of us would not feel comfortable employing these tactics, and Paul himself did not utilize them with all his churches. But they fit the psychology of the Corinthian church—a church that was not unlike many of our megachurches today. The Corinthian church prided itself on being the best spiritually and on excelling in everything (8:7). One of the reasons they were so disturbed by Paul's refusal to accept their financial support was that this was one way they measured their self-importance. "We support this big-name preacher or that big-name evangelist" was a badge of honor for the Corinthians. They would never be caught short in comparison with other churches, if they could help it.

We might say that by stooping to their level, Paul did something that is hardly worthy of a pastor, let alone an apostle! But here we need to keep in mind the collection's importance. First, its goal was to relieve desperate want in the Jerusalem church—a substantial point in and of itself. Second, it served as a concrete demonstration of the interdependence of the members of Christ's body and symbolized the unity of Jew and Gentile brought about through Christ's death and resurrection. And finally, it was intended to ameliorate the lingering suspicions of conservative Jewish Christians toward the Gentile mission—suspicions that the Corinthian church did little to discourage.

□ **Relevance**

The kinds of ministerial challenges Paul faced at Corinth are frighteningly similar to those that currently plague many of our churches: an emphasis on individualism, narcissistic attitudes and values, a need to be the best at everything and a focus on externals. At the core is a spiritual arrogance and a materialistic orientation that becomes evident in the importance placed on such showier gifts of the Spirit as tongues, knowledge and healing. It reveals itself in our judging others by how they look, rather than by what they say and do. It colors our expectations that the Christian life should bring health, wealth and prosperity. It surfaces in the glitz and stage performance of many worship services. It expresses itself in the mentality of "bigger is better"—the more members, programs, committees and the like, the more successful we think the church is. And it seeks power—power evangelism, power preaching and power spirituality.

By contrast, Paul sets before the church a model of pastoral care and self-sacrifice and a lifestyle of weakness. This model is set forth in two key statements: "We do not preach ourselves, but Jesus Christ as Lord, and ourselves as your servants" (4:5) and "we are weak in him, yet by God's power we will live with him to serve you" (13:4). Paul's statements go to the heart of what Christian ministry is all about. Richard Bauckham sums it up well when he says,

> To identify with Paul's experience we do not need to be shipwrecked or imprisoned or lowered in a basket from a city wall. Even without the physical dangers of Paul's career, anyone who throws himself into the work of Christian ministry of any kind with half the dedication of Paul will experience the weakness of which Paul speaks: the times when problems seem insoluble, the times of weariness from sheer overwork, the times of depression when there seem to be no results, the emotional exhaustion which pastoral concern can bring on—in short, all the times when the Christian minister or worker knows he nas stretched to the limits of his capacities for a task which is very nearly but by God's grace not quite too much for him. Anyone who knows only his strength, not his weakness, has never given himself to a task which demands all he can give. (1982:5-6)

Paul's relationship with the Corinthian church should be an encouragement to all pastors and church leaders who struggle with congregations that are more informed by the standards and expectations of society than by Christ's expectations for us as salt and light in our communities.

There is also warning here. The Corinthian church reminds us of how easy it is to be tempted to work from a position of power, wealth or knowledge. This is the model that our society offers. Paul, on the other hand, challenges us to seek our security in God and to boast not in personal successes but only in the cross of our Lord Jesus Christ (1 Cor 1:31; 2 Cor 10:17). The Corinthian church also serves as a reminder that spiritual giftedness does not equate with spiritual maturity and that doctrinal soundness should not be used as the sole standard for how a church measures up in God's sight. Despite the Corinthians' all-around spiritual giftedness and excellence, Paul commands them to examine themselves to see whether they are in the faith. Indeed, he wonders whether amid all the glitz and glamour of their superspiritual lives, they in fact do still belong to Christ (13:5-6). We do well as a church to heed his warning.

Outline of 2 Corinthians

1:1-2_____ **Paul Sends the Corinthians a Personal Greeting**

1:3-7_____ **Paul Praises God for Divine Encouragement in Times of Trouble**

1:3-6 _____ Suffering and Encouragement Go Hand in Hand

1:7_____ Paul's Hope for the Corinthians Is Firm

1:8-11_____ **Paul Shares His News of a Near-Death Experience**

1:12—7:16 ___ **Paul Defends His Ministry Against Criticism**

1:12—2:4 ___ The Corinthians Complain About Paul

2:5-11 _____ Paul Asks the Corinthians to Forgive the Repentant Offender

2:12-17 _____ Paul Recounts His Evangelistic Efforts in Troas

3:1-3 _____ The Corinthians Are Paul's Letter of Recommendation

3:4-6 _____ Ministerial Competence Comes from God

3:7-11 _____ The New Covenant Ministry Is Superior to the Old Covenant Ministry

3:12-18 _____ The New Covenant Minister is Superior to the Old Covenant Minister

4:1-6 _____ Paul Sets Forth the Truth Plainly

4:7-12 _____ God's Power Is Made Known Through Ministerial Hardships

COMMENTARY

☐ A Personal Greeting (1:1-2)

Just as we open our letters today with the conventional "Dear John," so Paul begins his letters in the way that was characteristic of the casual Greek letter of his day: A to B, greetings. How he elaborates this typical opening provides us with insight into his uppermost concerns at the time of writing (see the introduction). In 2 Corinthians Paul's concerns are three in number: (1) his apostleship, (2) God's ownership of the Corinthian congregation and (3) the church as the family of God.

The Sender (1:1) Paul's foremost concern is his apostolic standing in the Corinthian community. The very lack of elaboration in comparison with Paul's other letters highlights this at the start: *Paul, an apostle of Christ Jesus by the will of God.* The first-century writer used this part of the letter to strengthen family ties and friendships. Paul is no different. This is clear from his references to *Timothy our brother* (v. 1), *together with all the saints* (v. 1) and *our Father* (v. 2), by which he seeks to reinforce the idea of the church as the family of God.

The Readers (1:1) Corinth is distinguished, both in this letter and in 1 Corinthians, with the unique address *to the church of God.* The singular *church,* in contrast to the more commonly found *all* and *saints,* focuses attention on the unity of believers in the Corinthian locality. *Of*

God emphasizes divine ownership—an ownership that differentiates the church from a culture and society that were centered on idolatry (see the introduction).

It was common in Paul's day to include others beyond the immediate readers as independent witnesses of a letter's content and reception—somewhat like the function of our notary today. In the case of 2 Corinthians, *all the saints throughout Achaia* are called on to verify Paul's claim of apostleship—a claim that has been challenged from both inside and outside the Corinthian church and which, as we will see, Paul is at pains to defend throughout the letter.

The Greeting (1:2) Paul's greeting takes the form of an ancient Near Eastern blessing: *Grace* (or "mercy" in Jewish letters) *and peace.* Normally at this point, the first-century writer would go on to wish his reader(s) good health—much as we say, "Hope all is going well." Paul, instead, specifies the source of good health for the believer—*God our Father and the Lord Jesus Christ.* It is this kind of Christian blessing that he invariably uses to round off his opening greeting. *God* as a source of peace would be a typical Jewish thought. *Our Father,* however, brings Paul's greeting into the sphere of the familial—the exact way Jesus taught his disciples to address God in prayer. Yet, it is to be noted that while God is *our Father,* Jesus is not here spoken of as "our brother" but, rather, *the Lord. Kyrios* is placed first for emphasis. Grace and peace come from *the* Lord *Jesus Christ.* The concept of God as *Father* of the church and Jesus as her *Lord* captures two key distinctives of the Christian faith.

Notes: 1:1 Elaboration of the standard letter opening that signals Paul's immediate concerns is especially clear in Romans 1:1-7, where he comments at length on the essence of his commission as an apostle to the Gentiles, and in Galatians 1:1-5, where he expands the usual greeting to highlight the source of his commission and the redemptive work of Christ.

The brevity and almost mechanical phraseology of the opening verses of 2 Corinthians have led some to think that it is a circular letter. There is some support for this in the fact that Paul addresses not only Corinth but *all the saints throughout Achaia* (compare 9:2; 11:10). However, the specific references to the Corinthian situation in chapters 1—7 and the personal address to "you Corinthians" in 6:11 are against this.

Use of public attestation is also found in Philippians 1:1 ("To all the saints in Christ Jesus at Philippi, together with the overseers and deacons") and in Philemon 1:1 ("To Philemon . . . to Apphia our sister, to Archippus our fellow soldier and to the church that meets in your home"). Compare 1 Maccabees 14:20: "To Simon the high priest together

So Paul in these opening verses seeks to highlight both his apostolic and his family relationship to the Corinthians by calling on the witness of the broader community of Achaian believers and pointing to the filial bonds he and the Corinthians share. By making this most personal of letters "public," Paul holds the Corinthians accountable to the church at large.

□ Praise for Divine Encouragement in Times of Trouble (1:3-7)

Parents today commonly use the full name of their child to express rebuke. So too Paul's choice of the formal eulogy *(Praise be)* rather than the customary thanksgiving ("I thank") provides us with a definite clue that the news he received from Titus about his spiritual children in Corinth was not entirely to his liking. Paul's focus in these verses on his own situation and God's faithfulness, rather than his usual attention to the church's situation and its steadfastness, also suggests that something was amiss.

Encouragement in the Midst of Suffering (1:3-6) Rare indeed is the life that is free from all trial and hardship. Even for the carefree person a lingering illness, persistent obstacle or family tragedy can result in a rude awakening to life's vagaries. To many of us such a state of affairs is an outrage. For Paul, however, suffering is an inevitable part of the Christian life and an opportunity to learn how God goes about meeting our every need. This is reflected in the central theme of verses 3-6: divine provision of encouragement in the midst of suffering.

---

with the elders, the priests and the rest of the Jewish people."

1:2 3 Maccabees 3:12 is an example of the customary good health wish: "King Ptolemy Philopator to his generals and soldiers in Egypt and all its districts, greetings and good health."

1:3 Besides Paul's customary statement of thanksgiving, the usual intercession, remembrance and prayer for spiritual growth are also missing from verses 3-7. Compare Colossians 1:3-14: "We always thank God . . . when we pray for you, because we have heard of your faith. . . . We have not stopped praying for you and asking God to fill you with the knowledge of his will . . . bearing fruit in every good work, growing in the knowledge of God." All this points to an absence of those spiritual qualities that normally elicit thanksgiving. Paul is anticipating his need to rebuke the Corinthians for their lack of complete loyalty (6:1-13), continuing ties with idolatry (6:14—7:1), fractiousness (12:20-21) and immorality (12:21).

The formal antecedent of the eulogy is the Old Testament benediction. See, for example,

Praise be to the God and Father recalls the Old Testament psalter and synagogue liturgy. Paul gives a Christian twist to this eulogy with the addition *of our Lord Jesus Christ.* The result is a remarkable theological statement: *the God and Father of our Lord Jesus Christ.* Even so, Paul's concern at this point is not with theological precision but with personal experience. And his experience is of a *Father* who is moved to *compassion* and a *God* who responds with the provision of *comfort.* The word *compassion* (literally "mercies") refers to the exclamation of pity at the sight of another's ill fortune. By *comfort* he has in mind aid rendered in the form of encouragement, rather than consolation. Paul is drawing on the Old Testament image of God expressed by the psalmist when he says, "As a father has compassion on his children, so the LORD has compassion on those who fear him; for he knows how we are formed, he remembers that we are dust" (Ps 103:13-14).

Jews in Paul's day used the eulogy to commemorate acts of divine deliverance and provision. The provision that Paul celebrates is a God *who comforts us in all our troubles* (v. 4). By *us* Paul has primarily in view gospel preachers, who in their travels encounter *troubles* (v. 4) and *sufferings* (v. 5). *All* stresses the absence of any exception—no matter what the situation, encouragement is at hand.

Against the selfism that is prevalent even in Christian circles today, it is important to notice two things. First, this provision of comfort is not self-serving but is intended to equip for service to the church. God comforts us, Paul states, so that we, in turn, can *comfort those in any trouble* (v. 4). The trouble may vary (the sense is "whatever the trouble") but the comfort remains the same. *So that we can comfort* points to the

---

Genesis 14:20, where Melchizedek blessed Abram, saying: "Blessed be God Most High, who delivered your enemies into your hand."

To avoid speaking of "the God of our Lord Jesus Christ," some either treat verse 3 as two separate benedictions ("Praise be to God *and* to the Father of our Lord Jesus Christ") or translate *kai* as intensive ("Praise be to God, *even* the Father of our Lord Jesus Christ"). The single article plus *kai* rules out distinguishing "God" and "Father," and the intensive use of *kai* is rare indeed (although see Gal 6:16). Its reappearance in Ephesians 1:3, 17 shows that Paul is quite at home with this phrase. While we might initially balk at the subordination of the Son implied here, it is important to keep in mind that it is a subjection of the will and not an inferiority of nature or person that is in view. Compare 1 Corinthians 15:28, where Paul states that "the Son himself will be made subject to him who put everything under him, so that God may be all in all."

Oiktirmos and *paraklēsis* are used interchangeably in the LXX to render Hebrew words

fact that the means God uses to provide encouragement is other people. This was certainly the case in Paul's life. It is easy to talk about divine comfort in the abstract, but for Paul, God's comfort was very real. It was something he received with Titus's arrival from Corinth (7:6) and something he experienced on hearing the good news about the Corinthian church (7:4). In turn, the comfort that he gained when "harassed at every turn" (7:5) prepared him to give encouragement to those around him (1:5). Suffering, then, is a training ground for service to the body of Christ. It equips us so that we can better minister to those who, for the sake of the gospel, are going through trials and hardships. In this way we mediate God's encouragement.

Second, the provision is not deliverance "from" but encouragement *in* trouble (v. 4). The Christian is not promised release from trouble but help in the midst of it. The implication is that if we are serving Christ, we will encounter hardships. This is a given of the Christian life, as it was a given in Christ's life. As Paul puts it, *the sufferings of Christ flow over into our lives* (v. 5). The Greek verb translated "to flow over" means "to exceed the measure." Not only does God not deliver us from suffering, but he actually permits suffering to brim over into our lives. Yet this is not just any suffering but specifically *the sufferings of Christ*. What does this mean? It does not mean that we somehow complete what Christ failed to finish on the cross. The idea is, rather, that to identify with Christ is to identify with the suffering that was an essential part of his earthly ministry. What Paul articulates here is in essence what Jesus taught his disciples—to wit, that all who would come after him must deny self, take up the cross and follow him (Mk 8:34). Suffering

---

for God's being moved to show pity on his people.

1:4-7 That *parakaleō/paraklēsis* means "to encourage"/"encouragement" can be seen from Paul's statement in 7:4-7 that he was "encouraged" in his situation by Titus's arrival with good news about the Corinthians. Scott Hafemann puts forward the thesis that the suffering and comfort Paul experienced were uniquely his as an apostle: "Paul does not say that when they are afflicted he comforts them and when he is afflicted they comfort him" (1989:327-28). Yet this is exactly what Paul does say in 7:5-6. News of the Corinthians' longing and concern for him encouraged him when he was harassed at every turn in Macedonia. Indeed, one of the reasons he did not return to Corinth was that the Corinthians would not be in a position to make him "glad" (2:2). The point is an important one. The lack of mutual support between pastor and congregation is a major cause of ministerial burnout today. Pastor-congregation reciprocity is also a central concern of Paul's. See, for example, Paul's impassioned appeal in 6:11-13 for the Corinthians to open wide their hearts

overflowed into Christ's life; suffering overflows into ours. This is a hard truth for many of us to accept, and the Corinthians also had a problem in this area. In their case, they thought that they had "arrived" and had conquered the frailties of human existence (1 Cor 4:8-10). As a result, the sufferings that Paul underwent tended to discredit him in their eyes. In response, Paul attempts to drive home in verses 3-5 that both the gospel ministry and the lot of the Christian involve suffering.

Paul's purpose in this eulogy is not merely to praise God for personal comfort received or to discuss the nature of the gospel ministry. His primary concern is to show the Corinthians that their lives are inescapably intertwined, so that what impacts Paul impacts the Corinthians and what impacts the Corinthians impacts Paul. It is for their benefit, he says, that he encounters trouble. For, *if we are distressed, it is for your comfort and salvation; if we are comforted, it is for your comfort* (v. 6). Whatever he experiences, be it suffering or comfort, the Corinthians personally benefit. Paul then goes on to state an important but often neglected truth. Service to the body of Christ results in personal gain rather than personal loss. The experience of comfort received and imparted produces *patient endurance* (v. 6). The net effect is the ability to endure *the same sufferings we suffer* (v. 6)—that is, hardships and trials experienced in the course of proclaiming the gospel.

A Secure Hope (1:7) Paul concludes his eulogy with the statement *Our hope for you is firm, because we know that just as you share in our sufferings, so also you share in our comfort* (v. 7). Suffering is not incidental or even accidental to the Christian life. Paul does not say that

---

as he has opened wide his own.

1:4 When *pas* ("any") plus the article modifies a noun, it emphasizes the whole (*epi pasē tē thlipsei*—"in our situation of affliction"). When the article is absent, the anarthrous form stresses "each and every kind" (*en pasē thlipsei*—"whatever the trouble").

The noun *trouble (thlipsis)* can refer either to external suffering (as in Rom 8:35) or to mental anguish (as in Phil 1:17). In 2 Corinthians 7:5 both ideas are in view. The precise trouble is not spelled out. It is unlikely to have been a lingering illness. "Conflicts on the outside, fears within" in 7:5 points to persecution of some kind. Danger from "my own countrymen," danger from "Gentiles" and danger from "false brothers" seem the most likely possibilities (11:26). In fact, it could be any of the long list of missionary sufferings enumerated in 11:23-27.

1:5 By *the sufferings of Christ* Paul is not thinking of something Christ is currently experiencing. Nor is he suggesting that what Christ endured on the cross was in some

the Corinthians may share in his apostolic sufferings—they *will* share in them. This, however, results not in despair but rather in *hope*—a hope not in the Corinthians' ability to weather hardship but in God's ability to sustain and strengthen them (compare v. 3). This is why Paul can refer to this hope as *firm,* a term that has the sense of a legally guaranteed security. There is a note of warning here as well—a warning against placing confidence in our own spirituality. For it is those who consider themselves particularly spiritual who are most prone to fall when faced with hardship. But for those who trust in God, Paul expresses the certainty that they who share Christ's sufferings will also share God's comfort.

So this eulogy carries forward the theme of apostleship introduced in the opening greeting, an apostleship that is essentially characterized by hardship and affliction. Paul also seeks to strengthen his relationship to the Corinthians by showing how their lives are inseparably bound to his. For the church, this means recognition that the lot of those who proclaim the gospel includes suffering. Yet, there is in this the promise of God's comfort.

□ **News of a Near-Death Experience in Asia (1:8-11)**
Verse 8 of chapter 1 marks the point at which Paul moves from the eulogy to the body of the letter. *We do not want you to be uninformed, brothers* was a standard phrase that a writer in that day used to introduce new information. The new information that Paul wants to pass along to his readers is about the *hardships* he and his coworkers suffered while traveling through *the province of Asia.*

---

sense incomplete. The idea is rather that the gospel ministry is an extension of Christ's earthly ministry—a ministry that was marked by hardship.

1:6 *The same sufferings we suffer* can mean the same sort of sufferings, rather than the identical ones. Hardships and trials experienced in the line of duty as a gospel preacher are what is in view here.

It is unclear whether the latter part of the verse means "your comfort produces patient endurance" or "your comfort is produced by patient endurance." If *tēs energoumenēs* is middle, then it is "your comfort which works for itself endurance" (NIV, NASB, KJV, NKJV, REB); if it is passive, then it is "your comfort which is worked by endurance" (RSV, NRSV). The former produces the better sequence of thought. Paul would be saying that imparting comfort has the added benefit of building personal endurance.

Paul's consistent use of the first-person plural, *we,* in 1:3-14 and 2:14—7:2 suggests that hardship and divine comfort are a typical part of the gospel ministry.

Travel news, then as now, was a common way to begin the main portion of a letter. The news that Paul discloses, however, is most uncommon. For he refers to some kind of near-death experience that he and his coworkers *(we)* experienced while traveling from Ephesus to Troas. The severity of the experience is evident from the fact that Paul strains the language to the limit in an effort to express himself. *We were under great pressure* (literally, "weighed down") *far beyond our ability to endure* (literally, "utterly beyond our strength"). It was so severe, Paul states, that *we despaired even of living* (NIV *life*). The term for *despair* implies the total unavailability of an exit or way of escape. *Even of living* means that he was not certain of surviving the ordeal. *Indeed, in our hearts we felt the sentence of death* (v. 9). The tense of the verb stresses the permanent effects: "we received and still experience" (not the NIV *we felt*). *To apokrima tou thanatou* refers to a decision made in response to an official petition ("the answer of death"), not to a verdict rendered in a court of law (NIV *the sentence of death*). Paul reckoned his position to be like that of a man whose request for mercy had been denied and who was condemned to die. So futile did the situation appear that when deliverance occurred it was tantamount to resurrection: *God, who raises the dead . . . delivered us* (vv. 9-10). The verb "to deliver" denotes God's action to preserve or keep intact. The purpose of this near-death

1:8 Disclosure *(we do not want you to be uninformed)* is the way Paul usually opens the body or main part of his letters (compare Rom 1:13; 2 Cor 1:8; Phil 1:12-14; Col 2:1). This is not surprising since letters, then as now, were primarily intended to inform those at a distance of important developments. In Paul's day, items of news were introduced with a stereotyped statement that included, as here, a verb of desire *(we want)*, a personal pronoun of address *(you)*, a verb of disclosure *(to know)*, a vocative form *(brothers)* and relevant information *(about the hardships)*.

Although the NIV translates *adelphoi* as "brothers," it is nonetheless clear from the context that Paul is addressing the entire congregation. "People," "brothers and sisters" (NRSV), "dear friends" (NEB) and "my friends" (REB) are more accurate renderings.

The redundancy of expression underscores the severity of the trouble: *kath' hyperbolēn hyper dynamin ebarēthēmen*. What exactly Paul and his coworkers encountered is not stated. It is obviously different from what he describes in verses 3-7. There he speaks of divine comfort *in* the midst of trouble; here he refers to divine deliverance *from* a deadly peril. Although some locate this deadly peril in Ephesus, Paul's reference to *in the province of Asia* rather than "in Ephesus" suggests some place other than the provincial capital. The most likely point in time was while Paul was en route to Troas, where he planned to do some evangelistic work (2:12-13). Some think that Paul's vagueness shows that his readers were familiar with what he was talking about. But this overlooks the function of the letter carrier to fill in the details. The identity of the deadly peril is at issue. One common experience, Paul states, was to substitute dependence on God for reliance on self (v. 9).

To our loss, Paul does not provide any details about this near-death experience. This suggests that his primary concern is not to provide the Corinthians with a missionary update but something else. The customary function of the body opening in the letter of that day was to strengthen the writer's bond with the reader. Paul does this in verses 10-11, when he states that God *will continue to deliver us, as you help us by your prayers*. By this statement Paul ties his deliverance closely to the prayers of the Corinthians on his behalf. God has delivered and will continue to deliver, provided the Corinthians pray for him. The answer to their prayers will in turn, he continues, cause thanksgiving to overflow on the part of believers everywhere *(many)* for God's gracious dealings on behalf of Paul and his coworkers (v. 11).

A request for prayer usually appears in the closing section of Paul's letters. The fact that he departs from his usual practice and includes it here is noteworthy. Paul's request for prayer highlights what is probably the sore spot in his relationship with the Corinthians, namely, a lack of reciprocity. As Paul will say later, "We are not withholding our affection from you, but you are withholding yours from us" (6:12). There has been a cooling of the Corinthians' affection for Paul. So Paul seeks at the start

---

suggestion is some sort of crippling illness; another one is imprisonment (compare 2 Cor 11:23 "I have been in prison more frequently"). Those who opt for the latter frequently date Philippians at this time. A further possibility is some form of persecution. This is reasonable given the number of times that Paul had been beaten, stoned, flogged and "exposed to death" (11:23-25). That he had had his share of problems even in Ephesus is evident from references to the "many who oppose me" (1 Cor 16:9) and to Priscilla and Aquila risking their lives for him (Rom 16:3-4).

1:9 Colin Hemer has shown that there is no basis for understanding *apokrima tou thanatou* as a judicial metaphor (1972:103-7). Yet virtually all modern translations render this phrase as *the sentence of death. Apokrima* was used in the first century A.D. of an authoritative decision given in response to official petition. See Moulton-Milligan (1930) and Deissmann (1923).

In our heart (en heautois) can simply mean "it seemed to us."

1:11 The participle *synhypourgountōn* can be circumstantial *(as you help us by your prayers)* but is more probably conditional ("if you help out with your prayers"), since Paul is trying to show throughout chapters 1—7 how dependent he and his coworkers are on the Corinthians' involvement in their lives.

Many is literally "many faces." The image is of upturned faces expressing thanks to God.

The latter half of verse 11 is difficult to translate. *Hina* introduces the result of their

to rekindle that affection and concern by sharing with them how close he came to dying and how his very well-being is dependent on their taking a personal interest in his affairs. Perhaps he is even suggesting that his encounter with death was due to the fact that they had stopped praying for him. T. C. Hammond in an essay on prayer expresses a similar thought when he writes: "We are all bound together in the bundle of life."

So, Paul imparts the personal information that he does in verses 8-11 not primarily for its "news" content but to establish right at the start a relational basis between the Corinthians and himself. He is also anxious to show the impact that this mutuality has on the church universal. The Corinthians, like so many churches today, tended toward self-sufficiency. Paul's final comment is a reminder of our membership in the body of believers worldwide and of the interdependency of members in that larger body. Believers everywhere, Paul states, will give thanks that God preserved him for further ministry—a thankfulness that Paul hopes the Corinthians will come to share as well.

□ Paul Defends His Ministry (1:12—7:16)

We have all faced criticism at one time or another. In the church, the pastor(s) and leaders in particular bear the brunt of a great deal of griping. It was no different in the first century. The Pharisees and scribes were constantly criticizing Jesus. Even the churches that James wrote to had to be told to stop their grumbling and complaining (5:9).

The Corinthians' Complaints (1:12—2:4) The Corinthians were complainers as well (1 Cor 10:10, "Do not grumble") and took the opportunity of Titus's visit with the severe letter to communicate a number of criticisms they had against Paul. First, they said that Paul's

---

prayer: "if you pray for us, thanks *will be* given on our behalf." *Ek pollōn . . . dia pollōn* appears redundant. The best option is to take *ek pollōn* as masculine ("by many") and *dia pollōn* as neuter ("through many prayers"). Then the sense would be "many will give thanks for the way God helped us in response to many prayers." If, however, *dia pollōn* is masculine, Paul would be emphasizing the multitude of thanksgiving given "by many" and "through many."

1:12 The human conscience as a witness is also found in Romans 9:1, where Paul once again is at pains to emphasize the truthfulness of what he is about to say.

letters were hard to understand: "What is this fellow talking about?" (vv. 12-14). Second, they claimed that Paul was fickle. "He promises to visit us and then changes his mind without even consulting us" (1:15-23). Third, they thought that he had a domineering attitude toward them and wanted to show who had the upper hand (1:24—2:4). No doubt they were being egged on by visiting preachers who sought to displace Paul in the Corinthians' affections by pointing to his supposed character and ministerial deficiencies (see the introduction).

First Complaint: Obscure Letters (1:12-14) In chapter 1 verse 12 Paul begins to deal with the Corinthian complaints by pointing to the overall integrity of his conduct. *Now this is our boast: Our conscience testifies that we have conducted ourselves in the world, and especially in our relations with you, in the holiness and sincerity that are from God.* Paul's primary line of defense is personal commendation. *This is our boast.* The language of boasting (1:12, 14; 5:12; 7:4, 14; 10:8, 13, 15-17; 11:10, 12, 16-18, 30; 12:1, 5, 6, 9), commending (3:1; 4:2; 5:12; 6:4; 10:12, 18; 12:11) and having confidence (1:9, 15; 3:4; 5:6, 8; 7:4, 16; 10:2, 7) occurs more in 2 Corinthians than anywhere else in the New Testament. Paul also provides the Corinthians with three different résumés of ministerial credentials (4:8-9; 6:4-10; 11:22—12:6).

Even though résumés are a given in our society, many today take offense at Paul's boasting and view his self-commendation as a sign of personal arrogance. Three factors must be kept in mind. First, Paul does not engage in boasting in order to make himself look good. He is pushed to do it by the Corinthians, who placed great store in such things, and by his opponents, who enjoyed flaunting their credentials (5:12; 10:12). Paul stooped to their level in order to safeguard the church from placing its trust in those who were only out to exploit them (11:18-20). He is quite open about this. "We are not trying to commend ourselves to you

---

Tou theou is better translated "before God" than the NIV *from God.* Compare the similar phraseology in 2:17, where Paul says, "As those sent by God we speak with sincerity before God."

While *hagiotēti* ("holiness") has early (p⁴⁶ ℵ B) and widespread manuscript support, *haplotēti* ("frankness") is demanded by the context. *Haplotēti* has early support as well (D G vg it).

En sophia sarkikē is literally "with fleshly wisdom." Paul uses *sarkikos* to describe what is material and human as opposed to spiritual and divine.

again," he says, "but are giving you an opportunity to take pride in us, so that you can answer those who take pride in what is seen rather than in what is in the heart" (5:12). Second, the credentials Paul puts forward are job related. He speaks from the standpoint of his office, not his person, and phrases what he says in the plural "we," not the singular "I." It is as servants of Christ and ministers of the gospel that he commends himself and his coworkers. And, third, when Paul does boast, he boasts not in his achievements and accomplishments but in the hardships, struggles and trials of an itinerant missionary. "As servants of God we commend ourselves in every way: in great endurance; in troubles, hardships and distresses; in beatings, imprisonments and riots; in hard work, sleepless nights and hunger" (6:4-5).

Paul uses the language of the courtroom when he wants to underline the veracity of what he is about to say. *Our conscience testifies* (v. 12) means he has a clear conscience that is open to both divine and human scrutiny—an assertion that few indeed could make then or now. This is no idle boast on his part, for he makes this claim "before God" (v. 12; 2:17; see the note), who will judge the truthfulness of his words *in the day of the Lord Jesus* (v. 14). What he calls on his conscience to bear witness to is the "frankness and sincerity" of his conduct in the world and especially toward the Corinthians (v. 12). The word for "frankness" (NIV *holiness,* see the note) denotes simplicity of intent. Paul behaved with openness and candor, not holding anything back from them or attempting to deceive. Nor was he insincere in what he said and did—what we today would call a hypocrite. On the contrary, his affection for them was genuine. This was because he conducted himself not *according to worldly wisdom but according to God's grace.* In short, Paul did not allow society's standards to dictate how he spoke or acted. By society's standards his conduct would be deemed sheer foolishness. But God's standard of *grace* demanded that he reach out not primarily to the educated or power brokers of society but to the "nobodies" (1 Cor 1:28). "Not many of you were wise by human standards," he tells

---

1:13 The Greek is better translated "read and recognize," rather than the NIV *read and understand,* to reflect the play on words *(ana/epi + ginōskō).*

1:15 Paul actually changed his plans twice. In 1 Corinthians 16:3-9 his plan was to stay in Ephesus until Pentecost and then spend the winter in Corinth after passing through

them, "not many were influential; not many were of noble birth. But God chose the foolish things of the world to shame the wise" (1 Cor 1:26-27).

Even with such mundane activities as writing letters and making travel plans, Paul maintains that he acts with complete frankness and sincerity. Far from forcing the Corinthians to "read between the lines"—as they complained they had to do—Paul's intent was to write only what they could easily *read and understand* (v. 13). The first verb, *read (anaginōskō)*, is used for the reading of a letter aloud to an assembly; the second verb means not only to *understand* but also to give assent to what has been read (*epiginōskō*, "to recognize"; see the note). One of the functions of the letter carrier was to read the letter and answer any questions that the recipients might have. With Paul's letters, however, there are no hidden meanings or obscurities that require the on-the-spot explanations of a carrier. What he says is what he means.

Paul extends the idea of clarity in writing to a desire for complete understanding and clarity in all matters pertaining to his relationship with the Corinthians: *I hope that, as you have understood us in part, you will come to understand [us] fully* (v. 14). Through Titus's recent visit they have come to better understand something of Paul's motives (7:11). What Paul wishes for now is that they will have complete confidence in him, so that he might become a source of boasting for them, as they have become for him (v. 14).

Once again Paul emphasizes how intertwined their lives are—so much so that his apostleship has no meaning apart from those who have become his "children" (12:14-15). And when at last he must give an account on *the day of the Lord Jesus,* his basis for confidence and source of pride will be not himself but those who have come to faith through his ministry.

Second Complaint: A Change of Plans (1:15-22) It is a sad but true indictment of the church that we are too often program and people driven rather than mission and message oriented. An experienced

Macedonia. News of the deteriorating situation in Corinth led him to change this plan and go directly to Corinth, followed by a trip to Macedonia and then pay a return visit to Corinth. The Corinthians' complaint in verses 13-15 about not being able to understand his letters suggests that Paul communicated this changed itinerary either in a letter or a brief message

cotton-mill manager once said to Charles Hummel, the director of faculty ministries with InterVarsity Christian Fellowship, that his greatest danger was in letting the urgent things crowd out the important. In a rapidly changing and quickly paced society like ours, we as Christians live in constant tension between the urgent and the important. All too frequently it is the urgent that wins out. Paul faced this problem with the Corinthian church in his day. A canceled visit to Corinth led the church to label Paul as a fair-weather friend who, following the way of the world, made and changed his plans to suit himself and no one else. And if he was unreliable in small matters like this, how was he to be trusted in bigger matters like preaching the gospel? What the Corinthians failed to see, however, is that Paul's travels in serving the gospel were governed not by personal whim but by his mission and his message. God, not people or programs, dictated his schedule.

In an attempt to move his relationship with the church toward this fuller understanding of his priorities, Paul goes on in verses 15-22 to respond to a complaint that arose over some alleged miscommunication on his part about his travel plans. From Paul's comments in these verses it seems that he had planned to visit the Corinthians twice before heading to Jerusalem to deliver the relief fund (v. 15, see the commentary at 8:1). His intent was to come to Corinth first, move on to Macedonia and then return to Corinth, from where he hoped to be sent on his way to Judea with the money he had collected (v. 16). This would be the first time Paul had visited them since the founding of the church three years earlier. But the first of these two visits was so painful that Paul canceled the second one and returned to Ephesus, abandoning for the moment his Jerusalem collection efforts (see the introduction). The news of Paul's canceled visit was not well received at Corinth. They looked on his

via one of his deputies prior to the painful visit. Paul's failure to return to Corinth after his painful stay with them constitutes a second change. It is frequently said that his painful trip was done on the spur of the moment when, in fact, Paul's language in 2 Corinthians 1:15-17 indicates a well-thought-out plan (see the commentary). At the time Paul writes 2 Corinthians he is in Macedonia, following his original plan to go there first and then proceed on to Corinth.

1:16 The expectation that a traveler would be provided with whatever was needful for the journey ahead is found elsewhere in Paul's writing. See, for example, Titus 3:13: "Do everything you can to help Zenas the lawyer and Apollos on their way and see that they

willingness to forgo a return visit as a sign of a fickle person who can say yes one moment and no the next (v. 17).

Paul's initial approach to the Corinthian charge is to show that he is not fickle in his decision-making. *I planned,* he says, *to visit you first so that you might benefit twice* (v. 15). Paul chooses his words carefully. The Greek term for *planned* stresses a course laid out as a deliberate act of the will and is better translated "I determined" *(eboulomēn).* Far from telling the Corinthians one thing and doing another, his plan to visit them had been carefully thought out, and he had fully intended to follow through on it. Paul had also expected that the church would *send [him] on [his] way (propemphthēnai,* v. 16)—a technical term for furnishing a traveler with whatever provisions were necessary for the journey ahead. So he did not make these plans *lightly (elaphria),* a word commonly used of someone who makes a promise that they do not intend to keep (v. 17).

Paul goes on in verses 18-22 to answer the church's complaint from the standpoint of his role as a preacher of the gospel, arguing from the integrity of the message that he, Silas and Timothy had preached to them—and which they themselves affirmed by their *Amen* (v. 20)—to the integrity of the messengers themselves. Paul employs a greater-to-lesser line of argumentation that was in common use, especially in Jewish circles. *God is faithful* (v. 18). How do the Corinthians know this? They know this preeminently through *the Son of God* in whom there was and is no fickleness or inconsistency. *For no matter how many promises God has made, they are "Yes" in Christ* (v. 20). Put simply, Jesus is the very embodiment of God's faithfulness, for God has fulfilled and continues to fulfill *(gegonen)* every one of his promises in and through him *(en autō).* The Corinthians affirm God's faithfulness to his promises when *through* Christ they say

have everything they need." Compare Acts 15:3; Romans 15:24; 1 Corinthians 16:6; 3 John 6-8.

1:17 The negative *mēti* expects the answer no and can be translated: "Surely when I decided this, I did not do it in a lighthearted fashion." The article with the noun *elaphria* ("lightly") points to a Corinthian accusation and can legitimately be put in quotes. Compare Ephesians 4:9, where the article introduces an Old Testament quote: "What does 'he ascended' mean?" *(to de 'Anebē ti estin;* Blass, Debrunner and Funk 1961:no. 267).

1:19 The perfect tense, *gegonen,* is used of past action that results in a continuing state (Blass, Debrunner and Funk 1961:no. 318[4]). In and through Christ *(en autō)* the divine yes has come into effect as a permanent reality (M. J. Harris 1976:325).

"Amen" to the preaching of God's word (v. 20).

Two young girls were talking, and one said she had ten pennies. The other girl looked at her hand and only saw five. She said, "You only have five pennies."

The first girl replied, "I have five, and my father told me he would give me five more tonight. So I have ten." She understood that her father's promise was as good as done.

So it is with God's promises. And God's faithfulness in and through Jesus was preached by Paul without any wavering or inconsistency, so that the consistency of his message ensured the consistent character of his motives and actions. As the Corinthians themselves could verify, there was no "yes" and "no" about the Son whom Paul and his colleagues preached. His consistency in the greater matters ensured his reliability in the comparatively lesser matters.

Paul reinforces his argument by pointing in verses 21-22 to their joint possession of the Spirit, arguing that the God who gave them the Spirit to guarantee their common destiny (v. 22) is the same God who ensures the integrity of his conduct ([confirms] both us and you). So to doubt Paul's reliability in a trivial matter such as travel plans would be to also doubt the credibility of the Spirit's work in the Corinthians' own lives.

Paul chooses four terms drawn from the familiar world of law, religion and commerce to describe the Spirit's activity in the life of the congregation. The first is in the present tense, while the other three are past actions on which the Spirit's present activity is dependent: Having anointed, sealed and put his Spirit in our hearts as a deposit, God is now (through the Spirit) in the process of confirming both us and you in

1:20 Amen ("truly," "indeed") is from a Semitic root ('mn) that suggests solidity and firmness. It has its origin in the Jewish worship service, where it was spoken as a congregational response to a benediction or doxology (as in Neh 8:6: "Ezra praised the LORD, the great God; and all the people lifted their hands and responded 'Amen! Amen!' "). It expresses strong affirmation of what had been declared. See Galatians 1:5; Philippians 4:20; 1 Timothy 1:17; 2 Timothy 4:18.

1:21-22 The shift in tenses is noteworthy. The aorist participles define three actions antecedent to God's present stabilizing activity. The idea is that God's continuing activity in the church is dependent on his past work of anointing and sealing through the deposit of the Spirit in the human heart.

Christ, says Paul. To "confirm" (*bebaioō*, not the NIV *stand firm*) is a technical term for the legal guarantee that a seller gives a buyer to ensure the validity of the sale against any possible third-party claims. As applied to the Spirit, it depicts his job in confirming the ongoing validity of God's relationship to his people. "Anoint" (*chriō*) is a word used in the Old Testament for commissioning to a particular office (e.g., king, priest) or task (e.g., prophet). It is also used metaphorically of the Spirit's equipping for mission or service (e.g., Is 61:1). By the action of anointing, then, Paul has in mind the Spirit's empowering and equipping the church to carry forth Christ's mission in the world. To "seal" (*sphragizō*), in the commercial world of Paul's day, referred to the means by which money, goods or documents were secured for delivery. A seal was both a mark of ownership and proof that the goods in question had not been tampered with or falsified in transit. Nowadays we might think of the rancher in West Texas who makes it his practice to round up all his year-old calves each spring for branding. The brand, which is placed on the flank of the calf with a heated branding iron, is the rancher's mark of ownership. No one can dispute that the calf belongs to him. In the same way God has placed his mark of ownership on us by sealing us with the Spirit. No one can remove us from his ownership until the day of redemption.

The activities of confirming, anointing and sealing are dependent on what Paul calls the *arrabōn* of the Spirit in our hearts. *Arrabōn* is a legal term pertaining to contracts of sale or service. In the case of a contract of sale, the *arrabōn* in Hebrew law was something handed over as security to be reclaimed at a later date ("pledge," as in Gen 38:17-20), while in Greek law it referred to the earnest money that a buyer would give the seller prior to the actual sale and delivery of the item. Today

---

1:21 For the Spirit's anointing for service, see Isaiah 61:1, where "the Spirit of the Sovereign LORD is on me" and "the LORD has anointed me to preach good news to the poor" are parallel ideas.

1:22 It is unlikely that Paul has in mind the Spirit as a "pledge" that will be reclaimed by God at a later date. This conflicts with the notion elsewhere of the Spirit as a permanent possession of the believer. Some think in terms of the Spirit as a "warranty" or "guarantee," but this does not fit with extrabiblical usage. The idea of a "first installment" or "down payment" is the best option.

With a contract of sale, if the seller defaulted he was required to pay the buyer twice the *arrabōn*, while with a contract for services, it was the laborers who had to pay double the *arrabōn* to the hirer.

we might think in terms of the down payment *(deposit)* that we make on a house or car with the intent of paying the balance at some future point. In the case of a contract for services, the *arrabōn* was the first installment that a hirer would give the workers toward services to be carried out at a later date. Two letters from Paul's day illustrate this sense quite well. In one letter a servant writes to his master that he has paid Lampon the mouse-catcher an *arrabōn* of eight drachmas so that he will start work and catch the mice while they are still with young; in a second letter the provision is made regarding the engagement of certain dancing girls for a village festival who are to receive payment "by way of *arrabōn* to be reckoned in the price" (Moulton-Milligan 1930:79). Even today in Greece *bē arrabōna* is still used for "the engagement ring."

In what way, though, is the Spirit a first installment or *deposit?* The Spirit's activities of birthing (anointing, sealing) and guaranteeing the church's continuing existence leads one to think of the Spirit as the first installment of the church's future redemption. Paul develops this idea in Ephesians 5:25-27, where the church is portrayed as the bride-to-be and Christ as the expectant bridegroom. On his return they will be wed. Meanwhile, the church is in the process of being cleansed through the word, so that she might be presented to Christ as a "radiant" bride, without "stain or wrinkle."

To sum up, the Spirit's role in the life of the church is that of a first installment or down payment that guarantees God's indisputable relationship, commissions and equips for service, secures against falsification or tampering, and preserves the "goods" of this relationship until the day of redemption.

Third Complaint: A Domineering Attitude (1:23—2:4) We live in

---

1:23 Compare the oath taken under Augustus in the following Galatian inscription: "I pronounce a curse against myself, my body, soul, goods, children." Is Paul's oath contrary to Jesus' prohibition of oaths (Mt 5:34-37)? On the surface it would appear so. However, an examination of the context shows that Jesus is not dealing with pronouncing a curse against oneself but with the swearing of an oath to another person. The truly righteous person has no need to guarantee his or her commitments with an oath. A yes or no should be sufficient. In Paul's case, his word and conduct as a minister of the gospel has been called into question. A truly righteous congregation would have accepted his veracity at face value. But this was not the case with the Corinthians. And so he resorts to bolstering the truthfulness of his word with the strongest oath possible.

Epi tēn emēn psychēn is equivalent to the Hebrew phrase *'al-napšî* meaning "myself."

a day when the exercise of discipline in the church is fast disappearing or being replaced by self-image reinforcement, while in the home it is often frowned on as being antiquated or bordering on abuse. Yet discipline is firmly rooted in the biblical record, where it is presented as a positive, not negative, model. The preeminent model is God himself, whose dealings with his people are often pictured in terms of a parent-child relationship. Central to this relationship is discipline. It is a measure of God's love that he disciplines his children (Prov 3:11-12), but it is not without personal cost. In Hosea 11:8-9 God is portrayed as a parent pacing the floor, anguishing over the need to discipline his wayward child, Israel. Paul similarly anguishes over the need to discipline the Corinthian church.

In 1:23—2:4 Paul tells the Corinthians why he did not carry out his Corinth—Macedonia—Corinth travel plan. Today, to guarantee the truthfulness of what we are about to say, we use such phrases as "with God as my witness" or "I swear to tell the truth." Paul begins by swearing an oath in the strongest terms possible. *I call God as my witness* is literally "I call upon God as a witness against *(epi)* my soul *(psychēn)*." With this imprecation Paul invokes the wrath of God against himself (v. 23). He is willing to forfeit his very life if he is found not to be telling the truth. The term *soul* is commonly used in the New Testament of the "self." Paul employs it of the inner life of a person—equivalent to the ego or personality (e.g., Rom 2:9; 11:3; 13:1; 16:4; 1 Cor 15:45; 2 Cor 12:15). That Paul would bind himself in this way points to the seriousness with which he viewed the Corinthian accusation.

Legal terminology predominates in these verses. Paul pictures himself

Even in 1 Thessalonians 5:23 "spirit, soul and body" do not reflect different anthropological categories but the whole person viewed from three different modes of existence. See Vorländer and Brown 1978:682-84.

Earlier commentators assumed that Paul's painful visit was his founding visit recorded in Acts 18 and *ouketi ēlthon* the cancellation of a second, single visit. But there is nothing in the Acts account or in Paul's comments elsewhere that remotely hints at his first visit having been "painful" (2 Cor 2:1). Today most understand *ouketi ēlthon* to be referring to Paul's cancellation of the second of a two-pronged visit. See, however, Furnish (1984:138), who argues for the cancellation of an entire double visit subsequent to a painful second visit. For the reconstruction of events surrounding the painful visit (1:23) and severe letter (2:1-4), see the introduction.

on trial in a court of law. To *call upon (epikaloumai)* is a common legal term in the Old Testament for summoning witnesses to a trial—equivalent to our subpoena today. Under Jewish law any matter had to be verified by two or three witnesses (Deut 19:15; compare 17:6). Since there are no human witnesses who could testify about the intentions of his heart, Paul calls on *God* as his sole witness to testify to the fact that it was *to spare* the Corinthians that he did not pay them a return visit. Pastoral concern, not fickleness, caused him to change his travel plans.

But from what did Paul want to spare them? It is clear from his remarks both here and in chapter 13 that had he come again he would have had to discipline them (13:1-10), and this would have caused them *grief* (2:2). Paul exercised discipline very unwillingly and only as a last resort. When he did rebuke a church, it was done in *love,* never merely to hurt but to restore a broken relationship (2:4).

All of us who teach or pastor face the danger of thinking that our job is to force others to think as we do. So Paul immediately throws in a qualifier. To talk about sparing them discipline could sound like a threat. It could seem as if he is attempting to *lord it over* their *faith* (v. 24). On the contrary, he and his colleagues *work* together *with* them *(synergoi)* to secure their *joy.* When Paul rebuked, the last thing he wanted was to play the bully. Nor could he bully them if he wanted to, because it is *by faith,* not by pastoral coercion, that they *stand firm.*

In 2:1-4 Paul goes on to tell the Corinthians why he did not pay them a return visit. *I made up my mind,* he says, *that I would not make another painful visit to you* (v. 1). *I made up my mind* is literally "I judged this for myself," indicating a settled and carefully weighed decision. The

---

1:24 The dative in the phrase *tē pistei hestēkate* can be construed either as local ("you stand *in the sphere of* faith") or as instrumental ("you stand firm *by means of* your faith"). The perfect tense denotes that "you stood and now continue to stand."

Synergoi normally refers to Paul's colleagues. But given the emphasis throughout 2 Corinthians on the lives of apostle and congregation being inseparably linked, Paul may well be referring to the Corinthians as "coworkers." The contrast in verse 24 between *synergoi* and "domineering over" also suggests this construal. See also *synergountes* in 6:1.

2:3-4 Paul's severe letter in all probability is not extant. Earlier commentators tended to identify this letter with 1 Corinthians and the offender with the man who committed incest in 1 Corinthians 5:1-5. There is some support for this equation. Both involve an unnamed individual who committed a specific wrong, church discipline is called for in both cases, and Satan is mentioned in both accounts. However, against this identification

reason he gives for his decision is that his visiting them at this time would cause them to be sad and then there would be no one to make him *glad* (v. 2). So intimately was Paul's happiness bound up with theirs that he refrained from coming until it would be a time of gladness and nurture for both. So instead of paying them yet another painful visit, he decided to send them a letter that was intended to show how much he loved them but which caused him many tears to write due to its harsh character (vv. 3-4).

The events surrounding this painful visit and "severe letter" can be reconstructed to a large extent from 1 and 2 Corinthians (see the introduction). It appears that the relationship between Paul and the Corinthians deteriorated when a group within the church began to question his authority. There were "some" who were arrogantly claiming that Paul was not coming back to Corinth (1 Cor 4:18). They were also becoming suspicious of him because he would not accept financial assistance but worked instead to support himself (1 Cor 9:1-18). Perhaps, they thought, this was because Paul was not truly an apostle. News of this deteriorating situation reached Paul and resulted in a visit that was painful for both him and the Corinthians. It seems that during his visit someone in the congregation publicly insulted him and challenged his authority, demanding proof that Christ was speaking through him (13:3). What was particularly hurtful for Paul was the fact that the church sat by and did nothing to support him. After issuing a strong word of warning (13:2), he returned to Ephesus, abandoning his plan to visit the Macedonian churches, revisit Corinth (1:16) and then go on to Jerusalem with the relief funds that had been collected from the Gentile churches.

---

are Paul's statements in 2 Corinthians 2:5-11 about his personal forgiveness of the individual in question, his anguish at having to rebuke the Corinthian church for their lack of personal loyalty and the severe letter's primary intent to secure the Corinthians' obedience—none of which squares with 1 Corinthians 5:1-13. More recently it has been argued that 2 Corinthians 10—13 preserves at least a portion of this letter. But here too there are major discrepancies. Chapters 10—13 focus on outsiders who are trying to encroach on Paul's missionary field and not on the punishment of an individual who is a member of the Corinthian congregation. They also lack Paul's demand for discipline by the majority. Such difficulties have led most to conclude that the Corinthian church did not preserve this letter (see the introduction).

2:3 *Touto auto* can be taken adverbially, *I wrote as I did* (NIV, JB, RSV, LB) or as the object of the verb, "I wrote this very thing" (KJV, NEB).

When Paul returned to Ephesus he wrote the church a "severe letter" by means of which he hoped to avoid another painful encounter with them (2 Cor 1:23). In this letter he called for the Corinthians to discipline the individual who had "caused" him "grief" (2:5-11), rebuked the church for not coming to his aid (7:8-12), tested their obedience to apostolic authority (7:14-15) and questioned their personal support (2:3; 7:12-13). That this was a difficult letter for Paul to write is clear from his statement that he wrote it *out of great distress and anguish of heart with many tears* (2:4). *Thlipsis (distress)* and *synochē (anguish)* are virtual synonymns for personal pain brought about by oppressive circumstances. Here, they refer to the deep emotional turmoil that Paul experienced as he wrote this letter to the Corinthians, very much like the anxiety a parent feels when faced with the prospect of exercising discipline.

Disciplining a child is never an easy matter. That discipline can be motivated by love is exceedingly difficult for a child to comprehend. It must have been hard too for the Corinthians, who were "grieved" by the severity of Paul's letter (v. 4). Nonetheless, Paul intended that by this letter they might *know the depth of [the] love* he had for his spiritual children (v. 4). *Love,* which stands in an emphatic position in the clause, is the primary reason he gives for writing. It is all too easy to allow personal feelings to get in the way of ministry. But this was not the case with Paul. He could have used this letter to vent his anger and disappointment with his spiritual children. Instead, he saw past his own pain to what was needful from the pastoral standpoint.

Church Discipline and Forgiveness (2:5-11) Mention of the grief that the severe letter had caused the Corinthians leads Paul in verses 5-11 to

---

2:4 *Perissoterōs* could be "the love I have *especially* for you" or "the love which I have *in abundance* for you." The elative "especially" suggests that Paul is singling out the Corinthians over other churches. For this reason the positive "in abundance" is to be preferred.

2:5 "If *someone [tis]* has caused me grief" reflects Paul's practice of referring to the opposition in general terms rather than by name. Compare "some" (1 Cor 4:18; 2 Cor 3:1; 10:10), "many who" (2 Cor 2:17; 12:21), "those who" (5:12), "someone" (11:4) and "such people" (11:13). Only in the Pastoral Letters does he give the names of those who harmed him.

The precise sense of *apo merous* ("in part") is disputed. It can mean "a part of you" (that is, he grieved a portion of the congregation) or *to some extent* (that is, not all were

think as well of the pain that the offending person had caused the church. This, in turn, prompts him to consider the action that the congregation took in response to his letter and the need for forgiveness now that the individual in question had repented. Like some churches today, the Corinthian congregation was a church of extremes. When Paul was publicly challenged at Corinth, the church sat back and did nothing. But now when pushed by Paul to deal with the situation, they mete out punishment with a vengeance, even to the extent of losing sight of the remedial character of the disciplinary process.

Once again Paul is concerned to get the church to see how intertwined their lives are. In rather convoluted language, he shifts the focus from a personal insult to the corporate affront implied in the individual's attack against him. His pastoral tact is also in evidence when he refers to the blameworthy person as *anyone,* rather than by name. *If anyone has caused grief,* Paul says, *he has not so much grieved me as he has grieved all of you* (v. 5). Just as a slight to the father or mother cannot help but reflect on the children, so an affront to Paul as their spiritual parent cannot fail to reflect on them. Paul does *not* wish *to put it too severely,* so he qualifies *he has grieved all of you* with *to some extent.* Not all in the church may have been affected to the same degree by the offense. Indeed his reference in verse 6 to the punishment by the majority implies that a minority did not agree with the course of action decided on.

The Corinthians' course of action is described in verse 6 as *the punishment inflicted on him.* The word for *punishment* can denote a penalty, rebuke or censure and implies causing others to suffer what they deserve (Louw and Nida 1988-1989:38.6). The context gives the

---

equally grieved).

Epibareō means to "weigh heavily on," "bear hardly on." Most take *mē epibarō* as intransitive, "not to labor the point" (Phillips, JB, NEB, NIV, RSV), rather than transitive, "not to lay too heavy a burden on" (TEV, KJV, LB).

2:6 *Tōn pleionōn* ("the majority") could be a Hebraism for the entire congregation *(ha rabbîm)* or stand for the main portion of the Corinthian church. If it is the latter, then there is the question of the identity of the "minority." It could refer either to those who felt that the discipline was too lenient or to those who did not support the degree of discipline or perhaps even the need for it. Given the severity of the punishment (2:7) and indications of a lingering opposition (10:6; 12:20-21; 13:2), the presence of a nonsupportive minority seems the likeliest possibility.

impression of some kind of formal disciplinary action decided on and carried out by the congregation. Excommunication or at least the withholding of church privileges is suggested by the danger posed to the individual (v. 7, *so that he will not be overwhelmed by excessive sorrow.*

The responsible exercise of discipline was something that Paul had great difficultly instilling in his churches—especially a church like Corinth. It is the corporate responsibility of the church to punish wrongdoing (2 Cor 2:6; 10:6), to excommunicate in the case of persistent sin (1 Cor 5:2, 10-13) and to reinstate the repentant (2 Cor 2:7-8). Paul had to rebuke the Corinthians initially for not disciplining the individual in question (v. 9). Now the church has gone too far in the other direction (v. 6). Paul's counsel to them is threefold. First, the punishment by the majority *is sufficient* (v. 6). Mention of the man's *sorrow* (v. 7) shows that the punishment had its intended effect; the person has repented of his action. Reference to *the majority* points to the presence of a dissenting minority, who thought that the discipline was either too lenient or, more probably, too severe.

The Corinthians are instructed, second, *to forgive and comfort* the man rather than continue the discipline (v. 7). Instead of *aphiēmi,* the customary word in the Gospels for forgiveness, Paul uses *charizomai,* which means to "give freely" and so to forgive on the basis of one's gracious attitude toward a person (Louw and Nida 1988-1989:40.10). God's gracious attitude toward us in the person of his Son is surely in the background here. It is likely that the man is becoming discouraged by the church's continuance of the discipline. What is needed at this point is for the Corinthians to stop the punishment and to "encourage" (rather than the NIV *comfort;* see the note).

The third and last piece of advice Paul gives the church is to *reaffirm*

2:7 *Parakaleō* most commonly means "to request." Other frequent uses are "to exhort" and "to encourage." "To comfort" is a rare meaning, attested only in the biblical materials, and seems unsuitable here. Encouragement, not comfort, is what we give to someone who has repented.

2:10 *I have forgiven in the sight of Christ for your sake* shows that the offense involved some injury to Paul himself. Paul's offer of personal forgiveness and his understatement of the seriousness of the offense would be totally inappropriate if the offense were the case of incest mentioned in 1 Corinthians 5. See the introduction.

their *love* for the man (v. 8). The verb "to reaffirm" *(kyrōsai)* means "to confirm" or "ratify." It was commonly used in Paul's day of a will, treaty, law, decree, bill of sale or other legal document coming into force (Behm 1965:1098-99). Paul is probably thinking of a public reinstatement as a means of reassuring him of the congregation's love. That they are to confirm their *love* for the man shows that Christian discipline is always intended to be remedial, never merely punitive. The Corinthians had to be reminded of this. But it is not much different today. Many churches have equal difficulty knowing when to discipline and when to forgive.

These verses point to two dangers in carrying discipline too far. First, there is a danger for the individual. What starts out as godly sorrow can unwittingly lead to a consuming guilt or to an overpreoccupation with one's sin (v. 7). The Corinthians are to forgive and encourage the man so that he will not be *overwhelmed by excessive sorrow*. The picture is of a drowning person who is in danger of being swallowed up by his grief, as by a rushing river or flood of water. Discipline that goes beyond the stage of "godly sorrow" becomes strictly punitive and nonredemptive (7:10).

There is also a danger for the congregation. The Corinthians are to forgive the man *so that Satan might not outwit* them (v. 11). The word for *outwit (pleonekteō)* means "to take advantage" of someone with the intent to cheat or exploit them. Overdiscipline can provide Satan with just the foothold into the life of a congregation that he covets. *For we are not,* Paul continues, *unaware of his schemes* (v. 11). The NIV misses the wordplay here. The Greek is literally, "we are not unmindful of his mind," which in the case of Satan is a scheming, plotting mind. What kind of plotting is in view? It is possible that Paul is thinking of how Satan can take advantage of the discipline process to alienate a person from the church or even from Christianity. The presence of the plural,

---

In the sight of Christ has been interpreted to mean (1) in light of future judgment, (2) with Christ as witness or (3) in light of the forgiveness we have all received through Christ. It is difficult to decide which interpretation is the correct one, but it would be appropriate for Paul, having begun this section invoking God as his witness, to conclude by calling on Christ to testify to the genuineness of his forgiveness.

2:11 *Pleonekteō* is often associated with thieving and robbery (e.g., 1 Cor 5:10; 6:10). Some, as a result, prefer "rob" to the NIV *outwit*. On this reading, the Corinthians are to forgive the man in order that Satan might not rob the church of one of its members.

"that *we* might not be outwitted," suggests, however, that the congregation is in mind. Paul could well be thinking of how Satan can take advantage of an unforgiving, overly legalistic attitude to sow division and dissension in the church. Mention of the majority suggests that a difference of opinion existed within the Corinthian congregation that Satan could easily exploit. This is probably why in verse 10 Paul says, *If you forgive anyone, I also forgive . . . for your sake.* He also understates the seriousness of the offense in his qualification *if there was anything to forgive. If you forgive anyone* is literally "whom you forgive something" and assumes that they will in fact do as he has advised. Otherwise, Satan stands a chance of outwitting them—but not because the church has not been forewarned. *We are not unaware of his schemes,* Paul states (v. 11). One of the Christian's best defenses against Satan's ploys is prior awareness of his purposes and methods (M. J. Harris 1976:330).

Paul offers his own forgiveness *in the sight of Christ.* At the start he invoked God as a witness to his wanting to spare the church pain on a return visit (1:23). Now as he concludes this section, he calls on Christ as a witness to the genuineness of his forgiveness of the man who had caused him pain on the previous visit. Paul's personal forgiveness of an individual who had deeply hurt and publicly humiliated him provides an important model both for the Corinthians and for us today. It is a reminder of what Jesus taught his disciples about forgiveness. If we ask God to forgive our sins, we ask because we ourselves are willing to forgive anyone who sins against us (Lk 11:4). Someone once made the comment to John Wesley, "I never forgive," to which he aptly replied, "Then, sir, I hope that you never sin." Wesley's quick-witted response highlights the truth that it is only as we are willing to forgive others that God extends forgiveness to us.

Paul's initiative in offering his personal forgiveness also points up his primary reason for writing the "severe letter." To be sure, he wanted to see justice served. But even more important, he wanted to see if the Corinthians themselves *would stand the test and be obedient in everything* (2 Cor 2:9). The NIV *stand the test* is literally "to know the proof

---

2:12 Troas was the port city for travel between northwest Asia Minor and Macedonia (see Acts 16:8, 11; 20:5; 2 Tim 4:13). Paul states that he came *eis tēn Trōada.* Some take the definite article to be referring to the Troad, a fifty-mile-wide promontory. But the same

of you." *Dokimē* is the "proof" that comes from such a test of someone's or something's worth or genuineness. The Corinthians' response to the "tough love" expressed in Paul's letter would show their true character. Although Paul is concerned to know if they are on his side, it is their being *obedient in everything* that is the real issue. It is impossible to separate the person from the office. When Paul acts, he acts as an apostle of Christ. So to accept his reproof is to accept Christ's reproof, and to reject him is in effect to reject Christ. To the Corinthians' credit, they responded to Paul's rebuke with "godly sorrow" and an "eagerness to clear" themselves (7:11). When confronted with the facts of the situation, they were more than willing to admit they were at fault for not coming to his defense. One wonders whether many churches today—often the home of what J. I. Packer described as a "hot tub religion" that embraces anything that makes people feel better—could and would respond to a pastoral word of rebuke in like fashion.

Evangelism in Troas (2:12-17) Rather than fickle, as the Corinthians have charged, Paul has shown himself willing to adapt to their changing situation. He also acted for their benefit and not his own, choosing the course of action that spared them the most pain. Now in verses 12-17 Paul concludes his defense of his conduct by showing how even his efforts to preach the gospel in Troas were affected by his pastoral anxiety for the church. A friend of mine recently wrote that he has been grappling with the problem of "people or plans." While rushing to get an outline on the blackboard in the few minutes that remained before Sunday school, one of the church members stopped him to talk about a personal problem. The outline never made it to the board. In much the same way, Paul's plans for ministry in Troas were cut short because of his more pressing concern for Titus and his Corinthian friends. Friends or ministry strategies? People or plans? This is a tension that those in leadership roles in the church constantly face.

In what at first glance appears to be an abrupt change of topic, Paul at verse 12 recounts his travel itinerary subsequent to his return to

phrase occurs in Acts 20:6 where the reference is clearly to the seaport town of Troas ("we sailed from Philippi and came *eis tēn Trōada*").

Ephesus. A closer look, however, shows that he is still dealing with the charge of fickleness. When he left Ephesus and *went to Troas* it was not due to some sudden whim but in order *to preach the gospel of Christ* (literally, "for the gospel of Christ"). It is the gospel, not his own personal desires, that determines his travel plans. That Paul would plan an evangelistic outreach in the city of Troas is logical given its significance. Strabo, a first-century geographer, calls it one of the notable cities of the world. Troas was an Aegean seaport town located at the northwest corner of Asia Minor on a fifty-mile-wide promontory called the Troad. Founded as Antigonia in 334 B.C., it was renamed Alexandria Troas in 300 B.C. in honor of Alexander the Great. Construction of an artificial harbor provided for the first time a secure shelter within a few miles of the mouth of the Hellespont and led to the city's quick growth and subsequent prosperity (Hemer 1975:79-92).

Paul, however, is not merely interested in demonstrating that he went about the business of setting up his itinerary in a responsible fashion. His reference to Troas is important because it shows just how dear the Corinthians were to him. The severe letter that Paul wrote after his painful experience with the Corinthian church was carried to Corinth by Titus, one of Paul's coworkers. Shortly after, Paul made plans to travel to Troas to engage in a new work of evangelism. On his arrival in this bustling seaport town, Paul found that *a door* for evangelistic outreach "stood open" (NIV *had opened;* see the note) for him "in the Lord." An "open door," an idiom we use today for an opportunity set before a person, is how Paul routinely describes evangelistic opportunities (e.g., 1 Cor 16:9; Col 4:3). "Stood open" shows that this was more than an

---

Eis + *to euangelion* denotes purpose, "for the purpose of [preaching] the gospel." The genitive in the phrase *to euangelion tou Christou* is most commonly construed in Paul's writings as objective, "the gospel about Christ."

The perfect tense *aneōgmenēs* denotes a present state resulting from a past action. A door for evangelism opened for Paul and his coworkers on arriving at Troas and remained opened during their stay. For this reason, "stood open" is to be preferred to the NIV's *had opened.*

2:13 F. F. Bruce speculates that Paul interjects his experience in Troas at this point in the text because it proved a notable instance of one of Satan's schemes (2:11). By exploiting Paul's unhappiness over Corinth, Satan was able to hinder the advance of the gospel in Troas (1971:186).

Paul might well have waited until sea travel stopped for the winter months to be sure

impromptu evangelistic foray. It had apparently been arranged that Titus was to meet Paul there with news about the Corinthian church. But after spending a short time in Troas, Paul became so disturbed that he *did not find Titus there* that he gave up a successful outreach to set out on the road toward Macedonia in the hopes of meeting him along the way (v. 13; see the introduction for further discussion).

Paul describes his psychological state while waiting for Titus at Troas as without *peace of mind* (v. 13; literally, "I had no relief in my spirit"). The word translated *peace* in the NIV refers not so much to "rest" (KJV, NKJ, RSV, NRSV) as to "relief" (REB, NEB) or "relaxation." The NIV *of mind* is, literally, "in my spirit"—the seat of human emotion and sensation (Plummer 1915:65). The JB "I was continually uneasy in mind" and TEV "I was deeply worried" catch the sense quite well. Today we would say that Paul was uptight—so much so that he *said good-by* to the new believers at Troas *(to them)* and *went on to Macedonia.* The word for *good-by* is literally "to take leave of" and suggests a reluctant departure. The reference to *them* indicates that Paul was at Troas long enough to establish a church (see Acts 20:6-12). That he would head for *Macedonia* probably means that he took the overland route hoping to catch Titus on the road that wound its way through the major cities along the Eastern seaboard of the province. It is quite possible that part of Titus's mission was to firm up the collection efforts among the Macedonian churches after his visit to Corinth.

At verse 14 Paul suddenly shifts from anxiety (*I still had no peace of mind,* vv. 12-13) to thanksgiving: *But thanks be to God, who always leads us in triumphal procession,* v. 14). This shift has generated considerable

that Titus would not be arriving by boat. In this case he would most likely take the overland route to Macedonia to be certain that he did not miss Titus. Murray J. Harris (1976:331) and C. K. Barrett (1973:94) speculate that Paul's anxiety was partially a concern for Titus's safety, especially if he were carrying contributions for the Jerusalem collection.

The variation between *oudemian eschēken anesin hē sarx hēmōn* ("our *flesh* had no relief," 7:5) and *ouk eschēka anesin tō pneumati mou* ("I had no relief in my *spirit,*" 2:13) shows that Paul is not making a sharp distinction between "flesh" and "spirit." Regarding the use of the perfect tense *(eschēka)* for the aorist in historical narration, see Blass, Debrunner and Funk 1961:343[2]. Paul is not saying that he continues to lack peace of mind, as the perfect tense would normally indicate, but that he had lacked it at one point in the past.

discussion. Some argue that 2:14—7:4 is a letter fragment that the editor of the Pauline corpus inserted at this spot in our canonical 2 Corinthians (see the introduction). Others maintain that the shift is of Paul's own making. Explanations include a premature expression of his relief on meeting Titus, a shift in gears after a dictation pause, a sudden realization of the need to deal with themes that he failed to touch on in his opening eulogy and an instance of the Pauline theme of divine power overcoming human weakness. It is the last proposal that offers the best explanation. A look at the broader context of the letter shows that this kind of mood shift is part and parcel of Paul's repeated emphasis on God's ability to triumph over the frailties and fallibility of the gospel preacher (see the introduction). God's power is able to overcome any and all human weakness (Perriman 1989:39-41).

This realization causes Paul to break out in a joyful exclamation of *thanks to God, who always leads us in triumphal procession* (v. 14). When the Spartans marched into battle, they advanced with cheerful songs, willing to fight. But when the Persians entered the conflict, you could hear the crack of the whips with which the officers drove the soldiers into the fray. It is no wonder that a few Spartans were more than a match for thousands of Persians. So it should be with preaching the gospel. "If we were enthusiastic soldiers of the cross," writes Spurgeon, "through

---

2:14 Some claim that the meaning "to triumph over" for *thriambeuō* is not attested this early, but Liddell, Scott and Jones 1978 gives numerous examples of this usage.

Victor Paul Furnish thinks that *thriambeuonti hēmas* is a picture of the apostles being paraded about by God in humiliation and shame ("put on display as if we were prisoners in a triumphal procession" [1984:187]); P. Marshal argues that Paul's metaphor is drawn from the arena, picturing the vanquished person as a figure of shame and ridicule (1983). The difficulty here, though, is that apostolic weakness is not in view. Rather, verses 14-17 depict the glorious advance of the gospel and the apostolic task as dispensing a message that has the power to kill or to make alive (v. 15). P. B. Duff proposes that *thriambeuonti hēmas* depicts an epiphany procession of a deity (1991a). R. B. Egan maintains that *thriambeuō* has no triumphal overtones and merely means "to make known, visible, public" (1977).

The integral placement of 2:14—7:4 in 2 Corinthians 1—7 is being called into question with increasing frequency today. It is generally argued that Paul's travel narrative is abruptly broken off at 2:13 and not resumed until 7:5; the apostolic defense in 2:14—7:4 has little, if anything, to do with the surrounding travel narrative; the polemical tone of 2:14—7:4 is in conflict with the conciliatory tone of the surrounding material; it is psychologically improbable that Paul would have broken off the narrative at just this point, thereby leaving the reader in suspense about Titus and the Corinthian congregation; and the presence at 2:14 of a conventional thanksgiving is at odds with

God's help nothing would be able to stand against us." This was Paul's experience as he left Troas and moved on to Macedonia. Even though he had difficulty keeping his mind on his ministry because of gnawing concern for the Corinthian church, he knew that it is God alone who can claim the victory and overcome any deficiencies in his ministry.

Thriambeuō, the word translated in the NIV as *leads . . . in triumphal procession,* is a much debated term. The KJV "cause us to triumph" was not a meaning in use in Paul's day, so modern interpreters have turned to other possibilities. In classical and Hellenistic usage it can mean (1) to triumph over, (2) to lead in triumph, (3) to make a spectacle of and (4) to noise abroad. If we follow either "to lead in triumph" (NIV, RSV, NASB) or "to make a spectacle of" (Col 2:15; compare 1 Cor 4:9), Paul would be drawing on the picture of the Roman *triumphus,* where the victorious Roman troops led the conquered enemy down a processional route in the city of Rome to the temple of Jupiter. The route was lined with spectators who applauded as the victors passed by (Josephus *Jewish Wars* 7.5). Paul would then be thinking of himself and his coworkers either as God's willing captives (TEV, NEB) or as victorious partners with God (JB, Phillips) in the triumphal procession of the gospel. While this is an attractive possibility, it is more likely that he is using the term in the simpler sense of "to triumph over" and thinking of God's ability to

the mood of haste and anxiety in the preceding verses.

Two theories are most commonly put forward. One is that 2:14—7:4 (except 6:14—7:1) is the first of a series of four or five letters that arose out of a situation of developing tensions between Paul and the Corinthians over the intrusion of itinerant preachers who sought to divert Corinthian support from Paul to their own cause. The second is that 2:14—7:4 combined with chapters 10—13 forms Paul's severe letter, written at the height of interaction with his opponents at Corinth and followed by a letter of reconciliation reflecting a resolution of the conflict in Paul's favor.

In reality, interpolation theories create more problems than they solve. There is no manuscript evidence to suggest that 2 Corinthians circulated in any form other than its present one. Moreover, if it is hard to see why Paul would have broken off his travel narrative at this point, it is equally difficult to imagine why an editor would have inserted a fragment at such an unlikely spot. Then too, the arguments commonly put forward lose their cumulative force on closer inspection. The line of continuity between 2:12-13 and 7:5-16 is more apparent than real. Verses 12-13 deal with evangelistic ineffectiveness, while 7:5-16 has to do with divine comfort in the midst of trials. Also, there is a commonality of themes and terms in 2:12-17 and 7:3-16 that belies disunity. While evangelistic terminology dominates 2:12-17, it is the language of "confidence," "boasting," "comfort" and "joy in affliction" that unify 7:3-16. In addition, a polemical note is already struck in 1:12-24 with Paul's defense of his conduct as a church planter (see the introduction).

overcome ministerial weaknesses and ineffectiveness. Regardless of
Paul's state of mind while in Troas, the gospel message went forward.
While God chooses to work through us in spreading the good news, he
does not depend on our personal abilities—or even our stability—for
the message to be effective in the life of the listener. In the final analysis,
it is God who gets the job done.

What, then, is the nature of the gospel ministry? And what kind of
competency do we look for in the gospel minister? These are two key
issues that Paul introduces in verses 14-17 and develops in chapters
3—7. The task of the gospel preacher, Paul states, is to be God's
instrument in advancing the gospel (v. 14). It is *through us,* he says, that
the gospel *spreads everywhere.* The role of the evangelist is pictured as
that of channel for disseminating *the fragrance of the knowledge of
him*—an attractive idea expressed by means of a characteristically
ambiguous string of genitive constructions. The first genitive can indicate
the source of the fragrance, "the fragrance which comes from knowing
him," or its content, "the fragrance which is knowing him." The former
suggests that as our personal relationship with the Lord grows, we give
off a fragrant odor to those around us—a provocative notion, to say the
least. It is the latter construal, however, with knowledge depicted as a
sweet-smelling perfume that permeates the world, that best fits the
central thought of the gospel preacher as God's channel for spreading
the good news. The second genitive provides the object of the knowledge—*knowledge of him.* But which *him* is Paul thinking of—God or
Christ? Both are found in the context (vv. 14-15, 17). But God is the
primary subject. When "Christ" occurs, it is in phrases like "the gospel
of Christ," "the aroma of Christ" or "in Christ."

Knowledge of God reappears in chapter 4, portrayed as light rather
than scent (4:6). Yet it is not knowledge of God in the abstract but "the
light of the knowledge of God in the face of Christ." Indeed the light of
the gospel (4:4) and knowledge of God (4:6) are presented as parallel
notions. The point is not a trivial one. The emphasis among evangelicals
today is, as it should be, on a personal relationship with Christ. And yet
it is often forgotten that such a relationship is not possible apart from

2:15 The present tenses of the articular participles in verse 15 indicate process. "Those

knowledge of God. J. I. Packer writes, "Knowing about God is crucially important for the living of our lives. As it would be cruel to an Amazonian tribesman to fly him to London, put him down without explanation in Trafalgar Square and leave him, as one who knew nothing of English or England, to fend for himself, so we are cruel to ourselves if we try to live in this world without knowing about the God whose world it is and who runs it" (1973:14).

The term in verse 14 for *fragrance (osmē)* is used of both pleasant and unpleasant odors. In verse 15, however, Paul shifts to *euōdia*, which refers only to agreeable smells, and further defines this odor as an *aroma of Christ* to God. A number of backgrounds that Paul may be drawing on have been proposed. For the Jew, Paul's language would immediately bring to mind the scent of burnt offerings, which in the Old Testament are described as a "pleasing aroma to the Lord" (for example, Lev 23:18; Num 28:2-6), while to the Gentile *euōdia* would recall the smell of incense being burnt as a fragrant offering to the gods. If, on the other hand, the Roman triumph is in view, Paul might well be thinking of the smell of sacrifices offered when the procession reached the temple of Jupiter or the odor of incense burned along the processional route.

The focus shifts in the second half of verse 15 from the effect of Paul's preaching on God (a sweet-smelling aroma of Christ) to its effect on his audience. *Among those who are being saved,* it is the *fragrance of life,* whereas *among those who are perishing,* it is *the smell of death.* Paul divides humanity into two groups: those on the road to salvation and those on the path to destruction (compare 1 Cor 1:18). Because of the cross, "two roads diverged in a wood"—to reapply Robert Frost's familiar words—and all of humanity past, present and future travels one road or the other. This is a sobering thought. There is no middle ground here. And if we preach anything else, we do not preach the gospel. Jesus employed essentially the same image when he said to his disciples, "Wide is the gate and broad is the road that leads to destruction, and many enter through it. But small is the gate and narrow the road that leads to life, and only a few find it" (Mt 7:13-14).

To the former group the preaching of the gospel is, literally, "an odor

who are in the process of being saved" and "those who are in the process of perishing" give the sense of the text.

from life to life." To the latter it is "an odor from death to death." But what does Paul mean by "from life to life" and "from death to death"? Most interpreters understand "to" *(eis)* as pointing to the end result. Acceptance of the gospel ultimately results in life, while rejection concludes in death. "From" *(ek)* is more problematic. *Ek* + genitive commonly defines source: "an odor issuing from death/life." But what in practical terms does this mean? It is also possible that *ek* defines the nature of the smell: "a deadly odor" or "a life-giving fragrance." It can likewise be a Hebraic idiom to express the concept of increase ("the odor of an ever-increasing death"; "the fragrance of an ever-increasing life") or suggestive of a condition that goes from bad to worse ("an ever-worsening odor") or from good to better ("a fragrance that gets better and better").

In any case, it is the progressive element that is primary. The idea is that the preaching of the gospel causes either death or life to become increasingly more rooted in the hearer. To those who are on the road to destruction the gospel is like a noxious fume that relentlessly carries the unwary to their death. To those on the road to salvation it is comparable to a compelling fragrance that invigorates all who come in contact with it. Jim Elliot once prayed, "Father, make me a crisis man. Bring those I contact to decision. Let me not be a milepost on a single road. Make me a fork, that men must turn one way or another on facing Christ in me."

Given the life- and death-wielding character of the gospel, Paul raises the question, *Who is equal to such a task* of being a gospel preacher? (v. 16). The expected answer is a resounding "no one" in and of themselves. Paul is very aware that his competency as a gospel preacher does not reside in himself but in God. It is God who triumphs over the weaknesses of Paul and his coworkers (v. 14), God who sends them out (v. 17, *from God*) and God who holds them accountable (v. 17, *we speak before God*).

2:16 Some maintain that Paul's question *Who is equal to such a task?* expects the answer "I am." But he categorically denies any self-capability in 3:5. It is more likely that the Corinthian intruders are the ones who made this kind of claim.

2:17 *Hoi polloi* ("the many") is another way of referring to the majority of people. Compare "the masses" (Furnish 1984:178).

Some think that *peddle for profit* makes a comparison to merchants who watered down

There were those, however, who thought themselves quite capable to carry out the role of gospel preacher. *Unlike so many,* Paul continues, *we do not peddle the word of God for profit.* There is a subtle shift at verse 17 from answering the complaints of the Corinthians to responding to the criticisms of an as-yet-undefined adversary. Here we catch the first hint that behind the church's grievances against Paul lurk outsiders who have insinuated themselves into the good graces of the Corinthian church. Paul goes on the offensive against, literally, *the many (hoi polloi)* who preach for the sake of financial gain. The term translated *peddle for profit (kapēleuō)* means "to be a retail-dealer," "to drive a petty trade" (Liddell, Scott and Jones 1978). In Paul's day it was figuratively applied to those who made a trade of selling their teachings for profit. But it is not getting paid for preaching per se that is at issue. Paul argues at length in 1 Corinthians 9 for the right of the itinerant preacher to receive financial support, even though it was a privilege that he himself forwent. What he is concerned about is *why* one preaches the gospel. The motivation of *the many* was money. Like the Sophists of that day, the majority showed more interest in lining their wallets than in preaching the truth (LB, RSV/NRSV, NIV, NEB, NKJ). By doing so, they were in effect treating God's message like so much cheap merchandise (TEV).

This was not so with Paul. His motivation was not greed but *sincerity (ex eilikrineias).* Yet couldn't these visiting preachers ostensibly make the same claim? This is most likely why Paul goes on in the second half of verse 17 to shore up his claim with what amounts to an oath. He speaks as someone who has been *sent from God,* that is, as someone who has been commissioned like the prophets of old. But unlike them, he speaks *in Christ,* that is, as Christ's representative. Paul's commission as Christ's representative amounted to calling "people from among all the Gentiles to the obedience that comes from faith" (Rom 1:5; 15:15-16). He also speaks *before God.* "In God's sight" *(katenanti theou)* catches the sense better. The idea is that because Paul leaves himself open at

---

their merchandise to make a bigger profit ("who adulterate the word of God"—KJV, NJB, REB, Phillips). Hafemann has convincingly shown that there is no extrabiblical evidence that the *kapel*- word-group directly signified ideas such as "watering down," "adulterating" or "falsifying" or that these ideas were ever present as part of the wider semantic field of the verb (1990:101-25). Moreover, the point of contrast is motivation for preaching the gospel, rather than changing or "adulterating" the actual content of the gospel message.

all times to God's scrutiny, the truthfulness of what he says can be divinely verified.

That Paul would need to appeal to divine witnesses to assure the Corinthians that his motives in preaching the gospel are honest ones says more about his culture than about any criticisms that may have come his way. In Paul's day, many made their living by their skill at speechmaking. Sophists in particular were known for their ability to move an audience through their artistry and rhetoric. It was how they said it rather than what they said that impressed the average listener. So Paul is attempting to distance himself not so much from those who sold their gospel "wares" for a living as from those who were out to make big bucks from preaching. If we take an even closer look at Paul's language in verses 14-17, we find that he chooses his words in light of the impact that these money-motivated preachers were having on the congregation. The Corinthians were being influenced by the triumphalist tone (v. 14) of those who claimed professional competency (v. 16) and were out to make a good show (v. 14) with culturally approved credentials (see 3:1-3).

We face much the same problem today. Evangelists and preachers can get easily sidetracked either by the lucrative potential evangelistic ministry presents or by the praise and applause a skillfully wrought sermon elicits. In many respects it is we the audience who are to blame in that congregations are increasingly placing more value on the art form than on the message. An article in *Christianity Today* highlights the consumerism, or "McChurch," mentality that pushes pastors to market themselves and their church competitively. Many people nowadays approach a sermon the way they approach fast-food restaurants. Today it might be McDonald's, tomorrow Burger King and the next day Wendy's (Colson 1992:29).

Paul's Letter of Recommendation (3:1-3) It is unthinkable in our

---

3:1 The word *again (palin)* can modify either *archometha* ("Are we once again beginning to commend ourselves?") or *synistanein* ("Are we beginning to once again commend ourselves?"). Either rendering raises the question of what previous occasion of self-commendation is in view. Some have argued that Paul is referring back to statements he made in the "previous letter." The first-person plural is to be noted, however (*Are we*

society to present yourself to a prospective employer without a résumé in hand and a list of references at your fingertips. It was much the same in Paul's day. He lived in an equally mobile society that placed similar value on personal achievements and introductory letters. Itinerant speakers, in particular, were expected to carry letters of reference with them as they traveled from place to place. It was often the only means by which they received hospitality and provisions for the journey ahead. *Zenon Papyri* 2026 is a typical letter of this sort:

> Asklepiades to Zenon, greeting.
>
> Philo, the bearer of this letter to you, has been known to me for a considerable time. He has sailed up in order to obtain employment in certain sections of the bureau of Philiskos, being recommended by Phileas and other accountants. Be so good, therefore, as to make his acquaintance and introduce him to other persons of standing, assisting him actively, both for my sake and for that of the young man himself. For he is worthy of your consideration, as will be evident to you if you receive him into your hands.
>
> Farewell.

Paul too wrote letters of recommendation, especially for colleagues who represented his pastoral interests in the various Gentile churches he had founded. A number of his letters bear witness to this practice (e.g., Rom 16:1-2; 1 Cor 4:17; 2 Cor 8:16-24; Phil 2:19-30). He did not, however, personally carry letters of this kind, although he made use of them prior to his conversion (Acts 9:2; 22:5). This gave Jewish-Christian missionaries who were attempting to gain a foothold in the Corinthian community an opportunity to discredit him in the eyes of the church.

At 3:1 Paul attempts to forestall a wrong conclusion. The JB captures the sense admirably: "Does this sound like a new attempt to commend ourselves to you?" Much as itinerant speakers would present their credentials to gain a hearing in a given location, Paul's review of what his ministry entailed, his commissioning by God to be Christ's repre-

---

beginning . . . ?). Paul uses it throughout 2:14—7:7. This suggests that he is thinking of an occasion that included at least Timothy (1:1), if not Silas (1:19), which eliminates the "previous letter" ("*I* wrote you," 2:9; "*I* caused you sorrow by my letter," 7:8). He could be thinking of either 1:12 ("Now this is our boast") or 2:17 ("Unlike so many, we do not peddle the word of God for profit"). He may also have in mind his founding visit, when it would

sentative and the divine scrutiny that his ministry undergoes on a daily basis could well have sounded to Corinthian ears as if he were attempting in 2:14-17 to reintroduce himself and his coworkers all over again to the congregation. *Or do we need, like some people, letters of recommendation to you or from you?* (3:1) The "many" who peddle the word of God for profit (2:17) begin to take definite shape as the *some (tines)* who take pride in *letters of recommendation* that they are able to present *to* the Corinthians and solicit *from* them to carry along to the next church on their travel circuit. *To you* and *from you* shows that these missionaries were not interested in planting churches through their own efforts but profiting from (2:17) and taking credit for *(from you)* the efforts of others.

Paul's approach to these intruders is quite insightful. While he does not condemn their use of such letters, he does point out to the church that the reason he and his coworkers had not brought any letters to Corinth was because they had come as church planters, ready to begin a new evangelistic work. So it is the church formed as a result of their labors *(you yourselves),* not a *letter written with ink* (v. 3), that serves as their letter of reference.

Two aspects of this letter are highlighted in verse 2. It is a letter *written on* the *hearts* of Paul and his coworkers *(engegrammenē en tais kardiais hēmōn)* and it is a letter *known and read by everybody (ginōskomenē kai anaginōskomenē hypo pantōn anthrōpōn).* "Heart" is

---

have been natural for him and his coworkers to acquaint the fledgling church with their credentials and mission, or, in effect, "to introduce" themselves—a common use of *synistanein.* Chapter 3:1 would then translate: "Does this sound like we are introducing ourselves to you all over again?" This follows nicely after 2:14-17 (see the commentary).

Paul's letter to the Romans reads very much like a letter of introduction, especially chapters 1—8, which spell out in great detail the nature of Paul's commission as an apostle to the Gentiles. It may well give us a picture of the kind of self-presentation that Paul made to churches that did not know him.

Are we beginning to commend ourselves again? does not expect—as some would argue—a negative answer. *Mē* appears only with the second rhetorical question. In fact, Paul quite explicitly commends himself and his coworkers three times in this letter (4:2; 6:4; 10:12-13). But he does it in a way that distinguishes him from his rivals—that is, "as a servant of God" (6:4) rather than as "self-competent" (3:4-5). Here it is likely that Paul is merely acknowledging that the way he has been talking in 2:14-17 may indeed sound as if he were introducing himself to them all over again.

From whom did these intruders get their letters of recommendation? Some think that

used here in the Semitic sense of the inmost self and center of the personality, not in the English sense of the seat of emotions and feelings. It is the locus of a person's spiritual and intellectual activity and, as such, the place where God begins his work of renewal (Sorg 1976:181-83). The perfect tense, *written (engegrammenē)*, points to a letter that has been indelibly etched on Paul's heart. *Known and read* is a rather peculiar order of things until one recognizes the play on words *(ginōskomenē kai anaginōskomenē)*. The term for *read* means "to know" something well enough that you can recognize it again (as one does with words on a page). It is similar to our expression "he reads me well" and might best be translated "known and recognized by all." Paul's first comment is initially somewhat puzzling. While it is fitting to talk of the changed lives of his converts as the only recommendation he requires, it is less clear how this letter can be written on his own heart and, even more so, how it can be known and recognized by all. While Paul might be pushing the limits of his analogy, the point he is making is an important one. By *written on our hearts* he means that the gospel has an impact not only on those who hear it but also on those who preach it. *Known by everybody* (v. 2) and *you show* (v. 3) suggest an obvious and widely perceived impact. By contrast, the Corinthian intruders present pieces of paper that are seen by only a few and have a limited, temporary effect.

The notion of an evangelist who does not become personally

only the Jerusalem church (see Barrett, Bruce, Käsemann) or its Pharisaic wing (see M. J. Harris) could have supplied them with letters that would have carried any weight in a large, urban church like that at Corinth. That they were Jewish Christian missionaries is clear from later references in 2 Corinthians. But Paul makes no explicit comments about whom they represented. The practice was so widespread in the Greco-Roman Empire that their use of such letters need not in and of itself point to the mother church. In fact, Acts 18:27, where Luke refers to a letter of introduction written by the Ephesian church to the Corinthian church on Apollos's behalf, suggests otherwise.

3:2 Some maintain that only the variant "on *your* hearts" *(hymōn)* makes sense in the context. The better-attested reading, however, is "on *our* hearts" *(hēmōn)*. *Hymōn*, though having early support, is found exclusively in Alexandrian manuscripts (א 33 88 436 1881) and versions (ethiopic^ro). *Hēmōn*, on the other hand, has early support (p^46 B D it vg), wide geographical distribution and strong genealogical backing (B D G). It is also intrinsically the more difficult reading, for it is easier to picture a scribe making a change from *our* to "your hearts" than from "your" to the more difficult *our hearts* (see the commentary).

involved in the lives of his or her converts is one that is foreign to the New Testament. Unfortunately, it is all too common today. The job of witnessing often amounts to giving someone a tract or telling them that God has a plan for their life.

The story is told of a new homeowner who worked fruitlessly for several hours trying to get a broken lawnmower back together. Suddenly one of his neighbors appeared with a handful of tools. "Can I help?" he asked. In twenty minutes he had the mower functioning beautifully.

"Thanks a million," the new homeowner said. "And say, what do you make with such fine tools?"

"Mostly friends," the neighbor smiled. "I'm available anytime."

In a schedule-driven society like ours, the kind of commitment to people that this neighbor evidenced is quickly becoming extinct. Paul, however, became involved in the lives of people to whom he witnessed and in so doing was himself affected. So great, in fact, was the personal impact that no matter where he traveled it was evident to all. Nor was Paul's relationship with the Corinthian church an isolated case. In 1 Thessalonians 2:8 he says that he and his coworkers shared with the Thessalonians not only the gospel but their very lives, because they had become so dear to them.

And what about a résumé? What credentials does Paul present to prospective listeners in order to gain a hearing? Again, his response is instructive. For the only credential a gospel preacher can in reality bring to an unevangelized field like Corinth is not a list of personal accomplishments but the presence and power of God's Spirit working to convict the listener of the truths of the message about Jesus Christ. *You are a letter from Christ, the result of our ministry, written . . . with the Spirit of the living God* (3:3).

Four things characterize this letter of reference. First, it is *a letter of Christ (epistolē Christou)*. While Paul could be thinking of a letter "about Christ" (objective genitive; Phillips), in light of the analogy employed it is more likely a letter "from Christ" written on Paul's behalf (genitive of source; most modern translations).

Second, it is a letter that is mediated by Paul. The NIV *the result of*

3:3 The anarthrous form of the participle *zōntos* stresses the nature of God—the God

our ministry is literally "ministered by us" (KJV, NKJV). The aorist *(diakonētheisa)* points to a specific ministry occasion, most likely Paul's founding visit. Translations are evenly divided as to whether it is the role of a secretary ("drawn up by us"—LB, JB, NRSV) or the job of a letter carrier ("delivered by us"—TEV, RSV, NEB, REB, Phillips) that is depicted here. In either case, the NJB's "entrusted to our care" catches the sense, if not the picture.

Third, it is a letter written *not with ink but with the Spirit of the living God* (v. 3). Ink, in Paul's day, was a black carbon mixed with gum or oil for use on parchment or with a metallic substance for papyrus. It was applied by means of a reed that was cut to a point and split like a quill pen. The phrase *living God,* which is a familiar one in the Greek Old Testament, is found six times in the Pauline writings. It is normally employed to distinguish God from lifeless idols (Acts 14:15; 1 Thess 1:9; 2 Cor 6:16). Here it is used of what is animate *(God)* as opposed to what is inanimate *(ink).* The new element in verse 3 is *the Spirit* of the living God. The characteristic mark of Christianity as contrasted to Judaism was, and remains, the work of the Spirit in the life of the believer and congregation. Under the old covenant, God made his will known externally through the law. Under the new covenant his presence is revealed internally through the Spirit.

Fourth, it is a letter written on *tablets of human hearts* rather than on *tablets of stone* (v. 3). The word *tablet* probably describes the form (rectangle) rather than the material. Even so, the introduction of *stone* tablets is unexpected. The writing implement used with stone surfaces was a chisel, not a reed pen with ink. Letters in Paul's day were written on either papyrus or parchment—or, in a pinch, on a piece of pottery. So why the shift to stone tablets? The contrast itself is between what is pliable ("fleshly," not the NIV *human)* and internal *(hearts)* as opposed to what is fixed and external *(stone).* But the point could have been made by following through on the analogy of the letter of recommendation. What is Paul up to here? The connection is to be found in the idea of a divine composition. *Stone tablets* recalls the two tablets of the Decalogue inscribed by the finger of God (Ex 31:18; Deut 9:10). "Fleshly

who is *alive.*

hearts," on the other hand, brings to mind the new covenant expectation of God's law written on the heart (Jer 31:33). This feat is accomplished by God removing the "heart of stone" and replacing it with his Spirit (Ezek 11:19; 36:26).

His critics solicited human references. Paul turns, instead, to divine references. For the credential that he has to offer is Christ's own letter written with the Spirit of the living God on the hearts of his converts. His critics boasted, as well, of the presence and power of the Spirit in their ministry. But for them it was the Spirit's presence as manifested in and through the working of signs, wonders and miracles (12:11-12). Paul, on the other hand, looked to the inward change of heart as the primary evidence of the Spirit's presence. It is changed lives, not sensational feats, that are the true sign of a Spirit-directed ministry.

Qualifications for Ministry (3:4-6) It is all too easy to be overly impressed with a list of credentials and to lose sight of the fact that inward change, not outward achievement, is what validates someone in God's eyes. Such a misplaced emphasis often follows from the need for some kind of objective standard by which to evaluate a person's competence. Paul faced this problem as well. So he tries to give the Corinthians an objective standard by which to judge his competency as a minister of the gospel (5:12). But he also recognizes that competency in the ministry is something that is God-given rather than humanly achieved—a fact that is often forgotten in a twentieth-century culture that is oriented toward such overt signs of approval as applause and kudos.

Paul fears that his claim to possess divine references could be construed as overconfidence. To forestall such an allegation he interjects a series of disclaimers. His first disclaimer is that *such confidence* as he

---

3:4 *Pros* + the accusative normally defines orientation or movement "toward" rather than proximity *before* (NIV, JB) or location "in" (TEV, Phillips). The NIV *such confidence is ours before God* is better rendered "toward God" (Blass, Debrunner and Funk 1961:no. 239).

3:6 Canon 59 reads: "Let no private psalms nor any uncanonical books be read in church but only the canonical ones of the New and Old Testament."

In Hellenistic Greek *diathēkē* is normally used of a disposition made by one party with plenary power, which another party could accept or reject but not alter (e.g., a will or

exhibits *before God* is his only *through Christ* (v. 4). *Before God* is better rendered "toward God" (see note). *Through Christ (dia tou Christou)* defines the basis for his confidence. Paul is probably thinking of his commissioning by Christ on the road to Damascus as apostle to the Gentiles (Acts 9:15-19; 26:12-18). It was a commissioning uniquely his, yet not because of any competency that he himself possessed. Indeed, Paul freely admits elsewhere that he is the "least of the apostles" (1 Cor 15:9) and the "worst of sinners" (1 Tim 1:15). Here he merely states, as a second disclaimer, that he does not possess any competency in and of himself (v. 5). The Greek is literally "not that we are competent to reckon anything as of ourselves" *(ouch hoti . . . hikanoi esmen logisasthai ti hōs ex heautōn)*. The Greek verb for *to reckon* means "to credit to one's own abilities." "There is nothing in us that allows us to claim that we are capable of doing this work" (TEV) catches the gist of Paul's statement. Competency in our society is largely determined by whether we are able "to get the job done." Ministerial competency, by contrast, issues not from self but *from God,* who *has made us competent as ministers of a new covenant*—Paul's third and final disclaimer (vv. 5-6).

Verse 6 functions as a transition to an extended treatment of the superiority of the new covenant or *Spirit* ministry over the old covenant or *letter* ministry. The emphasis throughout is on ministry. The terms *diakonia (ministry)* and *diakonos (minister)* occur five times in verses 6-11. In fact, close to 40 percent of all Pauline uses of both nominal and verbal forms appear in 2 Corinthians. Paul's point is that competence as a minister lies in the competency of the ministry represented. Paul's competence stems from being a minister of a *new covenant. Diathēkē* should be translated *covenant,* not "testament" (KJV; corrected in the NKJV), and it should not be capitalized. There were no Old and New Testaments in Paul's day, only

---

testament; Moulton-Milligan 1930:148-49). But in the LXX it is also employed of bilateral agreements between two parties (Guhrt 1975:365-66). The meaning of *diathēkē* in the New Testament must therefore be evaluated on a case-by-case basis.

The only other occurrence of *new covenant* appears in the tradition Paul received regarding the institution of the Lord's Supper: "In the same way, after supper he took the cup, saying, 'This cup is the new covenant in my blood; do this, whenever you drink it, in remembrance of me.' For whenever you eat this bread and drink this cup, you proclaim the Lord's death until he comes" (1 Cor 11:25).

"the Scriptures." "New Testament" applies to the Christian writings that were given canonical status alongside the Jewish Scriptures. The process of canonization was a long one. Clement of Alexandria (c. 215) and Origen (c. 250) are the earliest church fathers to distinguish between "old" and "new testament" writings. Canon 59, which was issued by the Synod of Laodicea in A.D. 363, is the first church document to use the phrase "new testament" of a distinct body of literature. The actual phrase "canon of the new testament" does not appear until about A.D. 400 in Macarius Magnes's *Apocriticus* 4.10 (Belleville 1994:375-76).

The language of *new covenant* comes from Jeremiah 31:31-34, the only place in the Old Testament where this phrase occurs: " 'The time is coming,' declares the LORD, 'when I will make a new covenant with the house of Israel and with the house of Judah. It will not be like the covenant I made with their forefathers.' "

A *covenant,* simply put, is an agreement into which two parties enter. It can be a bilateral agreement between equals or a unilateral arrangement where the terms are dictated by one, superior party. God's covenants with his people are of the latter kind.

The word *new (kainos)* denotes that which is qualitatively better as compared with what has existed until now (Haarbeck, Link and Brown 1976:670). This is borne out in how Paul describes the new as opposed to the old arrangement between God and his people. The character of the old covenant is that it is *of letter (grammatos)* and *kills*. The new covenant, on the other hand, is *of Spirit (pneumatos)* and *gives life*. Both nouns are in the genitive case and lack the article. *Letter* and *Spirit* are therefore descriptive terms, setting forth the quality or nature of their respective covenants. What is qualitatively better about the new covenant is that it is not a *letter* covenant—that is, an external code—but a *Spirit* covenant—that is, an internal power. A covenant that is *letter* in nature *kills* because it makes external demands without giving the

---

The contrast in the first half of verse 6 between *gramma* ("letter") and *pneuma* ("spirit") has commonly been taken in the following two ways: (1) *gramma* refers to the concrete demands and written form of the Mosaic law; *pneuma* refers to the internal principle of moral life under the new covenant; (2) *gramma* and *pneuma* are literal and spiritual understandings of Scripture respectively. The former fits better the contrast in verses 7-11 between the Mosaic law and the new covenant. Yet in the broader context, *pneuma* refers

inward power for obedience, while a covenant that is *Spirit* in character *gives life* because it works internally to produce a change of nature. Paul describes this change of nature elsewhere as a "new self" created "to be like God in true righteousness and holiness" (Eph 4:24).

The Superiority of the New Covenant Ministry (3:7-11) By a covenant of *letter* Paul has in mind the Mosaic covenant. His reference in verse 7 to the shining face of Moses on his descent from Mount Sinai with the tablets of the law makes this clear. The Mosaic covenant was a unilateral agreement that structured every aspect of Israel's social, religious, physical and civil existence from the time of Moses until Paul's day. The sum total of commandments that regulated the Jew's life were numbered at 613. This did not include rabbinic interpretations of the law (the Tannaim of the Mishnah), which were also considered binding. Paul, however, now calls this covenant "old" (v. 14). Ever since, Judaism—not to mention certain branches of Christianity—has been loath to agree.

Someone once said that "second-best is the worst enemy of the best." People have always tended to cling to the old even when something far better is offered (Barclay 1954:191). Most of us have been in churches with diehards who insisted that the old way of doing something was necessarily the right way. There is security in clinging to the familiar, even when the familiar leads eventually to our undoing (*death*, v. 7; condemnation, v. 9). Paul faced this difficulty at Corinth—How to convince the diehards in the church that the new way, and not the old, was the right way?

Paul's shift from letters of recommendation to a consideration of the old and new covenants is judged problematic by most. What prompts him to consider these two covenants in such great detail (and in such stark contrast)? Some think that a letter written on the heart (v. 3) leads Paul to think of the new covenant promise of Jeremiah 31:33 and, in

---

to "the Spirit of the living God" (3:3), *the Spirit* that *gives life* (3:6) and "the Spirit of the Lord" (3:17). It is probably best, therefore, to translate *pneuma* in the first part of verse 6 as "Spirit" (so NIV) and understand the lack of an article as pointing to the qualitative difference between "letter" and "Spirit."

3:7-11 Compare the *qal wahomer* argumentation of *Mekilta* "Beshallah" 1.100: "If Elisha the disciple of Elijah could make the iron come to the surface, *how much more* could Moses the master of Elijah do it."

turn, the old covenant engraved on stone tablets. Others suppose that the letter written by the Spirit in verse 3 calls to mind the finger of God on the stone tablets of the law. Recent studies seek an explanation in a Moses polemic of rival missionaries (for example, Georgi 1986). This seems likely; otherwise verses 7-11 give the impression of being no more than a temporary excursus.

Paul's emphasis in particular on the greater glory of the new covenant suggests that his opponents associated themselves in some fashion with Moses and the law—but not with its legalistic side, since there is no mention of circumcision or obedience to the law (see the introduction). In view of Paul's use of the Jewish tradition of the overpowering splendor of the Mosaic ministry, it is probable that these intruding missionaries appealed to Moses as a model of spirituality and to the law as the key to a victorious Christian life. Moses, who was accredited by God through the working of wonders, signs and miracles, would have been the ideal figure to lend credibility to their ministry. And the tablets of the law, which came in such a blaze of glory, would have functioned as the perfect letter of reference.

What to do when old ways die hard? Paul's overall approach is not to denigrate the Mosaic covenant but rather to demonstrate the superiority of the new covenant over the old. To do this he uses a Jewish form of argumentation called *qal waḥōmer,* or what today we would label an a fortiori argument (from lesser to greater). His line of reasoning is that if the glory of the old covenant was transient yet came with such overpowering splendor that the Israelites could not look steadily at the face of its minister as he descended from Mount Sinai with the tablets

---

3:7 *The ministry that brought death* is incorrect. Death came through Adam and "reigned from the time of Adam to the time of Moses" (Rom 5:14). The NEB's "dispensed death" is a better translation.

Neither the inability of Israel to look steadily at Moses's face nor the dwindling character of Moses's splendor is found in the Exodus narrative. All Exodus 34:29-30 says is that Moses' face shone to such an extent that Israel feared to approach him. These are details that Paul derived from Jewish tradition. For example, Philo states: "Moses descended with a countenance far more beautiful than when he ascended, so that those who saw him were filled with awe and amazement; nor could their eyes continue to stand the dazzling brightness that flashed from him like the rays of the sun" (*The Life of Moses* 2.70). Of special interest is *Zohar* 3.58a, where the wording is almost identical with what is found in 2 Corinthians 3:7: "Now if merely because of this remnant of brightness the children of Israel

of the law, *how much greater* must the new covenant be, whose splendor is permanent and whose glory does not fade. The implication is that though the Mosaic covenant can impart an initial glory and credibility to its ministers and adherents, because of its transitory character it has no lasting effect. Therefore for these visiting preachers to link themselves with a covenant that is fast becoming obsolete is to suggest that their competency is fading and their credentials are of no lasting importance. It is only the new covenant with its enduring splendor that can impart a permanent and lasting credibility to its ministers.

Paul's evaluation of the Mosaic ministry is even more to the point. Far from being the key to the victorious Christian life, it is in reality a ministry that brings nothing but *death* (v. 7) and condemnation (v. 9) to those of God's people who strive to live by it. To be a minister of the old covenant is therefore to be an instrument of death and destruction. The new covenant ministry, on the other hand, brings *the Spirit* (v. 8) and *righteousness* (v. 9). So to be a minister of this covenant is to be an instrument of life and salvation.

The role of the law in the life of the Christian is an important issue in the church today. Is Paul saying that the Christian is to have no contact with the law whatsoever and to do so is to bring about one's own condemnation and death? How can this be, since elsewhere he speaks of the law as "holy, righteous and good" and "spiritual" (Rom 7:12, 14)? The key phrase in the discussion is "under law," which Paul uses in Romans 6:1-23 and Galatians 3:21—4:31; 5:13-26 to refer to the role of Mosaic law in strictly supervising every aspect of the life of God's people (Belleville 1986:59-60). It makes clear to us our obligation, oversees our

could not look steadfastly at the face of Moses, how glorious must the splendor have been in its original state" (Belleville 1990:31-35, 63-72).

There is a fair amount of rabbinic speculation concerning the origin of Moses' facial splendor. The most common traditions suppose that he received it from (1) the hand God used to cover him with as he passed by the cleft of the rock, (2) the rays of the divine light that made their way into the cave, (3) the sparks that shot out of God's mouth when Moses was being taught the Torah, (4) the portion of the tablets not grasped by either himself or God, (5) the tablets as they passed from God's hand to his own, (6) the radiance that God spread over him to protect him from the angels around his throne or (7) the ink that clung to his forehead when he passed the pen used to write the commandments through his hair (Belleville 1990:64).

conduct and rebukes and punishes our wrongdoing. The difficulty is that it does not give us the ability to overcome the prevailing influence of sin in our lives. So, as with any legal code, to break the law is to incur judgment. And we all inevitably do break God's law because our sinful nature inclines us in this direction. Lamentably, the penalty for breaking God's law is death (Rom 7:10-11).

Paul, nonetheless, can say that the Mosaic law is holy, righteous and good. This is because its demands reflect the character of its Creator. But the breaking of the law incurs God's judgment. This is why the role of the law was only a temporary one—"until Christ came" (Gal 3:24, TEV, RSV, JB, NEB). With the advent of Christ came a new covenant, one that is based on a familial, not a legal, relationship to God. We are still commanded not to kill, steal and so on—not because it is our obligation in a covenant relationship, but because it is appropriate behavior for a member of God's family. What is also needed is a change of nature. This too is provided for under the new covenant. With Christ's coming, the Spirit, rather than sin, becomes the controlling principle in the life of the believer. The power that was lacking under the old covenant is now there for us to be the kind of moral people God intended. This is essentially what Paul means in verses 7-11 by the ministry that brings *the Spirit* and *righteousness* as opposed to the ministry of *death* and condemnation.

The grammar in verses 7-11 is difficult to follow, but the point in each case is clear. *Engraved in letters on stone* (v. 7) recalls Moses' descent from Mount Sinai with the two tablets of the law. Stone tablets were normally used for royal, commemorative or religious texts, or for public copies of legal edicts. A metal chisel or graver was used to carve the letters onto the stone face. The tablets themselves were normally rectangular in shape and measuring no more than 17.5 × 11.7 in. (45 × 30 cm). The use of the perfect tense (*en* + *typoō,* "to hammer in") points to a permanent, unchangeable state of affairs. The letters that were chiseled into those two rectangular stone tablets were there to stay.

Paul distinguishes these tablets in two ways. First, he calls them "a ministry of death" (v. 7). The genitive can be descriptive ("a deadly ministry") or, more likely, objective ("a ministry that dispensed death," NEB, RSV). *Death* is the penalty for being a lawbreaker under this covenant. Second, he says that these stone tablets came with glory. The term *glory (doxa)* is the LXX's translation of the Hebrew word *kābôd*, which comes from a root meaning "to be heavy, weighty." Here it applies to something that is weighty in outward appearance. Nowadays we would call someone described in this way "flashy" or "handsome." Here it refers to the fact that Moses' face shone as he descended with the tablets of the law. So bright in fact was this splendor that Israel *could not look steadily at the face of Moses because of its glory, fading though it was* (v. 7). The verb *atenizō* means "to look intently at," "to gaze earnestly at." Today we might say that the Israelites could not keep their eyes glued on him, much as they were fascinated by the spectacle of his shining face. The word for *fading (kata + a-ergon)* means "to cause to become idle" or "to render ineffective or powerless," not "to abolish" (KJV). To cause light to become idle or inactive is effectively to cause it to "fade" (virtually all modern translations). The present tense indicates that Moses' splendor was "in the process" of fading *(tēn katargoumenēn)*. Paul's point is that although the brilliance of Moses' face was overpowering, it was a brilliance that immediately began to fade, symptomatic of the transient character of the ministry that it represented.

By comparison, the new covenant ministry will be *even more glorious* (v. 8). Why? Because it is a ministry not of *death* but *of the Spirit*. The two genitives must be taken in the same way. If the Mosaic covenant is a ministry that "dispenses death," the new covenant is a ministry that "dispenses the Spirit" (objective genitives). More than this Paul does not say. But elsewhere it is clear that the gift of the Spirit is the centerpiece of the new covenant (e.g., Gal 4:4-7). The future tense of the verb is to be noted. While the old covenant ministry *came (egenēthē)* with glory *(en doxē)*, the new covenant ministry *will be (estai)* with glory *(en doxē)* (vv. 7-8). Paul is undoubtedly thinking of "the glory that will be revealed in us" when Christ returns (Rom 8:18). This future glory is "our adoption, the redemption of our bodies" of which the gift of the Spirit is the "firstfruits" (Rom 8:23). The same idea occurs in 2 Corinthians 5:5, where Paul states that God "made us for this very purpose and has given us the Spirit as a deposit, guaranteeing what is to come." He may also be thinking of Jesus' teaching that he will come again "on the clouds of the sky with great power and glory" (Mk 13:26 and parallels).

To speak of the Mosaic covenant as a ministry that dispenses death would have sounded blasphemous to Jewish ears. It was the uniform opinion of the rabbis that what Moses gave the people of Israel were "words of life," not words of death (as in *Exodus Rabbah* 29.9).

Paul goes even further in verse 9 to call the Mosaic covenant a "ministry of condemnation"—something that incurs God's judgment, not his blessing. In line with the previous genitives, the genitive here should be construed as objective *(the ministry that condemns)*. The Greek word for "condemnation" *(katakrisis)* is a rare one, occurring in the Greek Bible only here and in 7:3. It refers to a verdict of guilty or to the passing of sentence against someone.

In contrast, the new covenant is a "ministry of righteousness." The term *righteousness (dikaiosynē)* is common in Paul. Normally it refers to the act of doing what is right or what God requires. Here, however, as a counterpoint to "condemnation" it is to be understood in the legal sense of being declared innocent (TEV) or acquitted (NEB). Paul's contention is, then, if the Mosaic covenant is a ministry that condemns and yet is accompanied by splendor, how much more glorious must be the ministry that declares people innocent!

In verses 10-11 Paul takes his argument one final step and advances the idea that the splendor of the old covenant is not only dwindling but also completely eclipsed by the surpassing glory of the new covenant. This is because the Mosaic ministry is temporary, while the new covenant ministry is permanent. In short, with the arrival of the new covenant, the Mosaic covenant is no longer the "big kid on the block." The text reads literally: "For that which has been endowed with splendor is now not endowed with splendor on account of the surpassing splendor." The grammar is at best tortuous. The idea is that the greater light obscures the lesser—or as someone once said, "When the sun has risen the lamps cease to be of use." The covenant that was once glorious now scarcely appears so in light of the splendor of the new. *In comparison with* is literally "in this part." Paul could be saying that the Mosaic covenant "was endowed in part with splendor" (that is, had a limited glory) or, as is more likely, that the Mosaic covenant "in this case

---

3:10 "In this part" *(en toutō tō merei)* can modify either *to dedoxasmenon* or *ou dedoxastai*. If it modifies the former, it would be referring to "that which had been glorified had no splendor at all" (that is, on account of the surpassing splendor of the new covenant).

The shift from feminine (the splendor of Moses' face, v. 7) to neuter (the splendor of the Mosaic ministry, vv. 10-11) is to be noted. The Mosaic covenant is pictured as belonging to a vanishing order, an economy that began to fade immediately after its inception, as was typified by the dwindling splendor of Moses' face (M. J. Harris 1976:336). The conclusion Paul draws from this fact is that if the ministry that was vanishing was ushered in with great pomp and circumstance *(dia doxēs)*, how much more spectacular must be the ministry that lasts. These are amazing statements for a Jew to make—albeit a Christian one—and ones to which Jews in Paul's day did not on the whole take kindly. For the Jew, the law was eternal and lifegiving. While there are occasional expressions in Jewish literature of an expectation that the law would suffer modification in the messianic age, there is every belief that it would endure forever.

The Superiority of the New Covenant Minister (3:12-18) At verse 12 Paul turns from a consideration of the merits of the old and new covenants to what it means to be a minister of each. What most likely prompts this discussion is the fact that rival missionaries at Corinth were looking to Moses as the consummate minister. Only in this way can Paul's contrast in verses 12-18 between Moses and the new covenant minister be explained. An additional reason Paul pursues what he does in these verses is the evangelistic conundrum that existed both then and now. One of the most difficult audiences to reach with the gospel today is a Jewish one. This is an amazing fact considering that the gospel is the good news of God's fulfillment through Jesus of his promises to his people Israel. The Jewishness of the gospel is reflected in the early Christian preaching that Jesus is the Messiah of Jewish expectation and in the attempt to prove from the Scriptures that the Messiah had to suffer and rise from the dead (Acts 2:22-36; 13:26-39; 17:2-3; 18:4-5). No one struggled with this conundrum more than Paul. His own success rate among his people was so low that it caused him "great sorrow and unceasing anguish"

---

in part"; if it modifies the latter, it would read "it had not been glorified *in this case."*

(Rom 9:1-3). The "why" of this state of affairs was something that constantly preyed on his mind. 2 Corinthians 3:12-18 is a brief version of Paul's lengthier reflections in Romans 9—11.

The Unveiled Face of the New Covenant Minister (3:12-13) Paul's train of thought in verses 12-18 has long been considered obscure. In part this is because he is dealing with two different but related criticisms. It appears that he was accused at some point of professional arrogance. Verses 12-13 and 18 address this matter. It also seems that his opponents were pointing out his lack of success among his own people. Verses 14-17 tackle this issue. Interestingly, Paul does not deny either charge.

We are very bold, he tells the Corinthians (v. 12). But it is only because they *have such a hope* that they act in such a fashion. By *we* Paul has in mind the minister of the new covenant, as 2:14—3:11 makes clear. The Greek word for *bold (parrēsia)* originally referred to the right of a Greek citizen to freedom of speech (*pas* [full] + *rhēsis* [speech]). In Paul's day it was applied, as well, to behavior befitting this constitutional freedom. Here he has in mind conduct befitting a minister of the new covenant (v. 12). But what kind of conduct would this be? "Bold" (TEV, NIV, RSV, NEB), "frank and open" (Phillips), "confident" (JB) and "plain" (KJV) have all been suggested. Each has its merits. Paul, however, goes on to draw a contrast with the veiled behavior of Moses (v. 13), suggesting that "open" (that is, "public") is the best option. Unlike Moses, who veiled his face to prevent public scrutiny of the fading character of his ministry, the new covenant minister is very up-front.

Paul, in particular, has made every effort to act with clarity (1:13; 11:6) and openness (3:3; 5:11-12) toward the Corinthians. What allows him to do this is the *hope* that he possesses. *Such a hope* (v. 12) looks back to verses 7-11 and the superior character of the new covenant ministry over the old. Paul calls this ministry a *hope* because its full splendor is yet to be seen. By using this word he is not suggesting that there is any doubt about the outcome. It is not a matter of wishful thinking on his part. This is how

3:12 The NEB translates *parrēsia* as "speak out boldly" (compare KJV's "plainness in speech"; NKJV's "boldness of speech"). Paul, however, is at pains in 2 Corinthians to defend his conduct, not his preaching. This narrative, in particular, is action-oriented. Verses 12, 13 and 18 contrast Moses, who veils his face, with the gospel minister, who does not. Verses 16 and 17 compare the unveiled face of Moses with the unveiled heart of the Jew.

3:13-18 The kind of expansion and interpretation of the Old Testament text found in

secular society understands hope. Seneca called hope "the definition of an uncertain good." For the Christian, however, hope carries an unconditional certainty within itself that God's promises will be realized. For this reason, Paul never loses his enthusiasm for the gospel, even when some labeled his ardor as professional arrogance.

Alfred Plummer has described 2 Corinthians as a "trackless forest" (1915:xiii). At first glance the line of argument in verses 13-17 appears very much so. In part this is because we tend to apply twentieth-century logic to the text. If we think like a first-century exegete, the pattern becomes clearer. It is important to notice that verses 13-17 are a commentary on Exodus 34:29-35. Paul cites from his text and then comments on it phrase by phrase. The reader should beware, though. Paul expands his "text" to include Jewish haggadah (traditions that have wide currency) and his own interpretive comments. As a result, his Old Testament text ends up looking quite paraphrastic—somewhat along the lines of the Living Bible or the Amplified Bible. The passage can be mapped out roughly as follows: (1) verses 12-13a: opening statement, (2) verses 13b-14a: Exodus 34:33, (3) verses 14b-15: commentary, (4) verse 16: Exodus 34:34, (5) verse 17: commentary and (6) verse 18: Exodus 34:35 and commentary intermixed.

Not like Moses at verse 13 introduces Paul's citation of Exodus 34:33, where it is observed that at the point Moses finished speaking to Israel, he *would put a veil over his face. Would put* translates the habitual action of the imperfect tense *(etithei)*. Moses customarily put on a face veil after communicating God's law to Israel. Why did he do so? A great deal of interpretive energy has been expended trying to answer this question. Some think that Moses wanted to hide the fact that the Mosaic covenant was only temporary. Others suggest personal embarrassment over the dwindling character of his facial splendor. Still others believe that Moses did it out of a righteous concern for exposing God's glory to a sinful people (and justifiably so, after the episode with the golden calf). The

---

these verses was very common in Paul's day. The rendering in *Targum Pseudo-Jonathan* of Exodus 16:4 is a case in point. The additions are bracketed: "Behold I will cause to descend from heaven [the] bread [which has been laid up for you from the beginning]. And the people shall go out and gather the matter of a day by the day that I may try them whether or not they will keep [the commandments of] my law."

difficulty is that the Exodus narrative does not help us one way or another.

The second half of verse 13 does give us a motive of sorts. Paul says that Moses did this *to keep the Israelites from gazing at [his face] while the radiance was fading away.* The NIV has done quite a bit of interpreting here, but a neutral translation is virtually impossible. The verb *atenizō* means "to look intently at," "to gaze earnestly at" (see v. 7). It is human nature to stare at a spectacle, whether it be gapers at a traffic accident or kids at a firework display. The Israelites were no different. But what exactly were they staring at? The NIV impies that it was Moses' face. The text merely reads "down to the end of *that* which was in the process of fading." But the shift from the feminine (v. 7) to the neuter (vv. 11, 13) shows that Paul is thinking more broadly of the Mosaic ministry and not just of Moses' face. The Greek word *telos* can refer either to a "goal" or an "end" (missing in the NIV). If the former, then Moses sought to prevent Israel from looking at Christ as the "goal" or fulfillment of the Mosaic covenant. If the latter, as seems likely from the context, then Moses covered his face so that Israel could not gaze "right down to the last glimmer," similar to an infant who continues to stare at a windup toy long after it has stopped moving. That Paul can speak of Moses' facial splendor and the glory of the Mosaic covenant in the same breath is not surprising since to the average Jew, Moses and the Torah were virtually interchangeable. Indeed, Paul can easily shift between the two, as "when the old covenant is read" and "when Moses is read" in verses 14-15 show.

Israel and the Old Covenant (3:14-15) Israel's response to this habitual performance of Moses' was a dulling of the mind (v. 14). The verb translated *made dull* means "to petrify" or "to cause a stone or callus to form" and in the passive (as here), "to become hard" or

---

3:13 *Pros to* + infinitive can give the result ("with the result that they could not look at the fading glory") or purpose ("in order that they not look at the fading glory"). The latter, which provides a motive for Moses' behavior and a counterpoint to Paul's *but* at the beginning of verse 14, is the better option.

3:14 The relationship of verse 14 to what precedes is obscure. Some translate *alla* as "indeed" (TEV) or "still more" (Phillips). But neither translation alleviates the sequential problem.

While *epi* + the dative can have a temporal sense *(when the old covenant is read)*, this

"thickened." When applied to the mind it means "to become obtuse" or *dull*. Paul introduces this state of affairs with the word *but (alla)*, as a point of contrast to the preceding thought. In spite of the Mosaic veiling, their minds became dull. The aorist *(epōrōthē)* is ingressive, denoting a settled condition. Israel "became and remained" mentally sluggish (versus the NIV *made dull*).

But what does a sluggish mind have to do with Moses' practice of veiling his face? The exegetical difficulty is that Paul's comment in verse 14 does not follow logically after verse 13. The thought runs, It was Moses' custom to veil his fading splendor, but Israel became mentally dull. It is tempting to link Paul's *but* with verse 12 instead of verse 13. The new covenant minister, although up-front in preaching the gospel (unlike Moses), nonetheless makes no impression on the Jewish audience because of a condition of mental stupor. Yet the aorist indicative places the first half of verse 14 firmly in the historical context of the Exodus narrative.

One solution is to link Israel's condition of mental stupor with Moses' *motive* in veiling his face. Perhaps Moses habitually veiled his face so that Israel's attention should not become so obstinately riveted on him that they fail to understand the significance of the fading splendor— namely, that the Mosaic covenant was only temporary (v. 11) and already at its inception was becoming "old" (v. 14). But if this was Moses' game plan, it did not work. Despite his repeated efforts, Israel's perceptions became dulled to the point that they could not even entertain the notion that the Mosaic covenant was anything but "eternal and lifegiving" (*b. Šabbat* 30a). This remains one of the most difficult truths to communicate to a Jewish audience. Jews even today are so caught up in the greatness and glory of the Mosaic covenant that they are unwilling to consider that something greater has come.

But their minds were made dull is Paul's interpretive comment. No

---

is a usage that is seldom found outside of poetry. Its more usual sense is to denote location "on" or "over." In putting a veil over his face, Moses also veiled the Mosaic covenant—a state that has continued even down to Paul's day.

It cannot be the *same* veil that Moses wore over his face. Nor can it be, as some suggest, an inward veil of unbelief, since the idea of a heart-veil does not appear until verse 15. It is best to understand *same* in terms of function. This veil serves the same function that Moses' veil did in covering a dwindling splendor.

such state of affairs is found in the Exodus narrative. All Exodus 34:30 says is that Israel was initially afraid to approach Moses. How did Paul arrive at this conclusion? He reached it by looking at Israel in his own day. Here is part one of Paul's explanation for why Israel was not responding to the gospel. *For to this day,* he says, *the same veil remains when the old covenant is read.* The *same veil* is the veil that Moses used to cover the splendor of the Mosaic covenant reflected on his face. Only, instead of lying over Moses' face, it now lies over the Mosaic covenant (*epi* + dative).

The word for *covenant* is not to be translated "testament" (KJV), which can be misunderstood as referring to the Old Testament. Paul is referring, instead, to the agreement that was established between God and his people at Mount Sinai (see v. 6). The written form of this agreement, which he calls *old,* is found in Exodus 20—40 and the book of Deuteronomy. By *old* he means that the Mosaic covenant has outlived its ministerial usefulness (vv. 7-9). But Israel can not see this because a veil exists anytime the Law *is read. Is read* is literally "the reading," signifying a public occasion. It was and still is customary in the synagogue service to read a selected passage from the Law and then one from the Prophets.

When the Law is publicly read the Mosaic veil functions, Paul says, to "not reveal *[mē anakalyptomenon]* that *[hoti]* in Christ its glory is dwindling" (*katargeitai;* see the note). It is important to notice Paul's use of the present tense. It is not that the Mosaic covenant's glory *has* dwindled but that it is in the process of dwindling (see vv. 7, 11). With the establishment of a new covenant, we would expect the former. But the splendor of the new covenant ministry is not yet complete as the future tense "will be glorious" indicates (v. 8). The splendor of the Mosaic

---

The position of the participial phrase *mē anakalyptomenon* is ambiguous. If it modifies the preceding clause, then the sense is "the same veil remains *unlifted"* (NIV *it has not been removed*). But this leads to an unnatural construal of the remainder of the verse. It requires the insertion of *only* and translating *katargeitai* as *taken away* instead of "fading" or "dwindling" as in verses 7, 11, 13. If *mē anakalyptomenon* introduces the clause that follows, the sense is "the same veil remains and does not reveal that the glory of the old covenant is dwindling." This is a better fit with the overall context. *Hoti* can be either causal *(because in Christ)* or explanatory ("that in Christ"), depending on what is done with the participial phrase in question.

How one translates *katargeitai* is dependent on what the subject is seen to be. Some

covenant, as a result, has not been completely overshadowed *in Christ*. *In Christ (en Christō)* is ambiguous. The last time Paul used this phrase it meant "as Christ's representatives" (2:17). Here it may be equivalent to the new covenant as a counterpoint to the old covenant, to which he has just made reference.

Verse 15 introduces part two of Paul's rationale for Israel's nonresponsiveness to the gospel. But *to this day*, he says, *when Moses is read, a veil covers their hearts*. Paul portrays Israel's mental stupor in terms of a veil that has settled over the heart of the nation. The "but" (NIV *even*) that introduces this thought parallels the *but* clause of verse 14. The structure of verses 14-15 can be set out as follows:

Moses' action (v. 13b) → Moses' intent (v. 13c) → Israel's response (*but*, v. 14a)

The veil's action (v. 14b) → the veil's intent (v. 14c) → Israel's response (*but*, v. 15)

The lack of an article with *kalymma (veil)* indicates a different veil from the one lying over the old covenant. The shift from dulled perceptions (v. 14) to a veiled heart (v. 15) is probably Paul's attempt to go to the crux of the matter. To a Jew the heart represented the innermost self and center of a person's spiritual and intellectual activity (Sorg 1976:181-83). A veil covering the heart evokes images of darkness and ignorance (compare Rom 1:21; Eph 4:18). The plural *their hearts* is to be noted. It is corporate darkness that is in view here. *To this day* refers to the nation's inability down through the centuries to discern the truths of salvation history because of a condition of spiritual blindness. Paul is not alone in making this judgment. The Qumran community was of the opinion that those in Jerusalem "do not know the hidden meaning of what is actually taking place, nor have they ever understood the lessons of the past" (1QMyst 2-3). The Essenes

take the subject to be *the veil* over the reading of the old covenant and translate the verb as "is abolished" (RSV, NRSV, KJV) or *is removed* (TEV, NIV, JB, REB, NKJV, NASB). Others see the subject as "the glory" of the old covenant and render the verb "is dwindling" or "is passing away" (though see the NEB's "is abrogated"). The latter is to be preferred, based on consistent usage of the verb in the previous verses (vv. 7, 11, 13). The present tense precludes translating it as an accomplished fact ("has been lifted," Phillips; or "has dwindled").

3:15 The reading of *the old covenant* (v. 14) and the reading of *Moses* (v. 15) show how closely the minister and the covenant were associated in Paul's thinking.

likened the nation to "the blind and those that grope their way" (Cairo *Damascus Document* 1:8-9).

A Word of Hope (3:16-17) Isaiah 6:9-10 attributes Israel's condition to God's command to his spokesperson to "make the heart of this people calloused; make their ears dull and close their eyes." Paul, himself, does not take this step in this passage (although the NIV does in v. 14), but puts forward the hope that *whenever anyone turns to the Lord,* the *veil* of spiritual darkness *is taken away* (v. 16). Moses now becomes a model to be emulated rather than shunned; for Paul's hope is based on Exodus 34:34, where Moses, in coming before the Lord to speak with him, removed his veil. The LXX imperfect *periēreito* ("he used to remove") indicates that this was Moses' habitual practice on entering the tent of meeting.

Although Paul cites Exodus 34:34 almost verbatim, there are four significant modifications. First, he shifts to an indefinite subject, thereby moving the reader beyond the historical setting of the Exodus narrative *(whenever anyone turns).* Second, the action shifts from past to present *(whenever anyone turns, . . . the veil is taken away).* This shows that Paul is interested in this narrative primarily for his own situation.

Third, in the Exodus narrative Moses removes his own veil. In Paul's account, it is either God (passive, *the veil is taken away)* or the individual (middle, "he removes the veil")—or perhaps both. Quite often divine sovereignty and human responsibility work together in Paul's thinking, especially where individual salvation is in view. For instance, Paul can in one breath command the Philippians to "work out your salvation with fear and trembling" and in the next say that it is "God who works in you to will and to act according to his good purpose" (2:12-13). This is true throughout salvation history. Jeremiah 24:7, for example, attributes "turning" to the human will ("they will return to me with all their heart") and change of heart to God ("I will give them a heart to know me").

Fourth, instead of "to enter" *(eisporeuomai),* Paul uses "to turn" *(epistrephō; whenever anyone turns to the Lord).* This term marks the

---

3:16 The subject of *periaireitai* is not clear. If the verb is passive, then *the Lord* is the one who "lifts the veil"; if it is middle, it is *anyone* turning to the Lord who "lifts the veil."

3:17 During the patristic period there was a tendency to take *to pneuma* as the subject of the clause and interpret *ho kyrios* adjectivally: "The Spirit is divine." But this approach was fueled by the controversy at that time regarding the person and nature of the third

characteristic attitude of the Jew within the covenant relationship. To turn to the Lord in the Old Testament is to turn away from foreign gods (as in Jer 4:1) and to listen to God's voice (Deut 4:30) and commands with all your heart and soul (Deut 30:10). It is also the appropriate response to the gospel under the new covenant, regardless of whether one is a Jew (Acts 3:19; 9:35) or a Gentile (Acts 11:21; 14:15, 15:19; 1 Thess 1:9).

Whenever a person gives his or her thoughts and life a new direction, it always involves a judgment on previous views and behavior. So it comes as no surprise that repentance and turning to the Lord are closely related ideas in the New Testament (Laubach 1975:353). Peter, for instance, calls his Jerusalem audience to "repent and turn to God" (Acts 3:19).

To whom is Paul offering this word of hope? Israel is the most obvious choice, since it is they that have a veil over their heart (v. 15). Yet Paul's shift from the plural "they" (v. 15) to the singular *anyone* (v. 16) suggests that the individual Israelite, and not the nation, is in view. His point would be that in spite of national blindness—which explains why Israel as a whole is not responding to the gospel—there is still the possibility of a personal response. For, until today, whenever Moses is read a veil covers Israel's heart. Yet, if someone turns to the Lord (as Moses did), the veil is removed (as it was in Moses' case; vv. 15-16). The *Lord* to whom Moses turned in the Exodus narrative was Yahweh. The *Lord* to whom a person must now turn *is the Spirit* (v. 17).

Paul's statement *Now the Lord is the Spirit* has mystified theologians for centuries. At face value he seems to be equating two members of the Trinity. Which two depends on whether *Lord* is understood to be Yahweh or Christ. In previous years it was just assumed that Paul meant Christ and discussions focused on the precise relationship between the two. Quite often the Spirit's person or work got lost in the exegetical shuffle. It is common to read statements like "the essence of Christ in his resurrected and ascended state is that of Spirit" or "Christ is experienced and operative in the church through the Spirit." Some tried

member of the Trinity and not by careful exegesis. Some think that Paul is stating that the counterpart to the Yahweh of Israel in the old covenant is the Spirit in the new covenant. Others shy away from a personal understanding of *to pneuma* and interpret it in a qualitative sense (for example, God is no longer remote).

The method of text interpretation employed by Paul in 2 Corinthians 3:16-17 can also

to get around the theological difficulties by reading *pneuma* as lower case "spirit" and translating, "Christ is spirit" or even "Christ is the spiritual sense of the Old Testament." This, however, is just plain wrong. For one, Paul uses the article with *pneuma* twice in the space of two verses *(the Spirit)*. Two, he distinguishes *the Spirit* from *the Lord* and treats him as a distinct entity in the second half of verse 17.

Given Paul's dependence in verse 16 on Exodus 34:34 an increasing number of exegetes are identifying *Lord* in both verses 16 and 17 with Yahweh. On this reading the article is anaphoric, referring the reader back to verse 16: "Now by 'Yahweh' is meant the Spirit." But the reader is still left with an equation of Yahweh and the Spirit that has to be finessed in some fashion. Another approach is to think of verse 17 as Paul's commentary on Exodus 34:34 and treat *kyrios* as a citation. *Lord* would then be put in quotes and translated: "Now the term 'Lord' refers to the Spirit." Paul would be following a method of text interpretation commonly utilized in Jewish literature by which various terms of the biblical text are assigned a more meaningful, often contemporary equivalent. What this means is that Paul need not be construing *Lord* at the beginning of verse 17 in any personal sense. It is merely a term in his text that finds its meaning and application in the contemporary situation of his day. Nonetheless, in identifying the Spirit with the term *Lord*, Paul makes a profound theological point. Moses turned to Yahweh for the removal of his veil. With the advent of the new covenant, the Spirit becomes the prime mover in the lives of God's people.

Paul concludes his commentary on Exodus 34:34 with the statement *where the Spirit of the Lord is, there is freedom* (v. 17). The word *freedom*

---

be found in Galatians 4:24-26, where Hagar is identified with "Mount Sinai in Arabia," and Romans 10:6-8, where each quote from Deuteronomy 30:12-14 is assigned a more meaningful, contemporary equivalent. Philo uses much the same technique. In *On Flight and Finding* 57, for example, the citation "You are alive today" (Deut 4:4) is followed by "Now 'today' is the limitless age that never comes to an end" (compare *Allegorical Interpretation* 19). In many cases the terms themselves lose their original contextual associations. This is particularly the case with proper names and pronouns, which are often treated in an impersonal fashion. For instance, in *On the Change of Names* 117 Philo equates the word "man" with "the world which reason alone discerns." Similarly, in *Exodus Rabbah* 2.6 the term "Elohim" is identified with "Moses" (Belleville 1990:263-67).

3:18 It is often more or less assumed that *we . . . all* is Paul's way of including all believers, whereas up to this point discussion has centered on the gospel minister. But the imagery of an *unveiled face* is part and parcel of the contrast drawn in verses 12-18 between the public, upfront behavior of the new covenant minister and the veiled, nondisclosing

strikes a particularly resonant chord with those of us who live in a nation that places great importance on the possession of inalienable rights and freedoms. What did this word mean to Paul? Elsewhere it refers to freedom from death (e.g., Rom 8:2), sin (e.g., Rom 6:18, 22), the law (Gal 5:1-3) and condemnation (Rom 8:1-2). Here it means to be free of barriers that would impede spiritual understanding. It is the work of the Spirit to remove such spiritual impediments. *Freedom* also looks forward to the gospel minister in verse 18, who unlike Moses has the liberty to minister with an "unveiled face." This freedom to be open and public in the exercise of his ministry Paul also attributes to the work of the Spirit *(where the Spirit is)*.

The Freedom of the New Covenant Minister (3:18) Verse 18 is the capstone of Paul's reflections in this chapter. It picks up the two major ideas of verses 12-17, namely, the open conduct of the gospel minister and the Spirit as the prime mover of the new covenant, and weaves them together into a clinching argument against those who would depend on the way things were under the Mosaic covenant. To start with, Paul introduces a final point of contrast between Moses and the new covenant minister. *We, who with unveiled faces all reflect the Lord's glory, are being transformed into his likeness with ever-increasing glory.*

We . . . all might well be Paul's way of broadening his point of reference to include all believers. Even so, the focus is still on the new covenant minister. *With unveiled faces* invites comparison with Moses, but Moses in which role? Moses with unveiled face in the tent of meeting? Or Moses with his face veiled before Israel? Much depends on how one translates *katoptrizomenoi.* The verb is a rare one, and in the middle it

conduct of Moses. *We . . . all* merely emphasizes what is characteristic of the new covenant ministers as a group, namely, an ever increasing glory. Peter's use of "we all" to distinguish the disciples as a group (Acts 2:32) and Paul's "we all" to distinguish the Jews as a group (Eph 2:3) are cases in point.

The genitive *pneumatos* in the phrase *kathaper apo kyriou pneumatos* has been construed as possessive ("the Lord of the Spirit"), objective ("the Lord who sends the Spirit"), qualitative ("the Lord who is experienced as Spirit") and appositional ("the Lord, namely, the Spirit"). Virtually all modern translations take *pneumatos* to be appositional and render it *the Lord, who is the Spirit.*

It is possible that Paul is employing the same exegetical method that he used in verse 17 of assigning a contemporary equivalent to a term in his biblical text. If so, "as from the 'Lord,' that is, the Spirit" would be Paul's interpretive comment on "until he entered to talk with the Lord" in Exodus 34:35 (Belleville 1990:294-95).

can mean either "to behold oneself in a mirror" or "to serve as a mirror"—that is, "to reflect." Transfiguration through beholding God's glory is an attractive idea that a number of translators have opted for (KJV, NKJV, RSV, REB). Yet if Paul is continuing his commentary on the Exodus 34 narrative—with verse 35 being next in line—then he is thinking of how Moses habitually veiled his face on leaving the tent of meeting until his next encounter with Yahweh. New covenant ministers, by contrast, leave their face *unveiled* and in so doing *reflect* God's glory. Paul is drawing on the function of a mirror to pick up the light rays from an object and to reflect that light in the form of an image. The image that the new covenant minister reflects is identified in the text as *the Lord's glory*. This is a familiar phrase in Scripture. Here it anticipates "the light of the knowledge of the glory of God [reflected] in the face of Christ" (4:6) and, by association, reflected in the faces of Christ's representatives.

As gospel preachers do their job of reflecting knowledge of God to those around them, transformation occurs. The text reads, *And we who reflect the Lord's glory are being transformed into his likeness with ever-increasing glory* (v. 18). The word *transformed* means "to take on a different form or appearance." It can refer to an outward change or, as here, to an inward change. The present tense denotes an ongoing process: We are "constantly being transformed." *Transformed into his likeness* is literally "transformed into the same image." It is taken as a matter of course by many that the image Paul has in view is Christ's image (NIV *into his likeness*). He could also be thinking of how gospel ministers should be carbon copies of one another, if they are truly carrying on Christ's ministry of reflecting God's glory to a dark world.

Transformation is not a one-shot affair. It is transformation into a likeness that is *with ever-increasing glory* (v. 18). *With ever-increasing glory* is literally "from glory to glory." The phrase denotes a splendor that steadily grows, in contrast to the short-lived glory of Moses' face. It was the property of mirrors back in those days (which were made of a flat, circular piece of cast metal) that the more polished the surface, the clearer the image. Continuous elbow grease was needed to keep away corrosion. The picture is a provocative one. The life and ministry of the believer are depicted as a mirror that is in need of continual polishing so as to reproduce to an ever-increasing extent the glorious knowledge and truths of the gospel.

This ever-increasing glory, Paul states, *comes from the Lord, who is the Spirit*. As the unveiled glory of Moses' face is ascribed to his coming before Yahweh, so the unveiled, glorified face of the gospel minister is attributed to the activity of the Spirit. It is the third member of the Trinity and his work that take center stage in this chapter. The Spirit brings about understanding regarding the temporal character of the Mosaic covenant (3:13-17) and makes known in *unveiled* or plain fashion the truths of the gospel through the preaching and transformed life of the new covenant minister (vv. 2, 18). It is also because of the Spirit that the gospel minister has the freedom, unlike Moses—and perhaps unlike Paul's opponents—to unveil his or her face (v. 17). This durable glory, according to Paul, stems from the new covenant as a covenant of the life-giving Spirit rather than a death-giving letter (3:6-11).

Setting Forth the Truth Plainly (4:1-6) There is a constant temptation in the ministry to preach what people want to hear rather than what they need to hear. Sermons that confront a congregation with their spiritual shortcomings do not usually result in a pat on the back. Instead, they quite often yield criticism and hostility. David Wells argues that the pastoral task of brokering the truth of God to God's people has, for this very reason, largely fallen by the wayside in evangelicalism today (1993:1-14). To preach in a way that serves Christ and not people's egos takes courage. But it is easy to become disheartened when people turn a deaf ear to preaching that tells it like it is.

Paul repeatedly had to deal with discouragement in his ministry. There were plenty of preachers whose motives were less than pious and who would do whatever they had to to gain a following (v. 2). There were also churches who were readily seduced by flattering speech and winsome ways. It would have been all too easy for someone who remained faithful in preaching Christ and not themselves (v. 5) to grow weary of the downside of human nature (v. 1).

Paul, however, did not give in to discouragement. What heartened him were two things: the character of his ministry and the mercy of God. *Since through God's mercy we have this ministry,* he says, *we do not lose heart* (v. 1). *Through God's mercy* is literally "as we have been shown mercy." Paul looked on his ministry as something he received not because of any personal merit but on account of God's favor. Nor was this a matter of theoretical knowledge. Paul experienced God's mercy firsthand when he was stopped dead in his tracks while pursuing Jewish Christians who had fled Jerusalem for the safer haven of Damascus (Acts 9:1-9). Then there was the surpassing splendor of the new covenant *(this ministry)*. The privilege of being a minister of such a covenant more than compensated for the trials and tribulations that he experienced as an itinerant preacher.

As a result, Paul did *not lose heart (enkakoumen,* v. 1). The Greek verb means "to act badly" in the face of difficulties; "to give up" or "grow weary" while pursuing a worthwhile goal. Paul, however, would not allow any obstacles inside or outside the church to pressure him into abandoning his ministry. Instead of giving in to discouragement, he deliberately and categorically "renounces" the kind of behavior that characterized much of the itinerant speaking of his day. He describes this behavior as *secret and shameful* (v. 2). The phrase is literally "the secret things of shame." "Secret things" are a person's innermost thoughts and intentions (Furnish 1984:218). The genitive "of shame" can be descriptive: "shameful secret practices" (Phillips) or subjective: "actions kept secret for shame" (NEB, REB). Deeds one hides because of their shameful character is probably the thought here. Paul rejects two types of shameful deeds. First, he *does not use deception. Use* is literally "to walk" *(peripateō)*—a verb that occurs frequently in Paul's writings to describe the Christian life. The Greek term for *deception* means "capable of anything" *(pan + ourgia).* In the New Testament it refers to those who use their ability unscrupulously and denotes cunning or slyness. Not only does Paul not resort to deception, but, second, he does not *distort the word of God.* The verb *distort (doloō)* is commonly employed of adulterating merchandise for profit. Paul refused to follow in the

---

4:1 Furnish maintains that the parallelism between 4:1 and 3:12 requires the translation "we do not shrink back" for *ouk enkakoumen* (1984:217). It is a meaning, however, that is not attested in Liddell, Scott and Jones 1978.

4:2 Paul may be responding to an accusation that he had acted in an unscrupulous fashion. "Crafty fellow that I am, I caught you by trickery" in 12:16 seems to reflect just such a charge. Reading between the lines, it appears there were insinuations that Paul's Jerusalem collection was merely a smoke screen for the personal support he would not

footsteps of others who tamper with God's word in order to make it more palatable to the listener or more lucrative for themselves.

In short, Paul eschewed any behavior that was not in accord with the character of the gospel that he preached. His opponents, however, had no scruples in this regard. They quite willingly exploited the Corinthians for financial gain (2:17; 11:20). Paul, instead, *set[s] forth the truth plainly.* The Greek term translated "sets forth" *(tē phanerōsei)* refers to an open declaration or full disclosure. The contrast is between a straightforward and open, as opposed to deceptive, presentation of the gospel—what we call "telling it like it is."

By setting forth the gospel in a plain-spoken way, Paul "commends" himself to *every* person's *conscience.* The *conscience* is where conviction takes hold that what one is hearing is *the truth.* Paul does not seek to commend himself to a person's ego or intellect but appeals to their capacity to distinguish between right and wrong. Nor does he simply trust human judgment but commends himself *in the sight of God.* He is aware that what he does is done under the perpetually watchful eye of the Lord.

Paul goes on in verses 3-4 to deal with the accusation that his message is *veiled (kekalymmenon).* It would appear—if we can read between the lines—that Paul's critics reasoned from the absence of large numbers of converts (especially from among his own people) to some fault in his preaching. Paul is the first one to recognize that he is not an overly impressive speaker, as speakers go. This was deliberate on his part, as he would have his audience know only "Jesus Christ and him crucified" (see 1 Cor 2:1-5). So it is not surprising that he does not deny the charge. The conditional form that he chooses acknowledges their claim: *If* [as you claim] *our gospel is veiled, it is veiled to those who are perishing (ei* + indicative). But what he does not allow is that there is some fault with the message that he preached. If the content of his preaching is veiled, it

---

overtly accept.

All manner of translations have been suggested for *ta krypta tēs aischynēs,* including "the behavior that shame hides," "the things that one hides from a sense of shame" and "secrecy prompted by shame." One of the most provocative translations is "shameful intrigues that have been hatched in secret."

4:3 *Ei* + present indicative is a condition of fact, but the fact is probably only in the minds of Paul's opponents *(If [as some claim] our gospel is veiled).* The present participle

is not because he did not present the truths of the gospel plainly (v. 2).

The fault lies rather in three areas. First, the audience is at fault. If there is a hidden aspect to what he preaches, it only appears so to *those who are perishing*. As in 2:15-16, Paul divides humanity into two groups based on their destiny: those who are on the road to destruction *(tois apollymenois)* and, by implication, those who are on the road to salvation. To the one the gospel makes no sense (v. 3), while to the other it is plain as day (v. 6).

The fault lies, second, with the situation. The *minds* of those who are perishing have been *blinded*. The blindness is of a particular sort—it is a blindness to *the light of the gospel of the glory of Christ* (v. 4). The piling up of genitives both here and in verse 6 is typical of Paul. *The light of the gospel* is probably a genitive of source: "the light which *radiates from* the gospel." *Of the glory* is most likely descriptive, "the light of the *glorious* gospel." As the Mosaic covenant shone with glory, so the gospel shines with glory. *Of Christ* is plausibly construed as objective: "the glorious gospel *about* Christ."

Christ is further described as "the image of God." To be an image is to be a true representation. We say today that a child is the "spitting image" of his father or mother. Wisdom is similarly described as "a reflection of eternal light, a spotless mirror of the working of God and an image of his goodness" (Wisdom of Solomon 7:26). Paul states that Christ *is,* not was, God's image, for he alone brings to visible expression the nature of an invisible God (Col 1:15). So, to see Christ is to see God and to not see Christ is to not see God.

The fault lies, third, with the source of the blindness. Unbelievers cannot *see* the gospel's light because their minds have been blinded by

---

en tois apollymenois denotes process. The gospel is hidden to those who are "in the process of perishing." Compare 2:15-16. John A. Bain has argued that this phrase should be construed as neuter and translated "in the things that are perishing"; Paul would then be saying that his gospel is hidden by the material world (1906-1907:380). Samuel Davies understands the phrase as a reference to the "furniture and ceremonial of the Mosaic economy" (1868:27). The difficulty with both interpretations is that *en tois apollymenois* is explicitly used in 2:15 of people who are perishing, not things.

4:4 *Eis to* + the infinitive denotes purpose ("to keep them from seeing the light") rather than result ("with the result that they cannot see the light"). Satan's intent is to blind people to the truth.

Augasai is usually intransitive ("so that the light cannot *shine forth*"), but the transitive

the god of this age (v. 4). This is the only place where Paul refers to the adversary of God's people as a *god*. He is usually called Satan or the devil—although in Ephesians 2:2 he is named "the ruler of the kingdom of the air." It could well be that these are traditional formulations Paul used because of their familiarity to his readers. But there is no denying the power of this being. He can destroy the flesh (1 Cor 5:5), masquerade as an angel of light (2 Cor 11:14) and empower his servant, the antichrist, to work all manner of miracles, signs and wonders (2 Thess 2:9). Paul's thorn in the flesh is attributed to him (2 Cor 12:7), as is tempting (1 Cor 7:5), scheming against (2 Cor 2:11; Eph 6:11) and trapping (2 Tim 2:26) the believer. On more than one occasion Paul experienced firsthand his active opposition to the gospel (1 Thess 2:18).

The preacher in our media-oriented society is pressured to use the pulpit as a stage for displaying eloquence, dramatic skill and fine oratory. Congregations add to this pressure with their desire to be amused and entertained. As a result, preaching is often seen by outsiders as just another stage performance. And what is hailed as a successful ministry is sometimes little more than good acting. But to his credit Paul can say of himself and his coworkers that *we do not preach ourselves, but Jesus Christ as Lord, and ourselves as your servants for Jesus' sake* (v. 5).

The emphasis in terms of word order is on *not ourselves* (*ou heautous kēryssomen*, "not ourselves do we preach"; v. 5). It is hard to determine whether Paul is on the offensive or defensive here. He certainly accuses the Corinthian intruders later in the letter of putting on airs (10:12-18). But he also appears to have been faulted for ministerial arrogance (3:12—4:3)—although his claim to preach Christ and not himself was not an idle one. In 1 Corinthians 2:1-4 he reminded the Corinthians that

fits the context better: *The god of this age has blinded the minds of unbelievers so that they cannot see the light.* Parallelism with 3:13 regarding the Israelites' inability to look intently at Moses' shining face also favors the transitive. Satan as a blinder of the human mind is not a new idea. This attribution is also found in Jewish literature. *Testament of Judah* 19.4, for example, reads "The prince of error blinded me and I was ignorant."

4:5 Some manuscripts have *dia Iēsou* ("through Jesus") instead of *dia Iēsoun* ("because of Jesus"; *for Jesus' sake*). With the former, Paul would be saying that he is the Corinthians' servant as a result of his commissioning by Christ. Use of "Jesus" as opposed to "Christ" points, however, to the latter option. Paul counts himself as their servant because of him who first took on the form of a servant (Phil 2:7) and then commanded his disciples to do the same (Jn 13:14-17; Plummer 1915:119).

on his founding visit he did not come to them with eloquence, superior wisdom or wise and persuasive words. This was so that they might know nothing while he was with them except Jesus Christ and him crucified. Now he is concerned that they know not only the crucified Christ but also Jesus as *Lord,* that is, Jesus as master of their congregational life.

What then is Paul's role? In 1:24 he said that he does not lord it over the church but works together with them. Here he goes even further in defining his role as that of a *servant (doulos).* As an apostle of Christ, he could have merely said the word and commanded their obedience. Domination, however, was not Paul's style. He was there to serve them and used a command only as a last resort. This is an important reminder for pastors today. If Christ is to be truly Lord of the church, then pastors must be content with the role of servant.

Paul goes on to explain why he preaches Jesus Christ as Lord. *For God . . . made his light shine in our hearts to give us the light of the knowledge of the glory of God in the face of Christ* (v. 6). There is a piling up of genitives here in a similar way to verse 4. *The light of the knowledge* could well be "the light that comes from knowing" (genitive of source). The familiar caricature of sudden understanding as a light bulb going on in a person's mind captures the idea. Knowing what, however? In verse 4 it was knowing the good news about Christ. Here it is "knowing God" (objective genitive)—or more specifically, knowing "God's glory" (possessive genitive).

This knowledge, Paul says, *God made shine in our hearts.* The aorist indicative, *made shine (elampsen),* suggests a point in time. It is commonly thought that Paul is referring to his Damascus Road encounter. But Luke describes that experience as "a light from heaven [that] flashed around him" (Acts 9:3), while here it is a light that illumines the heart. Paul also uses the plural *our* hearts, indicating that this was (and should be) the experience of all gospel ministers. Some aspect of his conversion experience is undoubtedly in view. Perhaps it was the point at which, as he puts it, "God was pleased to reveal his Son in me so that I might preach him among the Gentiles" (Gal 1:15-16).

4:6 The genitive in the phrase *phōtismon tēs gnōseōs* can be plausibly construed as either a genitive of source, "the light *which comes from* knowing God's glory"; a genitive of content, "the light *which is* the knowledge of God's glory"; or even an objective genitive,

Paul pictures the conversion experience as a new creation (v. 6). For it is the God who said, *Let light shine out of darkness,* who illumines the human heart through knowledge of himself. The phraseology recalls Genesis 1:3 and the first day of creation ("Let there be light"). The key thought is that God's light dispels darkness, whether it be the physical darkness of night or the spiritual darkness of human ignorance. The idea of light dispelling darkness is a recurring one in the Old Testament. Perhaps the most familiar texts are Isaiah 9:1-2, where it is promised that those who walk in darkness in the land of Zebulun and Naphtali will see "a great light," and Isaiah 49:6, where it is said that God will make his "servant . . . a light for the Gentiles."

The light that dispels darkness in the human heart is found *in the face of Christ.* Paul is undoubtedly thinking of the Incarnation. The *face* is the image that we present in public. Christ's *face,* then, is what he presented during his earthly ministry. This is the second time Paul links knowledge of God irrevocably with Jesus Christ. The connection is a relatively simple one: To know Christ is to know God; to not know Christ is to not know God.

God's Power Is Made Known Through Ministerial Hardships (4:7-12) Virtually every archaeological dig in the Middle East has unearthed innumerable pieces of pottery from earliest civilization forward. Pottery seems to have been a favorite material for fashioning a wide variety of utensils. It was not a costly material. The well-to-do turned to materials such as ivory, glass, marble, brass and costly wood. Pottery, on the other hand, was the material of the common person. It was used to make everything from pitchers, oil jars and bowls to griddles, washbasins and pots. Coarse clay was preferred for utilitarian ware. For more expensive vessels, the potter first refined the clay by treading it out in water. Clay pots found many uses. Items of value could be kept in them, and clay jars were especially popular for storing liquids because the pottery hindered evaporation and kept the contents cool at the same time. Even broken

the light which enlightens with knowledge" (Phillips). The ready interchangeability of enlightenment and knowledge makes it difficult to decide.

pieces of pottery, or "shards," found a use as writing material for notes, receipts and messages.

In verses 7-15 Paul compares the gospel minister to a piece of Palestinian pottery. *We have this treasure in jars of clay* (v. 7). *This treasure* is the glorious good news about Christ (vv. 1-6). *Jars of clay* is actually "earthenware vessels" *(ostrakinois skeuesin)*. The noun *skeuos* refers to a vessel serving a specific purpose (such as a jug, cup, pan or pot). When used of people it often carries the sense of "implement" or "instrument" (Maurer 1971:358-67). So to be God's "vessel" is to be his instrument in carrying out a specific service—in this case, the gospel ministry.

The marvel of Paul's statement is not to be overlooked. The gospel minister is a vessel made of common, run-of-the-mill clay—fragile and easily broken. And yet God has entrusted the *treasure* of the gospel to such a vessel, just as Palestinians stored their valuables in common clay pots. Why does God do this? According to Paul, he does it *to show that this all-surpassing power is from God and not from us.* God uses what is fragile and yet serviceable so that there might be no mistaking the origin of the gospel minister's power. The adjective *all-surpassing (hyperbolē)* stresses the extraordinary quality or extent of something (Bauer, Arndt and Gingrich 1979). The "something" here is *power.* The Greek *dynamis* is the term from which we derive our English word "dynamite." The gospel is not merely a message that confronts the mind but an explosive power that turns a person's life upside down. On May 18, 1980, Mount St. Helens in the Cascade Range of Washington exploded with a stunning demonstration of nature's power. The explosion ripped thirteen hundred feet off the mountain and leveled 150-foot Douglas firs even seventeen miles away. We stand in awe of such force and yet forget the equally awesome power that is unleashed in the preaching of the gospel.

To develop this comparison of the gospel minister to the common clay pot, Paul employs an accepted literary form of the day called *res*

4:7 While the human body might initially come to mind as the clay pot in which the treasure of the gospel has been placed, it is the human being and not the body per se that is in view here. Hebraic thinking did not compartmentalize the human being (e.g., soul, body, mind). Rather, it viewed the whole person from different perspectives (e.g., material,

gestae, or "cataloging of deeds." Much like our curriculum vitae, it highlighted a person's exploits and accomplishments. Paul highlights four exploits that would not by any stretch of the imagination be considered impressive or desirable either in his day or in ours. All four point up the hardships and trials that confront the gospel preacher. *On every side* (v. 8) and *always* (vv. 10, 11) underline the extent and intensity of these so-called exploits.

First, he is *hard pressed on every side, but not crushed.* The verb *hard pressed* means "to press in hard against" someone, or, as we say today, to squeeze the life out of a person, while the term *not crushed* indicates that the pressure never got to the point where there was no escape or way out.

Second, he is *perplexed but not in despair.* There is a play on words here that the NIV misses. To be *aporoumenoi* is to be at a loss how to act, while to be *exaporoumenoi* is to be utterly at a loss (i.e., in extreme despair). Although Paul may have been at a loss about how to proceed, he never—as we say—went off the deep end.

Third, he is *persecuted but not abandoned.* The Greek verb means "to pursue" and is commonly used of tracking a prey or enemy. Paul was pursued from city to city by hostile Jews. But through it all, God never *abandoned* him. The idea here is that God did not leave Paul behind or in the lurch for the enemy to pick up.

Finally, he is *struck down* by the enemy *but not destroyed.* Paul was not only pursued by hostile Jews, but when they caught up with him, they stirred up trouble whenever they could. He may also be thinking of the time he was stoned at Lystra and left outside the city for dead. Yet he lived.

Hard pressed, perplexed, persecuted and *struck down* are summed up in the clause *we always carry around in our body the death of Jesus* (v. 10). *Carry around* refers to the itinerant life of the gospel preacher. *Always* points to the commonplace versus exceptional character of these experiences. *The death of Jesus* is actually "the dying of Jesus"—a term

---

spiritual, mental).

Duff maintains that the clay pot as a self-description calls to mind certain vessels carried in cultic epiphany processions that contained sacred objects manifesting the beneficent activity and saving power of the god or goddess (1991a:158-64).

that stresses the ongoing nature of the process. When we think of the "dying" of Jesus, we tend to think of the cross. Paul, however, has in mind the hardships, troubles and frustrations that Jesus faced during his three-year ministry—the loneliness, the disappointments with his disciples, the exhaustion, the constant harassment by opponents, the crowd's continuous demands, the incredulity of his family, the mocking and jeers of his foes, the flight of his friends, the hours on the cross, the thirst and then the end. "I die every day" expresses the same thought (1 Cor 15:31). Paul is acknowledging the wearing effect that the gospel ministry had on Jesus mentally, emotionally and physically. Nor is his a unique experience. Jesus taught his followers that if anyone would come after him, "he must deny himself and take up his cross daily and follow me" (Lk 9:23; compare Mk 8:34).

Paul further explains this thought in verse 11: *For we . . . are always being given over to death for Jesus' sake*. *Given over* is the legal term used in the Gospels of Jesus' being handed over to the authorities. If this is the sense here, then the gospel ministry is being pictured as a "delivering up into death's custody *[eis thanaton]*." The verb is present tense: "constantly delivered up." The NEB's "continually . . . we are being surrendered into the hands of death" captures well the sense. *For Jesus' sake* excludes a reference to the aging process or to the normal trials of everyday life. Paul is thinking of the hardships and troubles that he experienced as a result of carrying out his ministry. He catalogs them at some length in chapter 11.

To what end? Why does Paul put up with a life of hardship and trouble? It is *so that the life of Jesus may also be revealed in our body* (v. 10)—or as he says in verse 11, "in our mortal flesh." As Jerome Murphy-O'Connor notes, it is a Pauline paradox that "dying" should manifest "life" (1991:46). But this is why Paul likens the gospel minister to the expendable, perishable clay pot.

Christian reaction to adversity has tended to be "grin and bear it" or "keep a stiff upper lip." Paul's approach is to make clear that it is God's power (v. 7) and the life of Jesus (v. 10) that empower and sustain him,

---

4:11 *Dia Iēsoun* can mean *for Jesus' sake* (that is, "for his benefit") or, more probably,

and not his own fortitude. It has been debated whether by *the life of Jesus* Paul has in mind a human mode of existence or the power of the risen Christ. It need not be an either-or choice. The already/not yet character of salvation means that Christ's resurrection power is already impacting human existence. Paul acknowledges this very thing in his summary statement, *So then, death is at work in us, but life is at work in you.* While the Corinthians might have looked on hardship *(death)* as incompatible with a Spirit-directed ministry, it nonetheless produced a life that even now is at work, or better yet, is "energizing" *(en + ergeō)* them.

There is an important lesson here. The Corinthians, like many Christians today, believed that adversity was inconsistent with the Spirit-filled Christian life, let alone with the gospel ministry. At issue is how God manifests his power. Paul's opponents claimed that it is through the working of signs, wonders and miracles. Paul, on the other hand, maintained that God's power is able to make itself known most effectively through ministerial hardship and distress. His second catalog of ministerial troubles drives this point home even more forcefully: "Dying, and yet we live on; beaten, and yet not killed . . . having nothing, and yet possessing everything" (6:9-10). It is the "yet" side that attracts attention. How is it that gospel ministers live on? Certainly not by their own strength. Theirs is a position of weakness. But it is in their very weakness ("dying," "beaten," "possessing nothing") that the life of Jesus is revealed ("live on," "not killed," "possessing everything").

This is a hard message for the twentieth-century mindset. We like to be in control of our circumstances and operate from a position of strength. I doubt that a pastoral candidate who responded to the question "How has God been at work in your ministry?" with "To this very hour I go hungry and thirsty, I have nothing but rags to wear, I have been brutally treated by the community in which I have been ministering and I am currently homeless for Jesus's sake" (1 Cor 4:11) would be given further consideration. And yet in Paul's opinion this is exactly the kind of vita that authenticates the true gospel minister.

"on account of Jesus" (that is, in the service of the gospel).

A Faith That Prompts Outspokenness (4:13-18) Paul is not alone in his opinion. He finds the *same spirit of faith* in the psalmist's exclamation, *I believed; therefore I have spoken* (Ps 116:10). The Greek term *pneuma* can refer either to the divine Spirit or to a human attitude. The broader context of the psalm suggests that it is a commonality of attitude between himself and the psalmist that prompts Paul to cite this text. The genitive *of faith* is most likely subjective. Paul and the psalmist had in common a "faith that prompts outspokenness." The Old Testament quote is actually from the LXX rather than the Masoretic Text. In the LXX, the psalmist recounts how his faith gave him the courage to speak out despite opposition and how he was greatly afflicted because of his outspokenness. It is not clear whether the psalmist is speaking of a crippling illness, a mortal wound or a false accusation. Nevertheless, he, like Paul, felt crushed (Ps 116:10), dismayed (v. 11) and disillusioned (v. 11). And he, like Paul, possessed a faith that prompted him to speak out.

What motivates a person to speak out regardless of the personal consequences? This is a question that Paul raises twice in the space of two chapters. It is also one that we all ask from time to time. Why preach the gospel if it leads to ridicule, personal deprivation and hostility? For Paul it was not a matter of feeling that he was the best qualified or had superior credentials. It was, rather, a question of conviction—a conviction that constrained him to speak out, even when it was not to his advantage to do so. What was this conviction? It was not the belief that Jesus is the Christ—as we would expect of a Jew—but rather the certainty that he *who raised the Lord Jesus from the dead will also raise us with Jesus* (v. 14). *Raise us* points to a corporate event. *With Jesus* is best rendered "in the company of." Paul is thinking of the parousia, when "God will bring with Jesus those who have fallen asleep in him"

4:13 If *to auto pneuma* is a reference to the Holy Spirit, then the genitive *tēs pisteōs* is most likely objective: "the same Spirit who engenders faith."

The difficulty in construing the Hebrew of Psalm 116:10-11 is reflected in the wide variance among modern translations: (1) "I kept my faith, even when I said, 'I am greatly afflicted' " (RSV, NRSV, TEV); (2) "My trust does not fail even when I say, 'I am completely wretched' " (NJB); (3) "I was sure I should be swept away; my distress was bitter" (NEB, REB); (4) "I believed, therefore I spoke [said], 'I am greatly afflicted' " (NKJV, NIV) and (5) "I believed when I said, 'I am greatly afflicted' " (NASB). The Septuagint translator

(1 Thess 4:14). Paul could be saying that he speaks out despite the consequences because he knows that if death takes him, God can and will raise him up. But in light of verse 15 *(all this is for your benefit)*, it is more likely a recognition on his part of what hearers will miss out on if he fails to speak out.

Not only will God *raise us,* Paul says, but he will also *present us with you in his presence.* The Greek verb for *present* means "to cause to stand" or "to place beside." *In his presence* is not found in the Greek text. It answers the question: "Stand where?" It is Paul's conviction that God will raise and place before himself those who have heard and responded to the gospel—another reason to speak out. *All this (ta panta),* he reminds the Corinthians, *is for your benefit* (v. 15). What he undergoes as an itinerant preacher he undergoes not for his own sake but for theirs. As Paul's spiritual children, the Corinthians have been the direct beneficiaries of his willingness to preach the gospel regardless of personal cost.

The rest of verse 15 is a nightmare in terms of the grammar. The doxological cast results in syntactical imprecision. The two verbs, which are virtual synonyms, can be either transitive ("cause to increase/over-flow") or intransitive ("to increase/overflow") or any combination thereof. It is also difficult to determine whether *dia tōn pleionōn* (literally, "through the greater number") goes with the first or the second verb. Is it a matter of grace extended to more and more people *(grace that is reaching more and more people)* or thanksgiving being offered up by more and more people? A further problem is deciding whether *charis pleonasasa* refers to increasing numbers of converts, Paul's being delivered from a perilous situation (compare 1:10-11) or the spiritual growth of the Corinthian congregation. Since the subject matter is the gospel ministry, increasing numbers of converts is the most plausible

---

interpreted it as: "I believed, therefore I spoke. But I was greatly afflicted [for speaking out]."

Paul employs an unusual citation formula in verse 13: *kata to gegrammenon.* In fact, it is unique in the New Testament. He more commonly uses *kathōs gegraptai* (e.g., 2 Cor 8:15; 9:9), *kathaper gegraptai* (e.g., Rom 3:4), or merely *gegraptai* (e.g., 1 Cor 1:19).

4:14 *In his presence* can mean "before his judgment seat" or merely "close to him."

4:15 The aorist participle *pleonasasa* ("to increase") defines an action antecedent to the main verb *perisseusē* ("to overflow"): "grace having increased in turn causes thanks-

interpretation. God's *glory* most likely refers to his reputation. As more and more people give thanks, God's reputation is enhanced and extended.

A reasonable way to put the grammatical pieces together is as follows: As God's gracious invitation in the gospel extends to more and more people, the thanksgiving offered by the growing congregation of believers enhances God's reputation in the surrounding community (see the note).

At verse 16 Paul returns to the initial thought of verse 1: *Therefore, we do not lose heart.* He has given his readers four reasons that the demands made on him by the gospel ministry do not cause him to grow weary: (1) the privilege of being a minister of a covenant whose splendor will never fade (3:7-18); (2) the mercy God showed him on the road to Damascus (4:1); (3) the privilege of being God's instrument for revealing the life of Jesus (vv. 7-11); and (4) the enhancement of God's reputation through the growing community of faith (vv. 13-15)

Now he provides the Corinthians with yet another reason: *Though outwardly we are wasting away, yet inwardly we are being renewed day by day* (v. 16). Paul's *outwardly* and *inwardly* language is theologically somewhat confusing. How are we to interpret this antithesis? It has been commonly understood against the background of the Greek dualism of the outer body and the inner soul. Such a dualism, however, finds no place in Paul's thinking. Some have interpreted it in terms of the old nature of sin and the new nature of the Spirit, which, though central to Romans, Ephesians and Colossians, do not surface in 2 Corinthians.

If we take our cue from verses 7-12, Paul is viewing the self from two different vantage points. The outward person is that aspect of the self that is *wasting away*. This involves more than the body. It is the progressive weakening of our natural faculties, emotional vitality and

---

giving to overflow." Interpretations of "grace having increased" include (1) more and more people responding to the gospel, (2) more and more people hearing of the grace granted to Paul in his affliction and (3) grace expanding in the Corinthians' hearts and spurring them on to greater evangelistic efforts.

4:16 Some translate *hēmera kai hēmera* "every day" instead of *day by day* and

physical stamina. In one sense all human beings are in the process of wasting away. We begin to die as soon as we are born. The demands of the ministry merely exacerbate this process. Henry Martyn once said, "If I am going to burn out, let me burn out for God." The present tense denotes an ongoing process—we are in the process of wasting away. The passive suggests the inevitability of this process. The progressive weakening of our physical powers is a foregone conclusion.

The inward person, on the other hand, is *being renewed day by day*. *Day by day* accurately renders the Greek idiom *bēmera kai bēmera*. The idea is of a progressive renewal that matches step for step the process of physical decline. The Greek verb for *renew* means "to make new again" *(ana + kainoō)*. Paul appears to have coined the compound to express this developing spiritual reality. The deposit of the Spirit within us sets in motion a regenerative overhaul of the self that culminates in complete transformation at Christ's return (1:22; 5:5).

Alexander von Humboldt tells of a tree in South America called the cow-tree. It grows on the barren flank of a rock that its roots are scarcely able to penetrate. To the eye it appears dead and dried, but when the trunk is pierced there flows from it a sweet and nourishing milk. This is not unlike the Christian, who outwardly may appear to be withering and dying but within possesses a living sap that is welling up to eternal life.

It is in light of this ongoing renewal that Paul can view his *troubles* as merely *light and momentary* (v. 17). The noun for *troubles (thlipsis)* has the meaning of "pressure" in the physical sense (such as the pressure of the pulse) and "oppression" in the figurative sense. In both the Old and New Testaments it commonly denotes the affliction and harassment that God's people experience at the hands of the world (Schlier 1965:139-48). Paul uses the term eight times in 2 Corinthians, most often of the trouble and hardship that he experiences as a preacher of the gospel (1:4 [2x], 8; 6:4; 7:4). The word translated *momentary* is found only here in the New Testament. It emphasizes the temporary nature of

understand Paul to be speaking of a process that is repeated all over each day. See, for example, Phillips, "every day the inward man receives fresh strength," and the RSV, "our inner nature is being renewed every day." This is an unlikely rendering of the idiomatic expression, as the NRSV's change to "day by day" would suggest.

Christian adversity (Louw and Nida 1988-1989:67.109). *Light (elaphros)* was the term that the Corinthians used of Paul's supposedly capricious attitude toward them, as evidenced by his willingness to change his travel plans without first consulting them (1:17). Here, it denotes something that is light in weight. The troubles Paul faced were easy to bear because they were "without substance."

The troubles of the gospel ministry appear trifling in duration *(momentary)* and substance *(light)* in comparison with the *eternal glory that far outweighs them all.* There is a play on words here that is easy to overlook. The phrase is literally, "an eternal weight of weights." The term for *glory (doxa)* is used in the Septuagint to render Hebrew words with the root *k bd* "weighty" or "heavy." The noun *baros,* translated in the NIV by the verb *outweighs,* refers to a burden or heavy load. The trouble that Paul endures is producing a burden of a different sort, one that weighs in at an extraordinarily high figure. *Far outweighs* means all out of proportion or to the nth degree. This weight of glory is something all out of proportion in duration *(eternal)* and substance ("heavy load") to the troubles we now experience.

Paul is not speaking of the believer's future reward, nor is he talking about a recompense forthcoming to the Christian for enduring so much distress. This eternal weight of glory is something that our momentary, light troubles *are achieving for us* now. This takes awhile to sink in. Affliction does not give way to glory; affliction produces glory. The Greek verb for *achieve* means "to work out" *(kata + ergazomai).* Paul pictures the process of daily spiritual renewal in terms of a workout in the gym. Segments of our culture place a great deal of emphasis on bodybuilding and weightlifting exercises. Much physical exertion and strenuous effort are demanded. Such activities are not mastered overnight. It takes months of working out to build up the muscles of the body. In much the same way, suffering in the Christian life produces

4:17 In Hellenistic Greek *doxa* means "opinion" or "estimate." The translation *glory* is influenced by the Septuagint's use of *doxa* to render Hebrew words with the root *k bd* ("weighty"). See the text.

4:18 Paul uses the genitive absolute in verse 18 in an unusual way. Normally it precedes and defines the circumstances in which the action of the main clause takes place (as in "Dinner being over, the guests departed."). Here it follows the main clause: "Affliction achieves glory for us, *mē skopountōn hēmōn ta blepomena alla ta mē blepomena.*" The

muscles that become a permanent part of our spiritual physique.

A qualifier is thrown in at this point. This momentary, light afflic-tion is achieving for us an eternal weight of glory provided *we fix our eyes not on what is seen, but on what is unseen.* The key to the victor-ious Christian life is all in one's perspective. The genitive absolute *(skopountōn hēmōn)* most likely carries a conditional force. Affliction does its job of producing glory "as long as we fix our eyes on what is unseen" (see the note).

The verb *skopeō* means "to examine" or "consider" something with a critical eye to determine its worth or lack thereof (Fuchs 1971:414-16). What is of worth in this case is *what is unseen* as opposed to *what is seen.* Paul's contrast requires some explanation. A Greek would under-stand *what is seen* and *what is unseen* either as what is real versus ideal or what is material versus immaterial. Paul, however, is contrasting two realities, one transitory *(temporary),* the other permanent *(eternal).* The temporary reality is our present existence, which is declining with the passage of time. The permanent or *unseen* reality is that regenerative overhaul that the Spirit is undertaking, which is observable to the eye of faith but unobservable to those Satan has blinded (4:4). Critical observers will be able to distinguish between the two and keep from focusing on the former by judging its transitory value in the overall scheme of things.

The Christian Hope Beyond the Grave (5:1-5) Second Corinthians 5:1-10 is one of the most researched and written-about passages in Paul's writings—and for a good reason. Paul is tackling the topic of the Christian hope beyond the grave, and more specifically, what happens to the believer at the point of death. In our culture the subject of death holds a certain fascination as well as repulsion. On the one hand, we try to mask the fact of death with euphemisms such as "he passed on"

---

genitive absolute may be the equivalent of a temporal ("while"—KJV, NEB, NASB), causal ("because"—Phillips, RSV, TEV, RSV, NRSV) or conditional ("if") clause. (The NIV's *so* is a very unusual rendering of this construction.) A conditional sense provides the best connection with the preceding thought ("provided our eyes are fixed on the things that are unseen"—REB)—although a causal construal is by no means ruled out. See, for example, the RSV and NRSV: "because we look not at what can be seen but at what cannot be seen."

and "she went to a better place" and with funeral rites such as viewing the body, remarking how well someone looks and placing flowers on the grave. On the other hand, our culture, especially in recent years, has displayed an attraction to the topic of death in the form of accounts of near-death experiences, a resurgence of spiritism, the growing popularity of the New Age movement and the like. In fact, among the books on the bestseller list in the 1970s were Elisabeth Kübler-Ross, *On Death and Dying* (1970), and Raymond Moody Jr., *Life After Life* (1975); in the 1980s, Raymond Moody Jr., *The Light Beyond* (1988); and in the early 1990s, Betty J. Eadie and Curtis Taylor, *Embraced by the Light* (1992).

There was the same ambivalence toward death in Paul's time. Some viewed death positively as the release of the immortal soul from its mortal bodily tomb, while others looked on death as life's end—as the popular maxim "Let us eat and drink, for tomorrow we die" (1 Cor 15:32) attests. Paul, however, puts forward a different expectation for the Christian in 2 Corinthians 5:1-10. There is the certainty of physical resurrection and transformation (vv. 1-5), the confidence that death begins a journey in the realm of sight (vv. 6-7) and the assurance that death places us in the presence of Christ (v. 8). All this is confirmed by the *deposit* of the Spirit within us, guaranteeing what is to come (v. 5).

What motivated Paul to write on this subject? The notion in 4:16-18 of the decay of the outer self and the renewal of the inner self leads quite naturally to the question of what happens when these dual processes reach their point of completion. Yet, Paul's comments seem to go beyond routine doctrinal teaching. They have an air of correction about them, as evidenced by the repetitiveness of the instruction and the coining of terms. Twice Paul says that his current situation causes him to *groan* (vv. 2, 4), twice he states that he does not want to be *unclothed* but "overclothed" (vv. 2-3, 4), and twice he remarks that he

---

5:1-10 The body as the prison of the immortal soul was a view common to Orphic and Pythagorean philosophic schools. Belief in the immortality of the soul was by no means universal, though. Both Stoics and Epicureans rejected personal immortality. Stoics believed that the individual soul at death becomes submerged in the divine universal soul that permeates the cosmos. Epicureans thought that at death the atoms of the soul immediately disperse and all sensation ceases. The typical Greek looked on death as the end of life and therefore something terrible. Stoics consequently turned death into a human achievement: the goal was to live well and to die well. The early Jewish idea of Sheol was little better

is "confident" about what he is telling them (vv. 6, 8). There is also a piling up of compound verbs not found elsewhere in the New Testament, as Paul strains the limits of the language to express himself (*ependyomai, endēmeō, ekdēmeō*).

Whom and what is he correcting? It does not appear to be the Corinthians. When a problem exists in one of his churches, Paul normally tackles it head-on. He does not do that here. Mention in verse 12 of "those who take pride in what is seen rather than in what is in the heart" makes it likely that Paul's remarks are intended primarily as a criticism of outsiders who were attempting to convert the Corinthians to their way of thinking. What was this way of thinking? His emphasis in verse 7 that he lives "by faith, not by sight" points to those who valued the visible manifestations of the Spirit and took pride in visions, the working of miracles and ecstatic experiences (see the introduction). References to being found *naked* (v. 3) and *unclothed* (v. 4) suggest that Paul is also combating some form of Greek dualism, where immortality is viewed as the shedding of the physical body at death and the persistence of the soul beyond the grave. To a church that prided itself on having arrived spiritually (1 Cor 4:8) and tended to look at the physical side of things as a matter of indifference (6:12-13), this would be an especially appealing notion.

The NIV *now* obscures the connection with the preceding section. The opening *gar* (for) points back to 4:18 and answers why the gospel preacher focuses on what is unseen rather than on what is seen. It is because *we know that if the earthly tent we live in is destroyed, we have a building from God*. This is not new information that Paul is passing along to the Corinthians. He has dealt at length with the Christian hope of resurrection-transformation in his second letter to them (1 Cor 15). But he does make several advances over what he taught them earlier.

---

than this, for it was regarded as a dark land of oblivion (Ps 88:12) whose inhabitants cannot praise the Lord (Ps 115:17).

The coining of terms is particularly evident in this passage. *Ependyomai, endēmeō* and *ekdēmeō* are not found elsewhere in the Greek Bible. The hypothesis that *endēmeō* and *ekdēmeō* were borrowed from Paul's opponents is the simplest explanation. *Ependyomai* could merely be a stylistic variant of *endyomai*, but given the painstaking character of Paul's presentation, the double compound is probably a correction of an opposing position.

The Greek is literally "our earthly dwelling of tent" *(hē epigeios hēmōn oikia tou skēnous)*. The term *earthly* recalls the formation of Adam from the dust of the earth (Gen 2:7) and his return to dust at death (Gen 3:19). In Attic law the *oikia* (omitted by the NIV) was the "dwelling-house," while the *oikos* was the property left at a person's death (Liddell, Scott and Jones 1978). Our body is thus likened to a house that we dwell in during our sojourn on earth (contrast v. 1 *in heaven*).

The verb translated *destroyed* actually means "to dismantle" (*kata + lyō*, "take down"). Paul likens the process of physical decay and death to the dismantling of a tent-dwelling *(oikia tou skēnous)*. The Greek word *skēnē· (tent)* brings to mind the Old Testament tabernacle that could be dismantled and carried along wherever the people of Israel traveled. As something that can be easily swept away by storm, wind or other accident of nature, the comparison of the body to a tent is a particularly apt one—as the inexperienced camper can readily testify to. Paul would have had intimate knowledge of this kind of dwelling as a professional tentmaker.

All human beings experience the dismantling of their earthly tent-dwelling. Christians, however, look forward to *a building from God, an eternal house in heaven, not built by human hands*. In contrast to *tent (skēnē)*, the word *building (oikodomē)* denotes a stable and permanent structure. Paul's language has led some to think in terms of a literal house in heaven (Charles Hodge; compare Jn 14:2, "in my Father's house are many rooms"), a heavenly church (Earle Ellis; J. A. T. Robinson), a heavenly temple (Guy Wagner) or the realm of the unseen and eternal (Victor Furnish). Later references to what is mortal being swallowed up

---

5:1 *Skēnos* ("tent") was often used metaphorically of the physical body. See, for example, Wisdom of Solomon 9:15, "this earthy tent burdens the thoughtful mind" and 2 Peter 1:13-14, "as long as I live in the tent of this body" (Osei-Bonsu 1986:82).

5:2 *En toutō* can mean "in this state" (that is, "while in our tent-dwelling" we groan; NIV, JB, NEB, Phillips) or "for this reason" (that is, "out of longing to possess our heavenly house" we groan; LB, RSV). Some (such as M. J. Harris, Martin, Furnish) maintain that Paul's groaning is the eager, hopeful kind and not the despairing sort. But while it is true that despair has no place in the Christian life, Paul clearly did feel the burdens of the body.

5:3-4 Not all agree that Paul's unclothing/clothing metaphor applies to putting off the mortal body and putting on a transformed, immortal body. Furnish argues that "to clothe ourselves" is to put on Christ through baptism, "to be found naked" is to deny one's baptism and so alienate oneself from Christ, and "to clothe ourselves over" is to long for the

by life (v. 4) and being away from the body (v. 8) point, rather, to the believer's hope of a material existence beyond the grave. The present tense, *we have*, has suggested to some the expectation of a material mode of existence at death. But, as in English, the present tense in Greek can have a future sense—"we *will* have" (as in "I am going to the store after lunch"). Most, consequently, believe that Paul is talking about the resurrection-transformation of the believer at Christ's return.

All this, however, misses the point Paul is trying to make. The emphatic position of the verb stresses the certain possession of this building. God's intention for the believer is bodily existence, not disembodiment as some would claim. More specifically, those who face physical hardship and suffering as a result of their labors in the gospel ministry are assured that, come what may, a house of God's own designing *(ek theou—from God)* awaits them. This house is distinguished in three ways. It is of heavenly versus earthly origin *(in heaven)*. It is a permanent *(eternal)* as opposed to a temporary structure. And it is assembled by God rather than by human hands *(not built by human hands)*.

Meanwhile, Paul says, *we groan* (v. 2). *Meanwhile* is literally "in this state"—that is, while in our tent-dwelling. The verb "to groan" can mean to sigh out of longing for something or to moan in response to physical suffering, loss or distress. Paul sighs out of a *longing to be clothed with* his *heavenly dwelling* and be done with the burdens of this present existence. There is a shift of metaphors. While the culmination of physical decay is compared to dismantling a tent, the climax of renewal is likened to putting on an overcoat. *To be clothed with* is actually a

---

fulfillment of that salvation inaugurated in baptism (1984:297-98). Guy Wagner maintains that to "clothe ourselves" is to put on righteousness, "to be found naked" is to be without the clothing of righteousness and "to clothe ourselves over" is to put a glorified body on over the inner being of righteousness (1981:155-59). Murphy-O'Connor thinks that Paul is using the imagery of "clothed" and "naked" of God's favorable and unfavorable judgment of a person's moral life (1991:52). In support of the last interpretation, nakedness is taken to be a sign of God's judgment in both the Old and New Testaments (as in Is 47:3; Ezek 16:37-39; 23:28-29; Mt 22:11-14 [inappropriate clothing]).

5:3 There are two text variations in this verse. The UBS opts for *ei ge kai* ("on the assumption that" or, better, "but even if"), on the support of C and the majority of manuscripts. Most modern translations follow *eiper kai* ("since, indeed," "because, then"; the NIV drops the *kai*) found in p[46] B D F G 33 and 1175. Both constructions are employed

reflexive verb meaning to put on over something that is already in place *(epi + en + dysasthai)*. That which is perishable is pictured as clothing itself with an imperishable topcoat (compare 1 Cor 15:53-54).

Verse 3 is notoriously difficult. It is usual to treat this verse as a parenthetical remark explaining why Paul longs to put on his heavenly dwelling (so that he will not experience the nakedness of bodiless existence). But this is, by no means, the most plausible way to interpret the text. Most modern translations follow the reading *endysamenoi* and render the verse along the lines of the NIV: *because when we are clothed we will not be found naked*. But this makes verse 3 a mere repetition of verses 2 *(we groan, longing to be clothed with our heavenly dwelling)* and 4 *(we do not wish to be unclothed but to be clothed with our heavenly dwelling)* and, thus, without point or purpose in the paragraph. It is preferable to follow the Greek text adopted by the 4th edition of the UBS and the 27th Nestlé-Aland edition, which read "but even if we are *unclothed [ekdysamenoi]*, we will not be found naked."

What point would Paul be trying to make? It could be that he is repudiating the Greek idea that disembodiment is desirable. The noun *gymnos* was frequently used in Greek philosophy to describe the state of the soul separated from the body. That this was a common notion is reflected in the judgment of Wisdom of Solomon 9:15 that "a perishable body weighs down the soul, and this earthly tent burdens the thoughtful mind." He could also be reflecting Jewish feelings about nakedness. Unlike the Greeks, who gloried in the unclothed body, the Jews considered nakedness a disgraceful state. Nakedness and shame are equated in the Old Testament. Babylon's punishment is to have its nakedness exposed and its shame uncovered (Is 47:3), while Israel is

---

equally by Paul. *Ei ge* appears in Romans 5:6, Galatians 3:4, Ephesians 3:2 and 4:21, and Colossians 1:23, and *eiper* occurs in Romans 3:30 and 8:9, 17, 1 Corinthians 8:5 and 15:15, and 2 Thessalonians 1:6. The latter provides the smoother grammatical connection but makes sense only with the reading *endysamenoi* ("because when we put it [our heavenly building] on, we will not be found naked"). *Endysamenoi* ("to put on") is found in p[46] ℵ B D² itala vg, while *ekdysamenoi* ("to put off") occurs in D* itala. See the commentary.

It is from the verb *gymnazō* ("to train," "to exercise") and the noun *gymnasia* ("training," "exercise") that we derive our word "gymnastics." Since athletes in Greece performed without clothing, it is easy to see how *gymnos* came to mean "naked" or "bare." Usage of this word group in the New Testament includes being completely unclothed (Mk 14:52), lacking an outer garment (Jn 21:7, "stripped for work"), extreme poverty (2 Cor 11:27) and

to be left naked and bare and its shame exposed (Ezek 23:29). Indeed, *m. Berakot* 3:5 stipulates that a person must be clothed to recite the Shema—even if one's bathwater is the only handy covering at the time. Verse 3 is perhaps best construed against this latter background. What Paul longs for is to be overclothed with his heavenly body at the parousia. But if he should die before Christ returns, the dissolution of his body does not mean that he is left *naked.* That is the state of the non-Christian. Christians, by contrast, have been undergoing the progressive renewal of their inner person, which provides them with an appropriate covering at death. So even if Paul is in a state of undress (that is, lacking a physical body), he will nonetheless *not be found naked* (that is, in a state of shame), because his sufferings have been achieving for him "an eternal glory that far outweighs them all" (4:17). Taken in this way, the aorist is ingressive, "to enter into a state of undress" *(ekdysamenoi).* The form of the conditional statement (*ei* + aorist participle) admits the real possibility of this occurring (that is, that Paul will die before Christ returns). The passive "to be found" *(heuriskō)* is frequently used to denote the result of a judicial investigation (Bauer, Arndt and Gingrich 1979). To be found *naked,* then, would be to experience God's judgment and not the freedom from bodily existence that many Greeks (and perhaps some Corinthians) expected.

In verse 4 Paul repeats what he said in verse 2: *For while we are in this tent, we groan*—or more accurately, "for truly *[kai gar]* we groan." To this he adds *and are burdened. Baroumenoi (are burdened)* means "to be weighed down" or "made to carry a heavy load." The nominal form was used in 4:17 of the weight of eternal glory that affliction produces for those who serve Christ in the gospel ministry. Here Paul

---

lacking the appropriate garment (Mt 25:36-44). See Oepke 1964a:773-75.

Jewish abhorrence of physical nakedness is illustrated by the Mishnaic tractate *Berakot* 3:5, which stipulates that if a person does not have time after his early-morning bath to clothe himself before reciting the Shema, he must remain covered with water to recite it! For the view that Paul is expressing a Jewish fear that he will die before the parousia and so be without his bodily clothing for a period of time, see Cassidy 1971:214-15. On the other hand, Platonism, the dominant Greek philosophy of the day, looked on disembodiment as something desirable (Glasson 1990:145-48). Even some Jews were strongly influenced by it. See, for instance, Philo *On the Migration of Abraham* 9: "Away, my friend, from that earthly vesture of yours, escape from that accursed prison, the body, and from its pleasures and lusts, which are your jailors."

is weighed down because he does *not wish to be unclothed but to be [over]clothed* with his heavenly dwelling. The NIV translates the aorist infinitives as passives *(be unclothed/be clothed)* when in fact they are middles ("to unclothe/clothe ourselves over").

Why does Paul repeat himself? Some think that Paul's recent close encounter with death, related in 1:8-11, forced him to come to terms with the possibility that he would not be alive when Christ returned and in turn raised the question of the state of the believer between death and resurrection. Yet Paul is no stranger to perilous encounters. In 1 Corinthians 15:30 he tells the Corinthians that he risked his life "every hour." So the deadly peril that he faced in Asia was hardly a new experience for him. Being stoned at Lystra and left outside the city for dead certainly qualifies as a comparable ordeal (Acts 14:19). Others suppose that Paul is expressing his desire to avoid a state of bodily undress—as any pious Jew would.

Neither a close encounter with death nor a Jewish abhorrence of nakedness accounts, however, for the way Paul belabors the thought in verses 1-4. It is more likely that he is correcting what his opponents claimed to be a superior state of affairs—the soul's being stripped of the physical body. Like his opponents, Paul is burdened with a longing, but not a longing to be rid of the body and all that ails it (as these intruders would have it). His desire is rather to have his present existence with all its mortal ills *swallowed up by life* (v. 4). The metaphor once again shifts. The Christian hope of transformation, pictured as putting on an overcoat in verse 2, is now depicted as an animal swallowing its prey whole. The verb *katapinō* means "to gulp down" or "to consume entirely" *(swallowed up,* Goppelt 1968:158-59). As Jonah was swallowed up *(katapiein)* by a huge fish (Jon 2:1 [1:17]), *life,* as it were, swallows up the entirety of our earthly, fragile, expendable, clay-pot existence.

How can the Corinthians be sure that this expectation is correct? Paul goes on in verse 5 to provide them with two very good reasons. One, God *has made us for this very purpose;* and, two, God *has given us the Spirit as a deposit, guaranteeing what is to come. Made* is probably not the best translation. The verb *katergazomai* means "to equip" or "to prepare" someone for something (Bauer, Arndt and Gingrich 1979; TEV, RSV, NRSV, LB, NASB, NKJV). The something for which we are being prepared is to have our mortal existence swallowed up by immortality. This is accomplished through the Spirit given to us as an *arrabōn*.

Arrabōn (deposit) is a legal term pertaining to contracts of sale or service. The *arrabōn* was the earnest money that a buyer would give the seller prior to the actual sale and delivery of the item or that a hirer would give the laborers toward work to be carried out at a later date (see the commentary on 1:22). The idea is of a first installment or down payment of the full amount yet to come. In chapter 1 the Spirit was given as the down payment toward the church's full redemption. Here the Spirit is the first installment toward the believer's full possession of an *eternal house in heaven* (v. 1). The aorists *katergasamenos* (prepared) and *dous* (gave) point to a decisive moment in the past. Paul is undoubtedly thinking of the receipt of the Spirit at conversion.

The second installment he looks forward to is the complete transformation of our present perishable mode of existence into an imperishable one. The Spirit's job is not merely to point forward to or give assurance of this future transformation. He is currently working to bring it about through renewal of the inner self (4:17)—what Paul refers to in 4:12 as "life at work in you."

There is a great deal of controversy in the church today about what Paul teaches in these verses regarding death and beyond and what he does not. So it is important to be clear where the text is clear and to acknowledge where the text does not provide us with enough information to draw an exact conclusion. The following points are explicitly taught.

First, resurrection-transformation is the inevitable result of the Spirit's regenerative and renewing work within us. This is the privilege of the Christian, not the non-Christian. Second, the language of *building, house* and "overclothing" indicates that our future life with the Lord will involve some form of material existence. Disembodiment is not the hope of the Christian. This means that there is some manner of continuity between our present and future forms of existence. Finally, it is the down payment

"the down payment, that is, the Spirit."

of the Spirit that ensures continuity between present and future modes of existence.

To go beyond this is to speculate without textual justification. Whether we will possess a temporary body in the interim period or even receive our heavenly dwelling at death, Paul does not explicitly say—but neither possibility is explicitly excluded. Whether resurrection-transformation involves little or substantial physical change is impossible to determine. The fact of the matter is that Paul does not dwell on the details of the when and what of our future bodily existence. So we, in turn, do well to "not go beyond what is written" (1 Cor 4:6).

The Expectation of Eternal Life with Christ (5:6-10) What Paul does dwell on in these verses is how what we believe about the future should affect our lives today. It most certainly affected Paul. The knowledge that he possessed an eternal house in heaven allowed him to have a positive attitude toward life's adversities. *Therefore,* he says, *we are always confident.* The verb *tharreō* means "to be of good courage or cheerful." Paul maintains a cheery attitude toward his present circumstances. This is the opposite of losing heart or growing weary (4:16)—a temptation that all of us in full-time ministry face from time to time. Moreover, he is cheerful not only when things are going well but *always.* Not even the prospect of death affects his basic attitude.

Paul's cheerfulness stems in part from knowing that *as long as we are at home in the body, we are away from the Lord.* Some Greeks drew courage in the face of death from the belief that they possessed an immortal soul. Others, who had no such hope, felt only despair over their eventual demise (1 Thess 4:13). Paul, on the other hand, was cheerful about the

---

5:6-8 Paul's interjection at verse 7, *we live by faith, not by sight,* causes him to lose track of the grammatical flow. The two participial phrases *tharrountes pantote* and *eidotes hoti endēmountes en tō sōmati* in verse 6 are left hanging, while the possible misconstrual of *ekdēmoumen apo tou kyriou* (*away from the Lord* = "to be out of fellowship with Christ") is dealt with. The abandoned train of thought is picked up at verse 8 *(tharroumen de kai),* but the grammar of verse 6 is never brought to a closure. Nonetheless, the line of thought in verses 6-9 is clear: "Being of good cheer *(tharrountes)* and knowing *(eidotes)* that to be at home in the body is to be away from the Lord, we make it our goal to please him."

5:6 It is difficult to know how to construe *kai eidotes.* The participle could be concessive ("we are always confident *even though* we know that to be at home in the body is to be away from our home with the Lord"—NRSV) or causal ("we are always confident *indeed*

prospect of death. Death for him was not an enemy but a friend. This was because death, or being *away from the body,* meant being *at home with the Lord* (v. 8). The verbs *endēmeō* ("at home") *and ekdēmeō* ("away from home," "abroad") are found only here in the Greek Bible. The noun *dēmos* refers to the city or land where a particular group of people live (Grundmann 1964c:63). It is what we call our "hometown."

Cleveland is my hometown, the place where I grew up and where my mother and many of my friends still live. But Chicago is the city where I now make my home—where my colleagues, church family, spouse and children live. In a similar way, Paul speaks of *in the body* and *with the Lord* as two different homes in diverse locations. He cannot be in both places at the same time. And his preference is to be at home with the Lord (v. 8). But for this to happen he must be away from the hometown of his mortal body.

Has Paul slipped unknowingly into a dualistic way of thinking? Not at all. *Body* and *Lord* merely represent two different places that he can call *home*—like Cleveland and Chicago for me—without any necessary implication of a body-soul framework. *Body* is simply a catchword for his present mortal existence, much like the expression "home is where your heart is."

But what does it mean to be *away from the Lord* (v. 6)? To forestall misunderstanding, Paul adds parenthetically *we live by faith, not by sight* (v. 7). *Live* is literally "to walk" *(peripateō),* a word that Paul uses with regularity to describe the Christian life. The preposition *by* (*dia* + genitive) probably denotes realm (M. J. Harris 1978a:1182-83). To live by faith is to walk in the realm of faith. *By faith, not by sight* does not reflect a belief in the immaterial over against the material world but

because we know . . ."; compare KJV, NKJV). Paul never completes his thought in verse 6, so it is hard to figure out which he intended (see the previous note). The NIV's neutral translation is to be preferred: "We are always confident *and know* that as long as we are at home in the body . . ." The JB's rendering is on the wrong track: "We are always full of confidence, then, when we remember that to live in the body means to be exiled from the Lord."

The verbs *endēmeō* and *ekdēmeō* are not found elsewhere in the Greek Bible. Paul may well be borrowing the language of his opponents. Murphy-O'Connor thinks that verse 6 is a Corinthian slogan that Paul corrects in verse 8 (1991:55). Furnish believes that Paul is combating the identification of residence in the body and residence with the Lord (1984:302-3).

represents a conviction about what is yet to be seen compared to what can now be seen. This is similar to Hebrews 11:1, where faith is the assurance of things hoped for and the conviction of things not seen.

In religious parlance, to be *away from the Lord* (v. 6) can mean to be relationally distant from God. Paul, however, is speaking in spatial, not relational language. Our present existence offers to the visible eye merely a dim reflection of the Lord (1 Cor 13:12), so that our relationship with him, for the time being, is in the realm of faith, not sight. But at death we will see Christ "face to face" (1 Cor 13:12), for we will be *at home with the Lord* (v. 8). The preposition *pros* + the accusative *ton kyrion (with the Lord)* suggests not just impassive spatial proximity to Christ but dynamic, interpersonal communion with him (M. J. Harris 1978c:1205). Paul's use of the aorist tense (*endēmēsai/ekdēmēsai;* v. 8), as opposed to the present tense (v. 6), denotes a once-for-all turn of events (Martin 1986:112). This is why death is preferable to life in the mortal body. In fact, Paul can say to the Philippians that for him "to die is gain" (Phil 1:21).

In light of the expectation of face-to-face communion with Christ, Paul *makes it* his *goal to please him* (v. 9). The verb *philotimoumetha* means "to strive eagerly to do something," "to aspire earnestly" (Liddell, Scott and Jones 1978). The something Paul strives eagerly to do is to please Christ. His ambition is an eternal one. He makes pleasing Christ his goal, *whether at home in the body or away from it.* The NIV adds *in the body;* the Greek says merely "whether at home or away." Some consequently think that being at home or away from *the Lord,* not the body, is what is in view. If, however, verse 9 completes the thought left hanging in verse 6 (see the note), then Paul is speaking of life in or away from the body. This is suggested as well by the fact that Paul goes on in verse 10 to speak of our accountability for what we do through

5:7 *Eidos* can refer to the outward form of something (that is, "what is seen"; Furnish 1984:273) or to the act of seeing (that is, "what we see"; Martin 1986:111). The latter is the better option in the context. See the commentary.

5:8 Furnish argues that the issue in verse 8 is not one's present place of residence (that is, location) but what one gives as one's home address (that is, one's loyalty and longing; 1984:303).

Pros ton kyrion is to be understood as a reference to Christ. Paul's usual practice is to distinguish Christ from Yahweh by the use of the article (Zerwick 1963:no. 169).

(*dia* + the genitive) the body.

Either way, his lifelong and eternal ambition is to *please* Christ. David Brainerd expressed a similar thought when he said, "I do not go to heaven to be advanced but to give honor to God. It is no matter where I shall be stationed in heaven, whether I have a high or low seat there. . . . My heaven is to please God and glorify him and give all to him and to be wholly devoted to his glory." Second Corinthians 5:9 is the only place that Paul speaks of pleasing Christ. Elsewhere we are exhorted to find out what pleases God and then live that way (Eph 5:10). The Philippians' financial support of Paul (Phil 4:18), our offering ourselves as living sacrifices (Rom 12:1) and children's obeying their parents (Col 3:20) are examples of activities that are pleasing to God.

The second reason Paul strives to please Christ is the prospect of appearing before his judgment seat (v. 10). This prospect is an inclusive one, "we *all* must appear"—*pantas* placed first for emphasis. The tone is one of warning. *Must appear* evokes images of being called before the judge's bench to give an account of one's actions—though in Paul's day the judge did not sit on a highly polished piece of wood but on a stone seat or dais. The ministry of all who claim to be preachers of the gospel (including Paul's critics) will be subject to divine judgment. The Greek word *dei (must)* is commonly used of what is divinely ordained. Divine judgment is a requirement, not an option. Nor is this judgment to be taken lightly. In 1 Corinthians 3:10-15, Christian workers are cautioned that the quality of their work will be tested by fire. If what they have built survives, they will "receive a reward." But if it is "burned up," they will "suffer loss."

Divine assessment of our work will take place *before the judgment seat of Christ*. The *bēma* or *judgment seat* was the place where civil officials held session to hear certain legal cases and render judgment

---

5:10 There is a reversal of roles here. Jesus, who appeared before a human judgment seat on the basis of trumped-up charges, will one day sit in righteous judgment over all human beings.

The preposition *dia* + the genitive can be instrumental—"what was done *through* the body"—or temporal—"what was done *while in* the body." Given Paul's view of the unity of the person, the former is the likely option.

Article + *pas* + pronoun *(tous pantas bēmas)* emphasizes the whole or the entirety of something. Here it is gospel ministers as an entirety that are primarily in view.

(McComiskey 1976:369-70). Jesus was brought before the *bēma* of Pilate (Jn 19:13; compare Mt 27:19). Paul came before the *bēma* of Gallio in Corinth (Acts 18:12-17) and the *bēma* of Festus in Caesarea (Acts 25:6). According to Romans 14:10 we will stand before *God's* judgment seat, whereas here we come before *Christ's bēma*. These need not be two different occasions. In Romans 2:16 Paul states that God will judge the secret thoughts of all *through* (*dia* + the genitive) Christ.

This provocative text has elicited a fair amount of comment. Who is to be judged? What kind of judgment is this? When is this judgment to occur? Paul is not talking about the last judgment, when all of humanity past and present will be judged and those who have done good rise to live while those who have done evil rise to be condemned (Jn 5:28-29; compare Rom 2:6-11). *For we* at the start of verse 10 looks back to verse 9 and those who make it their aim to please Christ. So it is judgment of the believer that is in view. Paul's intention is to remind the Corinthians that all those who serve Christ will have to give an account of what they have accomplished for the Lord, not how they have increased their own reputation (5:12). Even the Corinthians are not exempt from this divine scrutiny and assessment. Though "washed, sanctified and justified" (1 Cor 6:11), they too will have to give an account of themselves (compare Rom 14:12).

How will we be judged? According to Paul, we are to *receive what is due* us *for the things done while in the body, whether good or bad*. While he began by saying that we as a whole must appear (*tous pantas hēmas;* literally, "the whole of us," v. 10), each, nonetheless, is responsible for his or her own actions (v. 10; compare Rom 14:12). The middle voice is reflexive: "to receive for oneself." The term for what is *due* refers to receiving one's just deserts. What our just deserts will be is determined by *the things done* through *the body*. It is a judgment based on works that Paul puts forward.

This could be construed as in conflict with salvation by grace (as in Eph 2:8), if it were a judgment that determined destiny or status. But this is not the case. Paul is thinking, rather, of a divine assessment that results in praise or blame (1 Cor 4:5). A final assessment of the Christian is a recurring theme in Paul. Christian slaves are instructed to serve their masters wholeheartedly, because the Lord will pay back all for whatever good they do (Eph 6:8) and for whatever wrongs they commit (Col 3:25). Paul does not say what the reward or punishment will be, so it is useless to speculate. The punishment is a real one, however. In 1 Corinthians 3:15 there will be those who will "suffer loss" even though they themselves "will be saved." Here, as well, it is written that Christians can expect to receive in kind for the good and the bad that they have done.

When will this happen? It is not clear whether judgment will occur at death or at the parousia. Paul does not say one way or the other. What he does say is that we will be held accountable for what we do through our body (*dia tou sōmatos;* v. 10). Paul's emphasis on our moral accountability with respect to the body is no accident. As F. F. Bruce observes, though the mortal body belongs to a passing order of things, we are nevertheless accountable for its deeds (1971:206). It is easy to think that because the body will eventually be dismantled (v. 1), it matters little what we do with our bodies. Some in the Corinthian church thought this (1 Cor 6:12-17), as have others since. Paul, however, did not. Indeed, he teaches elsewhere that the body is the temple of the Holy Spirit and, as such, the object of redemption. We are called, therefore, to honor God with our bodies (1 Cor 6:18-20).

One final question needs to be raised, especially since this is one of the few places that Paul touches on what happens to the believer at death: does the believer face an embodied or a disembodied existence in the interim between death and the parousia? The difficulty is that Paul does not explicitly address this issue. We must read between the lines, and as with any venture of this sort, there is a wide margin for error. This explains the current disparity of interpretations. Some argue on the basis of these verses that there is no period of disembodiment (for example, F. F. Bruce, Murray J. Harris). Others maintain that Paul is indeed acknowledging a time of disembodiment between death and resurrection. But perhaps even to phrase the question in this way misses the central truth of these verses. The question of life beyond the grave is primarily not a metaphysical one (that is, what happens to the body at death and when a new body is given) but a Christian one (that is, what happens to the *believer* at death; see, for example, Philip E. Hughes 1962:175). Embodiment or disembodiment is, at best, peripheral. What matters the most to Paul is that to be absent from this present world is to be *at home with the Lord* (v. 8).

This is absolutely critical to communicate to those grieving the death of a Christian loved one, facing a terminal illness or struggling with the concept of personal mortality. We do not float somewhere in limbo at death or sleep the sleep of the unaware—even though our language at times wrongly communicates this. For the believer, death initiates face-to-face fellowship and communion with Christ—a "going home," as it were.

A little girl whose father had just died asked her mother where he had gone. "To be with Jesus," replied her mother.

A few days later, talking to a friend, the mother said, "I am so grieved to have lost my husband."

The little girl heard her and, remembering the earlier conversation, asked, "Mother, is a thing lost when you know where it is?"

"No, of course not," said her mother.

"Well then, how can Daddy be lost when he has gone to be with Jesus?"

The little girl had hit the nail on the head. To say that at death a Christian "goes to be with Jesus" is not a euphemism but a reality.

Fear of the Lord Motivates Ministry (5:11-13) A call to evangelistic ministry is increasingly becoming a rarity. In part this is because many churches no longer highly value or support this type of call. Street-corner preachers are regularly dismissed as crackpots. Revival meetings are becoming a thing of the past or are commonly redefined as occasions to boost the congregation's spirits or to push for recommitment. The developer pastor who seeks to plant a church through new converts is becoming a vanishing breed. Pastors and churches committed to outreach in their communities have become the exception rather than the rule.

This state of affairs was brought home to me recently in a conversa-

5:11 *We persuade* is commonly taken as a reference to gospel proclamation. Yet elsewhere Paul denies using the art of persuasion so as not to detract from the cross of Christ (as in 1 Cor 2:4). Moreover, the immediately preceding verse speaks of judgment, not grace. Suggestions as to what Paul tried to persuade others of include his sincere motives and sound credentials, his authority as an apostle, the claims of the gospel and

tion with a newly elected member of an evangelism committee who expressed frustration with the task's being defined primarily in terms of communal nurture rather than community outreach. Paul had no such illusions. He understood quite well what a call to preach the gospel involved. It was a lofty call to be one of "Christ's ambassadors," with God "making his appeal through us" (v. 20). It involved exhorting others to "be reconciled with God" (v. 20). And it arose out of a fear of the Lord (v. 11) and a knowledge of "Christ's love" (v. 14).

Pursuing such a lofty call necessitates having the right motives (vv. 11-15). In chapter 4 it was Paul's conviction that "the one who raised the Lord Jesus from the dead will also raise us with Jesus" that compelled him to preach (4:14). Now he adds two further reasons. The first is found in 5:11. *Since, then, we know what it is to fear the Lord,* he states, *we try to persuade* others. What is this fear of which Paul speaks? The Greek term *phobos* ranges in meaning from panic and fright to awe and reverence. Yet when we are faced with the divine, fright and awe more often than not coalesce. The genitive *tou kyriou* can be objective ("the fear that we feel toward the Lord") or subjective ("the fear that the Lord inspires"). But in reality, both amount to the same thing. Fear in itself is not necessarily bad. To fear the Lord is what God required of Israel (Deut 10:12). And it is through the fear of the Lord that a person avoids evil (Prov 16:6).

But what is it about the Lord that elicits Paul's fear? The answer is found in the opening *oun (therefore),* which points the reader back to verse 10 and the future judgment that all those who serve Christ must face. By *fear* Paul does not mean terror. In certain places on Alpine summits the way is peculiarly dangerous on account of frequent avalanches and the traveler walks in dread of instant destruction. The Christian does not stand in terror of divine judgment as the traveler does of the Alps. On the other hand, we need to have a healthy respect

divine judgment. The last of these, divine judgment, is the only one explicitly found in the immediate context.

The present tense is most likely conative ("we *try* to persuade"— Barrett 1973:163; Turner 1984:63) and not durative ("we *are* persuading"—Furnish 1984:306) in force.

for the One who has the power to destroy both the soul and the body (Mt 10:28).

Fear can often result in paralysis; but not so with Paul. While the prospect of appearing before Christ's judgment seat provokes fear, it also prompts action. For the author of Proverbs 1:7, fear of the Lord meant "the beginning of knowledge." For Paul, it means the attempt *to persuade men*. The NIV *men* renders a Greek term that is gender-inclusive *(anthrōpous)*. Paul attempts to persuade "people" (JB) or "others" (NRSV). The present tense carries a conative nuance—"we *try* to persuade." The term *persuade* means "to strive to convince" by means of argumentation (Becker 1975:590).

Of what does Paul seek to persuade? He does not explicitly say; but in light of his preceding reference to the judgment of the Christian worker, it is not too improbable to suppose that the judgment of the non-Christian is in mind. Judgment is an uncomfortable subject in most Christian circles. Yet it was not long ago that "hellfire and brimstone" preaching was a staple of the evangelical diet. Nowadays we tend to shy away from topics of this sort. But a substantial part of Jesus' preaching had to do with warning his audience of impending judgment. Peter pleaded with his audience to save themselves from "this corrupt generation" (Acts 2:40). And mention of "the coming wrath" was a regular component of Paul's evangelistic preaching (see Acts 17:31; 1 Thess 1:9-10).

Paul interjects the comment *What we are is plain to God* (v. 11). A healthy respect for Christ as judge motivates Paul to discharge his ministry with integrity, a fact that is *plain to God* and would be apparent to the Corinthians if they stopped and thought about it. Paul uses the perfect tense: "What we are *has been and continues to be* plain to God." While a person's motives and intentions can be hidden from others, they cannot be hidden from God. Paul, however, makes his ministry available to the scrutiny of all who would care to inspect it, including the Corinthians.

Paul momentarily slips into the first-person singular in an effort to express a deeply felt concern: "I hope it is also plain to your conscience" (v. 11; Furnish 1984:307). What he hopes is that if his apostolic legitimacy is not immediately apparent to the Corinthians, at least his integrity will be evident to their *conscience*. The conscience is that capacity of a person to determine right from wrong. Stoics saw the conscience as a watchman bestowed by God on individuals to guide them to live according to nature and to direct their moral progress (Hahn 1975:349). In much the same way, Paul appeals to the Corinthians' conscience to judge the sincerity of his motives. This assumes, of course, that their conscience has not been dulled through misuse, ignorance or disregard.

Although this may sound as if Paul is commending himself to them again, all he aims to do is to provide the Corinthians with the ammunition needed to answer his critics (v. 12). This is the second time that Paul has admitted saying something that could be taken as praising himself. In fact, nine out of thirteen Pauline uses of the verb *synistēmi* (to commend) occur in this letter. Its frequent appearance shows that ministerial commendation was a bone of contention with the church. Four times in 2 Corinthians Paul is pushed by the Corinthians' expectations to commend himself. But in distinction from his rivals, he commends himself as a servant of God (4:2-5; 6:4) and on the basis of what God accomplished through him (3:5; 10:13), of which the congregation, it seems, needed to be reminded from time to time (5:12). They should have taken the initiative to defend Paul against his detractors. Perhaps they had become so taken with the current group of visiting preachers that they forgot the many reasons to be proud of their spiritual father.

In the second half of verse 12 Paul puts before the Corinthians the major distinction between himself and these intruders. His rivals take pride in the externals or *what is seen*. Paul takes pride in the internals or *what is in the heart*. To *take pride in what is seen* is literally "to boast in the face." The noun "face" *(prosōpon)* originally meant that which struck the eye. Here it refers to the features or outward appearance of a thing or person. To boast "in the face," then, is to place great store in outward appearances, like letters of recommendations, polished oratory and flashy presentations. Perhaps Paul is thinking especially of boasting in ecstatic experiences, since he goes on in verse 13 to say, *If we are out of our mind* (*ekstasis* = English "ecstasy"), *it is for the sake of God; if we are in our right mind, it is for you* (RSV, NEB). "Out of mind" is the general sense of the intransitive. Literally, it meant to become separated from something or to lose something (*ek* "away" + *histēmi* "put, stand")

and was used figuratively of losing one's wits (Bauer, Arndt and Gingrich 1979). Part of the difficulty is that Paul employs the verb nowhere else. Mark, however, uses it of Jesus, whose family thought him "mad" (3:21). Most translators follow suit here.

In what sense was Paul "mad"? On the face of it, the comment is obscure. This may well have been a charge leveled by his opponents. That Paul would consider persecution and adversity something to be proud of might well have appeared mad to those who judged by the world's standards (4:8-9). Yet, whatever Paul does, he does not out of self-interest but for God and the Corinthians *(for you)*. This is the essence of verse 13. *Theō (for the sake of God)* and *hymin (for you)* are most likely datives of advantage, designating the person whose interest is affected (Blass, Debrunner and Funk 1961:no. 188 [101]). There is a time for conduct which appears mad to the world but is in God's best interest. There is also a time for calm, sensible conduct, which is to the church's advantage. Paul was prepared to follow whichever advanced the cause of the gospel (Barclay 1954:208).

Christ's Love Compels Service (5:14-17) A further reason for preaching the gospel is found in verse 14: *For Christ's love compels us.* Conviction (4:14), fear (5:11) and now love motivate Paul to pursue his call. The text is literally, "the love of Christ." The genitive can be objective, "our love for Christ," or subjective, "Christ's love for us." Although we might instinctively incline toward the former, the latter is preferred by most modern translations. This is because Paul goes on in verses 14-15 to speak of Christ's dying on our behalf—the ultimate

5:13 The Greek verb *existēmi* (noun *ekstasis*) is the term from which we derive our English word "ecstasy." Although *existēmi* was used of extraordinary experiences (such as visions, ecstasies, revelations), it was also employed of religious fanaticism, emotional instability and mental imbalance (Oepke 1964b). Some think that Paul may be referring to an episode during an earlier, unhappy visit to Corinth when he lost control of himself. But it is difficult to see how this would be to God's advantage *(theō—for the sake of God)*. Others suppose that he is alluding to the Corinthians' tendency to prize ecstasy as a manifestation of the Spirit. In this case he would be saying that ecstasy is something to be experienced in private, while intelligent speech (that is, *right mind*) is the appropriate mode for corporate worship (Tolbert 1983:65).

5:14 Both our love for Christ (Eph 6:24) and Christ's love for us (Rom 8:35; Gal 2:20; Eph 3:18; 5:2) are found in Paul—although the latter is far more prominent. Christ's death

demonstration of love. The basic sense of *synechō* (to compel) is to hold something together so that it does not fall apart. From this we get the meanings to "hold fast" (that is, to not allow to slip through one's fingers) and to "surround" or "hem in" (that is, to not let escape; Köster 1971:883). The idea is that Christ's love completely controls and dominates Paul so that he has no option but to preach. The hymn writer George Matheson knew of this kind of constraining love when he penned the words "O love that wilt not let me go, / I rest my weary soul in Thee; / I give Thee back the life I owe, / That in Thine ocean depths its flow may richer, fuller be."

It is not the mere fact of Christ's death but a conviction about it that leaves Paul no choice but to carry out his call to preach the gospel. *We are convinced,* he says, *that one died for all, and therefore all died* (v. 14). *We are convinced* is actually "we have judged this" *(krinantas touto).* The basic meaning of *krinō* is to "separate" or "sift," and it is commonly used of a conclusion drawn after thoroughly evaluating the facts. Here it emphasizes a carefully considered judgment as opposed to accepting something on good faith. Paul has assessed the evidence and come to the carefully thought-out conclusion that *one died for all, and therefore all died.*

Much effort has been expended on determining the theological import of the second half of verse 14. It is important to notice that Paul does three things here. He states a conviction, *(one died for all)* he draws a conclusion, *(therefore all died)* and he articulates a rationale *(that those who live should no longer live for themselves but for him who died for them and was raised again,* v. 15). Paul's conviction is that *one died for*

is cited as a manifestation of his love in Galatians 2:20 ("who loved me and gave himself for me") and Ephesians 5:2 ("Christ loved us and gave himself up for us").

Paul uses *hyper* regularly with the meaning "in the place of." See, for example, Philemon 13: "I would have liked to keep him with me so that he could *take your place [hyper sou]* in helping me while I am in chains for the gospel" (compare Rom 5:7; 9:3). This is especially the case when Paul is expounding the work of Christ. See Romans 5:8, Galatians 3:13, 1 Timothy 2:6 and Titus 2:14. See also the discussion in Zerwick 1963:no. 91.

Barrett's interpretation *all died* as all humanity became *potentially* dead to their old way of life on account of the death of Christ (1973:168-69) is without support in the New Testament. See, rather, Plummer, who argues that *all* means "all in Christ," who *died* in the sense that Christ's supreme act of love extinguished in them the old life of worldly interest in which the center of gravity was self (1915:174).

all. But by *all* does he mean all believers or all people? The contrast between *one* and *all* suggests that the term is to be taken in the broadest sense. Even so, while Christ may have died for all of humanity, it is only believers who reap the benefits. This is why Paul can say elsewhere that "Christ died for *us*" (Rom 5:8; 1 Thess 5:10) and "Christ died for *our* sins" (1 Cor 15:3). The scope of Christ's redemptive work may be all-encompassing, but the application is particular.

A second exegetical problem is the force of the preposition *hyper (for)*. Does it mean "instead of" (= *anti;* that is, Christ died in our place) or does it bear its usual sense, "on behalf of" (that is, Christ died as our representative)? Paul routinely employs *hyper* where *anti* would have been expected, so too firm a distinction should not be drawn between the two prepositions. In most instances, one who acts on behalf of another takes their place (Moule 1959:64). Galatians 3:13 is a case in point, where Paul states that "Christ redeemed us from the curse of the law by becoming a curse in our place" *(hyper hēmōn)*. This may well be the primary idea here. Just as Christ took upon himself the curse that should have been ours, so too he died the death that we should have died.

A number of years ago, a young couple, knowing that a tornado was upon them and not having time to take cover, laid their baby on the floor of their living room and covered him with their own bodies. The tornado struck with devastating force and leveled a row of homes, including theirs. The next morning, as rescue workers were rummaging through the destroyed homes, they heard a muffled crying. They came upon the lifeless bodies of the young couple, with their baby still safe beneath their bodies. They gave their lives for their child. This is what Christ did for us.

The conclusion *(therefore)* Paul draws from the conviction that one died for all is that *all died* or, literally, "the all died." The article + *pas* emphasizes the whole as opposed to the part. The notion here is one of corporate solidarity. In placing our trust in Christ as Savior, we become united with him and all that he accomplished on our behalf. This is the

5:15 *Hyper autōn* ("for them") could modify *apothanonti* ("who died for them") or *apothanonti kai egerthenti* ("who died and was raised for them"). The word order suggests the former *(tō hyper autōn apothanonti kai egerthenti)*. If *hyper = anti* ("in the place of")

idea behind Paul's statement in Romans 6:3-5 that "all of us who were baptized into Christ were baptized into his death . . . buried with him" and "will certainly also be united with him in his resurrection." What is the nature of this death? Is Paul thinking of a physical death? The aorist indicative, "all *died*," suggests something other than this. Paul can hardly mean that we all died physically as a result of Christ's death. Some suggest spiritual death due to sin. Yet it was this very condition that necessitated Christ's death. It was while we were yet sinners and dead in our transgressions and sins that Christ died for us (Rom 5:8; Eph 2:1-2). The most plausible alternative is to understand *all died* as a death to our old way of life. This is supported by the sequence *all died . . . those who live* (vv. 14-15). It is also suggested by the shift from aorist *(apethanen)* to present tense *(hoi zōntes)*. Death to sin and self is a familiar theme in Paul. "I have been crucified with Christ and I no longer live, but Christ lives in me" (or a similar statement) is found in virtually every one of his letters (Gal 2:20, compare Rom 6:6-14; Eph 2:1-5; Col 2:20). When Augustine returned to his hometown after his conversion in Milan, his former girlfriend called to him: "Augustine, Augustine, it is I!" He turned to her and said: "Yes, but it is not I." Where there is no radical change of attitude toward life and self, there is no conversion.

Christ's self-sacrifice had a particular goal in mind. He died *that those who live should no longer live for themselves but for him who died for them and was raised again* (v. 15). The aorists *died* and *was raised* point to two historical facts. The active voice *he died (apothanonti)* denotes a voluntary action on Christ's part. It is followed, however, by the passive voice, *he was raised,* the deed in this case being performed by God. It is on the basis of these two facts that believers are constrained to live no longer for themselves but for Christ.

But what does this mean? In the first instance, it means that our life is not our own. We have been bought with the price of Christ's death and therefore are called to serve not self but Christ (1 Cor 6:19-20). Freedom is an illusion. We like to think along the lines of William Ernest Henley: "I am the master of my fate; I am the captain of my soul." The

---

it could only modify *apothanonti*. Christ died in our stead, but he was not raised in our place.

fact of the matter is that ours is to serve, not to be served. If we are not serving Christ, we are serving another master. To live for self is to serve sin. To live for Christ is to serve him—or as we say today, to allow Christ to be Lord of our life. The difference is between treating Christ as a houseguest and serving him as the house owner. Robert Munger in *My Heart—Christ's Home* (first ed. 1954) pictures the latter in terms of going to the strongbox, taking out the title deed to our life and signing it over to Christ for eternity. The central thought is a transference of ownership. Frances Ridley Havergal appropriately expressed this transfer in a hymn:

Take my will and make it thine,

It shall be no longer mine;

Take my heart—it is thine own,

It shall be thy royal throne.

From time to time we hear someone say that a particular experience has given them a whole new outlook on life. Changed convictions should result in changed attitudes. It did for Paul. His conviction that *one died for all, and therefore all died* (v. 14) changed irrevocably how he looked at people. Seneca once said, "I do not distinguish by the eye, but by the mind, which is the proper judge of the man" ("On the Happy Life" 2.2). It is all too easy to judge people by outward appearances— what kind of clothes they wear, how much education they have had, what neighborhood they live in, what kind of car they drive, what schools they went to, and so on. Paul had judged Jesus in this fashion and decided that Jesus could not be the Messiah because he did not fit the messianic mold. It was expected that the true Messiah would deliver Israel from the hand of the nation's Roman oppressors and restore the Davidic monarchy, thereby ushering in the eternal kingdom of God. Jesus did not do this. Even worse, he died on a cross, which was considered the ultimate sign of God's disapproval. The law-abiding Jew would know that anyone "who is hung on a tree is under God's curse" (Deut 21:23). So, to all outward appearances, Jesus was a messianic

---

5:16 If *kata sarka* is understood to modify *Christon*, it could refer to Paul's firsthand knowledge of Jesus' earthly ministry. But the phrase *kata sarka* typically follows the word it modifies, which in this case would be *egnōkamen*. What Paul rejects is not Jesus' earthly ministry but a human and therefore faulty knowledge of Christ *(a worldly point of view)*. Since Paul lived in Jerusalem during this time, it is quite possible that he had encountered Christ. Some even speculate that he was the rich young man who came to Jesus wanting

pretender who justifiably died a criminal's death.

Paul's encounter with the risen Christ on the road to Damascus forced him to do some reevaluating. He realized he had been wrong in his assessment of Jesus. Jesus died a criminal's death, but the criminal was actually everyone except Jesus. In short, *one died for all.* Paul initially came to a false conclusion because the standards he used to form his judgments were wrong. *We once regarded Christ,* he says, *from a worldly point of view* (NIV *in this way;* v. 16). The NIV is a free translation of *ei kai egnōkamen kata sarka Christon:* "Even if we knew Christ according to the flesh." Some have understood Paul to be rejecting knowledge of the earthly, physical Jesus in favor of the risen, spiritual Christ. But this is to take the verse out of context. He has just distinguished himself from those who form their judgments of a person on the basis of external appearances ("what is seen," v. 12). In particular, he is thinking of the Corinthian intruders who presented themselves as power evangelists and polished speakers, emphasizing the outward display of the Spirit in the working of miracles, revelations, ecstatic experiences, knowledge and charisma (see the introduction).

Being driven to reconsider his judgment of Christ also caused Paul to reassess the place of the non-Jew in salvation history. *From now on,* he says, *we regard no one from a worldly point of view. From now on* is probably calculated from the moment Paul became convinced that one died for all (v. 14). The emphatic position of *we* in the clause *we regard no one* may well indicate that others (like Paul's critics) do judge in this fashion (Murphy-O'Connor 1991:59). "To regard" translates two different Greek verbs that are virtual synonyms. *Oida* (perfect of *horaō*) is to see with the mind's eye (that is, "to know by reflection"), while *ginōskō* is to know by observation. Both *oida* and *ginōskō,* when used of persons, mean "to have knowledge of," "to be acquainted with." Here the sense is to have enough knowledge to form an opinion or estimate of someone. Formerly, Paul based his estimates of people "after the flesh"

to know what he had to do to inherit eternal life (Mt 19:16-30; Mk 10:17-31; Lk 18:18-30).

It is unlikely that *from now on* means after the writing of 2 Corinthians, as some would suggest. Paul may have in mind his conversion experience. But in the context, *from now on* is the point when he became convinced that one died for all (v. 14). See Martin, who argues that it marks the point of transition from the old to the new order (1986:151).

(kata sarka), a favorite phrase that occurs twenty times in his letters. The term *sarx* (flesh) can refer not only to what is physical but also to what is human or worldly. Thus to know someone "after the flesh" is to form an estimate of them on the basis of human standards *(regard . . . from a worldly point of view)*. Yet human standards are faulty because they are based on externals like heritage, intelligence, wealth and social status (2 Cor 11:22; 1 Cor 1:26).

Paul's new estimate is that Christ died not only for the Jew but also for the non-Jew. Caiaphas had advised the Jewish leadership that it would be good "if one man died for the people" (John 18:14). Paul's judgment is that *one died for all*—for the Jew and non-Jew alike. This was a radical shift for a Jew to make. Because of non-Jewish heritage, the Gentile's place in the kingdom was thought to be at best that of a second-class citizen. Now "in Christ" there is neither Jew nor Gentile (Gal 3:28). Indeed, Paul can go even further and claim that *if anyone is in Christ, he is a new creation; the old has gone, the new has come!* (v. 17). *Kainos (new)* denotes what is fresh or newly made. *Kainē ktisis* can mean either "there is a new creation" (RSV, NRSV, NEB, REB, JB) or "a new creature" (KJV, NKJV, TEV, LB, Phillips, NASB, NIV). The former has to do with the dawning of a new age, the latter with the creation of new life within. *Ktisis* is normally used in Paul's letters of creation in its entirety (Furnish 1984:314). But the previous verses speak of a new estimate of people, not things. It is the world's way of evaluating people that will no longer suffice; for if someone is "in Christ, he becomes a new person altogether" (Phillips).

The values of the world were evidently still having their way in the Corinthian community, influencing their judgments (5:12) and their behavior (12:20-21). Critiqued by the world's standards, Paul comes out looking like the underdog of humanity instead of the servant of Christ. In part, this is the fault of rival missionaries, who reasoned from outward conformity to the world's standards and values to ministerial credibility. Paul calls this way of viewing things *the old* way. *Archaios,* when used

---

5:17 The conditional clause is lacking a subject and verb in the apodosis. The Greek has only *kainē ktisis.* Either *he is* or "there is" must be supplied. If the former, the apodosis would be "he is a new *creature*"; if the latter, "there is a new *creation.*" Most translations opt for "a new creature" (see the commentary). Hughes, Furnish and other commentators

of things, as here, means "old-fashioned, "antiquated" or "worn out" *(ta archaia)*. This old way of thinking about things, Paul says, *has gone (parēlthen)*. The aorist points to something that has passed out of existence.

In its place *the new has come*. Paul's pronouncement is prefaced by *idou* ("look"; translated as an exclamation point in the NIV), a particle frequently used to arouse the attention of the listener or reader (Bauer, Arndt and Gingrich 1979). The word *new (kainos)* denotes that which is qualitatively better as compared with what has existed until now (Haarbeck, Link and Brown 1976:670). A better way of looking at things *has come*. The tense is perfect *(gegonen)*—a new set of standards and attitudes "has come to stay" (M. J. Harris 1976:353) so that a person is now to be judged in a completely new light. Paul has in mind specifically the person *in Christ*. This is a favorite phrase of his that more often than not means "to belong to Christ."

A Ministry of Reconciliation (5:18-21) Paul attributes his changed perspective to God, who did two things for him. First, he *reconciled* Paul *to himself through Christ,* and second, he *gave* him *the ministry of reconciliation* (v. 18). This is an amazing statement. The reconciled become reconcilers (Tolbert 1983:68). Paul is the only New Testament writer to use the noun *katallagē (reconciliation)* and verb *katallassō* (to reconcile). The basic idea is to change or make otherwise. In Greek social and political spheres the term denoted a change in relations between individuals, groups or nations, while in the religious arena it was used of relationships between gods and humans. In Paul's writings, God is always the reconciler. Those in need of reconciliation are hostile human beings (2 Cor 5:18-19; Rom 5:10-11). This is the reverse of Hellenistic religion, where it is the human being that seeks restoration of the gods' favor, and also of Judaism, where confession of sin and repentance are the means by which reconciliation with God is sought (as in 2 Macc 1:5; 7:33; 8:29, Vorländer 1978:167). The initiative now is

argue for "a new creation," primarily on the basis of the apocalyptic nature of Paul's language. The prospect of a new world order finds a parallel in Revelation 21:5: "Behold, I make all things new."

with God who changes a relationship of enmity to one of friendship. This is accomplished *through Christ,* that is, through his death on the cross (Rom 5:10). It is thus with good cause that we sing: "Lift high the cross, the love of Christ proclaim / Till all the world adore his sacred name" (George Kitchin).

The essence of the message Paul proclaimed as a minister of reconciliation is spelled out in verses 19-20. *God was reconciling the world to himself in Christ* . . . The syntax is ambiguous. The text can read, "God was *in* Christ, reconciling the world to himself " or "God was reconciling the world to himself *through* Christ." The emphasis in the former is on the incarnation ("God in Christ"), with Christ as the locus of divine revelation (M. J. Harris 1978b:1193). But this moves us away from the soteriological focus of these verses. The stress in the latter is on redemption. God used Christ's death on the cross (*God was reconciling* [periphrasis]) to bring about reconciliation (instrumental *en*).

To debate the issue is perhaps to lose sight of Paul's focus. *Theos* is emphatic: "*God* was reconciling to himself." God is the initiator, not the recipient, of reconciliation. The recipient is *the world. Kosmos* (*world*) is the world of human beings, not the cosmos. Reconciliation occurs because "God does not count *their* sins against *them*" (v. 19; not *men's sins*). To "count against them" *(logizomenos autois)* in the world of commerce referred to calculating the amount of a debt (Heidland 1967a:284-85). Today we might think of charges on a credit card for which we are held legally responsible. Here it means not posting debts to our account that should rightfully be ours. The debts are called *sins*—or better, "trespasses" (KJV, RSV, NRSV, NASB), a term that in Hellenistic Greek has to do with a false step, slip or blunder. The REB's "misdeeds" catches the sense. To the Greek *paraptōmata* are mistakes that result from ignorance. To the Jew they are deliberate actions knowingly committed against God (Bauder 1978:585-86). As someone

---

5:19 The force of *hōs hoti* is unclear. *Hōs hoti* can be equivalent to *hoti* and introduce a quote ("as it is said: 'God was reconciling' "—e.g., Furnish), a nominal clause ("namely, God was reconciling"—e.g., Turner 1963:137) or a reason ("since, God was reconciling"— e.g., Vulgate). Or it can be equivalent to *hōs* ("how" or "with the conviction that God was reconciling" [Blass, Debrunner and Funk 1961:no. 396.3]).

Ēn (taken in an absolute sense) + *en Christō* can be construed as the predicate with *katallassōn* modifying the previous clause ("God was in Christ, reconciling the world to

once said, "sin is a clenched fist and its object is the face of God."
As part of his message Paul included the fact that God *committed* to
him *the message of reconciliation* (v. 19). This occurred at the home of
Judas on Straight Street in Damascus shortly after his encounter with the
risen Christ (Acts 9:10-19; compare 22:12-16). The verb *committed*
(themenos) denotes a divine appointment (Maurer 1972:157). This was
a deliberate and carefully considered action on God's part.

The nature of Paul's appointment was to serve as one of *Christ's*
ambassadors. The verb *presbeuō (are ambassadors)* means to be "elder"
or "first in rank" (Liddell, Scott and Jones 1978). Here we might think
of the role of the statesman, where age and high rank often go together.
Then as now, an ambassador was someone who represented the
interests of his or her nation abroad. In the Old Testament the range of
duties included offering congratulations (1 Kings 5:1; 2 Sam 8:10),
soliciting favors (Num 20:14), making alliances (Josh 9:3-7) and protest-
ing wrongful actions (Judg 11:12). The Roman counterpart to the Greek
presbeutēs was the legate *(legatus),* who was duly appointed by the
emperor to administer the imperial provinces on his behalf. Paul was
similarly appointed by God to administer the gospel *on Christ's behalf*
(hyper Christou; compare Eph 3:2). It is as though God himself were
making a personal and direct appeal through Paul (v. 20).

Reconciliation is both an accomplished fact (v. 18) and a continuing
process (v. 19). Although it is a done deed as a result of Christ's work
on the cross, it nonetheless must be personally appropriated. This is
where Paul and the gospel ministry fit into the picture. He, and those
like him, function as God's agents in proclaiming what has been
accomplished. To use Paul's language, God has appointed them to
preach the word of reconciliation (v. 19) and so they proclaim: *Be*
reconciled to God (v. 20). Two things need to be noted. First, the verb
is passive. It is not that we must reconcile ourselves to God—as would

himself.") Or *ēn* + *katallassōn* can be interpreted as a periphrastic imperfect with *kosmon*
as the direct object and *en Christō* as a prepositional phrase denoting instrument or means
("God was reconciling the world to himself through Christ").

"The word" *(ton logon)* of reconciliation is the gospel message. Paul appears to be
particularly fond of using *logos* in this way (Hughes 1962:207). See, for example, Ephesians
1:13 ("the word of truth, namely, the gospel of salvation") and Colossians 1:5 ("the word
of truth, namely, the gospel").

be the case with the Greeks or Romans vis-à-vis their gods. Rather, we are to *be reconciled,* that is, to accept what God has already achieved. Second, the gospel minister's job is not to bring about reconciliation but to announce what has already occurred. In a real sense, he or she is the town crier or herald proclaiming a news item of earth-shaking significance. In fact we take on the role of the herald each Christmas when we sing the well-known lines by Charles Wesley: "Hark! The herald angels sing, 'Glory to the newborn king, / Peace on earth and mercy mild, God and sinners reconciled!' "

But what we recount in song Paul proclaimed in earnest. For all that remains for humankind to do is to receive what God has effected. Yet how can they receive it unless they have heard about it? And how can they hear without someone preaching to them (Rom 10:14-15)? "How beautiful . . . are the feet of those who bring good news!" (Is 52:7). The demand for heralds remains a pressing one today. For the need is still as desperate and the news just as vital.

The reason trespasses are not credited to our account is that God *made him who had no sin to be sin for us, so that in him we might become the righteousness of God* (v. 21). The fact that Christ *had no sin* is well documented in the New Testament. He was tempted as we are "yet was without sin" (Heb 4:15); one "set apart from sinners" (Heb 7:26). The NIV *had no sin* is actually "knew no sin" *(ton mē gnonta hamartian).* The verb *ginōskō* (to know) denotes personal acquaintance with something. Christ did not possess the knowledge of sin that comes through personal experience. He did not sin either in thought ("in him is no sin," 1 Jn 3:5) or in action ("he committed no sin," 1 Pet 2:22).

The rest of verse 21 is theologically elusive. The first problem is to determine the sense in which Christ was *made . . . sin for us.* There are three major approaches. One approach is to understand *made . . . sin*

5:20 It is not *as though* God were making an appeal but "with the conviction that" God is making an appeal *(hōs;* Blass, Debrunner and Funk 1961:no. 423.3). On the whole, the genitive absolute *(tou theou parakalountos)* is relatively rare in Paul's writings (Turner 1976:99).

It is to be noted that *deometha* lacks a direct object. Nor is one to be supplied in English, as the NIV does *(we implore you).* The Corinthians are not in view here. Paul is merely giving the substance of the call that he routinely makes following a presentation of the gospel message: "We make the request on behalf of Christ: 'Be reconciled to God.' " The

as "treated as a sinner." As our substitute, Christ came to stand in that relation with God which normally is the result of sin, that is, estranged from God and the object of his wrath (Barrett 1973:180). The second approach is to identify *made . . . sin* with Christ's assuming a human nature. Through the incarnation Christ was made "in the likeness of sinful man" (Rom 8:3). The final approach is to interpret verse 21 sacrificially as "made to be a sin offering." This draws on the Old Testament notion that God made the life of his servant a guilt offering (Is 53:10).

On the whole, this last interpretation seems the likeliest one. The equivalent Hebrew term *hatta't* can actually mean either "sin" or "sin offering" (as in Lev 4:8-35). Also, the logic of verse 19 almost demands it. If our debts are not posted to our account, it is because someone else has legally assumed them—much as the scapegoat did on the Day of Atonement (Lev 16) and the guilt offering did on other occasions (Lev 4—5). This is why God can make overtures of friendship toward those who are otherwise his enemies.

If the exact point of "made sin" is lost to us, the thrust is clear. So closely did Christ identify with the plight of humanity that their sin became his sin. In the final analysis this is not so different from the idea in 1 Peter 2:24 that Christ himself bore our sins in his body up onto the tree. Paul may well be thinking of Isaiah 53:12, where the servant of the Lord is to be numbered with the transgressors and bear the sin of many.

In identifying with our sin, Christ paved the way for us to become identified with *the righteousness of God*. The genitive can be subjective ("the righteousness that God gives"—that is, a righteous character), objective ("the righteousness we have before God"—that is, a right standing) or possessive ("the righteousness that God possesses"—that is, we share the righteousness that characterizes God himself). In Paul's

---

verb *katallagēte* can be either indicative ("You are being reconciled to God") or imperative ("Be reconciled to God"). The imperative is the likely choice in the context.

5:21 *Hyper hēmōn* normally means "on our behalf." But Paul quite often uses it with the sense "in our place" (Zerwick 1963:no. 91). Some argue that Christ did not actually become a sinner ("in our place") but merely took upon himself the responsibility for sins that were not his own ("on our behalf"). Yet *hamartian epoiēsen* implies more than this. Tasker suggests that "made to be sin" includes making friends of sinners and empathizing with their burden of sin (1934-1935:560-61).

writings the noun *dikaiosynē* typically is used of character. It is not merely that we acquire a right standing or do good works; we actually *become* righteous—although the latter may well presume the former. This is no legal fiction. For in Christ (or perhaps "through Christ," *en autō*) we truly assume his righteousness, just as Christ assumed our sin (Brown 1978:169).

A Plea Not to Take God's Goodness for Granted (6:1-3) In 1910 Julia H. Johnston penned the words

Marvelous, infinite, matchless grace,

Freely bestowed on all who believe!

You that are longing to see His face,

Will you this moment His grace receive?

We use the word *grace* a lot in evangelical circles. But what does it really mean? And how does it differ from God's mercy? Webster's Unabridged Dictionary defines *grace* as "the enjoyment of divine favor" and *mercy* as "compassion extended to someone instead of severity." Protestant scholastic theology understands *grace* as "the undeserved generosity of God toward humankind" and *mercy* as "God's compassion toward his fallen creatures" (Muller 1985:130).

One thing is certain. In God, mercy and grace are one. But as they reach us, they are seen as two related, but not identical, attributes. Mercy is God's goodness confronting human misery and guilt. Grace is the good pleasure of God that inclines him to bestow benefits where they are undeserved—to "pity the wretched, spare the guilty, welcome the outcast" (Tozer 1961:100). With grace the initiative is on God's side. As C. S. Lewis describes it, "God was the hunter and I was the deer. He stalked me, . . . took unerring aim and fired" (1956:169). Yet once we receive this grace, something is expected of us. Otherwise we face the danger, as Paul says to the Corinthians, of *receiv[ing] God's grace in vain* (v. 1).

At 6:1 we move to the heart of chapters 1—7. All that Paul has written up to this point is to prepare the Corinthians for the appeal he now makes. He spent five chapters presenting his credentials as a minister of the gospel. They may not have been the flashy credentials that his critics flaunted, but they were the ones that really mattered in the ministry and ones that should have elicited the Corinthians' pride in their spiritual father. Now, on the basis of this ministerial résumé, Paul makes a plea for their affection and asks them to open wide their hearts to him, as he has opened wide his heart to them (vv. 11-13). The final verses of the previous chapter nicely prepare the way for this appeal. God's act of reconciling the world to himself anticipates Paul's request for the Corinthians' acceptance. The gospel minister's call, "Be reconciled to God," paves the way for Paul's plea to open their hearts to him, and "the righteousness of God" looks forward to the ethical demand to not be unequally yoked with unbelievers.

Even so, the sequence of thought in 6:1—7:2 is initially somewhat confusing. Paul begins with what at first sight seems to be an evangelistic call (*I tell you, now is the time of God's favor, now is the day of salvation*), then defends the paradoxical character of his ministry (vv. 3-10), goes on to make an urgent appeal for their affection (vv. 11-13), follows this with a command to sever ties with unbelievers (6:14—7:1) and finally repeats once again his request for their affection (7:2). What is the logic behind the sequence of thought in these verses?

In making sense of this section it is helpful to see that Paul asks two things of the Corinthians (vv. 1-2, 11-13) and introduces two potential obstacles to carrying them out (vv. 3-4, 14-18). His first request is *not to receive God's grace in vain* by rejecting him as God's ambassador (vv. 1-2). There are potentially good reasons for a church to reject an itinerant evangelist like Paul. Traveling preachers were constantly faced with the temptation to adapt their life and message to what the world expected in order to gain acceptance. Paul, however, emphatically denies being seduced in this fashion (vv. 3-4), and his life of adversity bears witness to his resistance (vv. 4-5, 8-10). The Corinthians should therefore be eager to "open wide" their "hearts" to him—Paul's second request (vv. 11-12)—unless, of course, the obstacle lay with them. The danger for a Gentile congregation in a city like Corinth was in adopting the prevailing mores and attitudes of their culture. Today we call this "peer pressure." One of the main reasons for teenage pregnancies, drug addiction and alcoholism is that most young people are conformists. They, like their parents, do what everyone else does, feeling instinctively that if most people are doing it, it must be good to do. For this reason, the Corinthians are warned about yoking themselves unequally with non-Christians (6:14—7:1).

To cave in to peer pressure, Paul says, would be in effect to *receive God's grace in vain* (v. 1). *De kai* (now then), often dropped in translation, signals a major point of transition in Paul's letters. *We urge (parakaloumen)* is the verb Paul routinely uses to move from the "that" (or indicative) part of his letter to the "do" (or imperative) section. The Corinthians are now called to act in a way that is consonant with the facts presented up to this point. It is also the verb Paul tends to use when making a request of his readers. He does not, however, approach the Corinthians as equals. *Parakaleō* is used by someone who has the authority to command but the tact not to.

Paul and his colleagues make their request as *God's fellow workers*. The Greek text does not include the word *God*. This is an assumption of the NIV translators. *Synergountes* could equally be rendered "as your coworkers." Which is correct? The point was made early on that Paul is dependent on the Corinthians' help (*synhypourgountōn*, 1:11) and, in turn, works with them for their joy (*synergoi esmen*, 1:24). On the other hand, the warning not to accept God's grace in vain does not suggest a willing partnership in the gospel ministry—as much as Paul may have wished for it. On balance, "God's coworkers" seems the likelier option. Paul usually uses *synergeō* (and cognates) of teammates in the gospel ministry, but the term may also not be wholly inappropriate for what he describes in 5:20 ("God making his appeal through us").

So Paul appeals to the Corinthians as cooperators with God not to accept his grace *in vain*. The phrase *in vain* means "without effect or result." Paul's concern is that God's grace will not have any meaningful impact on their lives. Use of the aorist infinitive *(dexasthai)*

6:1 To be *God's fellow workers* in the gospel ministry, though rare in Paul, is not a totally strange idea. This seems to be the only way to read *Timotheon . . . synergon tou theou* in 1 Thessalonians 3:2—although some early manuscripts have *diakonon* instead of *synergon*, obviously because scribes found the notion theologically difficult.

Some suppose that *dexasthai* is a timeless aorist ("do not now or at any time receive God's grace in vain"); others think that it has the force of a past tense ("do not reject the grace you received at the time of your conversion"). The former is too general for the specificity of the context, while the latter really requires the perfect tense (indicating condition or state as a result of a past action). *Now is the day of salvation* (v. 2) suggests, instead, a simple action in the present ("do not now reject God's grace").

The force of Paul's appeal not to receive God's grace in vain has been debated. Some

suggests a danger that the Corinthians faced at this particular time. But what exactly was the danger? The answer depends in large part on what one understands by *God's grace (tēn charin tou theou)*. The Greek root *char-* is used of things that produce well-being. The noun *charis*, found eighteen times in this letter, is employed of God's favor or goodwill (1:2, 12; 4:15; 6:1; 8:9; 13:14), a monetary gift (8:6, 19), a human privilege (8:4), a spiritual endowment (8:7), divine enablement (8:1; 9:14; 12:9), an expression of gratitude (2:14; 8:16; 9:15) and a divine blessing (1:15; 9:8; Bauer, Arndt and Gingrich 1979). Here it refers to God's undeserved favor extended to us through Jesus Christ—or, simply put, salvation.

Is Paul suggesting that the Corinthians are in danger of losing their salvation? At first glance, the quotation from Isaiah 49:8 supports this conclusion: *In the time of my favor I heard you, and in the day of salvation I helped you* (v. 2). The time of divine favor in the context of Isaiah 49 is the point when God answers the prayers of his servant and comes to his aid. The servant had been despised and rejected by the nations. God now promises vindication, so that "kings will see you and rise up," and "princes will see and bow down" (Is 49:7). What Isaiah looked forward to, Paul says, is at hand: *I tell you, now is the time of God's favor, now is the day of salvation* (v. 2). The adverb *now* is placed first for emphasis. The particle *idou* is intended to arouse the attention of the listener: "Look! [NIV *I tell you*] Now is the time." The sense of urgency is unmistakable. The *time of God's favor* has arrived. The term *euprosdektos* (and its cognates) is used in the LXX of what is pleasing to God (Grundmann 1964a:58-59). It stands in parallel with *the day of salvation* in the next clause. The time of God's favor is in effect the day of salvation. It pleases God to display his good pleasure through human agents

---

think that he is warning the Corinthians about compromise with the world. This is certainly the case in 6:14—7:1 but does not explain Paul's self-commendation and plea for the church's affection in verses 3-13. Others suppose that Paul is cautioning them against thinking that they could still achieve their own salvation, while still others believe that he is alerting them to the possibility of losing their salvation. The expressions of confidence and pride in the Corinthians in the next chapter indicate, however, that salvation is not at issue. Lambrecht argues that the action called for is a decision to live the reconciliation they had already received (1989:388). Beale goes even further: to live reconciliation is to accept Paul as the Isaianic Servant (1989:562, 567-68). This nicely fits the broader context (see the text).

("ambassadors," 5:20; "coworkers," 6:1; "servants," 6:4), whose job it is to proclaim that the day of salvation has arrived.

Of what, then, are the Corinthians in danger? The fact that Paul can go on to say *We put no stumbling block in anyone's path* (v. 3) suggests that he is identifying himself with the servant of Isaiah 49:8 and equating receiving God's grace with accepting himself and his coworkers. For the Corinthians, then, to reject Paul would be in effect to reject God's grace. This is an audacious move on Paul's part. Yet for God's ambassador (5:20) and coworker (v. 1), it is not unjustifiable.

Why, though, would the Corinthians reject Paul? Did they understand the implications? It is certainly not because any fault can be found with his ministry. The language is emphatic: "We give no offense of any sort in any thing" *(mēdemian en mēdeni).* The Greek noun *proskopē,* found only here in the New Testament, refers to something that causes a misstep or provokes offense. While the gospel message itself may offend (1 Cor 1:23), the gospel preacher may not. So Paul has been careful not to do anything that someone could legitimately take offense at. This is so that his ministry will not *be discredited,* a term that means "to find fault with, to criticize."

The story is told of a small boy who closely watched a neighboring pastor build a wooden trellis to support a climbing vine. The youngster did not say a word the entire time that he watched. Pleased at the thought that his work was being admired, the pastor finally said to the boy, "Well, son, trying to pick up some pointers on gardening?"

"No," replied the boy, "I'm just waiting to hear what a preacher says when he hits his thumb with a hammer."

Paul's Ministry Credentials (6:4-10) This story points out how crucial

---

6:3 *En mēdeni* can be neuter ("in any way") or masculine ("to anyone"). If it is the former, Paul is saying that he avoids giving offense in any way (KJV, NEB); if the latter, Paul *puts no stumbling block in anyone's path* (NIV, TEV, JB, Phillips). On balance, the neuter provides the better counterpoint to "in every way" in verse 4. Some think that *didontes* has a conative force: "we *try* not to put obstacles in anyone's way" (for example, Bratcher 1983:64). But this incorrectly softens the force of Paul's claim ("in no way *[en mēdeni]* do we give offense but in every way *[en panti]* we commend ourselves," 6:3-4).

6:4-5 Von Hodgson (1983:59-80) and others have shown that tribulation lists were common in the first century. Parallels can be found in such diverse sources as Josephus, Jewish apocalyptic writings, the Mishna, Stoics, Cynics and Plutarch.

6:4 *Hōs theou diakonoi* is in the nominative. It is *as servants of God* (subject of the verb)

it is that our practice match our teaching and preaching. There will always be those who will judge the claims of Christ by we who claim to be his followers. Children are especially able to see through this kind of hypocrisy (often to the embarrassment of their parents). In the life of the person who truly serves God there can be no such discrepancy. As A. J. Gordon once said, "We do not stand in the world bearing witness to Christ, but stand in Christ and so bear witness to the world." Simply put, we do not witness to prove we are God's servants, we witness because we *are* God's servants.

This is why Paul is able to assert that it is *as servants of God we commend ourselves* (v. 4). The Greek word *diakonos* means "servant" or "messenger." The genitive *of God* is in all probability possessive. Paul and his coworkers are "God's servants" and, as such, take their orders from him. This is why they can commend themselves *in every way. In every way* is placed first for emphasis. The gospel ministry can admit no exception for the sake of credibility. This is the second of three places in the letter where Paul explicitly recommends himself to the Corinthians (4:2; 6:4; 11:16—12:11). The Corinthians have forced him to it (12:11) with their misplaced confidence in those who flaunt their credentials (5:12). Even so, Paul can bring himself to boast only in what his critics would consider ministerial failures rather than successes (4:8-9; 6:4-5; 11:23-29).

As a small boy walked on a beach one day, he spied a matronly woman sitting under a beach umbrella on the sand. He walked up to her and asked, "Are you a Christian?"

"Yes," she answered.

"Do you read your Bible every day?"

---

that Paul commends himself and his colleagues. "In everything we do we show that we are God's servants" mistakenly treats the phrase as an accusative (JB, KJV, LB, Phillips). Paul is not out to prove he is God's servant but to commend himself as such.

En hypomonē pollē could go with what precedes, "We try to recommend ourselves in all circumstances by our steadfast endurance: in affliction . . ." (REB; compare JB). But it is usually taken with what follows, *We commend ourselves in every way: in great endurance* . . . (NIV; compare Phillips, KJV, RSV, TEV).

Some speculate that Paul's *troubles* involved imprisonment either in Ephesus or somewhere along the route from Ephesus to Troas. Philippians is commonly dated during this period. See the introduction.

She nodded her head. "Yes."

"Do you pray often?" the boy asked next.

Again she answered, "Yes."

With that he asked his final question: "Will you hold my quarter while I go swimming?"

Trustworthiness is hard to come by. It is not implicit in the claim to be a Christian. We look for evidences of trustworthiness just as the small boy on the beach did. Paul lists twenty-eight reasons why the Corinthians should consider his ministry deserving of confidence (vv. 4-10). Some, like *troubles, hardships and distresses,* are not the kind of things that the Corinthians—or a lot of churches today, for that matter—would naturally appreciate. Yet they are the telltale signs of a successful ministry in God's eyes and for this reason alone should commend themselves to the church. But the Corinthians, like many of us, were so used to judging success by society's standards that it is a hard sell for Paul.

This is the second of three *res gestae* (cataloging of deeds) or curricula vitae found in 2 Corinthians. Like the list in 4:8-9, it highlights exploits and accomplishments that society would judge to be blameworthy rather than praiseworthy (such as *beatings, imprisonments and riots*). Unlike the previous résumé, it goes beyond the typical missionary afflictions to include such spiritual attributes as purity, understanding, patience and kindness, along with such divine credentials as the Holy Spirit, genuine love, the word of truth and the power of God (vv. 6-7). The finely shaped and stylistically well-balanced character of this section has led some to suppose that Paul is using a preformed text. Each of the first group of eighteen is introduced by the preposition *en* (in), the second group of three by the preposition *dia* (through) and the final group of seven by *bōs* (as).

The first grouping of eighteen can be divided into three subgroups: (1) missionary hardships and sufferings (vv. 4-5), (2) ethical virtues (v. 6) and (3) spiritual weaponry (v. 7). Paul starts with nine kinds of sufferings that he experienced as a gospel minister. Of the nine, only *riots* does not appear elsewhere in his tribulation lists. *In great endurance* heads the list. In chapter 1 *endurance* was the end result of divine encouragement received during trials. Here it denotes how one should go about handling adversity. Used positively, the term means "to stand firm" or "to hold one's ground" in the face of difficulties. This is in contrast to the Stoics, who taught that life's difficulties can and must be overcome.

The first group of difficulties that require a firm stance includes external and internal pressures of one sort or another: *troubles, hardships and distresses.* The Greek word for *troubles (thlipsis)* denotes the pressures and anxieties of life that come our way. These can be external ("conflicts without," 7:5) or internal ("fears within," 7:5), though the term is most often used of the harassment that God's people experience at the hands of the world. *Anankē (hardships)* signifies that which compels, forces or necessitates such adverse circumstances as calamity, torture or bodily pain. To experience *distress (stenochōria)* is to find oneself in a tight corner or in narrow straits with no apparent way of escape—not unlike an army under attack in a long narrow pass with no space to maneuver or retreat (Barclay 1954:213).

The next group are difficulties inflicted by others: *beatings, imprisonments and riots.* *Plēgai (beatings)* are physical blows that occur as a result of mob action or court punishment. Paul recounts having been lashed five times by Jewish authorities and whipped three times with Roman rods (11:24-25). As for *imprisonments,* Luke records only the imprisonment in Philippi prior to the writing of 2 Corinthians (Acts 16:16-40). Paul says in 11:23 that he had been jailed more times than his opponents, but we do not know when and where the other imprisonments took place. *Riots* happened in almost every city Paul visited. With few exceptions these were incited by Jewish antagonists who were envious of Paul's success among the Gentiles.

The final three difficulties are self-imposed: *hard work, sleepless nights and hunger. Kopos (hard work)* literally means a "striking" or "beating." It came to be used of labor that is physically exhausting—the kind that causes one to collapse at night from sheer exhaustion. Paul uses the term to describe both his trade as a worker of goats-hair cloth (1 Cor 4:12; 1 Thess 2:9; 2 Thess 3:8) and his missionary labors (2 Cor 10:15)—although the two are connected, since he plied a trade so as not to be a financial burden on his churches (2 Thess 3:8). *Agrypnia* denotes sleeplessness or wakefulness. For Paul, this was voluntarily imposed. If 11:28-29 is any indication, it was the result of prayerful concern for his churches. It can also be an indication that his tentmaking and missionary labors (preaching, discipling, prayer, correspondence) carried him well into the wee hours of the night. The last hardship is *hunger*. *Nēsteia,* as opposed to *limos* which is involuntary hunger, refers to self-imposed abstinence. Fasting was a common practice among pious Jews and was often done as a means of focusing one's energies on the task of intercession. There may also have been times when Paul went hungry to avoid being a burden on anyone (2 Cor 11:7-10).

At verse 6 Paul goes beyond what Chrysostom called "a blizzard of troubles" to include four moral attributes deemed essential for those who claim to be God's servants: *purity, understanding, patience and kindness.* None is unique to the gospel ministry. Two, in fact, appear among the fruits of the Spirit listed in Galatians 5:22 and in the same order (patience and kindness; compare 1 Cor 13:4).

Hagnotēs (only here in the Greek Bible) and the more common cognate *hagnos* range in meaning from an inward disposition ("pure of heart," 11:3) to outward behavior ("innocent," 7:11; "chaste," 11:2; "without defect," Phil 4:8; "blameless," 1 Tim 5:22). Since *hagnotēs* is linked with relational qualities like patience and kindness, it may well bear the sense of moral blamelessness in dealing with others—a point that Paul is concerned to underscore throughout the letter (1:12; 4:2; 6:3).

Although *knowledge (gnōsis),* second in Paul's list, can refer to a "grasp of truth" (NEB), it is "insight" (Phillips) or *understanding* (NIV) that best fits the context. Anyone can acquire head knowledge—that is, the mental accumulation and integration of facts. The Corinthians thought they possessed it (1 Cor 8:1-2), and Paul's opponents laid claim to it (2 Cor 11:5). Heart knowledge, on the other hand, is much harder to come by. It is the God-given ability to know the right thing to do in a given situation—what we call "wisdom" or "insight" (see 1 Cor 12:8).

The Greek word for *patience,* third in Paul's list, means "long-tempered" *(makro + thymia);* this word is frequently used in the Old

---

6:6 The adjective *hagios* ("holy") echoes *hagnotēs* ("purity") at the head of the list.

It is sometimes argued that it would be unlikely for Paul to refer to the Holy Spirit in a series of human ethical qualities or to place the Spirit in a subordinate position in terms of word order. Yet similar combinations of human virtues and divine references are readily

Testament of God's long-suffering attitude toward his people. In extrabiblical literature it denotes a human attitude of passive resignation or forced acceptance, but in the Greek Bible it is a positive attribute (Gal 5:22). More than simple endurance or forbearance, it expresses loving patience toward those whose failings would normally provoke irritation (Horst 1967:374-85).

Chrēstotēs, the fourth and final moral quality, is the capacity to show kindness even to the undeserving and to evidence a sympathetic interest in the problems of others.

Blamelessness, insightfulness, patience and kindness constitute Paul's moral imperative for the gospel preacher. The regularity with which the last two crop up in his ethical instruction (as in 1 Cor 13:4; Gal 5:22; Col 3:12) suggests a common growing edge in the churches that he pastored. It was not for want of a model in Paul, though. It may well have been that these churches were looking to the wrong model. There is every indication that they were listening to the wrong message (2 Cor 11:4; Gal 1:6; Col 2:18-23). But then, quite often wrong theology leads to wrong behavior (see 1 Tim 4:15-16).

The spiritual arsenal of the gospel minister is presented in the next group of four. Each is distinguished by a modifier that emphasizes what is uppermost in Paul's mind: *in the Holy Spirit and in sincere love; in truthful speech* and in *divine* power (NIV *the power of God*). It is an arsenal that in Paul's estimate his opponents on at least two counts lacked (11:4, "a different Spirit [see the commentary] . . . a different gospel").

En pneumati hagiō could denote the ethical quality of the human spirit ("with a holy spirit") or the divine Spirit ("by the Holy Spirit"). When the word *pneuma* (spirit) stands alone, it is sometimes difficult to determine which sense Paul has in mind. But when modified by the adjective *hagios* (holy), it invariably refers to the divine Spirit (e.g., Rom 5:5; 9:1; 14:17; 15:13, 16; 1 Cor 12:3; 1 Thess 1:5-6; Titus 3:5). Why would Paul include the Spirit in his ministerial arsenal? The combination of

---

found. For example, in Romans 14:17 *en pneumati hagiō* appears with such ethical qualities as "righteousness, peace and joy," and in Romans 15:13 *en dynamei pneumatos hagiou* is conjoined with "joy," "peace," "trust" and "hope."

purity (hagnotēs) and the power of the *Holy (hagios) Spirit,* to be sure, makes for an unbeatable credential. Still, Paul may have something more in mind. The grouping of Spirit, love, speech and power suggests the outward, validating signs that frequently accompanied the preaching of the gospel in the first century. Although Paul does not brag about them as his rival missionaries do, he does remind the Corinthians that the things that mark an apostle—"signs, wonders and miracles"—had been done among them (12:12). With the addition of the adjectives *holy, sincere* and *truthful,* Paul takes the offensive in pointing to the kind of inward, authenticating signs that should equally accompany gospel proclamation. The Spirit's inclusion in the missionary's weaponry underscores his role in confirming the message and convicting the listener.

The second weapon in Paul's missionary arsenal is *sincere love.* A love that is sincere is one without hypocrisy and free from artificiality. *Love* and *Spirit* is a familiar combination with Paul. Hope does not disappoint us, because "God has poured out his love into our hearts through the Holy Spirit" (Rom 5:5). Paul even solicits the Roman church's prayers "by the love that the Spirit inspires" (Rom 15:30 NEB).

Truthful speech, the third missionary weapon, is actually "the word of truth" *(logō alētheias).* This is an important distinction because Paul elsewhere equates the word of truth with the gospel message (Eph 1:13; Col 1:5). A better translation might be "the true message." His rivals, on the other hand, preach a distorted version of the gospel (4:2; compare "another gospel," 11:4) for the sake of financial gain (2:17) and to gain acceptance (3:1-2). Paul's last weapon is *the power of God.* The genitive is most likely descriptive: "divine power." Divine power undoubtedly includes both enablement to preach the gospel and confirmation of the message proclaimed (1 Cor 2:4; 1 Thess 1:5). In all cases Paul connects this power with the working of the Spirit.

The armory of the Holy Spirit—sincere love, the true message and divine power—is deployed *with weapons of righteousness in the right hand and in the left* (v. 7). Paul is fond of military language, whether to describe Christian self-control (1 Thess 5:8), the resources available to resist the devil's schemes (Eph 6:11-18) or, as here, the spiritual array

---

6:7 The genitives *en logō alētheias* and *en dynamei theou* are probably descriptive: "the

at one's disposal in preaching the gospel. The relationship between the two nouns *weapons* and *righteousness* is unclear. Are these weapons used to fight for righteousness, weapons that righteousness provides (Furnish 1984:346), righteousness used as a weapon (that is, a life of integrity; Phillips, TEV) or weapons that are righteous in character (Bultmann 1985:172-73)? The last option seems the preferable one. Paul's weapons were ones of notable integrity and not like those of his rivals, who utilized domination, exploitation and humiliation (11:20).

Roman soldiers carried a sword or spear *in the right hand* for attack and a shield *in the left* for defense. In this way they were well equipped to meet the challenges of battle. Paul too was well equipped for battle, a battle that he defines as demolishing arguments, pulling down every proud obstacle that is raised against knowing God and taking captive every thought to make it obedient to Christ (10:4-5).

At this point in his résumé, Paul turns to two opposite estimates of his ministry—two contrasting letters of reference, as it were. One letter reflects public opinion, the other, divine appraisal. According to public opinion he is a disgrace *(dishonor)*, a bad character *(bad report)*, an *impostor* and *unknown* (v. 8). The first two nouns are similar in meaning. *Atimia* in extrabiblical Greek signifies a state of social disgrace resulting from the loss of one's rights as a citizen. In the estimate of his social peers, Paul was someone to be shunned (compare Cotton Patch Version, "spit on"). The closely related term *dysphēmia*, found nowhere else in the New Testament, denotes an "ill word" spoken against someone so that they gain a bad reputation in the public eye. Both are potential hazards in the ministry. The one can discourage (4:1); the other can cause one to lose perspective (4:8). Paul is also perceived to be an *impostor (planos)*, who misleads and causes others to wander. In addition, he is an unknown *(agnooumenos)*, someone lacking stature who can be dismissed as unworthy of recognition.

But then Paul cared very little about how his social peers judged him—or even how the Corinthians evaluated him (1 Cor 4:3). The opinion that mattered to him was God's. And in God's opinion he is esteemed *(glory)*, of good repute *(good report)*, *genuine* and *known*.

true message," "divine power."

Doxa bears the Hellenistic sense of a favorable opinion or estimate (NRSV *honor,* not NIV *glory*). The closely related term *euphēmia* means a "good word" spoken on someone's behalf (that is, a *good report*). The Greek word *alēthēs* can mean "honest" (TEV, NEB, REB) or "genuine" (KJV, Phillips, RSV, NRSV, JB, NIV). The latter provides a better point of contrast to *impostor.* Although judged to be an imposter by some, Paul in reality is *genuine* (or, as we say, "the genuine article"). The word *known (epiginōskomenos)* means to be "recognized" for what one is. Even though society considered Paul a nobody, there is the divine recognition that as an ambassador and coworker he is a somebody.

Paul concludes with a list of five paradoxes that typify the gospel ministry. *Dying, and yet we live on* does not quite catch the sense of the first. "Dying, yet look! We live" is more the idea. The public perception is that Paul and his coworkers are in the process of dying (present tense)—and to all outward appearances they are. Paul himself said earlier that he always carries around the dying of Jesus (4:10). *Idou* denotes surprise: "Look!" Contrary to popular expectation and all outward appearances, they *live on* (present tense).

Second, they are *beaten, and yet not killed.* The Greek word for *beaten (paideuomenos)* actually means "chastened" and is commonly used of divine discipline. To the outsider Paul's suffering might well have seemed a sign of divine displeasure.

Third, they are *sorrowful, yet always rejoicing.* The cause of Paul's sorrow is not immediately obvious. It is unlikely to be sorrow over the fact that the ministry is wearing him down (4:16), since the end result is an eternal weight of glory (4:17). It could be sorrow over those who had sinned earlier and had not yet repented (12:21). But the present tense suggests something ongoing. Alternatively, the paradox may reflect an eschatological perspective. Paul's reaction to the prevailing

---

6:8 Verse 8 contains a chiasm: A *through glory* — B *and dishonor* — B *bad report* — A *and good report.*

It is difficult to know whose is the favorable estimate in verses 8-9 *(through glory . . . good report . . . genuine . . . known).* It most likely is God's estimate, but it may also be the opinion of Paul's coworkers or even that of most of his churches.

6:9 Martin thinks that "chastened yet not killed" is Paul's perspective (1986:182-83). While it is true that God chastens those whom he loves (Prov 3:12), *paideuō* is used here

influences of sin and death in this age is sorrow, while his response to the process of inwardly being renewed day by day is to always rejoice (compare Phil 4:4-7; 1 Thess 5:16).

The final two paradoxes express roughly the same thought. Paul is *poor, yet making many rich* and in the state of *having nothing, and yet possessing everything*. While some have thought that Paul is referring to spiritual poverty, the overall context of ministerial hardship and suffering suggests a lack of material goods (compare 11:27, "I have known hunger and thirst and have often gone without food"). But how can one possess *nothing* and *everything* at the same time? Paul could mean that although he was not well off in terms of material goods, because "the earth is the Lord's, and everything in it" (1 Cor 10:26) he too, in principle if not in fact, possesses everything. Or he may be contrasting possessing nothing in the way of material goods with possessing everything in terms of spiritual goods. He would not be alone in this belief. Philo expressed a similar thought: "The good person, though he possesses nothing in the proper sense, not even himself, partakes of the precious things of God so far as he is capable" (*On the Life of Moses* 1.157).

How Paul went about *making many rich* is also not at once apparent. He may be alluding to how he went without church support for the sake of collecting funds for destitute Judean churches. Or the contrast may have to do with physical deprivation for himself and spiritual blessing for others. His willingness to forgo personal comforts and even basic necessities undoubtedly would have freed up time for ministry and resulted in greater spiritual benefits for his churches.

All in all, Paul says that he knows what it is to be in need as well as what it is to have plenty, yet he can be content whatever the circumstances (Phil 4:12).

A Plea for the Corinthians' Affection (6:11-13) Paul's original appeal

of the world's estimate of Paul's ministry, not his own.

6:10 Having nothing in the material sense yet possessing everything in a nonmaterial sense is a familiar thought in Stoic and Cynic writers. For example, Pseudo-Crates states, "Although we possess nothing, we have everything, but you [wealthy], though you have everything, really have nothing because of your rivalry, jealousy, fear and conceit" (*Epistle* 7; Malherbe 1986:159).

not to receive God's grace in vain takes a personal turn at verse 11. Having demonstrated the blameless and sacrificial character of his record as a minister of the gospel, he now makes a personal plea for the church's affection: *We have spoken freely to you, Corinthians, and opened wide our hearts to you. . . . Open wide your hearts also* (vv. 11-13). The text is literally "our mouths are open to you." The perfect tense bears the sense "our mouths *stand* open" *(aneōgen)*. Barrett suggests that we translate verse 11 "I have let my mouth run away with me" in order to make the connection with verses 3-10 more apparent (1973:191). But the idea is that of being completely truthful with someone and not holding anything back (Louw and Nida 1988-1989:33.252; "frankly" [TEV, JB, NEB], "freely" [NIV], "hiding nothing" [Phillips]).

Not only has Paul been candid with them, but he has *opened wide* his *heart* to them as well (v. 11). The verb *platynō* means to "widen" or "extend." The perfect tense depicts a present state of affairs: "our hearts *are* wide toward you" *(peplatyntai)*. So *as a fair exchange* Paul asks them to *open wide* their *hearts also* (v. 13). The fact that Paul calls them by name *(you, Corinthians)* bespeaks the intensity of his feelings. He also addresses them as his children *(I speak as to my children)*. Through his preaching of the gospel they had become family; and like any father, Paul desires a place in their heart.

At the moment, however, the Corinthians' affections toward their spiritual father appear to be cramped (v. 12). To be sure, Paul is *not withholding [his] affection* (v. 12). His heart is wide open (v. 11). So, if there is any constraint, it is on their part, not his. The Greek verb *stenochōreō* ("withhold") comes from *stenos* ("narrow") + *chōria* ("space"), which in the passive means "to be in a narrow place" or

---

6:11 Paul rarely refers to his readers in the vocative. When he does, it denotes strong feelings, as in Galatians 3:1, where he admonishes the church ("you foolish Galatians!") and Philippians 4:15, where he expresses a deep sense of gratitude ("as you Philippians know . . . not one church shared with me in the matter of giving and receiving, except you only").

6:13 *Your hearts* is rightly supplied by the NIV. The clause in the Greek text lacks a predicate *(platynthēte kai hymeis)*.

Murphy-O'Connor argues that the lack of a possessive pronoun in the phrase *hōs teknois legō* shows that Paul is addressing the Corinthians "as children" (that is, immature) and not "cramped for space." The nuance is not easily captured in English. It is more than a withholding of affection (NIV) or restraint of feelings (Phillips). Paul used the nominal form earlier of tight corners in the ministry from which there is no apparent way of escape (6:4; compare 4:8). Here the sense is that the Corinthians have become constrained in their feelings for Paul, so that he is finding himself gradually squeezed out of their hearts.

To experience the withdrawal of the affection of someone close to us can be a devastating experience. Psychologists have shown that the human need for intimacy is so great that babies who are fed and diapered but receive no affection from their caregiver can become withdrawn, remote and even autistic.

The Corinthians were not deprived of affection from their spiritual caregiver: *We are not withholding our affection from you,* says Paul (v. 12). The noun *splanchnon,* translated *affection* in the NIV and "bowels" in the KJV, actually refers to the inward parts (heart, lungs, liver and kidneys). Like the noun *heart,* it was used metaphorically of the seat of a person's feelings—especially feelings of anger and love. Paul's feelings for the Corinthians are wide open. All he asks from them in return is a *fair exchange* (v. 13). *Antimisthia,* a word that has been found only in Christian writings, stresses the reciprocal nature of a transaction. Its meaning is similar to the Latin *quid pro quo*—something given in fair exchange for something received. What Paul asks for by way of a fair exchange is that the Corinthians open wide their hearts as he has opened wide his own.

Unequal Yoking with Unbelievers (6:14—7:1) Paul next issues a command: *Do not be yoked together with unbelievers* (v. 14). Actually

"as my children" (that is, family; 1991:67). Yet no point has been made in the context about the Corinthians' immaturity. Casting aspersions would hardly be the way to solicit their affection.

6:14—7:1 Additional theories put forward to explain the seemingly abrupt shift of topic at 6:14 include (1) a dictation pause, (2) Paul's tendency to stray off the topic and (3) the need to bring up lingering problems dealt with in more substantial fashion in previous letters.

Quite a good case can be made for the non-Pauline character of this passage. It contains a noticeably high number of hapax legomena *(heterozygeō, metochē, symphōnēsis,*

the command is even more pointed: "*Stop* yoking yourselves to unbelievers." Use of the present imperative shows that Paul is not merely
warning the Corinthians about a potential danger ("do not start") but
instructing them to stop an action already in progress. The command
appears to come out of the clear blue. Has Paul not been lobbying
strenuously for the Corinthians' affection? Has he not just asked them,
as his children, to open wide their hearts to him? Moreover, he resumes
his lobbying efforts at 7:2: "Make room for us in your hearts," he repeats.
What then are we to make of 6:14—7:1?

One common theory is that 6:14—7:1 is a letter fragment that was
misplaced within the Corinthian correspondence and inserted in its
present spot by a later editor of Paul's letters (see the introduction). This
is an easy solution to a complex problem. It is an easy solution because
it shifts the blame onto the shoulders of someone other than Paul without
really addressing the question, Why here? Some have been impressed
with the non-Pauline character of these verses and think that Paul may
be quoting a familiar sermon, a piece of traditional material or even an
Essene text that has been reworked to reflect a Christian point of view.
But while this helps to explain a number of unfamiliar words and
expressions, the question "Why here?" still remains.

Suggestions, fortunately (or perhaps unfortunately), are in abundant
supply. It could be that Paul is responding to news just received from
Titus about a continuing problem with pagan associations. Another
possibility is that having asked the Corinthians to "open wide" Paul is
now cautioning them about what not to be open to (compare the LXX
of Deut 11:16, "Do not open wide your heart *[mē platynthē hē kardia]*
and turn away to serve and worship other gods"). Judging from 1 Co-

---

synkatathesis, Beliar, pantokratōr and *molysmos).* Terms found elsewhere in Paul are used
differently here ("flesh," "share," "promises"). The phraseology is not particularly Pauline
(for example, *echontes oun* + hortatory subjunctive, pollution of the flesh and spirit, the
opening and closing citation formulas). There appear to be a number of non-Pauline ideas
such as cleansing from fleshly and spiritual pollution and the perfection of holiness. And
the rhetorical accumulation of synonymous phrases in verses 14-16 and the chain of Old
Testament citations are not characteristic of Paul. See the introduction.
   6:14 The present imperative usually addresses an action already in progress ("Stop . . ."),
while the aorist subjunctive warns of a potential danger ("Do not start . . ."). See Zerwick
1963:no. 246.
   The language of unequal yoking recalls the command in Deuteronomy 22:10 not to

rinthians 10:1-22, they would clearly have been in need of such guidance. It could also be that Paul is engaging in a little structural diplomacy. By starting and ending with statements of affection, he attempts to cushion the force of his command. The likeliest explanation is that Paul is specifying the cause for the Corinthians' constraint toward him: their ongoing partnerships with unbelievers. But there need not be just one explanation. A number of things could have led Paul to tackle the problem at this point and in this fashion.

What exactly is Paul prohibiting with his command? The range among translations shows that there is no easy answer to this question. TEV has "Do not try to work together as equals with unbelievers," the NRSV translates it as "Do not be mismatched with unbelievers," and the NEB renders it "Do not unite yourselves with unbelievers." The two key questions are who the unbeliever is and what the verb yoked together denotes. Fourteen out of sixteen Pauline uses of the term unbeliever (apistos) occur in 1—2 Corinthians. The majority appear in 1 Corinthians 7 and distinguish those who have made a commitment to Christ from those who have not (7:12, 13, 14, 15). The only other occurrence in 2 Corinthians is used of those whose minds have been blinded by Satan to the light of the gospel (4:4). Here, in 2 Corinthians 6:14, it refers to those with whom there is a conflict of interest stemming from incompatible loyalties.

Certainly not all contact with unbelievers is excluded. Paul corrects just such a misconstrual in 1 Corinthians, when he tells the church that to have nothing to do with immoral people would necessitate removing themselves entirely from the world (5:9-10). It is a particular *kind* of contact with unbelievers that is in view. What kind, though? Paul's quotation of Isaiah 52:11, where Israel is commanded to *come out from*

---

plow with an ox and a donkey yoked together (although the verb in the LXX is *arotriaō* ["to plow"] and not *beterozygeō* ["to be unevenly yoked"]). The nominal form *beterozygos* is found in Leviticus 19:19, where crossbreeding animals of different species is prohibited. Such unnatural combinations violated the purity of the species.

Concern for unequal partnerships with unbelievers is addressed in the Old Testament. For instance, in Exodus 23:1 God's people are commanded not to become partners with the wicked by being a malicious witness in a court of law (Derrett 1978:239). Some have argued that Paul is employing *apistoi* ("unbelievers") of Christian opponents (such as Judaizers [e.g., Collange 1972] or the *pneumatikoi* ["spiritual"] of 1 Corinthians who continued to oppose Paul [e.g., Murphy-O'Connor 1991]). Yet *apistoi* earlier in the letter refers unequivocally to unbelievers (*hoi apollymenoi*, "those who are perishing"—4:3).

them and be separate suggests contact of a compromising nature (v. 17). But what would constitute a compromising liaison? Would working with an unbeliever be forbidden, as Phillips ("do not try to work with them") and TEV ("do not work together as equals") suggest?

Atheists, gays and evangelicals recently joined ranks to oppose the proabortion policies of the current political administration in the United States. Are such collaborations forbidden? Marriage between a believer and unbeliever would certainly be a legitimate application of the command. But is it the only one, as "mismated" in the RSV and NEB leads us to believe? It may not even be the primary application, since the focus throughout is on the church, not the individual believer. This is especially clear from the Old Testament passages Paul invokes to support his prohibition. In each case they deal with God's covenantal relationship with Israel, which Paul reapplies to the church as *the temple of the living God* (vv. 16-18).

The command is literally *Do not be yoked together with unbelievers.* The verb *heterozygeō* is an agricultural term that refers to the practice of yoking to a plow two unequal kinds of animals such as an ox and a donkey. This would suggest that unequal associations between Christians and non-Christians are what Paul specifically has in mind. Five synonyms are employed to describe the kinds of associations that are forbidden. *Metochē* ("have in common"), found nowhere else in the Greek Bible, and *koinōnia* ("fellowship") mean to partner or share. *Symphōnēsis* ("harmony") signifies to be in agreement with or of one accord. *Meris* ("in common") denotes a shared lot or portion. *Synkatathesis* ("agreement") is commonly used of a decision arrived at by a group. Paul is clearly thinking of associations that involve a partnership rather than a casual or occasional working relationship.

The specific kinds of partnerships are left unnamed. A principle is merely articulated and understanding of its application assumed (compare Jas 1:27, "to keep oneself from being polluted by the world"). This

---

6:15 Use of a rhetorical question to drive a point home is common in both Hellenistic moral philosophy and Jewish literature. Sirach 13, which cautions against associations with the proud and the rich, is an excellent example: "Can the clay pot associate with the iron kettle? . . . What does a wolf have in common with a lamb? What peace is there between a hyena and a dog?"

may be because Paul dealt with specific instances in 1 Corinthians, so that the Corinthians understand quite well what kinds of partnerships are in view. For example, he had reprimanded them for allowing their legal disputes with one another to be arbitrated by the secular courts ("in front of unbelievers," 6:1-6). He had admonished them for participating with pagans in their cultic meals (10:6-22). And he had rebuked them for approving of sexual unions with prostitutes (6:12-20) and for taking pride in the sexual liaison between a Christian and his stepmother (5:1-13).

So it is unequal partnerships believers form with secular society (= *unbelievers*) that are of concern to Paul. Does this mean that it is not legitimate for the church to be active in society and its structures? Paul addresses this question by means of a series of five rhetorical questions that highlight recognized spheres of incompatibility between Christianity and the secular world. Each is introduced with the relative pronoun *tis* (what), each considers the partnership of acknowledged opposites (such as light and dark), and each expects the answer "No way."

The first two questions consider the partnership of moral opposites: *What do righteousness and wickedness have in common? Or what fellowship can light have with darkness?* (v. 14). The believer and the unbeliever are driven by a different set of values, the one characterized by righteousness *(dikaiosynē),* the other by lawlessness *(anomia).* There are no shared values because the one follows God's will and the other does not. So there can be no real partnership between them.

Light and *darkness* as descriptive of the way of the righteous and the wicked, respectively, are common imagery in the wisdom literature of the Old Testament (for example, "The path of the righteous is like the first gleam of dawn, shining ever brighter till the full light of day. But the way of the wicked is like deep darkness; they do not know what makes them stumble," Prov 4:18-19). In Paul's writings, light is christological in orientation. The lot of all is darkness until God shines the

Besides *Beliar,* the spellings *Belial* (a few Latin mss), *Belian* (D K) and *Beliab* (F G) can be found in the manuscripts and versions. The range of variants shows that there was considerable uncertainty about the last consonant. Without question the best-attested variant is *Beliar* (p[46] א B C P and some Latin manuscripts).

light of the glorious gospel about Christ in our hearts (4:4, 6). This light makes ethical demands on its recipients in the form of fruit that is "good and right and true" (Eph 5:9; Hahn 1976:494-95).

The second set of questions considers the partnership of personal opposites: *What harmony is there between Christ and Belial? What does a believer have in common with an unbeliever?* (v. 15). It is widely thought that *Belial* (Greek = *Beliar*) comes from the Hebrew term *b⁽e⁾liyya'al,* meaning "worthless, good-for-nothing" (Brown, Driver and Briggs 1953). Belial as a name for the devil is found only here in the New Testament. Paul usually refers to the Christian's archenemy as "Satan" (Rom 16:20; 1 Cor 5:5; 7:5; 2 Cor 2:11; 11:14; 12:7; 1 Thess 2:18; 2 Thess 2:9; 1 Tim 1:20; 5:15). In the Old Testament *b⁽e⁾liyya'al* also designates the realm of the powers of chaos and so comes to mean destruction, wickedness and ruin (as in Deut 13:13[14]; Judg 19:22; 20:13; 1 Sam 1:16; Ps 18:4[5]; 41:8[9]; 101:3; Prov 16:27; 19:28; Nahum 1:11[2:1]; Kaiser 1980:111). In the Qumran Scrolls *b⁽e⁾liyya'al* is the name of the highest angel of darkness and the enemy of the prince of light (Cairo *Damascus Document* 5:18), while in other Jewish materials Belial is the absolute enemy of God and chief of demons (as in *Testament of the Twelve Patriarchs; Jubilees* 1:20; *The Lives of the Prophets* 4:6, 20; 17:2; *Sibylline Oracles* 2.167; 3.64-74; *Ascension of Isaiah* 3-4; Böcher 1990:212). It is because the unbeliever's mind has been blinded by the devil to the truths of the gospel (4:4) that the believer and unbeliever hold nothing in common.

Paul's final rhetorical question considers the partnership of religious opposites, which goes to the heart of the problem at Corinth: *What agreement is there between the temple of God and idols?* (v. 16; compare Ex 20:2-6). Turning from idols to serve the living God was a regular part of the message Paul preached to Gentiles (1 Thess 1:9-10; compare Acts 17:22-31). Corinth was home to two renowned temples, the temple of Aphrodite (the goddess of love, fertility and beauty) situated on the Acrocorinth, an 1,886-foot-high fortified mountain, and the sanctuary of Asclepius (god of healing; see the introduction). The pagan temples, which were under the patronage of a particular god or goddess, were a focal point of social activity. Invitations along the lines of "So and so invites you to dine at the temple of Serapis" were a regular social possibility for those living in a city like Corinth.

To be sure, an idol is nothing in the world, and there indeed is no God but one (1 Cor 8:4). Yet to continue to be involved in the pagan cults is to suggest that an idol is in fact something, and to participate in cultic meals and temple worship is to seriously call into question one's loyalty to God. While the meat that has been sacrificed to an idol is itself indifferent, participation in the cultic meal is not. Such participation not only gives credibility to the idol but also forges a union with the patron god or goddess. Christian involvement leads others to think that there must be something to this after all. Moreover, while the idol itself may be nothing, there is a power behind the idol that is not to be overlooked. This is why Paul equates participation in cultic meals with becoming partners with demons (1 Cor 10:14-22).

To the extent that the structures of society espouse ethical *(wickedness, darkness)* or religious *(Belial, unbeliever, idols)* values and commitments that are diametrically opposed to those of Christianity, believers are forbidden to forge any partnerships with these structures. William Willimon, professor of Christian ministry at Duke University and a lifelong advocate of the public school system in the United States, recently withdrew his support because curricular materials reflect values that are in direct opposition to the Christian values on which the public school system was originally founded. Willimon is now of the opinion that this is a partnership in which most Christians should not be involved (1993:30-32).

Why so? For Paul, it is because the church is *the temple of the living God,* or, better, the "sanctuary" *(naos)*—the most sacred part of the temple structure (v. 16). Paul's choice of words is significant. *The temple of the living God* does not refer to a building. From the days of Solomon to the time of Christ, the temple was indeed a physical structure where God made his presence known to Israel. But with Christ's coming, God's temple became the people gathered in Christ's name. The first-person pronoun is placed at the head of the clause for emphasis—*We are the temple of the living God* (v. 16). This is a theological point not sufficiently grasped within Christendom today, where expressions like "going to church," "the church building" and "entering the house of God" lead insider and outsider alike to think of the church as a physical structure rather than as people.

To be *the temple of the living God* is to belong exclusively to God and to forsake all associations that would be incompatible with God's ownership. To drive home this point, Paul cites no fewer than six Old Testament passages that spell out what it means to be God's possession. In each case a text that deals with God's covenantal relationship with Israel is reapplied to the church (vv. 16-18). Phrases from each passage are woven together in an almost unprecedented way, recalling the testimonia collections of the early church.

The first, *I will live with them,* most likely comes from Leviticus 26:11 ("I will put my dwelling place among you"), but Ezekiel 37:27 is also a possibility ("my dwelling place will be with them"). The verb translated *live with (enoikeō)* means to "inhabit" or "be at home." The notion is active rather than passive. To be at home is to exercise one's rights as the proprietor of the house. So for God to inhabit his church is for him to establish his rule there. The next clause, *and walk among them,* is taken from Leviticus 26:12, with the minor modification of changing the pronoun from second to third person. To *walk among* is actually to "walk in and around" (*en* [in] + *peri* [around] + *pateō* [walk]). God does not merely exercise his rights as proprietor but moves with familiarity from one room in the house to the next.

The third quotation, *I will be their God and they will be my people,* is a recurring promise of Yahweh to Israel in the Old Testament. The first occurrence is in Leviticus 26:12, the most probable source of Paul's quote—although its appearance in the familiar texts of Jeremiah 31:33, 32:38 and Ezekiel 37:27 is also to be noted. The imagery shifts at this point from dwellings to treaties. The language is that of a sovereign to a vassal. In fact, in the immediately preceding verse, the LXX has "I will

---

6:16 Other examples of testimonia in Paul's letters include Romans 3:10-18; 9:25-29; 10:15-21; 11:8-10, 26-27, 34-35; 15:9-12—although none of these provides an exact parallel to 2 Corinthians 6:16-18. It is quite possible that Paul is using a preformed text that he adapted to his own use.

The verb *enoikeō* ("to inhabit," "to dwell in," "to be at home") is used of God (2 Cor 6:16), the Holy Spirit (Rom 8:11; 2 Tim 1:14), the word of Christ (Col 3:16), faith (2 Tim 1:5) and sin (Rom 7:17).

Codex Vaticanus and Codex Alexandrinus have *thēsō tēn diathēkēn mou* ("I will make my covenant") instead of *miškanî* ("my dwelling") in Leviticus 26:11.

put my covenant among you" (compare the Masoretic Text, "I will put my dwelling place among you"). Under the terms of the treaty that bound king and vassal together, the king agreed to protect the vassal, and the vassal promised sole allegiance and obedience. This is why worship of God and worship of idols are fundamentally incompatible. And while we no longer relate to God as vassals to a sovereign, the essential principle of exclusive possession underlying the Mosaic covenant still holds true (3:14).

Therefore, at the head of verse 17, introduces the practical implications of verses 14-16. The pledge of the sovereign's presence and protection also carried with it certain moral mandates for the vassal. The mandate for Israel was that they were to *come out from them and be separate. . . . Touch no unclean thing.* Paul quotes this time from Isaiah 52:11, changing the order of the commands and adding the phrase *says the Lord.* In Isaiah 52:8-12 the Israelites are warned as they leave Babylon that they are not to take any material goods acquired in exile back with them; and those who carry the sacred temple vessels, which had been carefully preserved in exile, are first to purify themselves. The concern is that Israel cut all ties with the idolatries, practices and impurities of their pagan captors. The same is true for the church. God always demands holy living from his people. Since he takes up lodging among us, we in turn are called to separate ourselves from everything incompatible with his holiness (Bruce 1971:215). The verbs are aorist imperatives *(exelthate, aphoristhēte).* Immediate and decisive separation is the appropriate course of action (Plummer 1915:209).

If the Corinthians do this, the pledge is that God *will receive* them and *be a father to* them. They, in turn, will be *sons and daughters* (vv. 17-18). *I will receive you* is probably drawn from Ezekiel 20:34 ("I will

---

6:17 Many of the Old Testament purity laws were attempts to keep Israel from becoming entangled in pagan religious practices. For example, ritual cleansing from contact with a dead body was intended to distance Israel from pagan cults of the dead (Num 19). Foreign territory was regarded as unclean since foreign gods were worshiped there (Amos 7:17). Even many of the regulations regarding clean and unclean animals were intended to guard Israel from the animal-worship practices of its neighbors (Lev 11).

6:18 The promise to David regarding his "son" is applied in the New Testament both to the Messiah (Heb 1:5) and to the messianic community (2 Cor 6:18). Second Samuel 7:14 is also cited in Revelation 21:7 as a promise to those in the last days who persevere in living holy lives.

receive you from the countries where you had been scattered," LXX). The second part of the pledge is taken from 2 Samuel 7:14 (2 Kingdoms 7:14): "I will be his father, and he will be my son." Paul sees God's promise to David that he will be a father to Solomon and Solomon will be a son to him fulfilled yet again in God's relationship to the church. The singular *son* is changed to the plural *sons,* and the phrase *and daughters* is added, probably under the influence of Isaiah 43:6 ("Bring my sons from afar and my daughters from the ends of the earth"). There are to be a family likeness and family affection between God and his people (Plummer 1915:210).

The entire string of Old Testament quotations concludes with the phrase *says the Lord Almighty.* The phrase is a familiar one in the LXX. The term *pantokratōr,* which translates the Hebrew *ṣᵉḇāʾōṯ,* is commonly rendered "almighty" but actually means "master" or "ruler of all" (Liddell, Scott and Jones 1978). With this phrase Paul emphasizes the awesome truth that it is the One who rules over all who chooses to dwell among us and be our Father.

Paul concludes this block of verses with an exhortation to be pure and holy: *Let us purify ourselves from everything that contaminates body and spirit, perfecting holiness out of reverence for God* (7:1). The language and phraseology are not typically Pauline. It may well be that he is quoting a familiar homily or a well-known ethical injunction. In the sphere of agriculture, *katharizō* ("purify") means to "prune away" or "clear" the ground of weeds—which may not be far off the mark here. The more usual way to construe the verb is to "wash" or "cleanse" of dirt or other filth. Paul's use of the reflexive *heautous* would support this sense ("to cleanse *yourselves*"). The aorist tense suggests a decisive action of cleansing *(katharisōmen).* Cleanliness as next to godliness fits well the religious mentality of Paul's day. Both Greek religion and Judaism placed an emphasis on physical and ritual purity. Within

---

7:1 The hortatory subjunctive (like "let us cleanse ourselves," *katharisōmen heautous*) was a common feature of first-century sermons (compare Rom 5:1; 1 Cor 5:8; 15:32; Gal 5:26; Phil 3:15; 1 Thess 5:6). The anarthrous *pantos* ("everything") stresses "each and every form of" defilement.

Sarx ("flesh") is used here of what is material or physical, as opposed to Paul's distinctive use of this term to denote the sinful nature of the human being (as in Rom 7:18; 13:14; Gal 5:16-17).

□ 2 CORINTHIANS 6:14—7:1

Judaism this mentality was grounded on the presupposition that uncleanness and Yahweh were irreconcilable opposites. The Essenes, in particular, were well known for their rites of purification and daily immersion practices (Link and Schattenmann 1978:104-5).

From what, though, are the Corinthians to cleanse themselves? According to Paul, it is *from everything that contaminates body and spirit. Contaminates* is actually a noun denoting that which stains, defiles or soils *(molysmos).* The noun is found only here in the New Testament, although the verb is used twice in Revelation (3:4; 14:4) and once in 1 Corinthians (8:7) of defiling the conscience through the indiscriminate eating of meat sacrificed to idols (compare 1 Esdras 8:83; Jer 23:15). This brings us back full circle to Paul's opening injunction to stop entering into unequal partnerships with unbelievers (6:14). The close association of *molysmos* with idolatry suggests that Paul is thinking especially of defilement that comes from dining in the local temples, membership in the pagan cults, ritual prostitution, active engagement in pagan worship and the like.

The defilement in view affects *body and spirit.* The Greek text is literally *"flesh* and spirit." Paul could be using popular language to designate the material and immaterial elements of a person (Plummer 1915:211). But the fact that he uses "flesh" and "spirit" interchangeably at 2:13 and 7:5 suggests that he is looking at the human being from two differing perspectives. This fits with Hebraic thinking, which did not compartmentalize the human being but viewed the whole person from different vantage points (such as physical, spiritual, mental).

The positive side of the exhortation is *perfecting holiness out of reverence for God.* The sense is not immediately clear. Is Paul commanding them to become perfect in holiness (Murphy-O'Connor 1991:70)? Or is he enjoining them to advance constantly in holiness (that is, to press on toward the goal; Hughes 1962:258)? The participle *(epitelountes)* may

---

The verb *epiteleō* means to "carry out," "achieve" or "accomplish" something. The prepositional phrase *en phobō theou* defines the circumstances or manner in which the exhortation is to be carried out. The Corinthians are to purify themselves with a view to holiness "in the fear of God." The TEV's "let us be completely holy *by* living in the fear of God" (compare Phillips) and the NIV's *out of reverence for God* (where *en* defines the motivation for holiness) appear off the mark.

well define the result of the action of cleansing *(let us purify ourselves . . . perfecting holiness)*. Looked at this way, holiness becomes a reality as we purify ourselves from physical and spiritual pollutants (Delling 1972:62). Purifying ourselves is to be done *out of reverence for God*—that is, in deference and devotion toward him to whom we owe everything (Hughes 1962:258). That we would strive to live a holy life is a wholly appropriate response to the promises of God's presence (v. 16), his welcome (v. 17) and his fatherhood (v. 18; *since we have these promises)*.

A Second Plea for Affection (7:2) At 7:2 Paul repeats his plea for the Corinthians' affection: *Make room for us in your hearts.* In verses 11-13 he asked the Corinthians to enlarge their hearts. Now he urges them to find room for him. Paul chooses a verb with a wide semantic range *(chōreō)*, playing on the meanings "to make room for another" and "to withdraw." "Withdraw" picks up the command in verse 17 to separate from pagan idolatries and practices. *Make room* recalls his appeal in verse 11 to enlarge their hearts. If they withdraw from idolatrous partnerships with the world, they will have plenty of room in their hearts for Paul.

Paul goes on to point out that there is nothing in his life or ministry that should prove an obstacle to responding to his plea (compare 6:3): *We have wronged . . . corrupted . . . exploited no one.* The trio of verbs is surprising. In light of the ministerial hardships and sufferings he presented earlier, this threefold denial looks somewhat out of place. This appears even more the case with the emphatic position of "no one" *(oudena)* at the head of each denial (*"No one* have we wronged"). All

---

7:2 *Adikeō* and its cognates frequently appear in legal contexts with reference to particular crimes like theft, fraud, incest and so on (Günther 1978:574). In 2 Corinthians *adikeō* is used of the injustice Paul had suffered at the hands of the "offender" (7:12), and *adikia* is employed of the supposed wrong he had committed by not asking the Corinthians for financial support (12:13). *Phtheirō* describes the intent of Paul's rivals to undermine the faith of the Corinthians ("as Eve was deceived by the serpent's cunning"—11:3). *Pleonekteō* is used of Satan's attempts to outwit the church (2:11) and of those who exploit the church to their own advantage (12:17-18). Martin believes that Paul is responding to the charge that he had "overreached" himself, promoting excessive disciplinary measures in the case of the individual who had caused him harm (1986:218).

7:3-16 Four elements appear with almost stereotypical regularity in the body-closing section of the Hellenistic letter: a motive for writing, expressions urging responsibility, a

three verbs were commonly used of wrongful financial activities. The verb *adikeō* denotes wrongful dealings that have the character of foul play about them (such as theft or fraud). *Phtheirō* means to "destroy," "ruin" or "corrupt." It has a wide range of usage, including "to bring about moral ruin," "to bribe," "to seduce a woman" and "to defile a virgin" (Merkel 1975:468). *Pleonekteō* means to "exploit," "take advantage of" or "defraud" and is often used of someone who is greedy and grasping after what others have.

Has Paul been accused of such things? There certainly would seem to be nothing in his life or ministry (6:4-10; 11:21-29)—or in the life and ministry of his coworkers (12:17-18)—to warrant such accusations. Perhaps his rivals at Corinth had been saying that the Jerusalem relief fund was merely a smoke screen for personal funds that he was unwilling to accept overtly (see the introduction).

Paul's defense is simply to insist that the charge is without foundation. The fact that he had often gone without food, adequate clothing and shelter is eloquent testimony in and of itself (11:27). He certainly was entitled to be financially supported by his churches (1 Cor 9:1-14). But he waived such support so as not to hinder the gospel of Christ (1 Cor 9:12).

Joy in the Midst of Distress (7:3-7) "Thank you kindly for looking into this matter," "your help is much appreciated," "hope to see you soon" and similar expressions tend to find their way into the concluding comments of our letters. This was also the practice in Paul's day. Expressions like "by so doing you will confer on me a kindness" (*Tebtunis Papyri* 766,15), "write to me for whatever you want" (*Bremer*

---

request for a letter and notification of a forthcoming visit. Paul's letters pretty much follow suit. But there are a few modifications. The motive for writing is regularly combined with expressions urging responsibility (such as "This is why I write these things when I am absent, that when I come I may not have to be harsh"—2 Cor 13:10). The nature of the relationship is typically spelled out (as in "my dear children . . . in Christ Jesus I became your father"—1 Cor 4:14-15). The routine request for a letter does not appear. But in its place are expressions of confidence (such as *I am glad I can have complete confidence in you*—2 Cor 7:16) or warning ("Examine yourselves to see whether you are in the faith"—2 Cor 13:5). The announcement of a forthcoming visit is expanded to include a desire and hope to see the reader(s), hindrances faced, the dispatching of an emissary, an invocation of divine approval ("if it be God's will") and the benefit (or lack thereof) to both parties (as in "Now I am ready to visit you for the third time," 2 Cor 12:14). See White 1972:93-99.

Papyri 52,9) and "I will try to come to you soon" (*Oxyrynchus Papyri* 1763,91f) were common fare in the first-century Greek letter. While we tend to include such phrases as a polite way of drawing matters to a close, the first-century letter writer chose his phrases and crafted his closing remarks with marked intentionality.

Paul in 2 Corinthians is no exception. *I do not say this to condemn you* at 7:3 signals the transition to a block commonly referred to in epistolary parlance as the body-closing section. In the Hellenistic letter this section functioned to underscore the reason(s) for writing (for example, "I have written to let you know," *Les Papyrus Grecs du Musée du Louvre* 43) and to further good relations with the reader(s). Often the latter was done by acknowledging the benefit to both parties concerned ("It is well for him to come quickly, for he will instruct you," *Oxyrhynchus Papyri* 743,⁴1f) and by expressing confidence in the readers' ability to do the right thing. Sometimes, however, a threat or warning was needed ("Take care that I do not come to quarrel with you," *Tebtunis Papyri* 759,9ff).

Paul's letters follow suit. Expressions of confidence appear with conspicuous regularity (e.g., "confident of your obedience," Philem 21). An aura of goodwill and family feeling generally prevails (e.g., "What is our hope, our joy, or the crown in which we will glory? . . . Is it not you?" 1 Thess 2:19)—unless the relationship has reached the point where only a threat will work (e.g., "Shall I come to you with a whip, or in love and with a gentle spirit?" 1 Cor 4:21).

Second Corinthians 7:3-16 is very representative of the Pauline closing section. This is Paul's final attempt in these chapters to get his readers to accept the legitimacy of his ministry and open their hearts to him. The tone is conciliatory and confident. His intent in writing is not to condemn them but to help them see that they are in his heart to live or die (v. 3). Expressions of joy and benefit predominate: the verb *chairō* ("I rejoice"; "I am glad") and the noun *chara* (joy) occur six times (vv.

7:3 The word order in this verse is curious. The RSV brings this out better than the NIV: "You are in our hearts, to die together and to live together." Why is it that Paul mentions death before life? Some speculate that the deadly peril he had recently faced made physical death a likely prospect for him. Others take it as a reference to being united in dying to sin but living for Christ. Still others suppose Paul is thinking of our union with Christ in

4, 7, 9, 13 [twice], 16), while the terms *comforted, encouraged* and *refreshed* appear eight times in all (vv. 4, 6, 7, 13). The Corinthians' obedient response to the severe letter is recalled (vv. 8-13), and mention is made of how it encouraged Paul in the midst of trials (vv. 5-7, 13). Confidence phraseology pervades: *I have great confidence in you* (v. 4), "I am glad that I can have complete confidence in you" (v. 16). Family feeling is evident throughout: *You have such a place in our hearts* (v. 3), *I take great pride in you* (v. 4), "I boasted to Titus about you" (v. 14).

Paul begins by reassuring the Corinthians that his purpose in writing is not condemnation. He abandons the first-person plural that he has used since 2:14 and takes up the first-person singular: *I do not say this to condemn you*. The Greek word for "condemnation" *(katakrisis)* is a rare one, occurring only here and in 2 Corinthians 3:9 in the Greek Bible. It means to bring a verdict of guilty or to pass sentence against someone. Paul has defended himself at length and made some strong denials throughout chapters 1—7 (as in 7:2: "we have wronged . . . corrupted . . . exploited no one"). In retrospect, he is aware that what he wrote could easily have sounded as if he was blaming and passing judgment on them. So he is concerned that they not misunderstand his intentions. Indeed, there can be no room for condemnation because of the secure place that the Corinthians have in his affections. What he *said before* he now says again: *You have such a place in our hearts that we would live or die with you*. When did Paul say this? No such statement can be found earlier in the letter, so it is likely that he expressed himself in this fashion either on his second visit (compare *proeirēka*, 13:2) or in a recent communication to them (perhaps in the severe letter).

The fact that he has to repeat himself shows that the depth of his commitment to them has not really sunk in (*I have said before*, v. 3). The place the Corinthians have in his heart is such that Paul can say, "Come death, come life, we meet it together" (NEB). His affirmation is a strong one and not unlike the wedding vows that couples have

---

death and resurrection. Paul, however, may merely be putting the more difficult commitment first by way of emphasis. The same thing is done in Romans 8:38-39: "I am convinced that neither death nor life . . . will be able to separate us from the love of God that is in Christ Jesus our Lord."

traditionally made to one another: "For better or for worse, for richer, for poorer, in sickness and in health, to love and to cherish, till death us do part" (Book of Common Prayer).

But Paul's commitment goes beyond this. The order of the words is significant. To *live or die with you* is actually the reverse: "to die with you and to live with you" *(eis to synapothanein kai syzēn)*. Paul puts the more difficult commitment first. His union with the Corinthians is not dissolved at death, as wedding vows are. Come what may, their destinies are inextricably linked both in this life and beyond. Paul expresses himself in the classical formula of his day for abiding friendship and loyalty. It is a pledge that is also found in the Old Testament. Ittai the Gittite's reply to David is nearly identical: "Wherever my lord the king may be, whether it means life or death, there will your servant be" (2 Sam 15:21). Nor is Paul alone in making this pledge. The first plural *we* indicates that his colleagues share in it as well.

Paul goes on to say that he has *great confidence* in them (v. 4). The range of meaning for *parrēsia* includes "confidence," "frankness," "boldness," "openness" and "public." Although sometimes translated as "frankness" ("I talk to you with utter frankness," Phillips; compare NEB), this overlooks the role that expressions of *confidence* regularly play in Paul's closing sections. The language is that of the optimist who finds an opportunity in every difficulty rather than a difficulty in every opportunity. Yet Paul's is not a blind confidence. The news Titus brought back from his visit to Corinth was that the church was duly repentant for not supporting him. The believers there had seen the error of their ways and punished the individual who had publicly humiliated him on his last visit. So Paul has every reason to be confident that they will take the next step and give him their complete support in the larger matters that he is now calling to their attention.

It is his confidence in the Corinthians that leads him also to *take great*

7:4 In the democracy of the Athenian free state, *parrēsia* originally referred to the right to say *(rhēma)* everything *(pan;* see the commentary and note on 3:12).

7:5 To say that Paul at 7:5 resumes the travelogue he had abandoned at 2:13 is not to suggest that 2:14—7:4 is a digression. There is nothing that connects 7:5 to 2:13 apart from the travelogue. On the other hand, there is much that connects it to what immediately precedes. Indeed, *kai gar* (for even) introduces the reason Paul can be encouraged and joyful in the face of affliction.

pride in them (v. 4). The notion is an active one. The text is literally "I do a lot of boasting on your behalf." Paul assumes the role of the father who not only takes pride in the accomplishments of his children but also actively boasts about them to anyone who will lend a willing ear. Is this a momentary euphoria stemming from Titus's good report? Not at all. Paul had boasted to Titus even prior to his Corinthian visit (v. 14). Nor has he suddenly become blind to the many failings of the Corinthians, as is the wont of parents when speaking about their children. But just as a parent will encourage a strong-willed child by praising her when she is obedient, so Paul encourages the independent-minded Corinthians by boasting about them when he can. Not only are the Corinthians a cause for pride, but they are also a source of encouragement. *I am greatly encouraged; in all our troubles my joy knows no bounds* (v. 4; compare the Cotton Patch Version: "I am bubbling over with joy").

At this point Paul resumes the travelogue that he had abandoned at 2:13. He had left a promising evangelistic field in Troas and gone to Macedonia in the hopes of meeting up with Titus and hearing news of the Corinthians' response to his severe letter (see the commentary on 2:12-13). But when he *came into Macedonia,* he was, instead, *harassed at every turn.* The Greek verb *thlibō* (v. 5) and noun *thipsis* (v. 5) are terms that frequently turn up in this letter (verb three times; noun eight times). *Thlibō* (and its cognates) means to put pressure on something or someone and so afflict, oppress or harass.

Paul does not provide any details about the harassment he encountered. The most he says is that it took the form of *conflicts on the outside* and *fears within.* The conflicts without are undoubtedly some kind of persecution or opposition. We know from Acts that Paul was pursued from city to city by a group of hostile, unbelieving Jews who stirred up trouble for him wherever he went. The term *conflict (machē* and its

Paul's use of the genitive absolute at verse 5 is to be noted (*elthontōn hēmōn,* "when we came"). The construction is somewhat rare in his writings. See Turner 1976:99.

If a distinction is to be drawn between "I had no relief in *my spirit*" (*ouk eschēka anesin tō pneumati mou,* 2:13) and *"our flesh* had no relief" (*oudēmian eschēken anesin hē sarx hēmōn,* 7:5), the former refers to mental anxiety and the latter to bodily fatigue. The two, however, often go hand in hand.

cognates) is frequently used in Hellenistic Greek for military combat or sporting contests (Bauernfeind 1967:527-28). Whether Paul's choice of words points to physical threats of some kind is not clear. In the Septuagint the literal sense predominates. But in the New Testament *machē* also is used figuratively of quarrels and fighting, and this could easily be what Paul intends here (2 Tim 2:23; Tit 3:9; Jas 4:1).

Paul also experienced *fears within*. Concern for Titus was certainly one of these fears. Has he been waylaid on the road by robbers? Did something happen at Corinth to delay him? These are some of the questions that must have been running through Paul's mind. The plural *fears* indicates that Paul faced more than one worry. Fear related to the opposition he encountered in Macedonia, which Titus's eventual arrival did not relieve, may well have been part of the picture (v. 4, *in all our troubles*). But what form did this fear take? Concern for his own safety does not square with Luke's picture of the apostle (as in Acts 20:22-24; 21:10-14). Fear about the safety of the Macedonian churches is more likely (see Acts 16—18). In fact, if Paul was in Thessalonica, much would be explained. The church there faced intense opposition on more than one occasion (Acts 17:1-9; 1 Thess 1:6-8; 2:2, 14; 3:1-5; 2 Thess 1:4)—so much so that Paul at one point was fearful his evangelistic labors there had been in vain (1 Thess 3:1-5). Then too, fear for the church at Philippi is a possibility. In his letter to the Philippians he tells them to "watch out for the dogs," those "mutilators of the flesh" and "workers of evil" (3:2) who are "enemies of the cross" (3:18).

The trouble that Paul faced in the province of Macedonia was such that his body *had no rest* (v. 5). The NIV's *body* is actually the word "flesh." But Paul is quite capable of using *body (sōma)* and "flesh" *(sarx)* interchangeably (as in 2 Cor 7:1; Gal 4:13-14; Eph 5:29; 1 Tim 3:16).

7:6 *Parekalesen* is better translated "encouraged" (TEV), not "comforted" (NIV). Paul was not sorrowing and in need of comfort but discouraged and in need of encouragement. *Tapeinos (downcast)*, though commonly translated "humble," can refer to position in society (that is, "poor," "powerless," "of no account"), to emotional states ("depressed," "downhearted," "downcast") and to attitudes ("subservient," "humble").

It is a curious fact that Luke does not mention Titus in his Acts of the Apostles. Barrett speculates on the reasons for this (1969:1-14). What information we have comes from Paul's incidental comments and the letter addressed to him.

"Flesh" is the physical side of things as impacted by external circumstances and inward state of mind. *Had no rest* is probably another way of saying that he was physically spent from worrying. Then too, he had no chance for respite *(anesis)*, because when he came to Macedonia he faced opposition at every turn (v. 5). The Greek word *anesis* refers not so much to *rest* (NIV, KJV, NKJV, RSV, NRSV) as to "relief" (REB, NEB) or relaxation.

While Paul did not experience respite, with Titus's arrival he did receive encouragement: *But God, who comforts the downcast, comforted us by the coming of Titus* (v. 6). With this statement we come full circle in chapters 1—7. Paul opened on a note of praise to the Father of compassion and the God of all comfort (1:3). Now we see exactly how the Lord comforted him. *Downcast* translates a Greek term that means "low" *(tapeinos)*. Paul had reached a low for which only divine comfort could suffice.

Three sources of comfort are specified. The first was *the coming of Titus* (v. 6). *Parousia (coming)* is commonly used of the advent of a notable personage, like a king or an emperor. One can almost hear the sound of trumpets heralding Titus's arrival, so palpable was Paul's relief. Nor was this an isolated case of anxiety for a colleague's mission. Paul had been similarly encouraged six years earlier when Timothy arrived with good news of the Thessalonican church's steadfastness in the face of intense persecution (1 Thess 3:6-7).

Paul's second source of comfort was news of the church's positive reception of Titus and the encouragement they had given him (v. 7). Precisely how they encouraged him Paul does not say. Part of it surely was the fact that they responded in obedience both to Paul's letter (v. 9) and to Titus himself (v. 15). Yet their response went beyond obedience. They also ministered to Titus. "His spirit," Paul tells the

7:7 *Eph' hymin* can mean "over you" (that is, Titus was encouraged about the Corinthians), "in you" (that is, Titus was encouraged by their change of attitude) or "by you" (that is, Titus received encouragement from the Corinthians). The last option seems the best. In verse 13 Paul recalls that the Corinthians not only obeyed Titus but also "refreshed his spirit."

Me mallon charēnai can mean "I became happy instead [of sorrowful]," "I also became joyful [rather than merely encouraged]," or, as seems likely, "I rejoiced still more." For *mallon* with the sense "still more," see Blass, Debrunner and Funk 1961:§§244.2. Titus's return brought joy (v. 7), but the good news about Corinth caused it to bubble over (v. 13).

Corinthians, "has been refreshed by all of you" (v. 13).

News of the Corinthians' Obedience (7:8-11) Confrontation is not easy for any of us. We tend to shrink from it or rationalize away its necessity. Paul, however, confronted the Corinthians directly, despite how much he stood to lose. He did it because he valued his relationship with the church more than his own reputation. Most of us would seek redress for a wrong done to us. This is especially the case where our rightful authority has been challenged and our reputation defamed. The stakes were even higher for Paul because it was his apostolic authority that was being attacked and his reputation as Christ's ambassador that was on the line. Yet his primary concern throughout is his relationship to the congregation. All else is secondary—even the injustice and public humiliation that he had suffered.

Paul's third and final source of comfort was Titus's report of the Corinthians' response to the severe letter. It is this piece of news that caused Paul to "nearly burst with joy" (Cotton Patch, v. 7). The Corinthians had reacted to his rebuke with a *godly sorrow,* just *as God intended* (vv. 9-10). Paul's letter had been written in the wake of a painful visit to Corinth. While there, someone publicly insulted him and demanded that he give proof of his apostleship (13:3, "proof that Christ is speaking through me"). What was particularly hurtful for Paul was that the church sat by and did nothing to support him. After issuing a strong word of warning (13:2), he returned to Ephesus and, instead of a promised return visit, wrote a letter in which he rebuked the church for not coming to his aid (7:8-12), demanded that the individual who had challenged his authority be punished (2:5-11) and expressed deep sorrow over the church's lack of support (2:3; 7:12-13).

The Corinthians' initial response had been distress: *I see that my letter hurt you* (v. 8). The Greek verb *lypeō* (hurt) means to cause pain or distress. This had not been Paul's intention. He had written not to grieve

---

7:8 *Pros hōran* is literally "for an hour" but can designate shorter ("for a moment," Gal 2:5) or longer ("for a little while," Philem 15) time spans.

7:9 *Hina* could define result *(and so were not harmed in any way)* or purpose ("in order that you might suffer loss in nothing," NKJV). The former provides the better

the church but to let them know the depth of his love (2:4). It had also caused Paul a great deal of pain to write such a letter. "I wrote," he says, "out of great distress and anguish of heart with many tears" (2:4).

Paul's initial reaction to Titus's news was *regret* for having caused such pain. The tense is imperfect. His was not a momentary pang of remorse but a time of sustained unhappiness over the affair. Many are the occasions when parents struggle over how severely a child should be punished. God repeatedly faced this challenge with Israel. In Hosea 11:8-9 he is pictured pacing the floor, anguishing over the need to discipline a wayward child: "How can I give you up, Ephraim? How can I hand you over, Israel?" This is what is commonly referred to as "tough love," a love that dares to discipline, dares to weep over the pain inflicted and dares to rejoice at the prospect of reconciliation and a better future secured for one's child. Paul went through this struggle in writing his severe letter to the Corinthians (2:4). And now when he is told of the grief that it caused the church, his first response is regret.

On reflection, however, Paul's regret changes to gladness. *Though I did regret it,* he says, *yet now I am happy* (vv. 8-9). Is this not a strange turnabout? What exactly led to his change of heart? Four things are specified. First, the Corinthians' sorrow lasted *only for a little while* (v. 8). They were not pained for any extended period of time, and so no permanent damage to the relationship occurred.

Second, God's hand was evident in the church's response. They had become *sorrowful as God intended* (v. 9). The phrase is literally "grieved according to God" *(elypēthēte kata theon)*. But what does this mean? Renderings include "sadness . . . used by God" (TEV), "suffering that God approves" (JB), "made sorry after a godly manner" (KJV, NKJV) and "as God would have had you sorry" (Phillips). The NASB's "made sorrowful according to the will of God" or the NIV's *became sorrowful as God intended* is probably the sense here.

The kind of sorrow that God intends results in a change of heart: *Your sorrow led you to repentance* (v. 9). This is the third reason Paul

---

sequence. Paul would be saying that if sorrow is of a godly sort no harm will come of it.

Metanoia (repentance) is a rare word group in Paul's writings. The noun is found four times (Rom 2:4; 2 Cor 7:9, 10; 2 Tim 2:25) and the verb only once (2 Cor 12:21). Two of five uses of the noun appear in this chapter.

can be happy. The Corinthians did not merely regret what they had done but repented of it (v. 9). *Metanoia (repentance)* denotes not just a change of mind about something but a reorientation of the whole person (Goetzmann 1975:357-58). Judas felt remorse for what he had done in betraying Jesus to the authorities (*metameletheis*, Mt 27:3), but his remorse did not issue in repentance. Repentance, to be sure, involves a recognition that a wrong has been committed. The Corinthians, when confronted with their failure to defend Paul in the face of his detractors, felt sorry for the pain they had caused him. This is remorse. But repentance goes further. It not only recognizes the wrong committed but also seeks to rectify it. This the Corinthians did by admitting their blame and by punishing the offender (2:6; 7:11).

The fourth and final reason Paul can be happy is that the church was *not harmed in any way* by the severity of his letter (v. 9). What kind of harm is in view? In the world of commerce the Greek verb *zemioomai* referred to loss or damage in money or material goods due to unfavorable conditions or circumstances (such as the loss in goods and lives caused by a storm at sea; Stumpff 1964b:888). The implication is that discipline can cause spiritual havoc or injury if not administered or received in the right way. This was Paul's concern for the offender whom the Corinthians continued to discipline even after he repented. Had the discipline continued, the man stood in danger of being overwhelmed by excessive sorrow (2:7).

To their credit, the Corinthians responded to the severe letter in the way God intended. Paul spells out what this way is in verse 10. It is only natural to experience pain and feel hurt when someone rebukes us for a perceived wrongdoing. And while we feel pain, it is what we do with our pain that counts. The Corinthians, despite their other failings, responded in a very mature fashion to Paul's rebuke. To be sure, they were hurt by what Paul said in his letter to them. But they did not allow their hurt to deepen into bitterness and resentment. Instead, they were able to get past their hurt to see that the rebuke rang true and that they needed to change their ways (v. 9). This is *godly sorrow*—one that recognizes the wrong committed and then does everything within its power to repair the damage. Simply put, godly sorrow is constructive.

Two people are chatting over coffee. In reaching for the sugar, one of them accidentally knocks her cup in the other's lap. A typical reaction would be "Look at the mess I've made. I'm so sorry." This is the voice of regret. A certain kind of person will continue to berate herself for her clumsiness. But constructive sorrow is different from either. It says: "Here are some napkins. I'll get the table cleaned up. And please let me pay the cleaning bill."

Constructive sorrow is the kind of sorrow that *leads to salvation and leaves no regret* (v. 10). Paul might not be thinking of salvation in the theological sense (that is, eternal life). The term *sōtēria* can also mean "self-preservation" or "well-being." Sorrow that turns outward to redress the wrong done leads to personal wholeness. *Worldly sorrow,* on the other hand, *brings death. Worldly sorrow* is that which turns in on itself and feeds off its ever deepening self-pity. It brings death because it breeds self-destructive resentment and bitterness that eat away at the person (Murphy-O'Connor 1991:71). It is said that a rattlesnake, if cornered, will sometimes become so upset that it will bite itself. That is exactly what the harboring of hate and resentment against others is—a biting of oneself. We think that we are harming others by holding these grudges and hates, but the deeper harm is to ourselves. This is a sorrow that will overwhelm and consume us in the end.

In the Corinthians we have an excellent model of godly sorrow that produces repentance and corporate well-being. Judging from the eight descriptive nouns found in verses 7 and 11, Titus must have given Paul a blow-by-blow account of the church's reaction to his letter. Their initial response was *alarm* (literally, "fear" *[phobos]*). Alarm at what? It could be that they feared divine reprisals for rejecting God's representative (see Héring 1967:55; Plummer 1915:223; Tasker 1958:106). It is also possible that they stood in dread of the discipline Paul would exercise when he came (Hughes 1962:274). The likeliest explanation, though, is that they were simply caught off guard. The voice of alarm says, "I had no idea. Is Paul all right?" They obviously had not taken seriously what had transpired between Paul and the offending individual, and they never guessed how deeply he had been affected by the whole ordeal.

The Corinthians moved then from alarm to *indignation. Aganaktēsis,* found only here in the New Testament, refers to deep vexation or profound displeasure. At what or whom were they vexed? The offender

2 CORINTHIANS 7:8-11 ☐ _____

and the rival missionaries (who quite likely egged the wrongdoer on) come immediately to mind. But it may well be that their indignation was aimed first at themselves. It would have been quite natural for them to turn in anger to one another and ask, "Who let this happen? Who is responsible?"

Then came the regret. "Titus told us of your deep sorrow," Paul says (see v. 7). *Odyrmos* commonly denotes wailing and lamentation, often accompanied by tears and other outward expressions of grief (Hauck 1967:116). In the New Testament it is found only here and in Matthew 2:18, where it is used of Rachel's weeping for her children and refusing to be consoled. It is, to be sure, a stronger word than the one Paul used to describe his own remorse at having to write such a severe letter (v. 8). What were the Corinthians lamenting? While they might have lamented the fact that Paul thought it best not to pay them a return visit (Barrett 1973:208), it is more likely that *odyrmos* depicts the deep sorrow and remorse they felt at having caused Paul such pain.

Once the Corinthians got past their initial shock over what had taken place, they reached out to Paul, *longing* to see him and assure him of their support (vv. 7, 11). *Epipothēsis* means a yearning for and desire in a good sense (Schönweiss 1975:458). They also hurried to clear themselves of blame. What *eagerness* Paul recounts. The word *spoudē* refers to the zealous pursuit of something. They must have made Titus promise that he would assure Paul of their noncomplicity in the whole affair: "Tell Paul we had nothing to do with this."

But while they had not taken the man's side against Paul, they had done nothing to support Paul either. So something more than earnest denials of complicity was needed. This led them to attempt to *clear* themselves. The term *apologia,* from which our word "apology" comes, is commonly used of a reasoned statement in defense of something or someone (Furnish 1984:388). The Corinthians' self-defense was apparently quite convincing, for Paul could say, *At every point you have proved yourselves to be innocent in this matter* (7:11).

The church also moved quickly to rectify the wrong that had been done by punishing the offender (*to see justice done,* v. 11). The language is judicial. *Ekdikēsis* can mean either to take revenge (KJV, NASB) or to punish (TEV, RSV, NRSV, Phillips). There is no hint in

198 _____

the broader context that the Corinthians sought to avenge themselves against the guilty party—although this might have been a natural reaction. Their concern was rather to see a wrong righted. *Readiness* (or perhaps "eagerness") *to see justice done* nicely captures the sense (NIV, JB, NEB, REB). Paul's choice of terms points to some kind of formal disciplinary action decided on and carried out by the congregation (see 2:6). Excommunication or at least the withholding of church privileges is indicated by the potential impact on the individual ("overwhelmed by excessive sorrow," 2:7).

The Corinthians set about their disciplinary task with great fervor (vv. 7, 11). The NIV *concern* is weak. *Zēlos* denotes "zeal." But zeal for what? Three possibilities readily come to mind. Paul could be thinking of the church's eagerness to discipline the offending party (Bruce 1971:218). Or he could have in view the Corinthians' zealous support in the face of his detractors (Martin 1986:235). He could even be referring to their enthusiasm in carrying out his instructions (Furnish 1984:395). Most likely all three are part of the overall picture. The apathy that they exhibited on Paul's last visit took an about-face. Now they are eager to demonstrate their support—or at least the majority are eager (2:6).

But as was their wont, the Corinthians went overboard to such an extent that Paul had to restrain their fervor (see the commentary on 2:6). All this proved to Paul that the Corinthians *at every point* were *innocent in this matter* (v. 11). *Hagnos* ("pure," "chaste," "holy") plus *einai* ("to be") carries the sense of legal blamelessness. The Corinthians' overall response was sufficient to clear themselves of blame (NEB) and prove themselves guiltless (RSV) with respect to the whole unfortunate affair.

Why does Paul recount the Corinthians' response to his letter at such length? Surely a statement acknowledging their obedience and expressing gratitude for their support—even if a bit late—would have sufficed. But Paul's relational skills are at work here. The Corinthians far exceeded his expectations. And so like a pleased parent he pulls out all the stops and basks in their affection and loyalty: *your longing for me, your deep sorrow, your ardent concern* (v. 7) and *what earnestness, what eagerness to clear yourselves, what indignation* (v. 11).

The Corinthians' favorable response provides Paul with a splendid opportunity to articulate his principal reason for writing such a severe letter. In chapter 2 he said that he wrote as he did to see if they would stand the test and be obedient in everything (2:9). It was not to cause them pain but to let them know the depth of his love for them (2:4). Now he adds, in a somewhat surprising vein, that he wrote *not on account of the one who did the wrong or of the injured party, but rather that before God you could see for yourselves how devoted to us you are* (v. 12). *Devoted* is perhaps better translated "earnest" *(tēn spoudēn)*. "Before God" is placed last in the clause for emphasis. A note of accountability is sounded here. The Corinthians are reminded that even their earnestness is played out under divine scrutiny.

Has Paul's sudden euphoria over the Corinthians' obedience blotted out all memory of the fears and anxieties that he had experienced while waiting for Titus? At this point he seems to be speaking in retrospect. When he wrote the severe letter he was not at all sure of the Corinthians' loyalty. In fact, he was so worried about their response to his letter that he gave up a promising evangelistic opportunity in Troas and went on to Macedonia in the hopes of meeting up with Titus and hearing news of the church (2:13; 7:5). But the church came through the test with flying colors (2:9). So perhaps this is Paul's tactful way of saying that his fears about them had been misplaced.

There certainly was a lot at stake. In writing such a letter, Paul had put all his apostolic labors in Corinth on the line. If he miscalculated in writing as he did, his relationship with the church might have come to an end (Murphy-O'Connor 1991:71).

Paul's Parental Pride in the Corinthians Proves True (7:12-16)
Much scholarly effort has been expended on determining the identity

7:12 Paul expresses himself in Semitic fashion, whereby the importance of one element is highlighted by negating others: "I wrote neither on account of the one who did the wrong nor for the sake of the injured party but rather that before God you could see how devoted to us you are." His primary purpose in writing is to salvage his relationship with the Corinthian church. Secondary reasons include the punishment of the offender *(the one who did the wrong)* and recognition of his apostolic authority *(the injured party.)*

The individual who had caused so much grief is not named. The Corinthians clearly knew to whom Paul was referring. Anonymity would prevent the wrongdoer from gaining unwanted notoriety as the letter circulated among the Achaian churches (1:1)—especially of *the one who did the wrong* (v. 12). The *injured party* is somewhat easier to ascertain: Paul is usually thought to be the probable candidate. But some have proposed Timothy (or another of Paul's coworkers). It is argued that the public challenge of Paul's authority occurred after he left Corinth and was directed at him through Timothy, his second-in-command. Otherwise he would have looked like an apostle turned coward (see, for example, M. J. Harris 1976:309). Yet this is exactly what some have been saying about Paul. He is "timid when face to face, but bold when away" (10:1). This is not to say that Timothy was not involved in some way. The fact that Titus replaced him as Paul's representative at Corinth by the time the severe letter was written (2 Cor 7:5-13) is indeed suggestive. But for Paul to use the language of a "painful visit" (2:1), "grieved me" (2:5) and "I gave you a warning when I was with you the second time" (13:2) indicates a direct versus indirect challenge. The alternative would have been to stay and discipline the Corinthians, which Paul was willing to do only as a last resort. Far from being cowardly, leaving could well have been the prudent course of action in a potentially explosive situation.

The offender's identity is more problematic. Use of the singular points to a single individual, and the masculine *(ho adikēsantos)* is indicative of gender. Beyond this the clues are scant. The individual in question has traditionally been identified with the Corinthian man who was involved in a sexual liaison with his stepmother at the time Paul wrote 1 Corinthians (1 Cor 5:1-5). The identification has been made primarily on the basis of parallel references to the activity of Satan, the authority of Christ and the corporate nature of the discipline (Lampe 1967:354). This proposal has been almost universally abandoned of late, and for good reasons. For one, the wrong committed is one that Paul takes personally, as "if someone has caused *me* grief" (2:5),

since he had repented (2:7).

Spoudē (devoted) occurs in the previous verse with the meaning "earnestness" and is perhaps best construed in like fashion here.

Enōpion tou theou (before God) could modify *egrapsa (I wrote)*, in which case Paul would be stressing that he wrote not in the heat of the moment but with a clear sense of his accountability to God. The emphasis in these verses, however, is on the Corinthians' response, not on Paul's conduct. It is therefore more likely that *enōpion tou theou* goes with *tēn spoudēn hymōn* ("your earnestness before God"). See the commentary.

"what *I* have forgiven" (2:10) and similar phrases make clear. Two, it is wholly inappropriate that Paul would offer to *personally* forgive someone who had been engaged in a form of sexual activity considered heinous even in Gentile circles (5:1, "of a kind that does not occur even among the pagans").

A more recent variation is that the incestuous person mentioned in 1 Corinthians 5 retaliated against Paul's call for excommunication (1 Cor 5:3-5, 13) by challenging his authority to issue such a directive (Kruse 1988:129-39). But the fact that Paul is willing to downplay the offense makes this construal improbable ("if there was anything to forgive," 2 Cor 2:10). An alternative suggestion is that the offender is the person in 1 Corinthians 6:1-10 who was accused of defrauding other members of the congregation. To be sure the same term is used *(adikeō)*. But beyond this, further parallels are lacking. And why Paul would construe this as a personal insult is not immediately evident.

The arguments also go back and forth on whether the guilty party was a member of the congregation or an intruder. In support of the latter is the fact that the whole church had been wronged by this individual (2:5). Moreover, if the man had been an insider, it would have been difficult for the church to prove "their innocence at every point" (7:11; Barrett 1970:154-55). But would the church have been in a position to exercise discipline if an outsider had been involved? And could an outsider have jeopardized Paul's standing in the community and caused the amount of pain that he did? Paul does not say in what exact way he was wronged. But from 13:3 we can surmise that it amounted to a public demand to provide proof that Christ was speaking through him.

The Corinthians' demonstrative support caused Paul to feel much better about things (v. 13). Actually, at this point he shifts back to the first-person plural that he has used throughout 2:14—7:2. His coworkers are once again included: *By all this we are encouraged* (v. 13). The tense is perfect *(parakeklēmetha)*. When he and his coworkers heard the news of the Corinthians' obedience to the directives of

---

7:13 Paul employs two comparatives to heighten the comparison. *Perissoterōs* means "beyond measure," while *mallon* means "more." A similar accumulation of comparatives

the letter, they were, and remained, encouraged.

Most translations place a full stop here and begin a new thought with the last part of verse 13 (LB, RSV, NRSV, NASB, TEV, NIV, NEB, REB). *By all this* would then point back to the earnest behavior of the Corinthians, and the second half of verse 13 would introduce a second reason for encouragement: *In addition . . . we were especially delighted to see how happy Titus was.* The cause of Titus's happiness was that *his spirit has been refreshed* by the Corinthian congregation *(by all of you).* The tense is once again perfect. Titus had been and remained refreshed *(anapepautai).* The verb translated *refreshed (anapauō)* actually means to cause to cease, stop or rest. The central idea is to bring about relief or relaxation. The implication is that Titus had ventured to Corinth with a certain amount of apprehension, perhaps due to negative reports that he had heard about the church. Such reports, however, did not come from Paul. He had done nothing but *boast* repeatedly (perfect tense, *kekauchēmai*) to Titus about the Corinthians (v. 14). On the other hand, Timothy might well have had a different report to give (1 Cor 16:10-11, "see to it that [Timothy] has nothing to fear while he is with you"). It also appears that travelers from Corinth regularly made their way to Ephesus and from time to time brought disturbing news about the church (1 Cor 1:11; 5:1; 11:18).

Of what exactly was Titus the beneficiary? It is possible that he had been spiritually *refreshed* from his time with the Corinthians (NIV, KJV, NKJV, NASB). Paul often speaks this way about his own visits to his churches (Rom 15:32; Philem 20). Titus could also have been the recipient of the kind of generous hospitality that Christians became renowned for in the first century (that is, physically *refreshed).* But it is more likely that "his mind" had been "put at ease" and his worries removed by the congregation (most translations). After all, his mission was hardly the kind to be eagerly anticipated. He had to deliver a letter of reprimand to the church and act in Paul's stead in carrying out its dictates. Paul's own mind had needed to be set at ease about the church

is found in Philippians 1:23 (Blass, Debrunner and Funk 1961:no. 60 [3]; 246).

just two years earlier (1 Cor 16:18), and even then the relief was short-lived (2 Cor 2:5). So regardless of his boasting, this is a church that would give even the most gifted minister pause.

Titus, however, was quite a capable deputy. Greek by birth (Gal 2:3), he had been converted at some point through Paul's ministry ("my true son," Tit 1:4). The first time his name appears he is a traveling companion on Paul's second postconversion trip to Jerusalem (Gal 2:1-3). He was also involved in the acrimonious exchange between the Antiochian leadership and some from the Pharisaic wing of the Jerusalem church who came to spy on the free exchange between Jew and Gentile in the church at Antioch (Gal 2:4-5).

The fact that Titus was selected for such a delicate mission at Corinth speaks volumes. That he would agree to visit Corinth after Paul's humiliating experience is remarkable, and the results of his mission bear marked witness to his abilities. Not only was he able to reinforce the dictates of the severe letter, but he was successful in reviving the church's flagging collection efforts (8:6). And if Romans 15:26 is any indication, on his second visit to Corinth Titus was able to consolidate Paul's authority and bring the collection to a completion (2 Cor 8:6, 16-24; 12:18).

Paul slips back into first-person singular at verse 14: *I had boasted to [Titus] about you.* It may have been that Titus's colleagues had been less hopeful than Paul about the Corinthians. But Paul typically provides more hope than a situation warrants (Martin 1986:242). And in the final analysis, the church did not *embarrass* him. The text is literally "I was not put to shame." The root *aisch-* referred originally to that which is ugly and disgraceful. So the verb *aischynō* came to mean that which disgraces or shames (Link 1978:562). Titus returned relieved and encouraged by his visit to Corinth, so that Paul had not been shamed. In fact, all that Paul had said to Titus about the church *proved to be true* (v. 14). It is one thing to be told something about someone; it is another to experience the truth of it oneself. Along similar lines, Job said of God, "My ears had heard of you but now my eyes have seen you" (Job 42:5).

7:15 *Perissoterōs* strictly speaking is a comparative: *bis affection for you is all the greater.* But this invites unnecessary comparisons—*greater* than what? The comparative is capable

It may seem as if Paul is belaboring the point. Yet Titus is going to be sent back to Corinth to complete the collection. Paul consequently does all he can to reinforce the mutual benefit and friendly feelings between Titus and the Corinthian church. But he cannot let an opportunity like this pass, so he adds that this shows *everything we said to you was true* (v. 14). Paul uses this occasion to strengthen his own case regarding the veracity of his dealings with Corinth. If his statements to Titus about the Corinthians were true, then his claims about himself and his ministry must also be true.

Memories are powerful things. As Titus dwells on his time at Corinth, his affection for the church becomes *all the greater* (v. 15). This is as it should be. We often like to take a stroll down memory lane, particularly if our memories are good ones. Titus took this stroll, and what came immediately to mind was how the Corinthians had received him. Two aspects are noted. In the first place, they had been *obedient* (v. 15). Did Titus make some demand of them (as suggested by Plummer 1915:228)? Or is he thinking of how they complied with the dictates of the severe letter (Furnish 1984:398)? Paul does not really say. What he does say is that it was not an obedience grudgingly given, for it was accompanied, in the second place, by *fear and trembling*. This is a strong phrase. It occurs four times in the New Testament (1 Cor 2:3; 2 Cor 7:15; Eph 6:5; Phil 2:12) and is used by Paul to describe the way he felt during his founding mission at Corinth (1 Cor 2:3). It may say something about the state of nervous anxiety the Corinthians had worked themselves into (Bratcher 1983:81). But the implication is that the church recognized Titus's official capacity and obeyed him as they would Paul.

The story is told of a little boy who was riding his tricycle furiously around the block over and over again. Finally a policeman stopped and asked him why he was going around and around. The boy said that he was running away from home. Then the policeman asked why he kept going around the block. The boy responded, "Because my mom said that I'm not allowed to cross the street." The point is clear—obedience will keep you close to those you love.

---

of doing duty for the superlative in the New Testament and can here be translated "his affection for you is very great."

Paul ends on a promising note: *I am glad I can have complete confidence in you.* A different word for confidence is employed than earlier in the chapter (see v. 4). The verb this time is *tharreō* ("to be of good courage," "to be cheerful," "to be confident"). Paul used it in chapter 5 of maintaining a cheerful attitude toward death, knowing that to be absent from the body is to be present with the Lord (5:6, 8). Here it refers to the confident attitude he has toward the Corinthians. Hughes calls Paul's pronouncement "the delicate pin around which the whole of the epistle pivots" (1962:282). The Corinthians have taken a step in the right direction. They followed Paul's directives with regard to the offender. They even exceeded his expectations with their earnestness, mourning and zeal on his behalf (v. 7). This affords Paul the perfect opportunity to expand their vision and encourage complete loyalty to him in the future.

□ Paul Sets Forth Guidelines and Models of Christian Stewardship (8:1—9:15)

Motivating Christians and congregations not only to give but also to be fiscally responsible in their giving is a difficult enterprise even in the best of circumstances. The needs are seemingly endless, and there are so many competing voices that the average Christian is stymied. Various and sundry organizations put forth their pleas for money constantly, sometimes relentlessly.

Fundraisers are frequently in a serious quandary themselves as they face the consumerism mentality of today's society. Books on how to corner the market are on the increase. Sophisticated marketing strategies abound. Then there are those who make a bad name for fundraisers everywhere by resorting to threats (such as to go without food until a certain dollar figure is met), sensationalism (such as showing pictures of children with severe deformities) and even warnings of impending doom for the organization if funds are not immediately forthcoming.

The Jerusalem Collection Paul faced many of these same chal-

8:1—9:15 In Acts 11:28 Luke records that a severe famine spread over the entire Roman world during the reign of Claudius (A.D. 41-54).

The Jerusalem church's practice was not a mandatory pooling of all assets. References to Joseph's field (Acts 4:37) and Mary's house (Acts 12:12) are evidence that private

lenges in his own day. Although he did not request personal support, he spent close to ten years soliciting funds for what is commonly referred to as the Jerusalem collection. This was a collection he took up among the Gentile churches to help Judean believers who were facing harder than usual economic times as a result of a famine during the mid to late 40s. Paul and Barnabas made an initial famine-relief visit to Jerusalem in A.D. 46 and delivered a monetary gift from the church at Antioch (Acts 11:29-30). At that time the Jerusalem church expressed the hope that the believers associated with Paul would continue to remember the Judean believers, which Paul was more than eager to do (Gal 2:10).

The collection effort was successfully completed in A.D. 57, and the funds were delivered by Paul and a group of delegates chosen by the contributing Gentile churches. In Romans 15:26 Paul states that the churches of Macedonia and Achaia "were pleased to make a contribution for the poor among the saints in Jerusalem," but the actual list of contributing churches is much longer. Luke's list includes delegates from Berea, Thessalonica, Derbe and Asia. The church at Philippi is without a delegate, but Luke himself may have functioned in this capacity (this is a "we" section of Acts). Timothy, who is included in the list, undoubtedly represented Lystra. Corinth was also without a delegate, but they may well, in the end, have asked Paul (or possibly Titus) to represent them.

A fundraising effort of this kind requires enormous investments of time and energy. Why did Paul do it? For one, the need was genuine. The Jerusalem collection was first and foremost an act of charity. Famine on top of persistent food shortages, double taxation and overpopulation crippled an already precarious Palestinian economy. The situation was undoubtedly aggravated by a voluntary pooling of assets in the early years of the church's existence (Acts 2:44-46; 4:32-37) and the constant need for the mother church to support the itinerant activities of its members and extend hospitality to visitors from other churches. Then too it was common, as it is today, for diaspora Jews to settle in and

---

ownership of property continued. A careful reading of Acts 2:45 and 4:34-37 shows that contributions were, in fact, voluntary and occasional. From time to time a member of the church would sell a piece of real estate in order to aid the needy within the congregation (imperfect tenses, *epipraskon, epheron, etithoun, diedideto*).

around the "holy city" at retirement; the result was a steady increase of widows and elderly in need of assistance.

Second, the relief fund served as an important, visible expression of the interdependence of believers worldwide. All of life is included in the shared concerns of those in Christ. For safety reasons, mountain climbers rope themselves together when climbing a mountain. That way, if one climber should slip and fall, he would not fall to his death but would be held by the others until he could regain his footing. In a similar way the Corinthians' surplus supplied the needs of the Judean churches so that the Judean churches could, in turn, meet the needs of the Corinthians (2 Cor 8:14).

Finally, the collection was a tangible representation of the heart of the gospel—that in Christ there is neither Jew nor Greek, neither slave nor free, not male and female (Gal 3:28). In particular, Paul may have had high hopes that the relief fund would allay any lingering fears and concerns Jewish Christians had regarding the Gentile mission. "Their hearts will go out to you," he says, "because of the surpassing grace God has given you" (2 Cor 9:14).

An unprecedented two chapters of 2 Corinthians are devoted to the Jerusalem relief fund. The length attests the seriousness with which the collection effort was viewed. What, then, was Corinth's role in the fundraising effort? According to 2 Corinthians 8:10, it was the first church not only to give but indeed to have the desire to do so. Paul must have made the Corinthians aware of the relief fund on his founding visit or shortly thereafter, for a little over a year later the church asked for his counsel on the best way to go about saving up such monies (1 Cor 16:1). His advice at the time was to do as he had instructed the Galatian churches: each person should set aside a sum of money every week in keeping with his or her income. In this way no collections would have to be made on Paul's next visit (1 Cor 16:2). The assumption that each person could do this shows that most members had surplus income. But it must not have been a very great surplus, since week-by-week savings were necessary for the contribution to be a generous one in the end (1 Cor 16:2; 2 Cor 8:20; Murphy-O'Connor 1991:77).

Between the writing of 1 and 2 Corinthians, the collection effort in Corinth fell by the wayside. In part this was due to intruding missionaries who raised questions about the legitimacy of the collection—perhaps with a view to diverting the funds into their own coffers (see the introduction). One of Titus's tasks after delivering Paul's severe letter was to rekindle interest in the relief fund. This he was able to do (8:6). But after he left Corinth, the collection effort once again came to a halt. Second Corinthians 8—9 is Paul's final attempt to get the Corinthians to finish what they had pledged to do the previous year (8:10-11).

Paul's Fundraising Strategy Paul's fundraising appeal is certainly well placed in the letter. He has just expressed his complete confidence in the church (7:16). Family feeling is high: the Corinthians have such a place in his heart that come what may, he will face it with them (7:3). Titus's affection for them and their obedient response to his demands have just been pointed out (7:13-15). This last fact, in particular, nicely prepares the way for Paul's announcement of his plan to send Titus back to Corinth to help bring the collection effort to a close (8:6).

To speak of "Paul's fundraising appeal," though, is to employ a kind of misnomer, for no direct appeal for funds occurs in these chapters. In fact, Paul does not even once use the term "money." His approach is much more subtle. His overall strategy is to provide the Corinthians with a number of powerful incentives for completing their offering. These incentives are for the most part tied to what he knows about the Corinthians rather than to any generic fundraising tactics. So what does Paul know about them? He knows that they are a fiercely independent and competitively minded congregation. This is why he cites the exemplary generosity of another church (8:1-5), compares the Corinthians' sincerity to that of others (v. 8) and puts before them the model of Christ himself (v. 9). He also realizes that they have a strong drive to excel at what they do and consequently pushes them to excel in the area of giving (v. 7). He is further aware of their fear of losing face before others. So he reminds them of the reputation that he has noised abroad about them (9:1-2), appeals to their embarrassment should visitors come and find them unprepared (9:4) and announces the forthcoming visit of one or more colleagues to make sure this does not happen (8:6; 9:3, 5).

Paul's approach is also realistic. He is keenly aware of the practical aspects of a collection effort such as this. This is evident in his concern to provide guarantees that the delivery of the funds will be handled in a responsible manner (8:16-24), to present the church with some practical guidelines for giving (8:11-15; 9:6-7) and to point out the benefits they will reap (9:8-15).

In many ways the cumulative picture is not a particularly comfortable one. Is it legitimate to use comparative strategies in fundraising? Is it wise to appeal to a church's ego to motivate giving? For all of Paul's talk in 6:14—7:1 of the need of Christians to sever their ties with secular society, is he not capitulating at this point to the way the world works? Our Western capitalistic society, in particular, is so competition-oriented—be it in business, education or sports—that it may not be spiritually healthy for the church to engage in such "let's get ahead of the next guy" tactics—or is it?

Several observations can be made. First, the strategy Paul employs is intended to motivate the Corinthians not to new giving but to follow through on a commitment already made. The distinction is important. Paul is not soliciting a pledge. In fact, it was the Corinthians who had expressed interest in the collection in the first place (1 Cor 16:1-2).

Second, Paul aims to motivate by comparing attitudes, not dollar amounts. It is the Macedonians' joyful, willing and earnest attitude that is set before the Corinthians, not the size of their contribution.

Third, the collection will not benefit Paul personally. He is not involved because it will look good on his résumé, enhance his reputation among the Gentile congregations or improve his relationship with the Jerusalem church. Indeed, at the time he gave the Corinthians an initial set of instructions, he was not even sure that it would be appropriate for him to travel to Jerusalem with the funds (1 Cor 16:4).

Fourth, the cause is an eminently worthy one. These are Christians of his own race who are in need of the basic necessities of life—food, shelter, clothing. Moreover, they are churches that Paul had started out persecuting. And even though he had done it out of zeal for God's honor, he never stopped thinking of himself as the worst of sinners because of it (1 Tim 1:15). A collection of this sort was a small step in rectifying the wrong that had been committed.

Finally, Paul is quick to point out that generous giving is an act of divine grace (8:1). It is only as God blesses and enables that we are able to give in the first place.

The Macedonian Believers Model Generosity (8:1-5) Instead of starting with a request for money, Paul begins with an example of sacrificial giving. *We want you to know* is the usual way he goes about introducing new information to his readers (v. 1). In this case, the new information concerns *the grace that God has given the Macedonian churches.* Edwin A. Judge (1982) describes Macedonia as a splendid tract of land, centered on the plains of the gulf of Thessalonica. It was a prosperous area. Running up the great river valleys into the Balkan Mountains, it was famous for its timber and precious metals. The *churches* of Macedonia had been planted by Paul on his second missionary journey—Philippi, Thessalonica and Berea. What is news-worthy about these churches is the *grace* that God has bestowed on them. The noun *charis* ("grace") appears ten times in chapters 8—9. Even within this short span of verses, the range of usage is surprising. It is employed of a spiritual endowment (8:7), divine enablement (8:1; 9:8, 14), a monetary gift (8:6, 19), a human privilege (8:4), a word of gratitude (8:16; 9:15) and divine favor or goodwill (8:9). Here it refers to the way that despite adverse conditions, God has enabled the Macedonians to financially assist destitute Christians whom they did not personally know.

Paul seeks to motivate the Corinthians by making reference to a longstanding competitor. Greece and Macedonia (called the "barbaric North") have a lengthy history of political rivalry. Although Philip of Macedon united all of Greece through brute force in 338 B.C., it was a union not destined to last. But now the Macedonians are put forward as a competitor of a different sort. These churches were experiencing *the most severe trial* (v. 2). The Greek is literally "a great testing of affliction." The genitive defines the content of the testing: "a severe test consisting of afflictions." The noun *dokimē* means a "testing" that proves someone's or something's worth or genuineness (compare 2:9). The term *thlipsis* ("pressure"), found nine times in this letter, is commonly used of the harassment that God's people experience at the hands of the world. No further details are provided about the nature of the harassment or the circumstances. But this may well be the same trouble that Paul faced prior to his rendezvous with Titus (7:5). If one can gauge from the frequency with which the topic crops up in Paul's letters, persecution was almost a way of life for these churches (Phil 1:29-30; 1 Thess 1:6; 2:14; 3:3-4; 2 Thess 1:4-10).

The severe trial that the Macedonian churches experienced was of a sort that left them in a condition of *extreme poverty*. The phrase is literally "down-to-the-depth poverty" (*hē kata bathous ptōcheia;* v. 2)—or, as Philip Hughes translates, "rock bottom" poverty (1962:288). James counsels his readers to consider it pure joy whenever they face trials (1:2). The Macedonian churches are a testimony that it is possible not merely to experience joy but to have it "overflow" in the midst of trials. Even more, just as persecution did not take away from their joyfulness, neither did poverty diminish their ability to be generous (Bruce 1971:220). Paul says that their poverty *welled up in rich generosity* (v. 2). The text is literally "a wealth of liberality" *(to ploutos tēs haplotētos).* The basic meaning of *haplotēs* is "singleness," and it denotes simplicity of character ("noble"), heart ("pure") or intent ("sincere"; Bauernfeind 1964). Here it signifies an openheartedness toward one's possessions ("generosity"). Sadly, it is often those having the least, rather than the most, who are the generous givers. Charles Spurgeon tells of receiving a wealthy man's invitation to come preach at his rural church to help the members raise funds to pay off a debt. The man also told Spurgeon that he was free to use his country house, his town house or his seaside home. Spurgeon wrote back, "Sell one of the places and pay the debt yourself."

It is easy to see how affluence can well up in generous giving. But how is it possible for extreme poverty to overflow in a wealth of liberality? Verses 3-5 provide the explanation.

First, it is because the Macedonians gave not just *as much as they were able* (literally "according to their ability") but *beyond* (v. 3). How

---

8:3 *Authairetoi (entirely on their own)* could go with what precedes: "they gave beyond their ability of their own free will" (KJV, NKJ, Phillips, JB, NASB, RSV, NRSV). Or it could begin a new thought: *Entirely on their own, they urgently pleaded with us* (TEV, NIV, NEB, REB). On the whole, the latter option seems preferable.

8:4 *Tēn charin kai tēn koinōnian tēs diakonias* is quite possibly a hendiadys (one idea expressed by means of two nouns separated by *kai*)—not "begging us for the privilege *and* sharing" but "begging us for the privilege *of* sharing." The genitive is objective: "sharing *in* this service." In Greek-speaking Judaism the term *diakonos* ("service") came to refer to the raising and distribution of charitable funds to meet the needs of the poor (Furnish 1984:401). The poor who received aid in Jewish society were the orphan, the widow, the

much beyond Paul does not say. But there is no hint that this was a reckless action on their part. The sense is that they determined what they could comfortably contribute and then went beyond this figure.

Second, what they gave, they gave *entirely on their own* (v. 3). *Authairetos (autos* = "self" + *haireomai* = "to choose") refers to something done of one's own accord or by a free choice. In essence, the Macedonians were not pressured into giving. They gave willingly. In fact, they *urgently pleaded* to be involved (v. 4). The thrust of the Greek is that they begged *(deomenoi)* Paul most earnestly *(meta pollēs paraklēseōs).* This was because they considered involvement in the relief effort a *privilege (charis;* see v. 1) and a *sharing (koinōnia,* v. 4). *Koinōnia,* commonly translated "fellowship" in the New Testament, means "that which we hold in common or have a share in." In Christian circles it came to denote the close union and common faith that believers have as members of Christ's church. Implicit in this close union is a responsibility to care for those in need in the family of God.

Finally, the Macedonian generosity was possible because they gave themselves *first to the Lord* and only then to Paul (v. 5). Their preeminent concern was how best to serve Christ. It is here that they exceeded Paul's expectations. They gave out of their poverty because of the sincerity of their commitment to Christ as *Lord (tō kyriō).* So great was their desire to serve Christ that they would not allow their economic situation to keep them from being involved in the Lord's work (Waldrop 1984:38). This is why Paul describes the collection as a *service* (v. 4). It is not just a financial obligation. It is a ministry opportunity *to the saints* (v. 4)—those set apart to be God's possession.

Paul Urges Titus to Finish the Work (8:6) The example of the

---

destitute and the helpless. *Testament of Job* 11:1—12:4 offers a striking parallel in language and thought to 2 Corinthians 8:2-5 and 9:7. Those without resources "begged" to be involved "in this service," and the "cheerful at heart" gave willingly *(hilaron . . . dotēn).*

The recipients of the collection are called *the saints,* not "the poor." The term is literally "holy ones"—those set apart to be God's own possession (1 Cor 1:2). Paul typically addresses his churches in this fashion when he writes to them (as in 2 Cor 1:1; Eph 1:1; Phil 1:1; Col 1:2).

8:5 *Tō kyriō* in all probability is a reference to Christ. Paul's customary practice is to distinguish Christ from Yahweh by use of the article (Zerwick 1963:no. 169).

Macedonian churches encourages Paul to call for the completion of the collection at Corinth (*so*, v. 6). To this end he announces his plan to send Titus to supervise the effort. This is a strategic move on Paul's part. Titus is someone whom the church knows and trusts. Plus, *he had earlier made a beginning* at Corinth. *Proenarchomai* ("to begin before," vv. 6, 10) is attested nowhere else in Greek literature. At face value it suggests that Titus had launched the collection effort. Yet technically Paul was the initiator (1 Cor 16:1-4). The choice of words may indicate that the offering had been so completely abandoned that Titus had to start effectively from scratch.

Although a latecomer on the Corinthian scene, Titus was nonetheless an important player. He was able not only to reinforce the dictates of the severe letter but also to revive the church's flagging collection efforts (see the commentary on 7:13-15).

The Corinthians Are Challenged to Excel in Giving (8:7) We humans are selfish by nature. Generosity is not something that comes naturally but is the result of God's grace in our lives. This is why Paul refers to the Corinthian offering as *this act of grace* (v. 6).

Charis is used both here and in the next verse of a spiritual endowment or gift of the Spirit. The Corinthians take great pride in their spiritual endowments. And well they should, since they do not lack a single one of them (1 Cor 1:7). Not only this but they *excel* in them—or at least in *faith*, . . . *speech*, . . . *knowledge*, . . . *earnestness* and *love* (2 Cor 8:7). Paul consequently pushes them to excel in *giving* as well *(see that you also excel in this grace)*. Giving is identified as a gift of the Spirit in Romans 12:8, where Paul exhorts the Roman believers that if one's gift is contributing to the needs of others *(metadidous)*, then that person

---

8:6 *Hina* can be imperatival: "We urged Titus: 'Bring to completion this act of grace.' " Or, more probably, it can define the content of Paul's request: *We urged Titus . . . to bring . . . to completion this act of grace.* The double *kai* makes for a cumbersome construction *(kathōs proenērxato houtōs kai epitelesē eis hymas kai tēn charin tautēn).* The first *kai* implies that Titus engaged in fundraising efforts on an earlier visit *(since he had earlier made a beginning, to bring also to completion).* The second *kai* modifies *tēn charin tautēn ("this gracious work as well").* The implication is that Titus's enforcement of the dictates of the severe letter and fundraising efforts were an act of divine *grace.*

The grammar does not demand a visit prior to 1 Corinthians, as Hughes (1962:293-94) and others claim. This visit could easily have been part of the mission described in 7:13-15.

should give generously (*en haplotēti;* compare 2 Cor 8:2).

All things considered, the list of endowments here is a modest one. The first three are gifts of the Spirit. *Faith* is grouped with gifts of healing and miraculous powers in 1 Corinthians 12:9-10. So Paul is probably thinking not of intellectual assent to a set of propositions but of a belief that God can and will act in a particular situation. This kind of faith, Paul says, is able to "move mountains" (1 Cor 13:2). *Speech* and *knowledge* are two areas of gifting that Paul refers to in 1 Corinthians (1 Cor 1:5). *Speech* may be a catchall term for such oral gifts as prophecy, teaching and tongues (1 Cor 12:10, 28). Similarly, *knowledge* may refer to the gifts of discernment, word of wisdom, word of knowledge and interpretation of tongues (1 Cor 12:8, 10).

Also among the things that the Corinthians excel at are *earnestness* and *love*. *Spoudē* denotes the earnest engagement or zealous pursuit of something. Paul has already made reference to the Corinthians' earnestness in trying to clear themselves of any and all blame regarding his public humiliation during his last visit (7:11-12). *Love* must accompany the exercise of the other four, otherwise nothing of lasting importance can come of them (1 Cor 13:1-3).

Paul Tests the Corinthians' Love (8:8-9) Paul is quick to say that he is *not commanding* them (v. 8). Although he has the authority to do so, he waives its exercise here. His game plan is of another sort. He seeks rather to *test the sincerity of [the Corinthians'] love by comparing it with the earnestness of others* (v. 8). In short, he tries to motivate them by means of some friendly competition. The term *test (dokimazō)* carries the positive sense of examining something to prove its worth or authenticity. The something here is *sincerity*. The term *gnēsios* means

---

In fact, the wording of 7:14 seems to require the conclusion that the Corinthian visit from which Titus had just returned was his first visit ("our boasting about you to Titus has proved to be true").

8:7 Both the UBS and Nestlé-Aland editions of the Greek New Testament have a slight preference for *hēmōn en hymin* ("our love for you"; C rating) over *hymōn en hēmin* ("your love for us"). Both readings have early manuscript support and modern advocates. But only the latter makes sense in the context.

Hina is imperative: *see that you also excel . . . (hina kai perisseuēte;* KJV, NKJV, RSV, NIV). Compare 1 Corinthians 5:2; Galatians 2:10; Ephesians 5:33; Colossians 4:16; 1 Timothy 1:3; Philemon 19 (Turner 1963:94-95).

"true-born" (Büchsel 1964a) and denotes what is genuine or legitimate (Liddell, Scott and Jones 1978). The Jerusalem relief fund becomes the Corinthians' opportunity to show, as the Macedonians have done, that the love they profess toward other believers is bona fide.

Paul turns not only to the Macedonian churches to test the Corinthians' sincerity but also to Christ himself, the supreme example of generosity. It has been said that no one can outgive God. There is no better proof of this than *the grace of our Lord Jesus Christ* (v. 9). *Grace* is used in its usual sense of divine favor or goodwill to those who do not deserve it. In this case it is divine favor extended to us by Jesus Christ (subjective genitive, *tēn charin tou Christou*). For *though he was rich, yet for your sakes he became poor* (v. 9). Paul is probably thinking of the riches of Christ's heavenly existence, which included equality with God and being in the form of God (Phil 2:6). But then Christ *became poor.* This was a voluntary action on his part. The aorist is most likely ingressive: Christ "entered into a state of" poverty. Paul undoubtedly has the incarnation in mind, when Christ gave up the "riches" of heavenly existence to assume an earthly state called "poverty."

What this state amounted to is debated. Paul could be thinking of how Jesus was born into a poor family and associated with those of low social standing. "Christ chose a stable in preference to a palace and consistently held to that even in death" (Macdonald 1986:5). This is, to be sure, an emphasis of Luke's Gospel (for example, 2:24; 6:20-26; 16:19-31). Or Paul could have in mind Jesus' identification with those who are "poor in spirit"—a stress in Matthew's Gospel (for example, 5:3, 6, 20; James D. G. Dunn). But perhaps the choice does not lie between spiritual and physical poverty. If Philippians 2:7-8 is any indication, then Paul is thinking of how one to whom honor and service was due voluntarily took the form of one from whom service was expected. Indeed, he "made himself nothing, taking the very nature of a servant . . . and became obedient to death—even death on a cross."

8:9 *The grace of our Lord Jesus Christ* is the customary phrase Paul uses to close his letters (Rom 16:20, 24; 1 Cor 16:23; 2 Cor 13:13[14]; Gal 6:18; Phil 4:23; 1 Thess 5:28; 2 Thess 3:18; Philem 25).

The participle *ōn* is concessive: *though he was rich.*

8:10 *Perysi* can mean *last year* (NIV, NEB, REV, TEV, NRSV) or "a year ago" (NASB, Phillips, KJV, NKJV, JB, RSV). So the Corinthians' pledge could have been made anywhere

"Ordinary charity," says James Denney, "is but the crumbs from the rich man's table; but if we catch Christ's spirit, it will carry us far beyond that" (1900:268). This is Paul's hope for the Corinthians.

William Barclay aptly observes that Christ's sacrifice did not begin on the cross, nor even at birth. It began in heaven, when he laid aside his glory and consented to come to earth (1954:229). Why did he do it? He did it, Paul says, so that we *through his poverty might become rich*. To put it another way, Christ went from riches to rags so that we might go from rags to riches. What are these riches? Although Paul referred two verses earlier to the Corinthians' rich spiritual endowments, it is more likely that here he is thinking of the riches of salvation. No fewer than eight riches have been mentioned thus far in the letter: the down payment of the Spirit (1:22; 5:5), daily renewal (4:16), an eternal weight of glory (4:18), an eternal house in heaven (5:1), unending fellowship with Christ (5:8), new creation (5:17), reconciliation (5:18) and righteousness (5:21).

The Corinthians Should Make Good Their Pledge (8:10-11) At verse 10 Paul once again stresses that he is only offering an opinion rather than giving a command: *Here is my advice about what is best for you in this matter*. His advice is quite simply to *finish the work* (v. 11). Two reasons are offered.

First, a considerable time has lapsed since the Corinthians first expressed interest. The year before they had been eager to contribute and had taken some initial steps to do so. But the tragedy of life so often is not that we lack good intentions but that we fail to turn them into action (Barclay 1954:229). Giving may start as a response of the heart, but it must move on to an act of the will. If the Corinthians do not finish the work, then in the final analysis all their good intentions amount to nothing.

Second, the Corinthians currently enjoy a twofold precedence over

from a scant month or two previous to just under two years earlier. The exigencies of travel make it likely that Titus's "beginning" (v. 6) occurred in the spring or summer of the previous year. While sea lanes were open from mid-March to mid-November, most travel by water occured from the beginning of June to mid-September. Little, if any, travel by foot happened during the winter months, especially in mountainous regions or plateaus.

the Macedonians in that they were *the first to give* and *the first . . . to have the desire to do so* (v. 10; M. J. Harris 1976:369). If they had also been the first to finish, they would have truly lived up to their reputation for excellence. But the Macedonians, who were latecomers to the collection effort, finished ahead of the Corinthians. So it is incumbent on the Corinthians now to bring their work to a speedy conclusion so that they do not lose what small advantage they still possess.

Paul's final strategy does not appear until 9:1-5, where he uses a little reverse psychology on the Corinthians. He began his appeal by pointing to the exemplary model of the Macedonian churches. At the end he admits that this sacrificial model is due in part to the boasting about the Achaian churches that he had done while in Macedonia. In particular, he had been bragging about the Corinthians' "eagerness to help" and "readiness to give since last year," which served to "stir most of" the Macedonian churches "to action" (v. 2). How would it look, then, if some visitors from Macedonia should come and find the Corinthians unprepared (v. 4)? It would be rather embarrassing for Paul—not to mention for them (v. 4).

Guidelines for Giving (8:11-15) Most of us, I daresay, associate the proverb "It is more blessed to give than to receive" with the offering on Sunday morning—even though for Paul (Acts 20:32-35) as well as for Jesus (Mt 10:8) it is a guiding principle for the Christian worker rather than the Christian giver. And while the principle is a helpful one when we consider the matter of financial contributions, questions of how much and to whom are still formidable ones for most Christians.

The Corinthians, to be sure, asked these same questions, and Paul responds with some practical guidelines for giving in 8:11-15. How helpful these guidelines are today will depend on how tied a church is to the legalistic practice of the "tithe." For it is curious that at no point here—or for that matter elsewhere in Paul's writings—is the tithe put forward as a guideline for giving. In fact, no New Testament writer either encourages "tithing" or presents it as the normative or even occasional

---

8:11 *Your eager willingness* translates a word *(hē prothymia)* that can mean "readiness,"

practice of the church. Yet many of our churches assume that this is the accepted New Testament standard.

Webster's defines "tithe" as "a tenth of one's income given voluntarily for the support of church or religious work." Although we commonly associate the tithe with Israel and Old Testament law, it was widely practiced by other ancient peoples and predates Mosaic times. For example, in Egypt, Joseph's family was required to give two-tenths of their harvest to Pharaoh (Gen 47:24). Samuel warned the Israelites that if they instituted a monarchy like their neighbors, they would have to give a tenth of their flocks and produce to the king (1 Sam 8:10-18).

Under Mosaic law Israel was commanded to give a tenth of its crops, herds, flocks and the fruit of its trees to support the Levites, who had no inheritance of their own (Lev 27:30-32; Num 18:21-24). The tithe was to compensate the Levites for the work that they did while serving at the tabernacle. The Levites, in turn, were required to give a tenth of Israel's tithe to the priests (Num 18:25-29; Thompson 1982:1205). They were permitted to pasture herds in forty-eight designated cities, to which they were forced to return during times of apostasy when the tithes were neglected (Num 35:1-8; Neh 13:10). In postexilic times it was the responsibility of the Levites (rather than the head of each household) to collect the tithe in the towns where they lived and deliver it to Jerusalem (Neh 10:37-39). The Levites were not the only beneficiaries of the tithe. At the end of every three years, the tithe of that year's produce was placed in storage in each town for the alien, the fatherless and the widow (Deut 14:28-29).

Although Jesus refers to the Pharisees' custom of tithing even herbs of the land (such as mint, anise and cumin) while neglecting the weightier matters of justice and love of God (Mt 23:23; Luke 11.42), he nowhere instructs his disciples that this is to be the practice of the church. But then would an Old Testament command tied to a largely agrarian economy and based on a theocratic form of government be applicable to an institution like the local church? The total silence of the New Testament writers in this regard is telling.

"willingness," "resoluteness" or "zealousness." "Eager determination" catches the sense perhaps the best.

This is not to say, however, that support of the Christian worker is abandoned. Paul argues strenuously in 1 Corinthians 9 that Christian workers deserve their wages. But the guidelines for giving that he puts forward are more in accord with a covenant of the Spirit than with a covenant of the letter (2 Cor 3:6).

The standard proffered is, in reality, a higher one than the traditional tithe. In counseling the Corinthians on the question of how much, Paul says that they are to give, in the first place, *according to [their] means* (8:11). The text is literally "out of that which you have." The implication is clear. We are not called to give or to pledge what we do not have. Contributions are to be based on actual income, not hoped-for windfalls or even anticipated earnings.

Giving is also to be in proportion to our earnings (*katho ean echē*, v. 12). It is not a fixed percentage but relative proportion that is key. In fact, beyond the tithe of livestock and produce to support the Levites, the standard for Israel's giving was a proportional one. The person with many possessions is to make her gift of alms "proportionately," and the one with few possessions is to give "according to" the little he has (Tobit 4:8). A similar guideline is given in 1 Corinthians 16:2, where Paul instructs the Corinthians that they are to set aside a sum of money each week "in keeping with" their income (literally, "however one has prospered").

Proportional giving actually turns out to be a fairer standard than the traditional tithe. Whereas a fixed 10 percent would most likely be negligible for someone with an income of $100,000, it could well cripple a person with an income of $10,000. This is why Jesus had such high praise for the widow who contributed two small copper coins to the temple treasury. She gave that which provided for her daily necessities ("all she had to live on," Lk 21:4), while the rich contributed out of their surplus. And while both may have given 10 percent, proportionately the widow put in more than all the others combined (Lk 21:3). This accords with Jesus' teaching elsewhere that we are responsible in direct proportion to how God has blessed us: "From everyone who has been given

8:12 *According to what one has* is misleading (*katho ean echē*). *Katho* denotes degree: "to the degree that" or "in proportion to."
For several centuries in the history of the church there was no such thing as a "tithe"

much, much will be demanded" (Lk 12:48).

Second, needs are to be met out of a person's surplus, not necessary income (that which one needs for life's basic necessities; v. 14). The Macedonian churches, in giving out of their poverty, were the exception rather than the rule. The norm is the Corinthians' *plenty* supplying what the Judean churches *need, so that in turn their plenty can supply what [the Corinthians] need* (v. 14).

Not all agree on what the Judeans' *plenty* amounts to. The obvious reading is that Paul contemplates the possibility of a reversal of economic circumstances. If this were to happen, then it would be incumbent on the Judean Christians to relieve the want of the Corinthians. For some scholars, however, the possibility of the Judean churches' possessing a material surplus is too remote. Paul is thought to be pointing instead to an existing reciprocity: the Gentile churches supply the mother church with material blessings, while the Jerusalem church provides the Gentiles with spiritual blessings (Nickle 1966:121; Bruce 1971:223). The fact that Paul goes on to cite an Old Testament example of material equality makes the former reading the likely one (v. 15, *as it is written: "He that gathered much did not have too much, and he that gathered little did not have too little")*. But rather than forecasting a reversal of economic conditions, Paul may be merely pointing to the kind of interdependency that should exist at all times among churches.

Third, there must be a genuine need. But what constitutes a genuine need? Some today think of themselves as needy if they lack private means of transportation or the funds for a college education; or perhaps their earnings fall below the governmental criteria for the poverty level. Paul, on the other hand, defines need as a lack or shortage of life's necessities (1 Tim 6:8). In the first century this amounted to a want of food, clothing or shelter (2 Cor 11:27). Paul himself voluntarily went without such necessities. But in the church such needs are not to go unmet—and not just within the local church. There are relatively few Christians in the Western world who lack such essentials, but in the church worldwide the need is staggering.

to support Christian workers; instead, freedom in giving was emphasized. In fact, church fathers like Irenaeus argued against the tithe (see Feinberg 1976:758).

In the final analysis, the key to giving lies in the attitude of the heart. In 8:12 and 9:7 Paul employs four adjectives that characterize the attitude that God finds *acceptable*. It must, in the first place, be a willing gift: *if the willingness is there, the gift is acceptable* (8:12). It is not the amount that counts with God. If a readiness to give is present, then the gift is gladly received, whether it be large or small.

Some years ago a woman was preparing a box to be sent to some missionaries in India. A child gave her a penny. The woman used this penny to purchase a tract for the box. Eventually the tract reached a Burmese chief and was used to lead him to Christ. The chief told the story of his conversion to his friends, many of whom believed. Eventually a church was established and over fifteen hundred people were converted to Christianity. The lesson is plain: no gift willingly given is too small for God to use.

The gift must also not be offered "reluctantly" (literally, "with pain"; 9:7). Nor should it be done "under compulsion"—that is, as though there were no other alternative (9:7). Arm-twisting is a common practice today. Pledge drives too often work this way. Instead of soliciting willing contributions, fundraisers bring to bear external pressure of one kind or another (such as making pledges public and applauding large donations), and people feel forced to give so as not to lose face. This is what Paul was hoping to avoid by sending Titus far enough in advance to allow for the contribution to be willing, not forced.

Finally, the offering that God finds acceptable is one that has been cheerfully given (9:7; *hilaros* = our English term "hilarious"). The cheerful giver is one who is happy to give and gives gladly. The sentiment is an Old Testament one. The last part of the verse is a free quotation of the Greek translation of Proverbs 22:8 (LXX): "God blesses a cheerful and generous person."

The aim of these guidelines is not an exchange of financial burdens.

8:13 The Greek verb *thlibō* and noun *thlipsis* are terms that turn up frequently in this letter (verb three times, noun nine times). The basic idea is pressure imposed by external circumstances.

8:13-14 A difficulty in punctuating verses 13-14 exists. *All' ex isotētos* at the end of verse 13 could be taken with what precedes: *Our desire is not that others might be relieved while you are hard pressed, but that there might be equality* (NIV, LB). Or it can begin a new thought: "But as a matter of equality your abundance at the present time should supply

Our desire is not that others might be relieved while you are hard pressed,
Paul says (8:13). *Thlipsis* ("hard pressed") is used of pressure of one
kind or another, while *anesis* ("relieved") denotes a relief or relaxation
of such pressure. Paul does seek the Judeans' relief from the pressure
of being in dire economic straits, but not to the extent that someone
else is financially strapped in the process. The objective is, rather, *that
there might be equality* (v. 13).

But what is meant by *equality?* Is Paul putting forward a kind of
biblical socialism, a leveling of rich and poor? Some have mistakenly
understood him to be advocating just this. Equality of provision so that
there is neither surplus nor deficiency is often taken as the aim (for
example, M. J. Harris 1976:370; Barrett 1973:227; Bratcher 1983:89). Yet
what Paul suggests as appropriate is equity of basic needs being met,
not equality of supply. *Isotēs* ("equality"), found only here and in
Colossians 4:1 in the New Testament, denotes what is "equitable" and
"fair." So it is equity and not equality that is at issue here. The TEV's "It
is only fair that you should help those who are in need" captures the
idea.

Paul is not saying that possession of a surplus of material goods is
wrong for a Christian. It is actually those who do possess a surplus who
are in a position to meet existing economic needs. This is clear from
verse 14, where Paul envisions the Jerusalem church's surplus providing
for the Corinthians' lack at a future point. On the other hand, for some
Christians to be living in luxury while other Christians go without food,
shelter or clothing smacks of gross inequity.

To illustrate the need for equity Paul turns to the account of God's
miraculous provision of manna in the wilderness (v. 15). *As it is written:
"He who gathered much did not have too much, and he who gathered
little did not have too little."* The quote is taken almost verbatim from
Exodus 16:18. Moses had instructed the people that they were to go out

their want" (RSV, NRSV, KJV, TEV, JB). It can even stand on its own: "It is a matter of share
and share alike" (Phillips, NEB, REB). While *alla* can introduce a new thought, the *ou . . .
alla (not . . . but)* construction is a very familiar one in Paul. For this reason the first option
seems preferable.

8:14 In view of the chronic poverty Palestine faced, Furnish (1984:420) and Héring
(1967:61) think that Paul is merely putting forward a theoretical possibility or a formal
statement of principle with no special thought for future implications.

each morning and gather enough manna for the day's need (v. 16). The Israelites did as they were told: some gathered much, and others gathered little (v. 17). But when it came time to measure by the omer (about two quarts or liters), the person who gathered much did not have too much, and the one who gathered little did not have too little (v. 18).

At first glance the Exodus narrative could be read to say that each Israelite ended up with the same amount regardless of how much or little was gathered. But in fact what the text says is that God made certain that no one had more or less than their fair share ("each one gathered as much as he needed," v. 18). Although the Israelites gathered varying amounts of manna, what they ended up with was the amount that met their individual needs. The key phrase in Exodus 16:18 is "as much as he needed." It is an equity of needs met rather than an equality of supply that the narrative illustrates. Even though some gathered more and some less, the needs of all were fairly met. In the wilderness it was God who ensured such equity. Today it is the responsibility of each believer.

Paul Sends a Team in Advance of His Coming (8:16-24) The administration of an effort like the Jerusalem collection could easily give rise to allegations of mishandling of funds. Today a charitable organization can employ a group that independently assesses its fiscal accountability and applies objective standards to its handling of donations (such as public disclosure of the percentage going to meet stated goals compared to salaries and administrative costs). In this way donors can be assured that all monies are being appropriately managed. But what about the first century? How could a donor be certain that his charitable contribution would not end up merely lining the pockets of an administrator? And what kind of assurances did a fundraiser give prospective contributors that their donations would be handled in a responsible fashion?

Verses 16-24 show the kind of precautions a first-century fundraiser took to ensure the responsible handling and transportation of a considerable sum of money. *We are taking pains,* Paul says, *to do what is right, not only in the eyes of the Lord but also in the eyes of men* (v. 21). *Taking pains* translates a verb that means to "think about beforehand, plan ahead of time" (*pronooumen;* Liddell, Scott and Jones 1978). Such advance planning was needed *to avoid any criticism of the way* the offering was being administered (v. 20). The term *stellomai* ("avoid") denotes shrinking from or standing aloof. Paul tries to have as little to do with the collection process as possible. In this way he hopes to eliminate any possibility of criticism (v. 20).

The extra care that Paul takes is understandable. His critics were quick enough to suggest that the collection was merely a covert way of receiving financial support (12:16-18). Moreover, the money involved is a *liberal* amount (v. 20). The term *hadrotēs,* found only here in the New Testament, means "abundant" or "lavish." Paul is anticipating a very large offering indeed, which is all the more reason for him to do whatever has to be done to guarantee its safe handling.

Paul was usually concerned with doing what is right in God's eyes rather than human eyes—especially since God's way and humankind's way are often in conflict. Here he takes the additional step of taking into consideration what is right in the eyes of others (v. 21). What this amounted to was making sure that everything not only was above suspicion *(right . . . in the eyes of the Lord)* but also looked so *(right . . . in the eyes of men).* Why? Because life and ministry are inseparable. There will always be those who judge the claims of Christ by the lives of those who claim to be his followers. If the conduct of the fundraiser can be faulted, then the gospel itself can be called into question. Not only this, but God's reputation can be damaged. The ultimate purpose of the collection was *to honor the Lord* (literally, "to advance the glory of the Lord"; v. 20)—an aim that could hardly be accomplished if any suspicions attached to the collection process.

The steps that Paul had already taken to avoid criticism are spelled out in 1 Corinthians. For one, he had insisted that the collection occur prior to his coming, so that he not be involved in the actual handling of the monies (1 Cor 16:2). Moreover, he had instructed the Corinthians to appoint their own representatives to accompany the collection, thereby exempting himself from any criticism regarding the transportation of the funds (1 Cor 16:3). Now, in 2 Corinthians Paul adds an additional precaution: he sends a trusted colleague to finish the collection effort, rather than going himself: *Titus . . . is coming to you* (2 Cor 8:17). This trusted colleague is well respected by the Corinthians and has already established a good working relationship with the church in the matter of giving (8:6).

The first time, Titus had to be encouraged to go to Corinth (7:13-14). This time no encouragement was needed. Paul made his *appeal (paraklēsis)*, and to his surprise, Titus *welcomed* it (v. 17). That Titus would welcome a visit so soon after returning from Corinth is surprising indeed. In part this is due to the church's warm reception and obedient response on his last visit. But it can also be attributed to *God, who put into the heart of Titus the same concern* for the Corinthians that Paul himself has (v. 16). *Concern* translates a term that is employed seven times in chapters 7—8 of the earnest engagement or zealous pursuit of something (Liddell, Scott and Jones 1978). The TEV's "Titus is eager to help you" captures the idea.

Just as we speak of an infectious laugh, in the case of Paul we can speak of an infectious love. His deep love for the Corinthians has rubbed off on Titus, so that the idea of a return visit is not only agreeable but one that he has embraced *with much enthusiasm* (v. 17). Ultimately, though, such love is the result of a divine work in the human heart, to bring about an affection for God's people that God himself possesses (v. 16).

Besides eagerly accepting the idea of a return visit to Corinth, Titus is coming *on his own initiative* (v. 17). The Greek term *authairetos* (*autos* = "self" + *haireomai* = "to choose") refers to something done of one's own accord, by a free choice. The word was used in 8:3 to describe how the Macedonians contributed entirely on their own, without any prompting at all from Paul. The implication here is that Titus had been thinking along these lines even before Paul approached him.

Fundraising is not an enjoyable activity, even in the best of circumstances. The fact that Titus had seen the need for a visit to Corinth so

---

8:17 The noun *paraklēsis* can refer to an appeal, an exhortation or an encouragement. The necessity of a return visit to Corinth so soon after the last makes an "appeal" the likely option.

The aorists in verses 17 (*exēlthen*), 18 (*synepempsamen*) and 22 (*synepempsamen*) could be epistolary—*he is coming* (virtually all modern translations)—or actual—"he came to you" (KJV, NKJV, NASB). It would be reasonable to assume that Titus was the carrier of 2 Corinthians and that 8:16-24 functioned as a letter of introduction for the two unnamed individuals on their arrival in Corinth.

soon after the last one says that the significance of the collection and Corinth's contribution to it goes beyond relief of economic need. A Gentile offering of this sort is a concrete manifestation of the unity in Christ that now exists between two ethnic groups that had been enemies for hundreds of years. In addition to a trusted colleague, Paul sends two church representatives of proven worth and recognized stature to help Titus with the collection effort (v. 23). The first is merely referred to in the text as *the brother* (v. 18); no name is provided. Some suppose that it was removed when Paul's letters were collected and edited for general distribution (see 9:4-5). But where a name is lacking, credentials are not. To the brother's credit is the fact that he *was chosen by the churches* to accompany the offering (v. 19). The verb *cheirotoneō* means "to stretch out" *(teinō)* "the hand" *(cheir)* to express agreement in a vote—or, as we say today, to elect by a show of hands. It may well signify the process by which church delegates were chosen. But the word was also used of choosing someone to carry out a specific task, apart from any kind of formal vote (as in Acts 14:23).

That this was a common precaution in the first century is suggested by Philo's similar reference to the selection of highly regarded people from every town to accompany the temple contributions to Jerusalem (*The Special Laws* 1.78; Lohse 1974:437). *The brother* was chosen not only to travel to Jerusalem with the relief fund but also *to accompany us* (*synekdēmos*, "fellow-traveler"; Liddell, Scott and Jones 1978). Somewhere between the writing of 1 and 2 Corinthians Paul had decided to go himself—but not without selected representatives of the contributing churches.

This brother is also someone *who is praised by all the churches for his service to the gospel* (v. 18). Although *praised by all the churches* could

---

Spoudaioteros can have a comparative ("all the more eager") or elative ("most eager" or "very zealous") sense. Cases of the latter are well attested in the New Testament (see Blass, Debrunner and Funk 1961:no. 244).

8:18 We cannot know for certain what "praised in the gospel" refers to. Murphy-O'Connor's hypothesis—that this individual is a Corinthian Christian who aided the spread of the gospel in Macedonia and established himself as an exceptional preacher—is to be commended (1991:86).

It has been proposed that *ton adelphon* be understood as "his brother"—that is, Titus's

be understood provincially (all the churches in Macedonia), the phrase could also point to someone who was highly regarded by all the Gentile churches contributing to the fund. Regardless, his fame shows that he is more than a local church leader (Furnish 1984:434). What he is famous for is *his service to the gospel.* The Greek text is literally "praised in the gospel" and may well indicate that he is an evangelist of some renown. There is no end of speculation as to who this individual could be. Luke, Barnabas, Aristarchus and Apollos have all been proposed at one time or another. *The* brother, as opposed to "our" brother, shows that he was not one of Paul's colleagues. Luke and Barnabas are thus eliminated from the list of likely prospects. Apollos was too well known to need the kind of official recommendation that Paul provides here (compare 1 Cor 16:12). Since Paul is writing from the province of Macedonia, it is reasonable to assume that *the brother* is a representative of the Macedonian churches. This would include Philippi, Thessalonica and Berea. From Luke's list of delegates in Acts 20:4-5, Sopater from Berea and Aristarchus and Secundus from Thessalonica are the most plausible possibilities.

The second church representative is unnamed as well. This individual, unlike the first, is well known to the congregation: *our brother* (v. 22). He is distinguished by Paul in two ways. First, *he has often proved in many ways that he is zealous* (v. 22). *Proved* is a verb that means "to test" in order to establish someone's or something's worth or genuineness (compare 2:9). It was used in 8:8 of testing the sincerity of the Corinthians' love by comparing it with the earnestness of others. In this case Paul does not specify the nature of the testing—only that it occurred many times *(pollakis)* and in a wide range of situations *(en pollois).* Each time, the brother was found *zealous (spoudaion).* Now he is *even more so* because of, second, *his great confidence* in the Corinthians. The language suggests a recent positive encounter with the Corinthians in a ministry capacity. But the clues are too scant to allow us to even speculate about who this individual may be. Later in the letter Paul makes mention of having sent "our brother" with Titus on the previous

own flesh and blood. For discussion, see Barrett 1973:228. While the possessive use of the article is common in the New Testament, nothing in the immediate context demands or even supports this interpretation. Nor is there anything in the context to support the

mission to Corinth (12:18), and this may well be the same individual.

Our brother raises the total that Paul sends in advance of his arrival to three persons. Would Titus alone not have sufficed? His ministerial abilities and affection for the Corinthians seem to be very much in evidence. Yet although Titus had had some success with the collection on his previous visit, it had not been enough to spur the Corinthians on to completion. In addition, Titus is Paul's colleague and representative, and there are now intruders on the scene raising doubts about the offering. So there is real value in sending persons who are not directly connected with the Pauline mission. Also, by sending two representatives of congregations that had already given, Paul can place a subtle pressure on Corinth to match the efforts of the other Gentile churches. Then too, the two delegates serve to guarantee the legitimacy of the endeavor. Their presence shows that the collection effort is not just Paul's sly way of raising personal funds for himself and his colleagues.

A summary of the credentials of the three individuals is provided in verse 23. Titus is distinguished as Paul's *partner and fellow worker*. The latter is the term Paul typically uses of his associates in the ministry. By virtue of his apostolic standing, he could legitimately have treated Titus as a subordinate. Instead he dealt with him as a partner and companion *(koinōnos)*. Titus is Paul's personally appointed representative. The other two brothers are designated *representatives of the churches*. The term is actually *apostles (apostoloi)*, which has both a narrow and a broad application in the New Testament. In the Gospels it is normally used of those Christ commissioned as his representatives to the world (the Twelve). In the epistles the term is extended beyond the Twelve to include those involved in church planting. This is why Barnabas (Acts 14:4,14; 1 Cor 9:5), James (Gal 1:19), Andronicus (Rom 16:7) and Junia (Rom 16:7) can be called "apostles." In a few cases the term appears to be used of those who are appointed by the local church to carry out a specific task on its behalf. This category includes the two *brothers* who serve as their church's delegates in delivering the Jerusalem collection,

suggestion that *all the churches* is to be identified with the Judean churches.

8:19 *Charis* denotes here a gracious work (compare 8:6).

and also Epaphroditus, who ministers to Paul on behalf of the Philippian church (Phil 2:25).

The two brothers are also distinguished as *an honor to Christ.* Nowhere else are individuals referred to in this way. The phrase is literally "the glory of Christ." The genitive can be objective—they are *an honor to Christ* (TEV, NIV, JB, NEB, Phillips)—or subjective—they are "a reflection of Christ's glory." If the former, then Paul is saying that their life and ministry are a credit to Christ (M. J. Harris 1976:373). If the latter, then the thought is that as church representatives they reflect Christ's glory (Furnish 1984:425).

Paul concludes by exhorting the Corinthians to do two things. They are to *show these men* their *love* and to demonstrate *the reason for [Paul's] pride* in them. What form this show of love was to take is debated. It certainly is more than extending a warm welcome and the customary hospitality. The noun *endeixis* means "proof." Earlier in the chapter Paul challenged the church to prove the sincerity of their love by completing the collection (8:8-12). Here the proof Paul has in mind is probably cooperating with the delegates' efforts to bring the collection to a speedy conclusion—although exhibiting a willing and generous spirit of giving may also be in view (Murphy-O'Connor 1991:88).

By showing Titus and the delegates their love, the Corinthians in turn demonstrate the reason for Paul's pride in them. He has been confidently boasting about them to the Macedonian churches (9:2). They are now called on to justify his boasting by fulfilling their pledge from the year before. And they are to do it *so that the churches can see it*—that is, the Corinthians are challenged to act as if the churches, and not just their delegates, were there to watch. Which churches are these? While it could be the Macedonian churches or even all contributing Gentile congregations, the churches that the two brothers represent are undoubtedly the ones Paul is thinking of.

Paul Employs Some Reverse Psychology (9:1-5) David Seabury once said, "Enthusiasm is the best protection in any situation and wholeheart-

---

8:24 *Endeiknymenoi* is taken as imperatival in force by virtually all translators. On the

edness is contagious." This is especially true when it comes to fundraising. A contagious enthusiasm is a very effective way to rouse a congregation to action. This was certainly Paul's experience. While visiting the Macedonian churches, he shared a ministry opportunity, and his enthusiasm carried the day (8:4). In fact, the Macedonians urgently pleaded for the privilege of sharing in "this service to the saints" in Jerusalem (8:4).

Paul also boasted, as proud parents are wont to do, about the Corinthians' eagerness to participate. But now a problem has developed. The Corinthians' initial eagerness has not translated into action. Titus was able to rekindle interest in the relief fund on his last visit (8:6). But after he left Corinth, the collection effort once again came to a halt. And now Paul is planning to travel to Corinth, and the Macedonian delegates who accompany him will see that all his boasting was so much hot air.

To prevent this from happening, Paul engages in a bit of reverse psychology with the Corinthians. To prevent embarrassment for all parties concerned, he does four things. He recalls their initial enthusiasm and how it had stirred the Macedonian churches to action (9:1-2). He refers to the Corinthians' loss of face should any Macedonian delegates come and find them unprepared (9:4). He announces the upcoming visit of *the brothers* to make sure this does not happen (9:3, 5). And finally he reminds them of the blessings that come from generous giving (9:6-15).

But isn't Paul going over much the same ground that he covered in chapter 8? The seemingly repetitive aspects of 9:1-5, in particular, have led some scholars to conclude that chapters 8—9 could not possibly be part of the same letter (see the introduction). For one, chapter 9 begins with a phrase that normally introduces a new topic ("Now concerning . . . "), and a full description of the collection reappears *(this service to the saints,* v. 1). How is this possible after Paul's call in chapter 8 to "finish the work"? Also, in chapter 8 the Corinthians' efforts are still in need of completion (vv. 6, 11), while in 9:2 it looks as if they have been ready since last year. Further, the mission of *the brothers* is presented differently. In chapter 8 they are delegates of the contributing churches,

---

participle used as an imperative, see Blass, Debrunner and Funk 1961:§ 468.2 and Moule 1959:179-80.

sent to ensure that the monies are handled in a responsible fashion; in chapter 9 they are Paul's representatives, sent to complete the offering before his visit to Corinth.

Three suggestions are commonly proffered to explain this state of affairs. One suggestion is that chapter 9 is a separate letter sent at the same time as 2 Corinthians 8 to communities in Achaia other than Corinth (for example, H. D. Betz 1985; Georgi 1986:17; Martin 1986:281). A second construal is that chapter 9 is a note sent after chapter 8 to firm up the collection effort that Paul had written about in his earlier communication. A third proposal reverses the chapters: chapter 9 is the earlier piece of correspondence, with chapter 8 sent to Corinth at the point that the good intentions Paul had boasted about to the Macedonians had not yet produced the desired results (Bultmann 1985:18; Héring 1967:xiii).

The idea of a separate letter, while attractive in theory, actually introduces as many problems as it solves. For one, the opening *gar* ("for") would be nonsensical as the start of a letter. Moreover, Paul's references to *the brothers* in 9:3-5 are quite unintelligible apart from the details of chapter 8. Then too, his mention of *the Macedonians* in 9:2-4 assumes the more explicit references in the previous chapter.

So what is the solution? In the final analysis, much depends on how the grammar of verse 1 is construed. The opening phrase, in point of fact, is "*for* concerning" *(peri men gar),* not "*now* concerning" *(peri de);* thus it links this section with what has come before rather than introducing a new topic. In addition, the article with *diakonia* could be resumptive—"concerning *this* service" *(peri tēs diakonias)*—a recognition on Paul's part that he has digressed a bit from his primary topic. The digression has in fact been a lengthy one (vv. 16-24), which would further explain why a full description of the collection *(the service for*

9:1 *Men* looks forward to the *de* in verse 3. The thought runs, "There is no need for me to write this to you, . . . but just in case, I am sending my personal representatives to make sure my pride in you is not unwarranted." *Gar* ("for") most likely refers back to Paul's appeal in verse 24: "Justify our pride in you, for I have no need to write to you about this ministry . . ." (compare Barrett 1973:232). Alternatively, it could pertain to *the brothers:* "I have commended the brothers to you (rather than commanded you to give), for I have no need to write to you about this ministry . . ." (Plummer 1915:253).

the saints) is included at this juncture.

A simple reordering of the clauses in 9:1 actually provides a ready explanation of what Paul is about here. If the main clause is the latter part of verse 1 and the first part of verse 1 is merely resumptive, then verse 1 and the first part of verse 2 can be translated "It is superfluous for me to write you about this service for the saints, for I know your enthusiasm . . ." Paul would then be saying that the advice he has offered them, after all is said and done, is probably not really necessary given the Corinthians' initial track record. Read in this way, 9:1 becomes not a clumsy transition but a pastoral affirmation that lets Paul express confidence in the Corinthians' good intentions and still voice concern that they not let him down by failing to translate their good intentions into action.

Paul's confidence is based on knowledge of the Corinthians' desire to be involved: *for I know your eagerness* (v. 2). The translation "I know your readiness" in the RSV and NASB is misleading. From 8:6 and 11 it is obvious that the Corinthians are far from ready—although the other Achaian churches may have been closer to the mark *(you in Achaia)*. *Eagerness to help* (NIV, JB, NEB, NRSV) and "how willing you are" (Phillips, TEV) are right on target.

The Corinthians' eagerness became common knowledge as a result of Paul's proud *boasting* to the Macedonians. The verb *kauchōmai* is present tense: "I am boasting." Paul has been criticized for being either hopelessly naive or overly optimistic about the Corinthians. In actuality, neither is the case. When talking about one church to another, he merely made a point of presenting the congregation in the best rather than the worst light possible—even if the latter is closer to reality.

What he specifically has been telling the Macedonians is that the Achaian churches have been ready *since last year*. Ready for what,

---

9:2 *Pareskeuastai* (middle voice) means "prepared" or "ready." Paul's use of *Achaia* rather than "Corinth" is probably to balance *Macedonia*—although some have argued on the basis of Paul's shift in language that chapter 9 is a circular letter to the Achaian churches. See the introduction.

I have been boasting . . . to the Macedonians indicates that Paul was in the province of Macedonia when he wrote 2 Corinthians. The present tense, "I am boasting," suggests that he has been moving from church to church, presumably in an attempt to finalize the collection.

though? If Paul is saying that their contribution was ready last year, this conflicts with his injunction in the preceding chapter to "finish the work" (8:11). If, however, he is saying that last year they were ready to be involved or prepared to make a commitment, this fits nicely with the broader context (*ready to give;* NIV, Phillips, TEV, JV, NEB).

Yet it was not their readiness to give that impressed the Macedonians but their *enthusiasm* (literally, "zeal" [*zēlos*]). "Zeal," used positively, denotes an intense and earnest effort to reach a goal (Hahn 1978b:1166). Paul could well be thinking of how the Corinthians not only were enthusiastic but also took the initiative in asking his advice on the best way to go about saving up for a generous contribution (1 Cor 16:1-4). The net effect was to stir the Macedonians—or at least *most of them—to action.* The verb *erethizō* usually means "to provoke," "irritate" or "rouse to anger." Here it is used in the positive sense of rousing to action by means of an encouraging example.

But enthusiasm is not easy to sustain over a period of years. So it is now the Corinthians' turn to be roused by the Macedonians' enthusiasm. Moreover, Paul will be accompanied by some Macedonians on his next visit to Corinth (9:4). If they come and find the Corinthians unprepared, this would make for a rather embarrassing situation for all parties concerned. To see that this does not happen, Paul takes the precautionary step of sending a team—consisting of Titus and the two companions—in advance to set matters in order (vv. 3, 5; compare 8:6). The plan is for them to visit first, and Paul plus the Macedonian delegates to follow after. Paul provides no further details about Titus's two companions *(the brothers).* In all likelihood this is because quite a lengthy recommendation has already been provided (8:16-24).

The task of Titus and his companions is twofold. Their first task is to make certain that the offering is ready by the time Paul comes *(finish the arrangements,* 9:5). Their second task is to ensure that the *generous gift* the Corinthians have pledged is freely and not *grudgingly* given (v.

9:3 The aorist *(epempsa)* could be preterite ("I sent") or epistolary ("I am sending"— most modern translations).

5). The noun translated *generous gift* means "a good word" *(eu + logia)* and is commonly used in the Greek Bible of a favorable word accorded God and others (as in 1 Cor 10:16; Rev 5:12, 13; 7:12). The term also came to denote a benefit or a bountiful gift bestowed on someone by someone else (Rom 15:29; Eph 1:3), which is the sense here. From all appearances, then, Corinth was a church with sufficient funds to make a sizable contribution.

Paul uses the term *generous (eulogia)* again in verse 5—this time as a point of contrast to a grudging *(pleonexia)* contribution. The exact contrast is difficult to determine. Since Paul has just reminded the Corinthians that they had promised a generous contribution, it is unlikely that he would hammer away at its size (a large and not a stingy gift [KJV]). The sense of freely as opposed to grudgingly offered is a possibility (NIV), as is voluntarily and not forcibly extracted (TEV, Phillips, JB, RSV, NEB). The last option fits the broader context the best. The TEV's "It will show that you give because you want to, not because you have to" is an apt rendering. The term translated "grudgingly" *(pleonexia)* derives from a verb meaning "to take advantage of" or "to defraud" and is often used of someone who is greedy and grasping after what others have. Here the term denotes selfish, greedy people who give only because they are forced to do so and not because they want to.

The point is well taken. If Paul waits until he arrives with the Macedonian representatives, then Corinth will feel compelled to give and the arrangements will be hastily made so as not to lose face. The preparatory visit of Titus and his companions buys enough time for the Corinthians' gift to be ready as a voluntary one.

Paul's precautionary measure of sending a team in advance prevents two embarrassing situations from occurring. The first is for Paul's *boasting* to prove *hollow* (v. 3). The verb *kenoō* means "to make empty or void"—or as we say today, to be "full of hot air." Paul's rivals have already been voicing criticisms about his credibility. If the Corinthians do not fulfill their pledge by the time he arrives,

---

9:5 *Prokatartizō (finish the arrangements)* means to "put in order" or "make ready in advance."

then his boasting will amount to a lot of fine-sounding words lacking any real substance. Not only this, but the Corinthians themselves stand to lose face. For Paul will be bringing some Macedonians with him when he comes, and how would it look to those who had made their contribution much earlier—and at grave personal cost—if the church's offering is not in order?

Thankfully, neither situation materialized. Titus and his companions fulfilled their mission, Paul made his promised visit, and the Corinthians, along with the other Achaian churches, were "pleased to make a contribution" (Rom 15:26). To Paul's way of thinking, this was only right. For "if the Gentiles have shared in the Jews' spiritual blessings, they owe it to the Jews to share with them their material blessings" (Rom 15:27).

The Results of Generous Giving (9:6-15) Paul concludes his appeal by pointing to the benefits the Corinthians will reap as a result of generous giving. Each generation takes delight in putting its practical wisdom in memorable form. For us it is maxims like "A stitch in time saves nine," "Don't count your chickens before they hatch" and "Look before you leap." In like fashion Paul sums up the benefits of liberality by means of a maxim: *Whoever sows sparingly will also reap sparingly, and whoever sows generously will also reap generously.* From all appearances Paul is quoting a popular saying. It is one that he finds useful, since it reappears in slightly truncated form in Galatians 6:7 ("A man reaps what he sows"). There is no exact scriptural parallel. A similar thought is found in a number of Old Testament texts (such as Job 4:8; Prov 11:24-26; 22:8-9; Hos 10:12-13). But the closest parallel actually appears in the teaching of Jesus: "Give, and it will be given to you. . . . With the measure you use, it will be measured to you" (Lk 6:38).

The principle is clear: we harvest in proportion to our planting—or, to use a contemporary maxim, "we get as good as we give." This applies as well to charitable giving—so much so that Paul takes eight verses to spell this out (9:8-15). But before doing so, in verse 7 he offers the Corinthians

---

9:6 Compare Proverbs 11:24: "One man gives freely, yet gains even more; another withholds unduly, but comes to poverty."

three guidelines for giving beyond what he has already listed in 8:11-15.

First, giving is to be an individual matter that is settled in the privacy of one's own heart. *Each,* Paul says, *should give what he has decided in his heart to give. Each* is placed first for emphasis. "How much?" is a question that each person must answer for herself. And it is never to be determined by how much "the Joneses" are contributing.

Second, giving requires resolve. The text reads *what he has decided* (literally, "as each has purposed"). The verb *proaireomai,* found only here in the New Testament, means "to choose deliberately" or "to make up one's own mind about something." It is a well-known fact that telethons that play on people's emotions to solicit contributions often end up with donors who pledge impulsively but not deliberately enough to follow through on their pledge. Paul says that giving is to be based on a calculated decision. It is not a matter to be settled lightly or impulsively.

Third, giving is to be a private, not a public, decision. It is to be decided in the *heart.* It is an unfortunate reality that some Christians will give only if there is some form of public acclaim or recognition involved. Endowed chairs, scholarship funds and building projects are rarely underwritten anonymously. Usually much pomp and circumstance is attached to these donations, with the contributor's name(s) prominently displayed and the donation itself frequently praised and honored publicly. The real reason to give is because one cannot help but give—or, as William Barclay puts it, because the "need wakens a desire that cannot be stilled" (1954:233). This desire is in fact to give the way God gave; it was because he so loved the world that he gave his only Son.

Paul identifies four beneficiaries of charitable giving in verses 8-14: the giver (vv. 8-11), the recipients (v. 12), God (vv. 11-12) and the church (vv. 13-14). In the first place, the giver benefits. God's response to generosity is *to make all grace abound* to the giver. The idea of grace abounding is a familiar one in these chapters. The verb "to abound" *(perisseuō)* is found six times. The noun *grace (charis)* is no stranger

---

9:7 There is an ellipsis in the Greek text. As it stands, verse 7 reads, "Each, as he has decided in his heart." A verb must be supplied to make the clause grammatically complete *(Each [person] should give . . .).*

either, appearing ten times in all. Here it refers to the giver's unmerited favor from God.

But what form does God's favor take? Is Paul thinking of spiritual benefits or material blessings? The focus in the context is clearly on material blessings. Yet Paul could well be thinking of all the benefits we receive from God. For inherent in the term *grace* is the idea that whatever we possess, be it physical or spiritual, we possess by reason of God's goodwill toward us, not because of personal merit.

We also possess it by reason of God's power. *God is able* is perhaps better rendered "God is powerful" (*dynatei ho theos;* v. 8). It is God Almighty who provides the means to be generous. This same thought is found in proverbial form in the teaching of Jesus: "Freely you have received, freely give" (Mt 10:8). The order here is important. It is only as we have freely received that we can, in turn, freely give.

God's abounding grace extends beyond the mere replenishment of resources. He is powerful not only to replace resources spent in Christian service but also to multiply them to the point that *at all times* and *in all things* we have *all* that we *need* (v. 8). *Autarkeia* ("all that is needed") means to be sufficient in oneself or self-supporting. Cynics and Stoics aimed at the kind of self-sufficiency that permitted indifference to other people and to circumstances. To a certain extent Paul aligns himself with this sentiment. Like the Stoic, the Christian aspires to be free from dependence on material possessions—or, as Paul puts it, "to be content whatever the circumstances" (Phil 4:11). To learn to be content with very little requires that one want very little: "If we have food and clothing, we will be content" (1 Tim 6:8). And the less one wants, the greater the means for relieving the needs of others (Plummer 1915:260).

9:8 It is hard to catch the alliteration and piling up of Greek terms in English. *Pas* occurs four times and *pantote* once: *God is able to make all grace abound . . . so that in all things at all times you have all that you need to abound in every good work.*

9:9 The aorists are probably gnomic, picturing the typical behavior of the righteous person: "he scatters abroad . . . ; he gives to the poor" (RSV, TEV, JB) and not "he has scattered . . . ; he has given to the poor" (KJV, NIV, NEB). The Old Testament concern for the destitute reflected in Psalm 112:9 continues in the New Testament. James, for example, defines "religion" as looking after widows and orphans (1:27).

For the identification of *dikaiosynē* with acts of piety, see Matthew 6:1-4. Paul normally

This is a very difficult notion for Westerners today, for the drive in our world too often is to get-get-get and buy-buy-buy. An attitude of contentment like Paul's presupposes trust and confidence in God to provide for our basic needs. If we are secure in his love and know that he undertakes to watch over our lives, then all anxiety for the future will be gone (Siede 1978:728).

Furthermore, Paul parts company with his Stoic contemporaries. For while he aims to be free of his circumstances, he does not aim to be free of people. The point of our resources' being replenished is so that we, in turn, can *abound in every good work* (v. 8). Money is given not to be hoarded but to promote good (Murphy-O'Connor 1991:91).

To illustrate this point Paul quotes the psalmist's praise of those who give freely to the poor: *He has scattered abroad his gifts to the poor; his righteousness endures forever* (v. 9; Ps 112:9 [LXX 111:9]). The person who dares to be generous toward those in need is compared to the farmer who scatters his seed while sowing. To sow by scattering is the opposite of sowing sparingly. The farmer who scatters seed is generous with it. *His gifts to the poor* is literally "he gives to the poor." The term for *poor* denotes someone who works for a living (the day laborer; *penēs*), not the destitute *(ptōchos)*. The Old Testament gleaning laws provided for the basic needs of those without any personal means of support, such as the widow, the alien or the orphan (for example, Lev 19:9-10; Deut 24:17-22). Beyond this, it fell to those with surplus income to meet other kinds of needs (see Ps 112:5: "Good will come to him who is generous and lends freely").

"Sow a thought and you reap an act; sow an act and you reap a habit; sow a habit and you reap a character; sow a character and you reap a

uses the noun *dikaiosynē* of moral uprightness and the verb *dikaioō* of a right standing with God. Ralph Martin (1986:291) and Alfred Plummer (1915:261) believe that the latter is in view here. But this introduces a notion that is alien to the context. Victor Furnish suggests that *dikaiosynē* is divine righteousness by which charitable persons live and in which they shall remain forever (1984:448-49). The referent of *autou*, however, is the charitable giver, not God. Henry Wicks is surely correct when he states that the context obliges us to understand *his righteousness endures forever* as meaning that those who are marked by thoughtful and glad liberality will have enduring high character as their reward (1917-1918).

destiny" (Samuel Smiles, *Life and Labor*). The destiny of the person who gives liberally is a *righteousness* that *endures forever* (v. 9). The sense is not immediately clear. *Righteousness* could refer to general moral uprightness (Barrett 1973:238) or to specific acts of piety (Plummer 1915:261). *Scattered abroad his gifts to the poor* suggests the latter, although generosity of the hand usually issues from generosity of the heart. Such righteousness *endures forever.* How so? The phrase could mean "is never forgotten"—that is, God will remember the givers' goodness and reward them with eternal life (Bratcher 1983:99)—or that their reputation for doing good will be recalled by subsequent generations (JB). Alternatively, the phrase could mean "never stops"—that is, the effects of their generosity will continue on from generation to generation (TEV, NEB). Personal renown seems to fit the context the best. For not only will the Corinthian offering meet a real need, but it will also overflow in many expressions of thanks to God (v. 12) and many heartfelt prayers for the Corinthians (v. 14).

Paul differed from the Stoic in one other significant respect. He pursued God-dependency rather than self-sufficiency. The generous giver, like the farmer, is dependent from start to finish on God: *he who supplies seed to the sower and bread for food will also supply and increase your store of seed and will enlarge the harvest of your righteousness* (v. 10). The idea is an Old Testament one. "Seed for the sower and bread for the eater" comes from Isaiah 55:10, while "the harvest of your righteousness" is taken from Hosea 10:12 (LXX). It was widely believed that material prosperity was the result of divine blessing. Paul to a certain extent reflects this belief. It is God "who richly provides us with everything for our enjoyment," he tells Timothy (1 Tim 6:17).

Take the farmer. God provides not only for his immediate physical needs in the form of a harvest of grain for his daily bread but also for his future needs in the form of seed for next year's planting (*supplies seed to the sower;* 2 Cor 9:10). If God routinely does this for

9:10 The fact that some in the early church had difficulty with the premise that material prosperity was the result of divine blessing is reflected in those manuscripts that have the

the farmer, he surely is able to do it for us—provided that we have good intentions. God supplies our seed and even increases it so that we *can be generous on every occasion* (vv. 10-11). The term *haplotēs* ("generous") denotes singleness of character ("noble"), heart ("pure") or intent ("sincere," "openhearted"; Bauernfeind 1964). Here, as in verse 2, it signifies openheartedness with one's possessions, or generosity.

The general principle is thus that the more we give, the more we will get from God. And the more we get, the more we are expected to give. John Bunyan wrote, "A man there was and they called him mad; the more he gave, the more he had." Of course Bunyan was writing of the Christian. To the world such a principle of giving is nonsense. But to Paul it is a reality of the Christian life.

The idea that God can and does multiply the generous giver's material resources is not well received today. Experience seems to indicate otherwise. The rich, who often are stingy with their wealth, seem to get richer, and the poor, who frequently are the most liberal givers, appear to get poorer. As a result, it is sometimes suggested that the "supplier" in verse 10 is not God but other Christians who come to the aid of those who put themselves at risk through generosity (Murphy-O'Connor 1991:93). Or it is proposed that *seed* and *harvest* are spiritual, not material, endowments (Martin 1986:292). But Paul goes on to tell the Corinthians that they *will be made rich in every way so that [they] can be generous on every occasion* (v. 11). The primary act of generosity that he has in mind is charitable giving, as *supplying the needs of God's people* in verse 12 makes clear.

Nonetheless, we do well to observe what Paul does not say. He does not say that wealth or surplus income is a sign of God's blessing. Nor is it giving per se that is applauded. It is, rather, a lifestyle of generosity that Paul commends. For those who give cheerfully and willingly, the promise is that God will provide all that they need to continue doing good.

Not only does the giver benefit from generosity, but the recipients benefit as well. *This service that you perform,* Paul says, *supplies the*

optative, "*May* God supply . . ." ($\aleph^2$ D^2 F G Ψ 0 0209 0243 1739 1881), rather than the indicative, "God *will* supply . . ."

needs of God's people (v. 12). The text is literally "the service *[diakonia]* of this service *[leitourgia]*." *Diakonia,* commonly translated "ministry" (3:7-9; 4:1; 5:18; 6:3) or "service" (8:4; 9:1), can refer more specifically to "aid" or "support," especially of the charitable variety (compare Acts 6:1; 11:29; Bauer, Arndt and Gingrich 1979). The aid Paul has in mind is the Corinthians' contribution to the Jerusalem collection, which is called a *leitourgia.* The word means "work for the people" *(ergon + laos)* and was used in Hellenistic Greek for service to the community that certain persons were under obligation to do because of the size of their income (Hess 1978:551).

How this applies to the Jerusalem collection is not immediately clear. Is the stress on performing a public duty (promoting the welfare of the community)? Or is the focus on carrying out a religious service (serving God through meeting the needs of his people)? Paul uses the term in Philippians 2:25 and 30 more generally of the "help" he received from Epaphroditus when he was in prison, and this may well be the sense here.

The specific help rendered by the offering is that of *supplying the needs* of the Judean Christians. *Hysterēma* ("needs") denotes a shortage or deficiency of basic necessities. In the first century this amounted to food, clothing and shelter (2 Cor 11:27). So the help offered through the Corinthians' contribution is by way of necessity, not luxury.

God is the third beneficiary of generous giving. *This service,* Paul states, *is also overflowing in many expressions of thanks to God* (vv. 11-12). The grammar of verse 12 is ambiguous. *Pollōn eucharistiōn* could be "many people who give thanks" (as in Martin 1986:294) or "many thanksgivings" (as in Plummer 1915:265). *Many expressions of thanks* catches the sense (NIV, NEB, Phillips). In any event, it is not the Corinthians who receive the recipients' gratitude but God, which is as

9:12 *Leitourgia* is used almost exclusively in the Septuagint for the cultic services of the priests and Levites. This sense is carried over into the New Testament, for example, in Luke 1:23, where Zechariah's priestly service at the temple is described as *hai hēmerai tēs leitourgias autou* ("his time of service").

9:13 The RSV understands the subject of the participle *doxazontes* ("glorifying") to be the same as that of the participle *ploutizomenoi* ("you will be enriched") at the beginning of verse 11—that is, the Corinthians. But since *doxazontes* does not stand in strict grammatical concord with anything in the immediate context, the subject is generally

it should be.

God is also the recipient of *praise* (v. 13). *Because of this service,* Paul remarks, *men will praise God.* The subject of the Greek participle *doxazontes* is not immediately clear. The RSV and NRSV take it to be the Corinthians themselves: "you will glorify God by your obedience." The KJV, LB, JB and REB, on the other hand, assume that the praise comes from the recipients ("those you help"). Phillips, NEB, NIV and TEV, yet again, construe the referent more generally as "many" *(men will praise God).*

On the whole, the second option seems preferable. Since the participle does not stand in strict grammatical agreement with anything in the immediate context, the subject must be supplied from the logic of the argument. And unless Paul has completely lost track of the argument, the logical subject is *eis autous* ("to them," v. 13)—that is, the recipients of the offering. Paul's point is that the church at large recognizes the collection for what it is: God's grace at work in the lives of the contributors. As in all areas of life, "the chief end" of humankind is "to glorify God and to enjoy him forever" (Westminster Catechism, question 1). So while the immediate aim of the collection is to relieve want, the ultimate goal is to bring honor to God—the enabler and provider of all that we possess.

The recipients' praise is grounded in two things. They will praise God, Paul says, first *for the obedience that accompanies your confession of the gospel of Christ* and, second, *for your generosity in sharing with them and with everyone else* (v. 13). The first phrase is literally "for the obedience of your confession." The genitive could be subjective ("the obedience that comes from your Christian profession"), objective ("your obedience to your profession"; RSV, NIV, JB, NEB, REB), adjectival ("your professed obedience"; KJV) or even epexegetic ("your obedience,

---

assumed to be the Jerusalem recipients (Bruce 1971:228). Ralph Martin, oddly enough, takes the referent to be those Corinthians who remained loyal to Paul's cause and to the collection (1986:294). Keith Nickle, on the other hand, argues that those who glorify God are not merely Jerusalem believers but also unbelieving Jews who will convert as a result of the Gentiles' demonstration of faith (1966:137-38).

The genitive in the phrase *to euangelion tou Christou* is probably objective: "the gospel about Christ."

namely, your Christian profession"; as in Furnish 1984:445; Martin 1986:294). The first two options best fit the meaning of the noun *homologia*, a term that in Hellenistic Greek denotes an agreement or compact (a common *[homo-]* statement *[logia]*). The opposite of an uncritical opinion, it implies assent to something felt to be valid and in such a way that it is followed by definite resolve and action (Michel 1967:200). "Profession" (JB, Phillips), the act of publicly declaring assent to commonly held beliefs, is perhaps a better translation than *confession* (NIV), which is usually associated with acknowledgment of sin or guilt. The common belief that is being professed is *the gospel of Christ* (or "the gospel about Christ"—objective genitive).

Paul's point is that to be vital and living, profession of faith must issue in works. The Corinthians' willing contribution to the Jerusalem collection shows that they possess a faith that accepts the claims of the gospel and obeys its dictates as well. Phillips's "that you practise the gospel . . . that you profess to believe in" captures the sense exactly. Paul is not alone in closely linking profession and practice. James similarly states that "faith by itself, if it is not accompanied by action, is dead" (2:17, 26) and "useless" (v. 20).

The Judean recipients will *praise God,* second, for the Corinthians' *generosity in sharing with them and with everyone else* (v. 13). This is the last of three occurrences of *haplotēs* ("generosity") in chapters 8—9. In all three cases the noun denotes simplicity of intent with respect to one's finances ("openheartedness"; 8:2; 9:11, 13). It is generosity of the heart, not the pocketbook, that counts. The recipients will praise God not merely for a gift of money but also for the fellowship in Christ that the gift expresses (Dahl 1977:35). *Koinōnia* ("sharing"), found four times in 2 Corinthians, refers to that which is held in common. In the New Testament it comes to denote the close union and caring concern of the members of Christ's body, the church (6:14; 8:4; 9:13; 13:13). It is a union that is forged by the Spirit (13:14) but that finds concrete expression in the contributions of the Gentile churches to meet the physical needs of their fellow believers in Judea.

9:14 *Kai autōn . . . epipothountōn* could be construed as a genitive absolute ("while

Paul enlarges the scope of recipients to include not only the Judean believers but also *everyone else* (v. 13). At face value the comment is obscure. The most reasonable construal is that *with them* refers to the Jerusalem church, which, in turn, would distribute the funds to *everyone else* in need. Alternatively, *kai eis pantas* may be Paul's way of pointing out to the Corinthians that what benefits the Judean believers benefits the whole body of Christians (Plummer 1915:267).

Fourth and finally, the church as a whole benefits from generous giving. Here is the key to the urgency of Paul's appeal. For the most part, the recipients were conservative Jewish Christians who still regarded the Gentiles with a certain amount of fear and suspicion. For them the collection proves the Gentiles' profession of faith (v. 13). *Dokimēs* (the noun behind the verb *proved* here) connotes a test in order to verify someone's or something's genuineness or worth. In this case the collection serves as the test by which the Gentiles' faith is shown to be genuine.

Paul anticipates that the offering will impact the church in two additional ways: *prayers* for the Corinthians will be offered, and a closer relationship between the Jewish recipients and the Gentile donors will be forged (v. 14). *Because of the surpassing grace God has given* the Corinthians, one expected result of the collection is that the recipients will pray for them *(their prayers for you)*. N. P. Willis once said, "Gratitude is not only the memory, but the homage of the heart rendered to God for his goodness." It is not enough to feel grateful for what others do for us. Heartfelt gratitude issues in prayer on the person's behalf. Prayer, in turn, has a way of bringing us into a closer relationship with those for whom we intercede. This is the second expected result that Paul anticipates. As the recipients pray, Paul says that their *hearts will go out to* the contributing churches (v. 14). *Epipotheō* ("go out to, yearn after") is another word that turns up a number of times in chapters 7—9 (7:7, 11; 9:14). As the Jewish recipients pray for their Gentile patrons, their hearts will be warmed toward them, and they will long to see and have a closer relationship with them (M. J. Harris 1976:378).

they themselves also . . . long after you"; Plummer 1915:267).

Paul caps off his appeal with what in form is a thanksgiving but in fact is a reminder of the supreme example of giving: *Thanks be to God for his indescribable gift!* (v. 15). We can never outgive God, for he gave beyond all human imagining. In fact, he gave what Paul calls an *indescribable gift.* The term *anekdiēgētos,* found only here in the Greek Bible (and only once outside the New Testament), denotes something that is beyond human description ("ineffable"—Liddell, Scott and Jones 1978). What, then, is this indescribable gift? Some suppose that this is Paul's final attempt to motivate generous giving by labeling the expected Corinthian gift as beyond all imagining. Others believe that Paul is describing the miracle of Jew-Gentile unity (for example, Plummer 1915:267-68) or the universal gospel (Martin 1986:295). Most, however, identify God's indescribable gift with Jesus Christ. We can give without loving, but we cannot love without giving. God so loved us that he gave the ultimate gift, whose cost can never be matched: the gift of his only Son.

Was Paul's appeal successful? Acts 20:2-3 would suggest so. Luke tells us that Paul made his announced third visit to Corinth and stayed three months. The length of his visit suggests that he received a ready welcome and that matters were in order regarding the Corinthians' contribution to the relief fund. Paul admits as much in Romans 15:26-27, when he states that "Macedonia and Achaia were pleased to make a contribution for the poor among the saints in Jerusalem." Yet Luke lists no delegate(s) for the Achaian churches. It may be that there was not sufficient time to arrange for a delegate to accompany the funds to Jerusalem. Or the Corinthians could have decided to forgo representation as a way of demonstrating their belated trust in Paul's integrity.

Paul and the delegates arrived at Jerusalem and were received "warmly" (Acts 21:17). Not a word is said, however, about the collection itself. Some conclude from Luke's silence that the offering was not well received. But arguments from silence are precarious ones at best. Moreover, the difficulty that captures Luke's attention is not the Jerusalem church's response to the collection but the trouble that unbelieving Jews from Asia caused Paul: "Jews from the province of Asia saw Paul at the temple. They stirred up the whole crowd and seized him, shouting, 'Men of Israel, help us! This is the man who teaches all men everywhere against our people and our law and this place' " (Acts 21:27-36). Paul anticipated encountering problems in Jerusalem and asked the Roman church to pray that he be rescued from unbelieving Jews in Judea (Rom 15:31). But the collection was far too important to deter him, for it symbolized, as it were, the very nature of the church—a community called out from many backgrounds to be "in Christ" (Craddock 1968:170).

□ Paul Tackles His Opponents: 10:1—13:11

Paul rarely identifies himself by name in the body of his letters (2 Cor 10:1; Gal 5:2; Eph 3:1; Col 1:23; 1 Thess 2:18; Philem 9 are the sole exceptions). When he does, it inevitably carries special significance. *I, Paul, . . . beg you that when I come I may not have to be as bold as I expect to be* (10:1-2). This rather startling comment at 10:1 marks the transition to the last of the letter's three major sections (1:1—7:16; 8:1—9:15; 10:1—13:13[14]). Indeed, so startling is Paul's statement, coming after his plea for the Corinthians' affection (chapter 6), his expressions of joy and confidence (chapter 7) and his fundraising appeal (chapters 8—9), that many today find it hard to believe that 1:1—9:15 and 10:1—13:13 originally coexisted in the same letter.

This is not the only difficulty. There are other aspects of chapters 10—13 that seem to be at odds with the rest of the letter. For one, Paul's remarks about his critics become much more pointed and strident. The "some" who peddle the word of God for profit (2:17) and carry letters of recommendation (3:1-3) are now called "false apostles," "deceitful workmen" and "[Satan's] servants" (11:13-15) who are out to enslave, exploit and slap the Corinthians in the face (11:20). Also, Paul's defense becomes much more impassioned: "What anyone else dares to boast about . . . I also dare to boast about" (11:21)—so much so that he admits to being out of his mind to talk as he is doing (11:23). Moreover, his tone is marked by biting sarcasm and scathing irony (for example, 11:19: "You gladly put up with fools since you are so wise!"). Indeed, translations average six exclamation points in rendering the Greek of chapters 10—12. Finally, Paul's attitude toward the Corinthians becomes threatening: "On my return," he warns, "I will not spare those who sinned earlier" (13:2). "Examine yourselves," he commands, "to see whether you are in the faith" (13:5; see the introduction).

A number of proposals have been put forward to account for this state of affairs. Some think that the explanation lay in Paul's frame of mind—that he penned chapters 10—13 after a bad night's sleep or that a lengthy dictation pause intervened. Others suppose that he received fresh news of an alarming character, prompting him to abruptly shift gears. Different audiences are sometimes proposed. Perhaps chapters 1—9 are addressed to the Corinthian congregation, while chapters 10—13 are directed at certain false apostles who have forced themselves into the congregation. Or maybe chapters 1—9 are intended for the majority who supported Paul (2:6), and chapters 10—13 are aimed at the minority who were still against him. It is even surmised that the abrupt shift is the result of Paul's habit of picking up the pen from his secretary and writing the final comments and greeting in his own hand (compare 1 Cor 16:21).

The difficulty, though, is that there are no contextual clues to alert the reader to a bad night's sleep, the receipt of disturbing news ("I hear that . . ."), a change of audience ("Now, to the rest of you . . .") or a change of writers ("I write this in my own hand"). This has led some to suggest that Paul intentionally reserved his criticism until he had regained the Corinthians' trust or that he first consolidated his apostolic authority and then exercised it. Yet the earlier chapters do not lack for criticism (in 3:1, for example, he says, "Do we need, like some people, letters of recommendation to you or from you?"). And Paul's authority is hardly a settled issue in the final chapters ("since you are demanding proof that Christ is speaking through me," 13:3).

The real problem that requires explanation is the sudden intensity of approach and stridency of tone at 10:1. How probable from a pastoral standpoint would it be for Paul to begin the letter with praise ("Praise be to the God and Father . . ." 1:3) and conclude with a sharp warning ("Examine yourselves," 13:5)? There is no real parallel to this in his other letters.

Many today consider the integrity of chapters 1—13 a hopeless cause and have abandoned ship in favor of one of two alternatives. One alternative is that chapters 10—13 are to be identified with Paul's "severe letter," sent prior to chapters 1—9 to rebuke the church for its lack of support and to call for the punishment of the individual who had challenged and humiliated Paul on his last visit (see, for example, Plummer 1915:xxxvi; Héring 1967:xii). The second alternative is that 2 Corinthians 10—13 was written after chapters 1—9 in response to reports of new developments at Corinth (e.g., Barrett 1973, Bruce 1971, Furnish 1984, Martin 1986, M. J. Harris 1976).

However, the lack of any manuscript or patristic evidence to suggest that chapters 10—13 circulated independently of chapters 1—9 is a major drawback of both of these alternatives (see the introduction). Also, it is not as if abrupt changes of tone do not occur elsewhere in Paul's letters (for example, Phil 3:2). Even so, "I am glad I can have complete confidence in you" (7:16) and "Examine yourselves to see whether you are in the faith" (13:5) do seem unlikely bedfellows.

As is often the case in life, the explanation probably lies in a combination of factors. "I, Paul," suggests that Paul now writes alone and with some urgency. Timothy, who is associated with Paul in the writing of 2 Corinthians (1:1), may well have served as secretary. Paul could have dismissed him at the conclusion of 9:15, intending to add a personal greeting and letter closing at his leisure. Disturbing news about the Corinthian church may have come in the meantime, leading Paul to confront the Corinthians in the personal and direct fashion that characterizes these final four chapters. His haste to address the problem may account, at least in part, for the abruptness of approach and stridency of tone.

Formally, 10:1—13:13 acts as a body closing section. It is the second such section in 2 Corinthians. Chapter 7:3-16 functions in much the same way (see the commentary). The presence of two body closing sections in a single letter is not without parallel in Paul's letters. Romans (1:10-15; 15:14-33) and 1 Corinthians (4:14-21; 16:1-18) are two noteworthy examples. First Corinthians, in particular, provides a close structural parallel. The question is, why two in this letter?

A careful look at both sections shows that they complement and balance one another. Chapter 7 states why Paul is not writing ("I do not say this to condemn you," v. 3), spells out the relationship between Paul and the Corinthians ("you have such a place in our hearts," v. 3) and provides expressions of confidence (vv. 4-16). Chapters 10—13, on the other hand, give Paul's explicit reason for writing ("This is why I write these things," 13:10) and announce his impending visit ("when I come," 10:2; "This will be my third visit to you," 13:1). In fact, what 7:3-16 lacks by way of Paul's future travel plans, 10:1—13:13 pursues with a vengeance (see the note on 7:3-16). The phrase "when I come" begins the section, and "this will be my third visit" concludes it. Sandwiched in between are expressions urging responsibility and threats of what will happen if responsible behavior is not forthcoming. Paul does obliquely speak of his upcoming visit at 9:4 ("if any Macedonians come with me"), but it is only in chapters 10—13 that an explicit announcement is made and details are given. Indeed, it would be a breach of epistolary etiquette for Paul to have written without formally announcing an upcoming visit. So chapters 10—13 fulfill a necessary function, without which chapters 1—9 would be incomplete.

Spiritual Weaponry (10:1-6) The exercise of discipline is never an easy matter. Because of the painful nature of the process, there is the temptation to put as much distance as possible between yourself and the person receiving the discipline. Written, as opposed to verbal, communication can be a less directly confrontational route, and hence more appealing. Where the tongue might get away from us in a face-to-face exchange, a letter permits a certain degree of perspective and objectivity. But avoidance of a face-to-face encounter can leave one

---

10:1 Paul customarily uses his name at the open and close of the letter, following the standard convention of his day (see the note on 1:1). All his letters start with a personal identification: Paul, . . . to the church in _____, greetings (see 2 Cor 1:1). Many of his letters also close with "I, Paul, write this greeting in my own hand" (1 Cor 16:21; Col 4:18; 2 Thess 3:17; Philem 19). Otherwise such personal references are rare indeed.

The body closing section of 1 Corinthians 16:5-11 both presupposes and supplements the content of 4:14-21. First Corinthians 4:14-21 states Paul's purpose in writing, notes the dispatch of an emissary and announces a forthcoming visit, while 16:2-10 includes information about the emissary he is sending, the reason for his own delay, why he will be coming, when it will occur and how long he plans to stay (Belleville 1987:29-31).

"Timid" when face to face . . . but "bold" when away is the opposition's critique of Paul. *Tapeinos* (and cognates) more commonly denotes humility, not timidity, and is extolled as a Christian virtue (for example, in Eph 4:2; Phil 2:3; Col 3:12).

R. Leivestad (1966) argues that *praÿtēs* and *epieikeia* denote the humble and patient submissiveness of a servant, rather than the gentle and forbearing attitude of a ruler. Yet

open to the charge of cowardice—a charge that Paul tackles head-on in chapter 10: *I, Paul, who am "timid" when face to face with you, but "bold" when away!* Paul is quoting the opposition, as the quotation marks around the terms *timid* and *bold* indicate (NIV, Phillips, REB). The word for *timid (tapeinos)* is commonly used in Hellenistic Greek to indicate a low social status, but it can also refer, as here, to the cringing, subservient attitude that sometimes accompanies humble circumstances. The Living Bible's "afraid to raise his voice when he gets here" catches the thought. But when Paul addresses the Corinthians at a distance (in writing), he becomes "bold." *Tharreō (bold)* was used earlier to speak of Paul's cheerfulness in the face of death (5:6, 8) and his confidence in the Corinthians (7:16). In this verse it connotes self-confidence or self-assurance of an unwarranted kind. In essence, Paul's critics are saying that he talks big in his letters (e.g., the severe letter) but is weak-kneed in person (e.g., the painful visit).

Indeed, in the minds of Paul's critics to resort to the pen is to *live by the standards of this world* (v. 2). The phrase is literally "to walk according to the flesh." "Walk" *(peripateō)* is one of Paul's favorite expressions to describe the Christian life (it occurs thirty-one times). Here it denotes a settled pattern of behavior. This pattern of behavior is described as "flesh," a term that ranges in meaning from what is physical, mortal or human to what is sinful or even sexual in nature. In this context it refers to a purely human way of doing things—which, for Paul's opponents, amounted to a weak way of doing things. They, by

---

Paul's stance in chapters 10—13 is authoritative and disciplinary, not humble and submissive. Compare Acts 24:4, the only other occurrence of *epieikeia* in the New Testament, where Tertullus, as he presents charges against Paul, begs the indulgence of the Judean procurator Felix.

The genitive *tou Christou* in the phrase *dia tēs praÿtētos kai epieikeias tou Christou* is subjective: "the gentleness and forbearance that Christ *showed.*" At first glance it seems odd that Paul would use *Christou* rather than *Iēsou.* The choice is probably due to the claim of some to belong to Christ in a special way (10:7; Plummer 1915:302).

10:2 To walk according to the flesh *(kata sarka)* in Paul's writings usually means to be "governed by human standards of behavior" (as in 2 Cor 1:17; 5:16). Here, however, the language is that of Paul's opponents, and the contrast is between "fleshly" and "powerful" modes of ministry (10:4). His critics could be referring to a want of visions and ecstatic experiences (for them the signs of a Spirit-empowered ministry). Or they could be equating a lack of self-assertiveness with spiritual inferiority (Barrett 1973:250). Gerd Theissen speculates, on the basis of 11:7 and 12:13, that Paul is responding to the

contrast, claimed to be spiritual people, boasting of their extraordinary experiences ("visions and revelations," 12:1) and Spirit-empowered ministry ("signs, wonders and miracles," 12:12). This would appeal to a congregation like Corinth, whose members thought they had arrived spiritually (they are "full," "rich," even "kings"—1 Cor 4:8). Paul's critics also asserted that he adopted human strategies of warfare (*wage war as the world does*, 10:3). *Strateuomai* means "to advance" with an army or fleet (Liddell, Scott and Jones 1978). His rivals claimed to fight with the armies of the Spirit, while Paul, they maintained, relied purely on ineffective, beggarly methods and resources to carry out his ministry.

Cowardly, weak and ineffectual—not an appealing pastoral portrait by any stretch of the imagination, and one that Paul dismisses out of hand. His introductory statement deserves careful attention. He begins with a warning. Yet it is a warning phrased in terms of a request, rather than a command: *I appeal to you . . . that when I come I may not have to be as bold as I expect to be* (vv. 1-2). The verb *(parakaleō)* is one commonly used by someone who has the authority to command but chooses not to.

Paul makes his request *by the meekness and gentleness of Christ.* At first glance this phrase seems out of sync with the forcefulness of what follows. But then Paul has been accused of "trying to frighten" the Corinthians with his letters (v. 9). So he takes pains to reassure his readers that he approaches them as Christ himself would. The adjectives are close synonyms. *Meekness (praÿtēs)* is descriptive of a gentle and friendly disposition, as opposed to a rough and hard one (Hauck and Schulz 1968:645-46; compare Mt 11:29, "for I am gentle and humble in heart"). *Gentleness (epieikeia;* only here and in Acts 24:4 in the New Testament) translates a term that denotes the yielding or forbearing disposition of those in positions of power—the judge who is lenient in judgment and the king who is kind in his rule (Bauder 1976:256; compare Phil 4:5, "let your forbearance [*epieikes;* NIV 'gentleness'] be evident to all"). Paul is

---

charge that he was too concerned with his livelihood and other worldly things and not trusting enough in Christ (1982:45). There is no basis whatsoever for Abraham Malherbe's contention that *kata sarka* is descriptive of mean, inconsistent and conniving conduct (1983:170).

gentle and forbearing as he approaches the Corinthians. Even so, this disposition does little to blunt the sternness of the warning that follows. Next time around Paul will exercise the discipline that he has been avoiding: when he comes, he expects to be *bold* (v. 2). Although his critics accuse him of being weak-kneed in person, Paul promises that he will be bold, if need be, on his next visit. Two terms describe the kind of boldness he will show. It will be, first, a self-assured boldness *(tharrēsai tēpepoithēsei)*—or, as the Jerusalem Bible translates, "with confident assurance." It will also be a courageous boldness. The verb *tolmaō* (missing in the NIV) means "to exhibit courage or daring" and is used of the confidence proper to those who are sure of their ground (Motyer 1975:365).

Paul's boldness will be directed on his next visit against *some* who *think* that he lives by worldly standards. The fact that he does not say "some of *you*" suggests that he is directing his comments at those who were intruding themselves into the Corinthian community. These meddlers remain unnamed throughout—although their opinions are quite explicitly named. They appear to be itinerant Jewish-Christian preachers who encroached on Paul's territory and claimed credit for his work. They disparaged him for refusing financial support from his churches (1 Cor 9:3-18; 2 Cor 12:13), not carrying letters of recommendation (2 Cor 3:1-3), being unsuccessful in reaching his own people (3:14—4:4) and being an unimpressive speaker (10:10-11). They flaunted their achievements, claiming a superior heritage to Paul's (11:22) and boasting of greater spirituality ("visions and revelations," 12:1; "signs, wonders and miracles," 12:12), knowledge (11:6) and speaking ability (10:10; see the introduction).

The verb translated *think (logizomai)* appears twice in verse 2. It means "to draw a logical conclusion" from a given set of facts (Eichler 1978:822-23). From the fact that Paul seemed to talk big in his letters yet had refrained from exercising discipline in person, his opponents drew the conclusion that he operated according to fleshly (that is, weak

---

Logizomai (and cognates) appears six times in chapters 10—12 (10:2 [2x], 7, 11; 11:5; 12:6). Victor Furnish may be correct in thinking that Paul is picking up a term from his opponents' arsenal (1984:456).

and ineffectual), not spiritual standards.

Paul accepts this estimate, to a point. "We do live in the flesh *[en sarki]*," he admits (*in the world,* v. 3). The change in preposition is crucial. His sphere of activity is indeed "the flesh"—the everyday world of human existence with all its limitations, frustrations, trials and tribulations. But while Paul lives out his life in the ordinary, mundane sphere of human existence, this does not mean that he conducts his affairs according to the flesh *(kata sarka)*—that is, as the world goes about things (*by the standards of this world,* v. 2). Nor does he wage war according to the flesh (*kata sarka—as the world does,* v. 3).

During the latter years of the Great Depression, the American people were faced with mobilizing themselves for a second world war. They rationed their butter, meat, gasoline and other basic items. With the money they had left after purchasing the necessities of life, they paid wartime taxes and bought war bonds to provide even more funds for mobilization. They also sent hundreds of thousands of their finest youth abroad. It was a massive effort, involving great sacrifices and a tremendous expenditure of resources (Waldrop 1984:42). Paul pictures himself as involved in a similar war effort. In his case, however, the battle is being fought on a spiritual front. And spiritual warfare requires spiritual weaponry, which Paul readily deploys. What distinguishes his weapons from those of the world can be summed up in one word—*power (dynatos).* The weapons Paul fights with have *divine power* and, as a result, can accomplish what the world's weapons cannot (*demolish stongholds,* v. 4). Paul does not identify these weapons here. But they certainly would include "the Holy Spirit," "sincere love," the true message and divine power (6:6-7). He may also have in mind "truth,"

10:3 Paul is fond of applying military language to the Christian life (compare Rom 13:12-13; 1 Cor 9:7; 2 Cor 6:7; Eph 6:10-18; 1 Thess 5:8; 1 Tim 1:18; 2 Tim 2:3-4). For examples of extrabiblical application of the metaphor of a siege to the rational faculties of the wise, see Malherbe 1983:143-73. Compare Proverbs 21:22, where the wise person "attacks the city of the mighty and pulls down the stronghold in which they trust."

The strategy of demolishing a city's fortified structures was a common one in ancient times. See, for example, 1 Maccabees 5:65-66, where Judas Maccabeus's attack on Hebron amounted to tearing down its strongholds and burning its towers on all sides.

10:4 *Dynata tō theō* can be construed as (1) an instrumental dative—"made powerful by God" (KJV), (2) a dative of advantage—"powerful for God" (JB, Phillips), (3) a dative of possession—"powerful to God" (that is, "God's powerful weapons," TEV, LB), (4) an

"righteousness," "the gospel of peace," "faith," "salvation" and "the Spirit," put forward as the Christian's armor in Ephesians 6:13-17. Paul's weapons are effective in doing two things. They can, in the first place, *demolish strongholds* (v. 4). *Ochyrōma* is a military term for a "fortified place" (Heidland 1967b:590; Malherbe 1983:147). The picture is of an army attacking and tearing down the fortified defenses of the enemy. In the ancient world a prosperous city would build not only a stout wall for its security but also, somewhere inside the wall, a fortified tower that could be defended by relatively few soldiers if the walls of the city were breached by an enemy. Once the stronghold was taken, the battle was over (Carson 1984:47). In ancient times this was commonly accomplished through a variety of siege machines, the most common being battering rams, mobile towers, catapults for throwing darts and the ballistae for throwing stones (Stern 1976). The strongholds that Paul's weapons lay siege to are *arguments* and *every pretension* (v. 5). *Logismous* are reasonings that take shape in the mind and are then worked out in life as action (Heidland 1967a:286; Malherbe 1983:147). *Hypsōma epairomenon* ("raised ramparts") are human "pretensions" (NIV) or "arrogances" (JB, TEV, REB, NEB, RSV, NRSV) that have built fortresses with high towers aimed at repelling attacks by *the knowledge of God* (v. 5; Malherbe 1983:147).

Such efforts, however, are to no avail. For Paul's weapons not only can demolish strongholds (v. 4) but also can *take captive every thought to make it obedient to Christ* (v. 5). The verb *aichmalōtizō* means "to take a prisoner of war" (Kittel 1964a:195). Paul pictures human thoughts as captured enemy soldiers. Once a city's defenses had been breached and its fortified places destroyed, conquered soldiers were taken in tow as prisoners of war. In

ethical dative—"powerful in God's sight" (Blass, Debrunner and Funk 1961:no. 188.2) or (5) a Hebrew intensive (an elative superlative)—"divinely [very, extremely] potent" (NEB, RSV, KJV, NIV; Moule 1959:184).

10:5 There is a division of opinion whether to begin verse 5 with the phrase *logismous kathairountes* (NIV, KJV, LB, RSV, NEB) or with *pan hypsōma epairomenon* (TEV, JB). Both phrases define the strongholds that need demolishing and should be kept together. The NIV versification is therefore to be preferred.

The genitive in the phrase *tēs gnōseōs tou theou* is most likely objective: "knowledge about God." Knowledge was important to the Corinthians (1 Cor 8:1; 12:8; 13:2; 14:6) and something that they excelled in (1 Cor 1:5; 2 Cor 8:7). *Tou Christou* in the phrase *eis tēn hypakoēn tou Christou* is also an objective genitive: "for obedience to Christ."

the Roman *triumphus,* the prisoners were paraded through the streets of Rome (see commentary on 2:14-16). Paul's objective, however, is not to put human reasonings and pretensions on public display but to take captive every thought for obedience to Christ (v. 5).

What does this mean today? We live at a time when the mind is deemphasized and the needs of the individual elevated—so much so that our generation has been dubbed "the me generation." By contrast, Paul affirms that the mind matters. Indeed, it is so crucial that he focuses all his efforts on taking every thought captive and making it obey Christ. Alister McGrath has written that the future of evangelicalism lies in the forging of rigorous theological foundations and intellectual credibility (1995:18). For this to happen, Christ must reign supreme in our minds.

So, far from being the spiritual wimp that his critics in Corinth make him out to be, Paul has at his disposal a divine arsenal, which he will use on his next visit *to punish every act of disobedience* (v. 6). The term *ekdikeō* means "to take vengeance for" or "punish" something—the something in this case being *disobedience (parakoē).* The noun *parakoē* (literally, "to hear aside") denotes a stubborn unwillingness to hear what is said and to act on it. The Corinthian intruders are primarily in view here—although any lingering dissenters at Corinth are not excluded. Their disobedience is not their unwillingness to bend the knee to Paul's authority but their attempt to subvert the gospel. "I am afraid that . . . your minds may somehow be led astray from your sincere and pure devotion to Christ," Paul says (11:3).

What the punishment will involve is left unstated. But Paul will be able to carry it out once the Corinthians' *obedience is complete.* Only with the church as a whole behind him can Paul operate from a position of

10:7 Verse 7 can actually be translated a number of different ways, depending on whether *blepete* is construed as an interrogative ("Are you looking?"), an indicative ("You are looking") or an imperative ("Look"). Of the three options, the interrogative fits the context the least well (KJV, NKJV). If Paul is giving a command, his point would be that his credentials are as plain as day, so that anyone looking at them cannot fail to see that he belongs to Christ just as much as the next person ("Look at what is before your eyes" [RSV, NRSV, JB, NEB, REB]). If he is stating a fact, then he is criticizing the Corinthians, as he did at 5:12, for judging solely on the basis of external appearances (*You are looking only on the surface of things* [NIV, TEV, LB, NASB]). *Blepete* is usually imperatival in Paul's

strength against his critics. But once he has their support, his troops stand at the ready to be deployed *(en hetoimō echontes*—"will be ready"). This is the reason for Paul's tough talk in his letters. By adopting a stern approach, he hopes to avoid acting as the disciplinarian in person—not because he is intimidated by the Corinthians but because he loves them. We always make the effort to avoid causing grief or pain to those we love. In many ways it is easier to bear hurt ourselves than to watch the suffering of someone we care about. Paul was no different. The severe letter he wrote to the church caused him great distress and anguish of heart (2:4). But he wrote it so that when he was next with them, he might be a source of joy (2:1-3) and love (2:4), rather than a cause of pain.

A Proper Use of Authority (10:7-11) Thomas Babington, Lord Macaulay, once observed that "the highest proof of virtue is to possess boundless power without abusing it." We have all seen authority abused in the church. "Power tends to corrupt and absolute power corrupts absolutely" (John E. E. Dalberg-Acton, Lord Acton). Those in positions of authority face great temptations to take advantage of the power inherent in their positions. It is rare indeed to find pastors or other church leaders deliberately holding back in the use of their authority. Anyone who shows such restraint should be applauded.

It was not so for Paul, though. He chose not to fully exercise his authority at Corinth, yet he was criticized for it. Why was this? Paul attributes it to the Corinthians' fascination with outward appearances (v. 7). The text literally reads, "You are looking only on the surface of things." That is, they were judging Paul and other itinerant missionaries by such externals as style, speaking ability and demeanor (compare

writings, but the indicative suits the argumentation better.

Ei tis pepoithen heautō is a condition of fact ("If [as is the case] anyone is self-confident . . ."). Paul has to contend with those who confidently claim that they are Christ's in a distinctive way. If they count themselves among Christ's original disciples, they may well have viewed Paul's authority as inferior to their own. Alternatively, their confidence may rest in a claim to possess a pneumatic relationship to Christ (see, for example, Bultmann 1985:187-88; Héring 1967:72). There is some basis for this, in that the intruders make much of spiritual feats like visions and revelations (12:1) and signs, wonders and miracles (12:12).

5:12). It is not much different today—equal, if not greater, value is placed on a speaker's imposing personality and oratorical skills. But appearances can be deceiving. Looking for a successor to Saul, Samuel went to the house of Jesse, where he saw Eliab and thought, "Surely the LORD's anointed stands here." In bearing and stature Eliab was presumably not unlike Saul, who had come from a family of some standing in the community and was a head taller than any other Israelite (that is, physically he was of kingly stature). But Eliab was not the Lord's choice. Samuel was told, "Do not consider his appearance or his height. . . . [For mortals look] at the outward appearance, but the LORD looks at the heart" (see 1 Sam 16:6-7).

By external appearances, Paul's rivals possessed a number of laudable credentials. They boasted an impeccable heritage (11:21-22), possessed first-rate letters of reference (3:1-3), laid claim to extraordinary and visionary experiences (12:1, 12), were skillful speakers (10:10; 11:6), exhibited erudition (11:6) and exuded a take-charge aura (11:20; see the introduction). On the face of things, these are admirable credentials. But what Paul's rivals did with their credentials was hardly admirable. For they used them as measuring sticks for determining whether a person did or did not *belong to Christ*. The phrase is literally "to be of Christ" (*Christou einai*, v. 7). The genitive could be possessive—"to belong to Christ," that is, to be Christ's person in a special way. Or it could define source—"to be from Christ," that is, to serve as Christ's authorized spokesperson. The latter provides the best connection in the context, where the demand is for Paul to provide proof that Christ is speaking through him (13:3).

Paul faces a catch-22 situation at Corinth. When he downplays or makes little of his credentials, the genuineness of his apostleship is questioned (v. 7). But when he emphasizes his apostolic authority, he is accused of being overly boastful (v. 8). Hastily drawn conclusions based on externals have led "some" to question whether Paul is in fact Christ's representative (v. 7). *Tis* ("anyone") is Paul's usual way of referring to intruding missionaries, who are attempting to displace him

---

10:8 Paul shifts to the first-person singular at verse 8 *(if I boast somewhat freely . . .)*. This is not surprising; for while his authority is a shared authority *(the authority the Lord gave us)*, his boasting is his own. *Ho kyrios (the Lord)* is clearly a reference to Christ. It is

at Corinth by raising questions about his apostolic credentials (compare 3:1; 10:2, 7, 12; 11:20). The fact that they claim to be Christ's spokespersons may indicate that they were commissioned by Jesus during his earthly ministry (or perhaps by the Twelve) and thus consider themselves to possess a superior right to such a claim. Whatever their relationship to Christ, it is a source of special pride to them (v. 7). But Paul's authority is in no way inferior to theirs. Indeed his authority equals, if not exceeds, theirs, for he was commissioned by the risen Christ himself (Murphy-O'Connor 1991:104). Moreover, while Paul himself admits that he does not cultivate an impressive bearing or polished speech, in all other respects he can match the opposition point for point (11:21—12:6).

So Paul challenges the Corinthians to look once again at the facts (*logizesthō*, "let a person reckon"), which when considered carefully can yield no other conclusion than *we belong to Christ just as much as* they (v. 7). Some might say that this is just another example of Paul talking big in his letters (v. 10). To this allegation Paul responds that he does boast *somewhat freely* about his authority (v. 8)—or, perhaps more accurately, "a little more than I should" (*perissoteron ti;* Bratcher 1983:107). Yet unlike his rivals, he cannot be charged with exaggeration. For his boasts can be substantiated from the results of his ministry. *The authority* that *the Lord gave* him builds up, whereas his rivals have done nothing since coming to Corinth but pull down (v. 8). *Oikodomē* ("upbuilding") is a favorite term that Paul uses for the church's growth toward spiritual maturity (Rom 14:19; 15:2; 1 Cor 14:3, 5, 12, 26; 2 Cor 10:8; 12:19; Eph 4:12, 16, 29). It lays emphasis on the process of construction, whether it be laying the foundation of a new church (1 Cor 3:10) or erecting the walls of a more established congregation (Eph 2:21). What Paul denies doing with his authority is *pulling . . . down (katheiresis).* The authority that he received from Christ was for constructive, not destructive, purposes (*eis* + accusative). Has Paul been accused of such a thing? Words such as "bold," *weighty* and *forceful* may

from the risen Christ that Paul received his apostleship and commission to preach the gospel among the Gentiles.

Kathairesis refers to the tearing down of buildings, houses and walls (Liddell, Scott and Jones 1978).

well imply an abuse of authority (10:2, 10). It is more likely, however, that "pull down" is Paul's countercharge. He builds up. His opponents tear down. He establishes. They try to undermine his work (10:13-14) and subvert the faith of his converts (11:1-4).

Paul's language echoes that of Jeremiah 1:10 and 24:6. Jeremiah was appointed over nations and kingdoms to "uproot and tear down *[kathelō]*, to destroy and overthrow, to build *[anoikodomeō]* and to plant." Paul's intent, however, is to build up the Corinthians and not tear them down. Nevertheless, if need be he will not hesitate to do in person what his critics claim he can attempt only at a safe distance.

Paul refrains from pursuing this point lest he appear to be *trying to frighten* the Corinthians with his *letters* (v. 9). The verb is a strong one (*ek* + *phobeō* intensifies the root). Some at Corinth think that he is aiming not merely to frighten but to terrify them into obedience. This, they claim, he does through the use of *weighty* and *forceful* letters (v. 10). If there is a difference between the two adjectives, it is that *barys* denotes the weightiness or heaviness of something (compare 4:17) while *ischyros* refers to brute strength. The Jerusalem Bible's "he writes strongly worded and powerful letters" catches the sense.

In person, however, it is alleged that Paul *is unimpressive and his speaking amounts to nothing* (v. 10). The text is literally, "His presence is of bodily weakness." This is probably more than a statement about his physique. Today we would say that he lacks presence. Patristic tradition bears this out. A presbyter in the province of Asia during the second century described Paul as "a man small of stature, with a bald head and crooked legs, in a good state of body, with eyebrows meeting and nose somewhat hooked, full of friendliness" (*Acts of Paul and Thecla* 3). That Paul was physically impaired in some way is suggested by his reference in 12:7 to a stake in his flesh which rendered him "weak" *(astheneia)* and led him to pray on three separate occasions for the Lord to take it away from him (12:8-9).

In the eyes of some, Paul's speaking ability was nothing to brag about

---

10:9 The structure of verses 9-11 is problematic. The *hina* clause at verse 9 can be construed as imperatival, with verse 10 supplying the reason for the command: "Do not think that I am trying to scare you by my letters; for some say, 'His letters are weighty . . .' " A second option would be to take the clause with the preceding thought: "The Lord gave

either. The NIV's *amounts to nothing* is somewhat weak. The term Paul's opponents actually used was "contemptible" *(exouthenēmenos)*—although the Living Bible's "You have never heard a worse preacher!" might be stretching it. Were they justified? Paul himself admits that he eschewed eloquence and rhetoric when preaching the gospel. It was not that he lacked the training. As a boy growing up in Tarsus and as a young man studying under Rabbi Gamaliel, he would have learned rhetoric as a routine part of his education. Nor did he lack the ability, as his letters eloquently attest. It was rather that he resolved to "know nothing" among the Corinthians "except Jesus Christ and him crucified" (1 Cor 2:2) and "Jesus Christ as Lord" (2 Cor 4:5).

Although Paul does not write with the intent to frighten the Corinthians, he does write to secure their obedience (Bruce 1971:232). And if that is not forthcoming through forceful words, he is more than able to secure it through a forceful presence. *Such a person should realize,* Paul says, *that what we are in our letters, . . . we will be in our actions.* In short, what he is in print he will indubitably be in person. The term translated "realize" *(logizomai)* means "to draw a logical conclusion" from a given set of facts (Eichler 1978:822-23). Those who criticize Paul for writing one way and acting another way have not adequately considered the facts. Paul prefers to come to them in love and with a gentle spirit. But if they push him to it, he will come with a rod (1 Cor 4:21).

Legitimate Spheres of Boasting (10:12-18) Fairly strict plagiarism laws exist to keep people from passing off the ideas or words of others as their own. But what about the ministry? How do we prevent others from taking credit for our labors? Or should the Christian worker even be concerned about this? Is not the important thing that Christ is preached, so that who does the preaching is of little significance (Phil 1:18)? Yet here in 2 Corinthians 10:12-18 Paul is concerned about this very thing. Itinerant preachers have come to Corinth and are taking credit for his apostolic labors: *We are not going too far* (as others are

us authority for building you up . . . lest I appear to be frightening you" (Plummer 1915:281). Or *hina + mē* can introduce a new thought that finds its completion in verse 11 (v. 10 being parenthetical): "Lest I should seem to be frightening anyone with my letters, I say: let that person consider . . ." (Martin 1986:310).

doing, v. 14) and we do not boast about work already done in another's territory (v. 15).

What is at stake for Paul is something more than pride of place. Today people often strive to get ahead in the workplace by raising doubts about the viability or integrity of the competition. Paul's opponents did this by saying that he possessed inferior credentials, thereby calling into question the authenticity of his ministry at Corinth. Their superior credentials, on the other hand, gave them the right to set the Corinthians straight about Paul and to claim credit for getting the church on the right track. There is every evidence that the Corinthians were listening to them (11:19-20). What the church failed to see, however, was that to raise doubts about Paul's ministry at Corinth was in effect to raise doubts about the viability of their own existence as a congregation. Simply put, if the validity of the preacher is called into question, then the content of the preaching also becomes suspect, and any congregation founded on that preaching is questionable.

In verses 12-18 Paul cuts to the heart of the problem by showing the Corinthians what the opposition is really after. It is not, to be sure, the spiritual welfare of the Corinthians. Their real goal is, instead, to expand their sphere of influence by encroaching on the territory of others and going beyond the boundaries God himself had established.

To demonstrate this, Paul goes on the offensive at verse 12 and levels three charges against his opponents. The first charge is that they lack basic intelligence. They use themselves as the standard by which they gauge their respective ministries, and then they take great satisfaction in finding that they always measure up (*they measure themselves by*

10:12-13 Paul's blunt language is possibly the source of the shorter reading in a handful of Western witnesses. "They are not very wise; we, however," is not found in D* F G it^ar,b,d,f,g,o vg^mss. It could also be a copying error, where the copyist's eye leaped inadvertently from *ou* to *ouk* and left out what falls in between. If the shorter text is followed, the sense is as in the NEB margin: "On the contrary we measure ourselves by ourselves, by our own standard of comparison" (omitted in the REB).

Some translations like the Revised Standard and the Living Bible begin a new paragraph at verse 13, rather than at verse 12. The fact that verse 12 begins with *gar*, tying it back to the preceding verses, offers some justification for this. But the idea of standards of measurement in the ministry is only first introduced in verse 12 and then developed in verses 13-18.

10:12 The verb *tolmaō* means to "dare" to do a thing in spite of any natural feeling. The idea here is of someone pushing himself forward so that he does not hesitate to speak *themselves,* v. 12). In so doing they give every evidence of not being very bright (*they are not wise,* v. 12). *We,* on the other hand, *do not dare to classify or compare ourselves* (v. 12). There is a play on words here that is easily lost in translation. *Enkrinō (classify),* found only here in the New Testament, means "to admit or accept into the same rank or class," while *synkrinō (compare)* means "to compare" or "measure" against something of equal value. The New English Bible's "We do not dare class or compare ourselves with any of those who put forward their own claims" is a fair rendering of the Greek. To this extent Paul's critics are correct in calling him "timid." He is by far too shy to engage in the self-admiration maneuvers of the opposition. Actually, the term Paul uses is even stronger. He does not *dare,* a verb that means "to make bold" or "to presume" in a bad sense.

Breach of contract is the second charge Paul levels against the opposition. *We . . . will not boast beyond proper limits,* he states (v. 13). The term *ametros (limits)* means "to be without boundary or measure" and refers to the unmeasured boasting of the opposition. Paul, by contrast, confines his boasting to "the measure of the field God measured" to him "as a measure" (a literal translation of v. 13). The Greek is intentionally redundant. Paul worked within clearly defined boundaries; his opponents did not. Paul defines these boundaries as a *kanōn* ("field")—the Greek term from which we derive our English word "canon." *Kanōn* in Hellenistic Greek was a rod or bar employed for testing the straightness of something—somewhat like our plumb line. It came to be used figuratively of the rule or standard by which something was measured. For example, in Galatians 6:16 it refers to the "standard"

or act on his own behalf (Martin 1986:319).

10:13 *Eis ta ametra* can mean beyond the proper limit (thus excessively) or outside the proper sphere. In the former case Paul would be saying that he does not make any "wild" claims (as in Phillips). With the latter he would be stating that he does not boast "beyond" his assigned sphere of ministry (most modern translations). The limiting of Paul's authority to Gentiles whom he or his converts were the first to reach may indeed explain why Paul's letters are directed almost exclusively to the Gentile constituency of churches with an explicit Jew-Gentile mix (1-2 Cor, Gal, Eph, Phil, 1-2 Thess). If no apostle was responsible for the founding of the church at Rome, this may also account for Paul's freedom to address the Roman church in an authoritative fashion.

Kanōn is a term found exclusively in Paul's letters (2 Cor 10:13, 15, 16; Gal 6:16). During the second century A.D. the term came to mean the "rule" or "essentials" of the faith to which Christian life and teaching was to conform *(regula fidei).*

by which Christian conduct is measured, while here in 2 Corinthians 10:13-16 it denotes the divine "yardstick" (JB) or "tape measure" used to establish the boundaries of a ministry field.

These boundaries were not of Paul's own making. They were boundaries that he and the "pillars" of the Jerusalem church agreed on during his second postconversion visit to Jerusalem. Paul was to preach to the Gentiles, and James, Peter and John were to go to the Jews (Gal 2:9)—a division that accords with Paul's own apostolic commissioning (Rom 1:5; 15:15-16; Gal 1:16; 1 Tim 2:7). It was an agreement based on recognition of divinely established spheres of ministry. God was seen to be at work in Paul's ministry as an apostle to the Gentiles and in Peter's ministry as an apostle to the Jews (Gal 2:7-8). So in coming to Corinth and treating this Gentile city as a legitimate sphere of ministry, the Jewish Christian missionaries were violating the evangelistic division of labor agreed on by Paul and the mother church almost eight years earlier (see the introduction).

But how did Paul know that Corinth was included in his rightful field? Were all Gentiles ipso facto considered to be his sole domain and all Jews a forbidden target group? That this was not the case is clear from the fact that his own evangelistic strategy involved an initial outreach in the synagogue (Acts 13:5, 14; 14:1; 17:2, 10; 18:4; 19:8). And while his commission was to proclaim the gospel to the Gentiles, it was Paul's unwavering policy to preach only in unevangelized Gentile areas so as not to build on another's foundation (Rom 15:18-20). So the Corinthians became part of his field not merely because they were predominantly Gentile but because he was the first apostle to reach them with the gospel (*ephthasamen;* 2 Cor 10:14).

10:14 The intrusion of rival missionaries into Paul's sphere of apostolic ministry may well be one of the acts of disobedience that Paul plans to punish on his next visit (v. 6).

Translators are divided on how to translate *ephthasamen.* The KJV, LB, RSV and NEB translate it "we were the *first* to come," while Phillips, TEV, NIV and JB render it simply as "we came to you." The primary idea is to come or do first or before another—although there are examples where the verb simply means to arrive or to come (Liddell, Scott and Jones 1978). Paul uses the verb in both ways ("to come first," 1 Thess 4:15; "to come" or "to attain," Rom 9:31; Phil 3:16; 1 Thess 2:16). But here it is the fact that he has come *first* to an unevangelized Gentile area that establishes Corinth as his legitimate sphere of ministry.

Paul has sometimes been accused of operating as a "lone ranger" evangelist who jealously guarded his turf and could not tolerate trespassers. But this was not at all the case. While he took seriously divisions of labor and allotted fields, he nonetheless viewed the task of evangelism as a cooperative effort, much like farming, where, as colaborers, one "plants" and another "waters"—but, in this case, it is "as the Lord has assigned" (1 Cor 3:5-9). Nor did Paul share the apostolic task grudgingly. He clearly welcomed others as colaborers.

The distinction lies in his understanding of authority. For while Paul can conceive of colaboring, he cannot admit the idea of coauthority. Authority, for Paul, resides in the father-child relationship that is established through the church-planting process. It is because Paul reached Corinth first with the gospel that he can address the Corinthians as "dear children" (1 Cor 4:14). It is this begetting "through the gospel" that gives him the right to ask his converts to "imitate" him (4:15-16) and explains the care Paul takes, in turn, to respect Peter's assigned field among the Jews (Gal 2:7) and James's evangelistic efforts in Jerusalem (Acts 21:20-26).

This points up Paul's third charge: *boasting of work done by others* (2 Cor 10:14-15). The term *kopos (work)*, literally a "striking" or "beating," denotes labor that is physically exhausting. Paul applies the term to both his trade as a worker of goat's-hair cloth (for example, 1 Cor 4:12; 1 Thess 2:9; 2 Thess 3:8) and his missionary labors (as in 2 Cor 10:15)—although the two are connected, since he plied a trade so as not to be a financial burden on his churches (2 Thess 3:8).

It is difficult to know what exactly the Corinthian intruders were taking credit for. They certainly did not discredit the Corinthians'

10:15 *En hymin* could be instrumental ("with your help") or local ("in your midst"). With the former Paul is looking to increase his geographical sphere of influence "with their help." If it is the latter, he is looking to increase their estimate of him so that he has a solid base from which to launch an evangelistic campaign in areas beyond them.

Area of activity renders a phrase that Paul used in verse 13 of the sphere of ministry that God had allotted to him.

Some suppose that Paul is equating *as your faith continues to grow* with obedience to his apostolate. But while apostolic loyalty may be what is necessary for him to preach the gospel in regions beyond them (v. 16), it is Christian maturity that is in view in verse 15.

The church at Cenchreae, about seven miles east of Corinth, may have been parented by the Corinthians, although it could also have been the fruits of Paul's own labors.

conversion and seek to rebuild the church from its foundation up. It is more likely from 2 Corinthians 11:22 that they claimed spiritual jurisdiction over Corinth because of their superior pedigree ("Are they Hebrews? . . . Israelites? . . . Abraham's descendants?"). In addition, they challenged Paul's right to offer authoritative spiritual direction, given what they felt to be his questionable apostolic standing ("Are they servants of Christ? . . . I am more," 11:23).

Another difficulty for Paul was that he operated in accordance with a clearly thought-out evangelistic strategy that was being compromised by the Corinthian intruders. Verses 15-16 provide us with a concise summary of this strategy: *Our hope,* he tells the Corinthians, *is that, as your faith continues to grow, our area of activity among you will greatly expand, so that we can preach the gospel in the regions beyond you.* There were two parts to Paul's strategy. Part one was to significantly expand his area of activity among his converts (v. 15). It was Paul's practice to focus his evangelistic efforts on the large urban centers with a view to enlarging his sphere of authority to outlying areas *(megalynthēnai kata ton kanona)* through the evangelistic efforts of his converts *(en hymin).* This was only possible to the extent that the *faith* of his converts continued to *grow* (2 Cor 10:15). Paul could be using *faith* in reference to a set body of beliefs. If so, he would be saying that growth in knowledge is a necessary prerequisite to evangelistic outreach. But growth in faith more likely refers to maturity of Christian life. As the Corinthians' commitment to Christ and to the demands of the gospel matured, outreach to those around them would quite naturally follow. Paul defines the kind of outreach he envisions as "greatly expanding our area of activity." The Greek is actually "to be enlarged *[megalynthēnai]* to a great extent *[eis perisseian]* in accordance with our field *[kata ton kanona bēmōn]*." Paul hopes to greatly expand his ministry, but within the limits of the field assigned to him.

If the outreach effort of the Ephesian church is any indication, this kind of expansion occurred through the parenting of a number of churches in outlying areas (Col 1:7; 4:15-16). Paul included within his "field" churches in Asia Minor that he had not personally planted (for

---

10:16 Some think that the phrase *regions beyond you* shows that Paul was geographi-

example, see Col 1:5-7). Given his policy of not building on another's foundation, it is reasonable to assume that he could include these churches because they had been planted by his converts. All told, three churches were established in this fashion (Laodicea, Hierapolis and Colossae). Paul now holds out the same *hope* for Corinth.

Part two of Paul's strategy was *to preach the gospel in the regions beyond* them (2 Cor 10:16). A significant time would be spent stabilizing a recently planted congregation, with the hope of using the newly formed church as a base of operation for outreach into "regions beyond." In the case of Corinth, regions beyond may have included other parts of the Balkan peninsula, like Dalmatia and Panonia to the northwest (Illyricum; Rom 15:19) and Moesia and Dacia to the north. But by the time Paul wrote Romans, he had set his sights on Spain and the western Mediterranean, for which the Roman church would serve geographically as a more appropriate base (Rom 15:24-28).

Consolidation, however, precedes advance (M. J. Harris 1976:384). Up to this point Paul has been expending all his energy in consolidating his sphere of authority in Corinth, so that he has been unable to reach beyond it in any significant way. The fact that he phrases his goal of expansion as a hope, rather than an accomplished fact, is a subtle reminder to the Corinthians that by not backing him, they are hampering the advance of the gospel.

The Corinthian intruders were quick to *boast about work already done in another man's territory* (v. 16). Paul, on the other hand, did not even claim credit for what occurred in his own territory, let alone the territory of others. If any boasting is to be done, it should be done in the Lord (*Let him who boasts boast in the Lord,* v. 17). The Old Testament quote in verse 17 is thought to come from Jeremiah 9:24 ("Let him who boasts boast about this: that he understands and knows me"; compare 1 Kingdoms 2:10). It appears as well in 1 Corinthians 1:31 as a corrective to boasting in personal achievements or pride of place (Bruce 1971:234). Here it is a corrective to taking credit for what others have accomplished.

Paul will go on in chapters 11—12 to boast about his pedigree, ministerial achievements and ecstatic experiences—but only because he

---

cally east of Corinth at the time of writing (perhaps in Ephesus), rather than north (Macedonia) as 9:1-5 implies.

feels pressured to do so. Even so, the ultimate credit goes to God, and it is God's approval—and his alone—that counts (Murphy-O'Connor 1991:104). Some Christian workers are like the woodpecker who was pecking on the trunk of a dead tree one day when lightning struck the tree and splintered it. Not realizing what had happened, the proud bird exclaimed, "Look what I did!"

Paul Unmasks His Opponents (11:1-21) Sometimes extraordinary circumstances can push us to abandon scruples that we otherwise cling to tenaciously. For example, when one of our children takes a tumble, our aversion to the sight of blood is forgotten. The sound of a fire alarm and the smell of smoke at night cause us to disregard our usual sense of modesty. In Paul's case, news of a worsening situation at Corinth leads him to abandon his normal aversion toward self-praise and proceed in chapter 11 to do the very thing that he eschewed earlier in the letter—boast in his ministerial achievements. He certainly is not comfortable in doing so, as "I have made a fool of myself, but you drove me to it" (12:11) shows. His willingness to lay down his scruples indicates how desperate the situation at Corinth had become.

The circumstances that drove Paul to commend himself are spelled out in 11:1-5. *I am afraid,* he says, *that . . . your minds may somehow be led astray from your sincere and pure devotion to Christ* (v. 3). His converts are being led—as we say—down the garden path by rival missionaries, and they are not even aware of what is going on (vv. 18-21). Paul's motivation is thus pastoral rather than personal in nature. It is his concern for the Corinthians' spiritual welfare, and not for his own reputation, that pushes him to engage in self-praise.

But why must he resort to boasting? Why not just expose the intruders for the frauds they are and leave it at that? Unfortunately, by the time the news reached Paul, the intruders had already made significant

---

11:1 Paul's analogy of the church as the betrothed of Christ is a particularly apt one. As Richard Batey observes, the church lives between the times, experiencing through faith the presence of her Lord and yet hoping for a future consummation (1963:182).

Ophelon is most likely a neuter participle used as a particle and equivalent to "would that." With the aorist indicative or, as here, the imperfect indicative *(aneichesthe),* it expresses an unattainable or, at best, an improbable wish.

Mou could modify *mikron ti aphrosynēs* ("a little bit of my foolishness"—KJV, Phillips,

inroads at Corinth. This was largely because of the Corinthians' penchant for impressive credentials (vv. 21-23), fine-sounding words (v. 6) and extraordinary shows of power (12:12). So in order to win the congregation's ear, Paul must match the opposition point for point: *What anyone else dares to boast about . . . I also dare to boast about* (11:21).

Paul's Reasons for Playing the Fool (11:1-5) There is a wistful edge to Paul's tone in these opening verses: *I hope you will put up with a little of my foolishness* (v. 1). The NIV does not quite catch the sense. The particle *ophelon* introduces an unattainable or highly improbable wish: "Oh that you would put up with me." Paul sets out to boast with the hope, however remote, of gaining a respectable hearing. To do so, though, is *foolishness*—a term denoting that which is in the realm of human folly or irrationality. What Paul is about to do is sheer nonsense in his eyes. But he is willing to do whatever it takes to forestall disaster at Corinth. The force of the second half of verse 1 is difficult to determine. It could be read either as an imperative—"do bear with me" (KJV, LB, RSV, TEV, NEB, Phillips)—or as an indicative—*but you are already [bearing with me]* (NIV, JB). The former actually provides the better connection. It is easy to see how an opening wish for their indulgence could move quickly to an entreaty: "Please bear with me" (REB).

The reasons for indulging him are three: first, Paul's divine jealousy for the Corinthians' purity; second, their willingness to put up with an aberrant message; and third, because he is in no way inferior to his rivals. *I am jealous for you with a godly jealousy,* Paul states (v. 2). Earlier Paul used the term *zēlos* of the Corinthians' "zeal" on his behalf (7:7, 11). But here it more likely means "jealousy"—yet of the divine sort rather than what we commonly think of as a human failing. The word denotes an intense concern for a person's honor or reputation. God's jealousy for Israel's reputation among the nations is a good example (e.g., Ex 20:5; Is 26:11; 42:13-17). Paul's jealousy stems from the fact that

NIV, NEB, JB), but its proximity to *aneichesthe* and the presence of *anechesthe mou* in the next clause makes modification of the verb more likely ("bear with me"—RSV, TEV). In this case *mikron ti* would be an accusative of respect: "Oh that you would bear with me *in* a little bit of foolishness."

Mikron ("little") can go with either *aneichesthe* ("bear with my foolishness for *a little while*") or *aphrosynēs* ("bear with me in *a little bit* of foolishness"—most modern translations).

he *promised* the Corinthians *to one husband, to Christ . . . as a pure virgin* (v. 2). In ancient Near Eastern culture, parents typically chose a wife for their son and arranged for the marriage by legal contract. It was then the responsibility of the father of the bride-to-be to ensure his daughter's virginity during the betrothal period. Betrothal was considered almost as binding as marriage itself. The betrothed couple addressed each other as "wife" and "husband" (Deut 22:23-24; Joel 1:8), and sexual faithfulness was expected. To this end, a bloodstained cloth was exhibited as proof of virginity on the wedding night (Wright 1982:743-44).

Israel as the betrothed of Yahweh is a familiar theme in the Old Testament (Is 54:5; 62:5; Ezek 16:9-22; 23:27; Hos 2:16-20). In the New Testament the bride-to-be is the church and the groom is Christ. As church founder, Paul pictures himself as the Corinthians' spiritual father, whose responsibility it is to ensure their faithfulness between birth (betrothal) and Christ's return (consummation), when the church will be *presented* as a *pure virgin* to her groom. But something now threatens to rob the Corinthians of their purity. Other suitors are on the scene, seeking to lure them away from fidelity to their betrothed. Paul's fear that their *minds may somehow be led astray* is well founded. The form of the conditional at verse 4 connotes fact (*ei* + indicative). Someone has come to Corinth and is successfully depriving Christ of a loyalty that is rightfully his. It is likely that only a small number have become prey to the intruders' ploys at the time Paul writes. But there is the real danger that the church as a whole may be carried along, as Paul's use of the second-person plural pronoun makes clear (*hymōn*, v. 3).

The Genesis 3 account of how the serpent deceived Eve into eating the forbidden fruit serves as a ready illustration of what Paul fears is

---

11:2 The betrothal ceremony was a formal occasion involving a marriage contract and betrothal gifts. The young man presented the young woman a gift of value and repeated, "Be thou betrothed to me with this gift" (*Qiddušin* 2.1). *Hērmosamēn* would normally mean "I betrothed myself" (middle voice). But this makes no sense in the context. The middle is occasionally found with an active sense, and so it should be understood here ("I betrothed you"; Blass, Debrunner and Funk 1961:no. 316 [1]). Mosaic law did not legislate penalties for broken betrothals, but the Code of Hammurabi stipulated that if the future husband broke the engagement, the bride's father retained the bride-gift, while if the father changed his mind, he repaid double the amount.

The genitive *theou* in the phrase *theou zēlō* could define quality ("with a godly jealousy") or source ("with a jealousy that comes from God").

going on at Corinth: *just as Eve was deceived by the serpent's cunning.*
Deceived translates a compound verb that has the intensified meaning
"thoroughly" or "utterly deceived" *(exēpatēsen)*. Eve's thorough deception is attributed to the serpent's *cunning*. The basic meaning of the
noun *panourgia* is "capable of all work" *(pan + ergon)*. In the New
Testament it refers to someone who uses his ability unscrupulously and
resorts to trickery and slyness.

In the case of the Corinthians, the deception is of a corrupting kind.
The NIV and RSV's *led astray* is not really the sense. The verb *phtheirō*
means "to destroy," "to seduce" or "to ruin." A corrupting influence that
leads to intellectual and spiritual ruin is most likely the idea (Martin
1986:333). Some think that Paul is drawing on a current Jewish legend
that Satan had sexually seduced Eve (as in *2 Enoch* 31:6). But the focus
in these verses is on a seducing of the mind *(ta noēmata)*, not a
corrupting of the will. Paul's fear is that as Eve was led astray by the
cunning argumentation of the serpent, the minds of his converts may
be similarly seduced by the trickery of his rivals.

The intruders' goal is to divert the Corinthians from a *sincere and
pure devotion to Christ* (v. 3). The Greek is literally "a whole-heartedness
toward Christ" *(apo tēs haplotētos tēs eis ton Christon;* compare 1:12; 8:2,
9-11, 13). *Haplotēs* ("sincere") in the New Testament denotes personal
wholeness or undividedness. As the bride-to-be is wholly focused on
her intended spouse, so the church is to be wholly undivided in its
devotion to Christ. If *kai tēs hagnotētos* (set off by square brackets in the
Greek text) is part of the original text, then the church's devotion is to
be marked not only by undividedness but also by "purity." Paul used
the noun earlier of the moral blamelessness that is to characterize the

---

11:3 Other than this text, reference to Eve in the New Testament is made only in 1 Timothy 2:13, where her deception is once again highlighted.

The earliest manuscripts have the longer reading, *apo tēs haplotētos kai tēs hagnotētos*
(p[46] ℵ* B D[vid] [reverses the order]), while ℵ[c] D[2vid] H Ψ Byz (KLP) support the shorter reading,
apo tēs haplotētos . It is easy to see how the eye of the copyist could have slipped from
the first -otētos to the second, thereby omitting what falls between *(kai tēs hagnotētos)*.
Alternatively, *kai tēs hagnotētos* could have arisen as a marginal gloss that got added to
the text by a later copyist. In view of the date and character of the evidence, the longer
reading is to be preferred. But in deference to the evidence for the shorter reading, *kai tēs
hagnotētos* should be enclosed in brackets (Metzger 1971:583-84).

life of the gospel preacher (6:6). Here it most likely signifies the kind of circumspect or chaste behavior that is to mark the life of the church.

A second reason for Paul to play the fool is the Corinthians' willingness to put up with rivals who present a different message: *If someone comes to you and preaches a Jesus other than the Jesus we preached, or if you receive a different spirit from the one you received, or a different gospel from the one you accepted, you put up with it easily enough* (v. 4). That Paul is dealing with a concrete situation and not just a hypothetical possibility is indicated by the form of the conditional (*ei* + the indicative). *Comes to you* suggests outsiders rather than opponents within the Corinthian congregation itself. Whether the singular *(someone)* points to the group's ringleader (Martin 1986:335) or is a generic reference to the group as a whole (Furnish 1984:448) is debated. The fact that Paul speaks of his opponent as "they" before and after verse 4 makes the latter the likely option. It is clear that the intruders came to Corinth of their own accord, rather than being sent at another church's behest. And they preached a message that the church has readily received: "you welcome it with open arms!" (JB). Unfortunately, it is not the message Paul had preached to them. Herein lies the difficulty. There is something defective about their preaching—so much so that Paul labels it *different (allon)* and "strange" (*heteron;* v. 4).

Verse 4 is one of the most scrutinized verses in the whole of chapters 10—13. In large part this is due to its perceived importance in identifying the Corinthian intruders and their teaching. In reality, though, the clues are few in number, and the terse "another Jesus/spirit/gospel" does not offer much help. Nonetheless, the triad is disturbing. As is typical of much false teaching in the church down

---

11:4 Speculation on the identity of Paul's Corinthian opponents is endless. The more popular suggestions include (1) Judaizing Jerusalemite Jews who, backed by the prestige of the mother church, constituted a rival apostolate to Paul's, (2) Hellenistic Jews who were preaching another gospel and another Jesus based on syncretic Gnostic principles, (3) Hellenistic Jews who patterned themselves after the Greco-Roman charismatic, miracle-working ecstatic and (4) ethnic and religious Jews who masqueraded as Christian leaders in an attempt to impede the gospel. Option 1 (Judaizing Jews) is still a commonly seen opinion (held, for example, by F. F. Bruce, C. E. B. Cranfield, C. K. Barrett, Fred Fisher, Philip E. Hughes, Murray J. Harris, Ernst Käsemann, Jerome Murphy-O'Connor and D. W.

through the centuries, the language of Paul's rivals has a very familiar ring to it. Yet what they mean by *Jesus, spirit* and *gospel* is so radically opposite to what Paul preached that nothing will do but to call it a *different* message.

What the intruders' preaching amounted to is difficult to assess. "Another Jesus" has commonly been understood to refer to Jesus either as a Hellenistic wonderworker (along the lines of the Greco-Roman "divine-man") or as a Jew who modeled obedience to the Mosaic law. It is hard to know whether by *a different spirit* Paul meant a human attitude (NIV, JB, Phillips, RSV) or the Holy Spirit (TEV, NEB). If the former, a spirit of legalism or an attitude of false spirituality could be the idea. A lifestyle antithetical to the gospel and someone's having fallen under the influence of evil spirits are also possibilities. From its position between *Jesus* and *gospel,* it seems probable, though, that *pneuma* denotes the Holy Spirit.

But in what sense was Paul's rivals' preaching *different?* Did they overemphasize their capacity for visionary and ecstatic experiences? Or did they lay claim to authoritative prophetic utterances, tongues, special revelations and the like? *A different gospel* sounds very much like the language Paul uses to describe the preaching of the Judaizers in his letter to the Galatian churches (compare "Unless you are circumcised, according to the custom taught by Moses, you cannot be saved"—Acts 15:1). Yet the topic of circumcision and law-obedience is strangely absent from 2 Corinthians. So we do well to look elsewhere for an explanation of Paul's language.

This bewildering array of possibilities points up the difficulties inherent in a reconstruction process such as this. Several of Paul's remarks in chapters 10—12 do, however, offer some helpful guidelines.

Oostendorp). But option 3 (Hellenistic Jews of a charismatic persuasion) is increasing in popularity.

The shift from *allon* ("another" of the same kind) to *heteron* ("another" of a different kind) can probably be attributed to stylistic variation.

A Judaizing reconstruction would see Paul's opponents modeling themselves after a Jesus who was a law-abiding Jew (another Jesus), encouraging a legalistic lifestyle *(a different spirit)* and preaching a gospel of human merit in addition to divine grace *(a different gospel).*

Are they Hebrews? Are they Israelites? (11:22) shows that the intruders are Jewish; but the lack of references to circumcision and the Mosaic law indicates something other than a Judaizing opponent (see above). The absence of theological argumentation suggests that doctrinal orthodoxy is not at stake. Indeed, most of Paul's efforts in 10:7—12:13 are spent combating the assertion that he possessed inferior credentials, not that he (or anyone else) preached an inferior gospel. It is also clear from the context that these intruders put great stock in things like an outward show of the Spirit, oratorical ability and heritage. "Signs, wonders and miracles" are "things that mark an apostle" (12:12). "Visions and revelations" are grounds for boasting (12:1). Eloquent speech (10:10; 11:6) and the proper heritage (11:22) are sources of pride. This fits with the epithet *super-apostles* (v. 5) and the portrayal of the intruders in chapters 1—7 as those who seek to legitimize their authority through letters of recommendation and who take pride in what is seen rather than in what is in the heart (5:12).

Putting all of this together, it is a reasonable conjecture that Paul's rivals were Palestinian Jews who, claiming the backing of the Jerusalem church, came to Corinth carrying letters of reference and sporting an impressive array of credentials (such as visions, ecstatic experiences and revelations). They sought to sway their audience through polished delivery and powerful oratory. They combined this with an outward show of the Spirit, appealing to the prominent role of the miraculous in Jesus' ministry. The intruders' focus on the extraordinary gifts of the Spirit, compelling rhetoric and Jesus the wonderworker may well be what Paul cryptically refers to as "another Jesus/Spirit/gospel." If so, their approach is not much different from what we call "power evangelism" today.

This raises the question of what constitutes a proper manifestation of the Spirit in the gospel ministry. To be sure, there is a place in preaching the gospel for persuasion and the working of "signs, wonders and miracles." Paul himself sought to reason with his listeners (Acts 9:29; 18:4). And he did preach a word accompanied by power, conviction and the Spirit (Rom 15:19; 1 Cor 2:4; 2 Cor 12:12; Gal 3:5; 1 Thess 1:5).

11:5 Some distinguish the *super-apostles* here from the itinerant intruders that Paul labels as *false apostles* in verse 13 (for example, Barrett, Käsemann, Thrall). Those who do commonly identify the super-apostles with the Twelve or with the "pillars" of

But the role of the miraculous was to validate, not displace, the gospel; and persuasion functioned to convince that "the Christ had to suffer and rise from the dead" (Acts 17:2-3). It is all too easy for an audience to fasten on an outward show and miss the intended message. This is why Paul concentrated on preaching "Christ and him crucified" (1 Cor 2:2). By focusing attention on what he was saying and not on how he said it, Paul prevented his listeners from getting distracted from the truly important.

William Barclay tells the story of a group of people at a dinner party who agreed that each should recite something after the meal. A well-known actor rose and, with all the resources of elocution and dramatic art, recited the Twenty-third Psalm. He sat down to tremendous applause. A quiet man followed him with his own recitation of this psalm. At first there were a few snickers. But by the time he had ended, his hearers had fallen into a stillness that was more eloquent than any applause. When he sat down, the actor leaned across the table and said, "Sir, I know the psalm, but you know the shepherd" (Barclay 1954:247). Similarly, Paul's opponents may have spoken with great skill and ability, but Paul preached from personal conviction. He knew the real Christ.

A third and final reason for Paul's playing the fool is the fact that he does *not think* himself *in the least inferior to these super-apostles* (v. 5). *Think* translates a term that means "to draw a logical conclusion" from a given set of facts (*logizomai;* Eichler 1978:822-23). A candid appraisal of Paul's credentials shows that he measures up at least as well as his rivals. Paul does not say that he is superior to these super-apostles—merely that he does not fall below them *(hysterēkenai)*.

The mention of "super-apostles" is intriguing. The phrase appears nowhere else in the New Testament. To whom is Paul referring? Some think that it can scarcely be other than the Jerusalem apostles, whose authority the Corinthian intruders invoked. Would this then be Paul's own sarcastic description of their exalted view of the apostles? Or is he merely quoting the intruders'—or even the Corinthians'—estimate of the

---

the Jerusalem church (Gal 2:9).
    The perfect tense, *hysterēkenai,* denotes a continuing estimate that Paul's credentials are inferior.

Twelve? Alternatively, "super-apostles" could be the intruders' own exaggerated appraisal of themselves—or even the opinion of the Corinthian church itself (McClelland 1982:84). On the whole, the latter seems preferable. Elsewhere Paul is careful to support and show respect for the Twelve, while further on he does not think twice about calling the intruders deceitful workers (v. 13) and servants of Satan (v. 15).

The Complaints of Paul's Critics (11:6-12) Paul goes on in verses 6-12 to deal with two specific areas of inferiority that his rivals have pointed to: his speaking ability and his lack of financial support. *I may not be a trained speaker,* Paul says, *but I do have knowledge* (v. 6). The NIV translation loses the force of the conditional. "Even if, as some claim" is the sense. Paul admits the possibility that he may not be as skilled a speaker as others *(ei de kai),* but he by no means concedes the point to his critics. The Greek *idiōtēs* ("not trained") refers to someone who has no professional knowledge or expertise in a particular area (that is, a layperson). In Paul's case, the charge is that he lacks expertise "in word" *(tō logō)*—that is, in well-fashioned phrases and lofty-sounding language (compare 10:10: "Some say, '. . . in person he is unimpressive and his speaking amounts to nothing' "). One can assume, then, that some of his rivals, in fact, possessed this expertise and used it to their advantage (Plummer 1915:300).

From 1 Corinthians 1—3 it is clear that the Corinthians placed a great deal of importance on oratorical skill. In this respect they are not much different from many churches today that are more interested in the outward wrapping than with what is in the package. In Paul's judgment, however, his *knowledge* more than compensated for any perceived lack (v. 6). *Gnōsis* most likely refers to an understanding of the truths of the gospel and insight into God's purposes, rather than to a "message of knowledge" spoken during worship for the edification of the church (1 Cor 12:8). It may be, though, that Paul is merely saying that he does "know what [he is] talking about" (Phillips) whereas his rivals do not.

11:6 It is quite possible that the intruders used Paul's lack of rhetorical flourish in speechmaking as evidence of a more fundamental lack of knowledge (Furnish 1984:505).
En pasin could be masculine ("among all people") or neuter ("in all things").
11:7 It has recently been argued that Paul refused financial support because it would have put him in a client-patron relationship with Corinth. See, for example, Judge 1980:214.

The Corinthians themselves had been endowed with knowledge (1 Cor 1:5). So they should have been the first to recognize that Paul possessed it too, especially since he had made this *clear* to them *in every way* possible (v. 6). But like so many of us today, the Corinthians got caught up in the outward form and appearance of things and lost sight of what was truly important.

It also rankled the Corinthians that Paul, unlike his rivals, preached *the gospel of God free of charge* (v. 7). Why did he do it? The intruders claimed it constituted an admission that he was a second-rate apostle. But Paul categorically denies this (*I do not think I am in the least inferior,* v. 5). In fact, he has already made it plain to the Corinthians that he waived support so as not to hinder reception of the gospel message (1 Cor 9:12). He did not want the gospel associated with a solicitation for money and rejected for that reason. Paul also refused to accept support in order to undercut the opposition (2 Cor 11:12). Like the Sophists of his day, a fair number of itinerant preachers showed more interest in lining their pockets than in proclaiming the truth. In doing so, they were in effect treating God's message like so much cheap merchandise (2:17 TEV).

Paul's response in verses 7-12 is noted for its biting sarcasm. *Was it a sin for me to lower myself in order to elevate you by preaching the gospel . . . free of charge?* (v. 7). Far from seeking to humiliate the Corinthians, he desired in fact *to elevate* them. With *elevate* Paul is probably thinking of the privilege of receiving the gospel and sharing in its riches (Bertram 1972:608). This same thought appears in slightly different form in 8:9, where Paul states that "though [Jesus] was rich, yet for [our] sakes he became poor, so that [we] through his poverty might become rich." Alternatively, he may be thinking of how the Corinthians had been elevated from a life of idolatry and sin (Bratcher 1983:117; M. J. Harris 1976:387).

Their elevation was made possible through Paul's own "lowering."

This became a particular sore spot with the Corinthian church, since he readily accepted financial support from the Macedonian churches (v. 9).

Robert Bratcher thinks that "humbled" *(tapeinōn)* may refer to the suffering and persecution Paul endured as a missionary (1983:118). The reflexive *emauton* ("I humbled *myself*") points, however, to something that was self-imposed.

Tapeinos means "low in stature or size." Paul may well be thinking of how he supported himself through a manual trade while planting the church at Corinth. It is quite likely that he came to Corinth initially to ply his trade as a tentmaker prior to the Isthmian games (Acts 18:2-3). He drew on the trade that was native to his home province of Cilicia—working with goats'-hair cloth, which was used to make cloaks, curtains, tents and other articles intended to give protection against the damp. The idea that Paul lowered himself by doing this is not his own. It undoubtedly was the estimate of his critics at Corinth. Within Judaism, manual labor was not denigrated. In fact, it was part of Paul's training as a rabbi that he be able to support himself through some form of manual labor. The attitude in Greek society, however, was quite different—especially among the upper classes. For the educated or the person of high social standing to have to do manual work was considered personally demeaning. The distinction between "blue-collar" (manual laborers) and "white-collar" workers in American society reflects much the same prejudice.

At some point Paul received sufficient funds from the Macedonian churches that he was able to drop his trade and give his full attention to evangelism ("when Silas and Timothy came from Macedonia, Paul devoted himself exclusively to preaching"—Acts 18:5). His reason for accepting their monetary help, he says, was to be better able to serve the Corinthians (2 Cor 11:8). It was his policy not to accept support from the church at which he was currently ministering. But once he left the area, he felt free to receive monetary gifts. Yet in the case of the Corinthian church, he continued to refuse financial assistance even after his departure.

Paul calls the money he received from the Macedonian believers *support* that he obtained by "robbery." The term *opsōnion* (literally "what is appointed for buying food") was commonly used in the first century of a soldier's pay or a state official's salary (Heidland 1967c:592). Here it refers to wages that would be one's due for services rendered. Paul says, however, that to receive these wages was in effect to "rob" the Macedonian churches. How so? The verb

---

11:9 This was not the first time Paul received funds from the Macedonian churches. After his founding visit, not one church shared with him in the matter of giving and receiving

sylaō, occurring only here in the New Testament, is a military term that means to "strip bare" or "deprive [a fallen enemy] of arms." Paul is making a bold statement. His ministry at Corinth was at no cost to the Corinthians because he had, as it were, plundered other churches of their funds instead of expecting the Corinthians to support him. What form this plundering took is debated. Quite likely it means that the Macedonian churches could not afford to give what they did but gave regardless.

Paul also reminds the Corinthians of how even after his personal funds were depleted and he began to feel needy, he still did not burden any of them (v. 9). *Hystereō (needed something)* means "to lack" or "to go short." During his stay in Corinth Paul reached the point of lacking the basic necessities of life—food, clothing and shelter (compare v. 27).

The life of an itinerant laborer was hard. A craftsman who stayed in one place and developed a regular clientele had to work from sunup to sunset every day to make ends meet. To be constantly on the road, as Paul was, meant that each time he went to a new town he had to start afresh. Opposition from competitors only increased his difficulties (Murphy-O'Connor 1991:112). It is not surprising, then, that he should often have been in want. But he was determined not to *burden* the Corinthians (v. 9). The verb *(katanarkaō)* means to "press" or "weigh heavily" on someone. Rather than place the burden of his daily needs on the shoulders of the Corinthians, *the brothers who came from Macedonia supplied what [he] needed* (v. 9).

Paul resolutely refused to abandon his policy of offering the gospel free of charge: *I have kept myself from being a burden to you in any way, and will continue to do so* (v. 9). In fact, his adamancy takes the form of an oath: *As surely as the truth of Christ is in me, nobody . . . will stop this boasting of mine* (v. 10). Paul calls this refusal to accept support from the Corinthians his "boast"—that is, something he can be proud of His boasting is not limited to Corinth but extends into *the regions of Achaia.* The Greek term for "region" *(klima)* normally refers to a district within the province. Here, though, it denotes the province as a whole

except the Philippian church (Phil 4:15). In fact, while he was in Thessalonica the church sent him aid "again and again" when he was in need (Phil 4:16).

(Bauer, Arndt and Gingrich 1979). No one in the province of Achaia *will* be able to *stop this boasting* (v. 10). The verb *phrassō* means to "stop up," "bar" or "stifle." The picture is of a dammed river or a roadblock. No matter what tactics Paul's opponents use, they will never be able to effectively blockade his policy of offering the gospel without charge.

Some suggest that verses 8-10 must be viewed against the patron-client relationship that existed in the first century, where to accept money from a donor was to place oneself under the obligation of gratitude to them (Judge 1980:214; Stambaugh 1986:113-27). If this is the primary background, then Paul refused to accept funds from the Corinthians so as not to put himself in a position of indebtedness to the church. This is not to say that Paul did not see himself as a servant of the church. He affirms this quite strongly elsewhere (1 Cor 3:5; 2 Cor 3:6; 6:4). But it is a known fact that a Christian worker's relationship to a local church changes when he or she moves from volunteer to paid staff. The tentmaking pastor, like Paul, has greater freedom to move in the direction God is leading. The salaried worker may feel obligated to follow the lead of the congregation or the denominational hierarchy. Consequently, staff workers can find themselves in situations where pleasing their church and pleasing the Lord are in conflict.

In verse 7 Paul said that his refusal to live at the Corinthians' expense was driven by a desire to elevate the Corinthians. Now in verse 11 he identifies an additional motive: his deep love for the church. Paul's critics claimed just the opposite. His refusal to accept support was evidence to them that he did not love the Corinthians: *Why [do I refuse support]? Because I do not love you?* (v. 11). Paul's response once again takes the form of an oath as he calls upon God's knowledge of his heart as a witness in this matter: *God knows I do!* So far from being a sign of indifference, his refusal to accept support is actually evidence of his love for the Corinthians. It is not as if Paul has not made this abundantly clear to the church. His purpose in

---

11:12 The second *hina* probably defines the content of *aphormēn:* "those who want an opportunity, *namely,* to be considered equal to us." The opportunity Paul seeks to deny the opposition is most likely that of goading him into accepting pay for preaching just as they do. Less likely is J. P. Mozley's suggestion that Paul's opponents desired to be considered equal to him in their disinterest in receiving financial support (1930-1931:212-

writing them a severe letter was so that they might know the depth of his love (2:4). Indeed, they have such a place in his heart that he "would live or die with" them (7:3).

But Paul is away from them now. And his rivals are the ones who have the Corinthians' ear. So he determines that he *will keep on doing* what he is doing—he will continue to boast in the fact that he preaches the gospel free of charge (11:12). On the surface this statement sounds odd. Did Paul not say at the end of chapter 10 that the person who wants to boast should boast in the Lord (10:18)? In Paul's case, though, the intent is not to draw attention to himself but to undercut the boasting of the Corinthian intruders who wanted to be considered his equals in the ministry: *I will keep on doing what I am doing,* Paul states, *in order to cut the ground from under those who want an opportunity to be considered equal with us in the things they boast about* (v. 12).

To cut the ground from is literally "to cut off" *(ek + koptō).* The image is of severing branches from a tree or cutting trees out of a wood. Today we might use the analogy of pulling the rug out from under someone's feet. The *ground* or rug that Paul aims to deprive his opponents of is *an opportunity to be considered equal with* him (v. 12). It is the Corinthians' perception that concerns him. The term *aphormē (opportunity)* was used in Hellenistic Greek of a starting point or base of operations for an expedition, and then more broadly of the resources needed to carry through on an undertaking. Paul's rivals wanted the church to believe that Corinth was within their legitimate sphere of ministry and hence part of their authorized base of financial support. One can easily see why Paul's policy of waiving support would have caused his rivals some consternation. And while they could assert that such support was a sign of apostolic legitimacy (12:11-13) or that Paul's refusal was evidence that he did not care about the Corinthians (11:11), the fact remained that they were a financial burden and he was not (Plummer 1915:308). Sooner or later the Corinthians would come to realize this.

13). It does not square with Paul's charge that his rivals were exploiting the church (v. 20).

En hō kauchōntai is literally "in that which they boast." Paul could be referring to his rivals' impeccable pedigree (11:22), their apostolic pretensions (11:23) or, as is probable, their right to consider Corinth within their sphere of ministry and hence part of their authorized base of financial support.

Paul Labels His Opponents "Servants of Satan" (11:13-15)
Meanwhile, there is an even greater danger. The fundamental reason
Paul cannot concede any ground to his rivals is that he sees them as
false apostles, deceitful workmen, masquerading as apostles of Christ
(v. 13). The language is surprisingly harsh. The phrase "false apostle"
does not occur anywhere else in Paul's letters. Some consequently
think that it may have been coined in the heat of the argument
between Paul and the Corinthian intruders (Furnish 1984:494). *False*
(pseudos) refers to that which is untrue or bogus. Although the
intruders claim to be Christ's delegates (*apo* + *stellō,* "to send forth"),
they in fact are not. How does Paul know? He can tell from their
methods, which mark them as *deceitful workmen.* There is more at
stake here than empty boasting and exaggerated claims. The noun
ergatēs is used in the New Testament of the worker who is employed
in Christ's service. The adjective *dolios* (only here in the New
Testament) and the verb *dolioō* are descriptive of someone who deals
dishonestly or treacherously with others. The intruders' misrepresentation of their missionary activity is not the result of self-deception
or careless exaggeration. It is quite deliberate and, for this reason,
treacherous in intent. The treachery stems from impure motives. The
intruders claim that their purpose in coming to Corinth is to serve
Christ, when in reality all they care about is serving themselves—and
at the Corinthians' expense (*exploits . . . takes advantage of,* 11:20).
In this way they are like wolves in sheep's clothing, *masquerading*
as apostles of Christ (v. 12).

Their behavior, Paul says, is not surprising, since *Satan himself*
masquerades as an angel of light (v. 13). The genitive can denote
material (that is, an angel made of light) or quality (a shining angel),
but the latter is the predominant use in the New Testament. Angelic
appearances are described as like lightning (Mt 28:3), gleaming (Lk 24:4)
and shining (Lk 2:9). The Greek term translated *masquerade* means to
"alter" or "change the outward appearance" of a person or thing. Satan

---

11:13 The noun *ergatēs* is normally used in the New Testament of the Christian worker
who is employed in Christ's service and sent into the world (for example, Mt 9:37-38; 10:10;
Lk 10:2; 1 Tim 5:18; 2 Tim 2:15; see Hahn 1978a:1150). It carries a negative connotation
both here and in Philippians 3:2 *(tous kakous ergatas).*

dons the outward guise of an angel of light in an attempt to conceal his true being. Nothing is said in the Old Testament about such an ability. For this Paul is drawing on a Jewish legend similar to what is found in the *Life of Adam and Eve* 9:1 and in the *Apocalypse of Moses* 17:1-2. In the former passage Satan transforms himself into the brightness of angels and pretends to grieve with Eve, who sits weeping by the Tigris River; in the latter Satan comes to Eve in the form of an angel at the time when the angels are going up to worship God and tempts her to eat of the fruit of the tree.

If Satan finds it advantageous to masquerade as an angel of light, *it is not surprising, then, if his servants masquerade as servants of righteousness* (v. 15). Paul's statement is sobering. Church leaders can seem genuine in appearance and profession and yet in actuality be Satan's minions. How one sees through the outward guise to the inner truth is not stated. But it is clear to Paul that the Corinthian intruders have disguised themselves in this fashion. The charge is a serious one. If the Corinthian intruders really are Satan's servants, then they are not merely Paul's opponents but also enemies of Christ. Paul said as much in the earlier part of this chapter, when he expressed his fear that the Corinthians were being seduced from their undivided commitment to Christ.

For the enemies of Christ only judgment waits: *their end will be what their actions deserve* (v. 15). The idea that all will have to give an account of themselves before God is thoroughly Jewish and one that Paul repeats elsewhere (for example, Rom 2:5-11; 1 Cor 3:10-15; 2 Cor 5:10; Gal 6:7-10). Many Jews believed that their deeds determined their ultimate destiny (Hahn 1978a:1149). For the Christian, however, judgment is defined in terms of rewards and punishments, not destiny or status (1 Cor 3:13-15; 2 Cor 5:10). Our labors may go up in a heap of smoke when subjected to divine scrutiny, but each of us individually will escape—albeit by the skin of our teeth ("as one escaping through the flames," 1 Cor 3:15). For the Corinthian intruders, however, Paul offers

11:14 The notion that Satan can transform his outer form at will is familiar in Jewish literature. For instance, in the *Testament of Job* he is said to have disguised himself as a beggar (6:4) and then as a bread seller (23:1).

no such hope. Their works will determine *their end*. The term *telos* in this context denotes end result or ultimate fate (Schippers 1976:61). They have done Satan's work; to Satan's fate they will go (Martin 1986:353). What this fate will be Paul does not say. Elsewhere, though, he states that the enemies of the cross of Christ will face eternal destruction, shut out from the presence of the Lord and from the majesty of his power (Phil 3:19; 2 Thess 1:8-9).

Paul Is Forced to Play the Fool (11:16-21) At verse 16 Paul finally gets on with playing the role of the fool. In verse 1 he had asked the Corinthians to bear with him in this matter ("I hope you will put up with a little of my foolishness"). But now he warns, *Let no one take me for a fool*. The term *fool* (literally "unwise") refers to someone who lacks sense or reason. It is not someone who is stupid or witless but rather someone whose self-perceptions are blown all out of proportion. The distinction is an important one. While Paul considers what he is about to do sheer folly (the act of boasting), nevertheless, what he is about to say is far from foolish (he is no blithering idiot). For if he chooses to boast, he would not be a fool (like his rivals) because he "would be speaking the truth" (12:6). The Corinthians will do well, therefore, to take what he has to say seriously. But should they be predisposed to do otherwise, he begs their indulgence to *receive [him] just as [they] would a fool*. After all, they are quite accustomed to putting up with fools—and in fact *gladly* receive them (v. 19). The fools Paul has in mind are the Corinthian intruders, who started this business of boasting ("that I may also boast," v. 18—NIV's *I too will boast*). So what will another fool matter among so many? If the Corinthians can tolerate the self-important jibberish of the intruders, they can also tolerate a little of Paul's boasting.

There is one qualification, however, that Paul insists on. They are not to receive his *self-confident boasting* as from the Lord (v. 17). The NIV translation *self-confident* is by no means certain, since examples of *hypostasis* used in this way are lacking (compare JB "certainty"; KJV,

---

11:16 Commendatory language (such as *synistēmi*) is found earlier in the letter, but it is of a general nature and includes Paul's associates. What distinguishes 11:16—12:6 is Paul's shift to the first-person singular (as in v. 21, *I also dare to boast*) and the specificity of the credentials (as in v. 25, *three times I was beaten with rods, once I was stoned*).

RSV, NSRV, REB "confidence"; Phillips "proud"). Of the possible meanings, the two preferable ones are "purpose" (as in "in this plan to boast") and "undertaking" (as in "in this matter of boasting"; Bratcher 1983:122). On balance, the latter is to be preferred.

In this matter of boasting Paul does not want to be taken as *talking as the Lord would*. The phrase is literally "according to the Lord" *(kata kyrion)*. What exactly does this mean, though? Paul could be saying that in boasting about his ministerial achievements he is not talking *as the Lord would* (NIV). But it is more likely that *kata kyrion* means "with the Lord's authority" (RSV, JB, Phillips) or "what the Lord would have me say" (TEV). The bragging Paul is about to engage in is not something the Lord would approve of; hence he does not presume to speak *ex cathedra* (as an apostle). Boasting of this sort is not the way of the Lord but rather the way of *the world* (v. 18). The Greek is literally "according to the flesh" *(kata sarka)*—a favorite phrase of Paul's (five times in 2 Corinthians). Typically it denotes operating the way the world does or being driven by human standards (compare 1:17; 5:16; 10:2, 3). When it comes to human pride, the way of the world is to boast in personal accomplishments. Many brag in this fashion, so Paul will too (v. 18).

The biting sarcasm of Paul's next remark is unmistakable. Having begged their indulgence, he now points out that bearing with his senseless boasting should pose no great problem for them, since they are used to putting up with fools. Paul minces no words when it comes to the Corinthian intruders. In verse 13 they were labeled "false" and "deceitful"; now they are called *fools* (v. 19). The term *fool* (*aphrōn*, "unwise") denotes a lack of sense or reason (see the commentary on v. 16). The intruders are fools on account of the exaggerated opinion they have of their self-importance. And the Corinthians *gladly* put up with them, thinking themselves to be *so wise* (v. 19). The position of *hēdeōs* ("gladly"), beginning the clause, heightens Paul's sarcasm: "*Gladly* you put up with fools." The Corinthians have been duped by the apostolic

11:17 Examples of *hypostasis* meaning "confidence" or "assurance" are lacking (Bauer, Arndt and Gingrich 1979).

The REB takes *kata kyrion* as equivalent to "like a Christian." Yet *kyrios* is not used elsewhere in this sense, and the phrase stands over against *kata sarka* in verse 18 (that is, "the human way of doing things").

pretenders. Yet they think themselves *so wise!* The irony of the situation does not escape Paul—nor does the danger. The Corinthians should have seen through these apostolic pretenders, but they chose not to. Moreover, they did not merely turn a blind eye to what they were about but received them with pleasure.

Is Paul being too hard on the Corinthians? The next verse suggests that he is not. For although the Corinthians thought themselves so wise in their dealings with the visiting missionaries, they actually allowed themselves to be walked all over (v. 20).

Five terms sum up how the intruders were taking advantage of the congregation. First, they were "enslaving" them. *Katadouloi* denotes absolute subjection or the loss of autonomy (Rengstorf 1964:279). Because the term is used in Galatians 2:4 of Judaizers who sought to enslave the Galatian churches to the rules and regulations of the Mosaic law, some have argued for the same sense here. But there is no hint of a Judaizing polemic in chapters 10—13. *Slaps you in the face,* at the tail end of verse 20, suggests, instead, subjection to a domineering style of pastoral leadership (Furnish 1984:497). "Treats you like slaves" (Bratcher 1983:123) or "orders you around" (TEV) catches the idea.

Second, Paul's opponents are "exploiting" the church. The Greek term *katesthiō,* commonly used of animals of prey, means to "eat up" or "devour." Paul undoubtedly is thinking of how the intruders set out to devour the Corinthians' finances. So C. K. Barrett's translation "eats you out of house and home" (1973:291) and the NJB's "eats up all you possess" may not be far off the mark.

Third, they are "taking advantage of" the church. In the realm of hunting or fishing, *lambanō* means to "catch" or "take unawares" through the use of alluring bait (Zerwick 1993:558). Paul uses the verb in 12:16 to denote catching through trickery, which may well be its sense here.

Fourth, they "push themselves forward." The verb is literally "to hold or lift up" *(epairō).* The picture is of individuals who have a lofty or stuck-up opinion of themselves—constantly keeping their nose in the air.

Finally, they are "slapping" the church "in the face." The Greek verb *derō* means to "flay" or "skin" (as in "to beat a dead horse"). It usually refers to a physical beating or flogging (Mt 21:35; Mk 12:3, 5; Lk 12:47,

48; 20:10, 11; 22:63; Jn 18:23; Acts 5:40; 16:37; 22:19), but it is also used figuratively for insulting behavior.

The overall picture is appalling. It would be appealing to say that Paul is only anticipating what could happen at Corinth. But the form of the conditional at verse 20 connotes fact (*ei tis* + indicative). Some have indeed come to Corinth and are employing these kinds of browbeating tactics. Paul, however, will not stoop to such levels. *To my shame,* he admits, . . . *we were too weak for that!* Biting sarcasm is once again in evidence. It is probably best to put *too weak* in quotes. This is the voice of the opposition speaking rather than Paul's own self-estimate. He has been accused of being bold enough when away but timid when actually face to face (10:1).

We may be quick to scoff at a church like Corinth. How could a church permit itself to be browbeaten like this? What kind of wimps were they to so readily accept such leadership? But are the Corinthians really so different from some of our contemporary churches? A take-charge, strong-arm style of leadership is valued by many within evangelicalism today. Those who lead in this way typically claim to be exercising their God-given authority. Interestingly enough, though, Paul rejects this style of leadership in his own ministry ("not that we lord it over your faith," 1:24)—as do other New Testament writers (for example, see Mt 20:25-26; 1 Pet 5:3). In fact, the language of "bearing rule," "governing" and "exercising authority" is not used by the New Testament writers to describe the leadership role in the church. It is employed only of the apostles and the congregation, not of an individual within the local church context (Belleville 1993a).

Paul Matches His Opponents' Boasting (11:21—12:10) *I am speaking as a fool,* Paul reiterates. But now at last at verse 21 he proceeds to boast. His plan of attack is to meet the opposition point for point: *What anyone else dares to boast about . . . I also dare to boast about.* The verb *tolmaō* ("dare") is used of the confidence proper to a person who is sure of her ground (Motyer 1975:365). Paul's confidence, in large part, resides in his heritage and ministerial achievements. The list, which continues into chapter 12, includes heritage (v. 22), service record (vv. 23-25), dangers and deprivations (vv. 26-27), pastoral concerns (v. 28), daring escapades (11:31-33) and ecstatic experiences (12:1-6). The basic categories are, undoubtedly, not those of Paul's own choosing. Since he was forced into this exercise in futility, we can be fairly sure that these categories were prompted by the claims of the intruders and the expectations of the Corinthians. On the other hand, what he singles out as exemplary is wholly his own. Where we might expect the opposition to make much of the number of churches planted, sizes of congregations, numbers of programs and the like, Paul turns instead to what many a search committee would view as pastoral handicaps and not strengths: ministerial trials and tribulations.

Heritage (11:22) Paul begins with his heritage. This may be because his opponents placed this at the top of their list of credentials. All indications point to the fact that the intruders extolled their Jewishness. They were trueborn Jews from Palestine—*Hebrews . . . Israelites . . . Abraham's descendants*—and not outlanders like this upstart from Tarsus (Fahy 1964:215). Paul's response is simply, *So am I* (v. 22). At the time Paul writes, *Hebrew* designated mother tongue and place of upbringing. So what he is affirming is that, like his rivals, he looks on Palestine as his home and Aramaic as his native language. This accords with Acts 22:3, where Paul states that although he was born in Tarsus of Cilicia, he grew up in Jerusalem. It also fits Philippians 3:5, where he claims that he is "a Hebrew of Hebrews." Second, he is an *Israelite*—that is, a member of God's chosen people (Gutbrod 1965:386). Third, he is one of *Abraham's descendants*. The Greek is literally translated "the seed of Abraham," which for a Jew amounted to circumcision on the eighth day in accordance with Mosaic law (again, compare Phil 3:5).

Service Record (11:23-25) Paul matches the Corinthian intruders' boasts with respect to heritage point for point. When it comes to service records, however, Paul can confidently claim that his surpasses that of his rivals: *Are they servants of Christ? . . . I am more* (v. 23). *Are they*

11:22 Ralph Martin (following Dieter Georgi) thinks that "seed of Abraham" refers to Abraham's role as the first believer and a person of the Spirit (1986:375). But its association with *Hebrews* and *Israelites* is against a figurative reading. "My father was a wandering Aramean" is how the father begins to instruct the youngest son during the Passover seder (Deut 26:5-10; *m. Pesahim* 10.4).

11:23 *En thanatois pollakis* is literally "[I surpass them] in deaths many times over." The plural "deaths" could refer to general threats to life ("mortal dangers"). But it more

servants . . . ? is perhaps better translated "Do they claim to be servants . . . ?" While this might be a given in their minds, it certainly is not in Paul's. In truth they are false apostles and servants of Satan (11:13-15). Paul parenthetically adds: *I am out of my mind to talk like this.* If his boasting thus far has been foolishness (v. 1), now it moves into the realm of sheer madness. The NIV translation *I am out of my mind* is a fairly cautious one. In today's parlance we might say, "I am a madman" or "I have gone off the deep end."

The first three boasts in the list appear as well in 2 Corinthians 6:5: *I have worked much harder, been in prison more frequently, been flogged more severely. Worked . . . harder* translates a Greek term commonly used of physical labor that causes one to collapse in bed at night from utter exhaustion *(kopos).* Although it is used in 10:15 to describe Paul's missionary labors, here it may refer to the long, grueling hours he worked as a tentmaker. He did this to avoid being a financial burden on the church at which he was currently ministering. The plural *kopoi* ("labors") may indicate that Paul had to work more than one job to keep himself financially afloat.

Been in prison more frequently piques the curiosity. Prisons back then were used to detain an accused person who was awaiting trial rather than to punish someone for breaking the law. Luke records only one imprisonment of Paul prior to the writing of 2 Corinthians (Acts 16:22-34). It is possible that Paul's near-death ordeal in the province of Asia (recounted in 2 Cor 1:8-11) hints at a second imprisonment. But this is merely speculation.

Paul's next boast can be translated either "flogged countless times" or *flogged more severely.* The main idea of the adverb is "to throw over or beyond" a mark *(hyper + ballō),* while the noun *plēgē* refers to a "stroke" or "blow." Flogging was a common punishment employed by both Jewish and Roman courts for a wide range of offenses. It was

---

likely refers to life-threatening experiences that Paul encountered on his missionary travels. "We . . . are always being given over to death for Jesus' sake" in 4:11 communicates much the same thought.

11:24-25 Tabulations of exploits, as in 2 Corinthians 11:24-25, are commonly found in the *res gestae* literature of the day. See, for example, *Acts of Augustus* 1.4: "Twice I triumphed with an ovation, thrice I celebrated curule triumphs . . . thirteen times I had been consul."

sometimes severe enough to kill a person—which is what Paul probably means by *exposed to death again and again* (compare JB's "whipped . . . often almost to death"; TEV's "near death more often"). The kinds of blows that almost killed him on numerous occasions are specified next. Five times he had received from the Jews *the forty lashes minus one*, three times he was *beaten with rods*, and once he was *stoned* (v. 25). The beatings administered by Jewish authorities are absent from Luke's account—although clearly remembered by Paul (*Jews* is placed first in the word order for emphasis). Mosaic law prescribed a maximum of forty lashes to be meted out as punishment for an offense (Deut 25:3). The number was lowered to thirty-nine to keep the flogger from accidentally miscounting and thus becoming a lawbreaker himself. In fact, if the person was given one stripe too many and died, the scourger was held responsible. In preparation for flogging, the person's two hands were bound, one on either side, to a pillar, and his clothing was torn to expose the chest and back. The lashes were administered with a strap consisting of three hide thongs. Twenty-six blows were given to the back and thirteen blows to the chest (*m. Makkot* 3:10-14).

Beaten with rods (erabdisthēn) was a Roman form of punishment. Of the three beatings Paul received, Luke records only the one in Philippi, where the chief magistrates of the city ordered Paul and Silas to be stripped and beaten (Acts 16:22-23). The rods, similar to our billy club, were made of birchwood. Such beatings occurred on the main square before the judgment seat. Technically a Roman citizen could not be publicly beaten and imprisoned, as Paul and Silas were, without due process. But there were a number of legal exceptions (Sherwin-White 1963:71-78).

Paul's one stoning was in the streets of Lystra during his first visit there (Acts 14:8-20). Certain Jews from Pisidian Antioch and Iconium had followed him to Lystra and stirred up the crowd against him. He was stoned, dragged outside the city and left for dead. Stoning was technically a Jewish form of punishment for capital offenses like idolatry, blasphemy, soothsaying, profaning the sabbath and adultery (Lev 20:2, 27; 24:14; Deut 13:10; 17:5; 22:22-24; *m. Sanhedrin* 7).

Paul concludes his service record with *three times . . . shipwrecked* and *a night and a day in the open sea* (v. 26). There is no account in Acts of any of these events up to this point in his ministry. That he had been shipwrecked three times is not surprising, however, given the peril involved in this mode of transportation in the first century and how often Paul traveled by sea (Acts 9:30; 13:4, 13; 14:25-26; 16:11; 17:14-15; 18:18-22; 20:6; 21:1-8; 27:1—28:13). The night and day adrift at sea was probably the aftermath of a shipwreck. Paul most likely found himself clinging for dear life to a piece of wreckage or ship's cargo while awaiting rescue (Bruce 1971:243). The ordeal apparently lasted twenty-four hours ("a night and a day"). Use of the perfect tense *(pepoiēka)* suggests that the memories of this experience were still vivid for Paul.

Dangers and Deprivations (11:26-27) Paul proceeds next to list dangers that he has encountered and deprivations he has endured in the line of duty as a gospel preacher. The dangers include natural enemies like *rivers* and the *sea* and human enemies like *bandits, my own countrymen* and *Gentiles.*

River hazards involved dangerous crossings and rivers that overflowed their banks. Floods and bandits were notorious problems for those attempting travel over the seven-thousand-foot Taurus Mountains (Acts 13—14). The floods of the Pisidian highlands are mentioned by Strabo, who wrote of how the Cestrus and Eurymedon rivers tumbled down the heights and precipices to the Pamphylian Sea and of the wild clans of Pisidian robbers who made these mountains their home (Williams 1985:220). Even the relatively populated stretch of road between Athens and Corinth, called the Sceironian Rocks, was infamous for its highway robbers (Murphy-O'Connor 1985:44).

Incidents involving Paul's *own countrymen* are too numerous to recount. Not only did he face active hostility from Jewish authorities in virtually every city he visited, but Luke also states that Jews followed him from city to city, stirring up trouble whenever they could. Three times they succeeded in inciting the Gentiles of the city (Acts 13:50; 14:2; 17:5). Failing that, the Jews were not averse to going straight to the local authorities (Acts 18:12). Luke records that Paul faced *Gentile* opposition twice—in both cases from those whose livelihoods were threatened by the gospel (16:19-21; 19:23-41).

Dangers were also faced *in the city* and *in the country.* The distinction is between densely and sparsely populated regions (*erēmia* = "desolate," "lonely," "solitary"). The hazards faced in each respective region would have been quite different. Mob action and crowd control were real problems in urban areas (for example, Acts 17:1-9; 19:23-41), while native superstitions and legends tended to thrive in rural areas such as Lystra (Acts 14:8-20).

Dangers *at sea* are listed as well. The general attitude toward sea travel is aptly summed up by Horace's statement that the boat was first conceived by a sadistic degenerate whose mission was to destroy humanity (*Odes* 1.3.9, 16; Murphy-O'Connor 1985:47). Given that ancient sailing vessels carried no lifeboats or life jackets, travel on the Mediterranean could be truly dangerous (Furnish 1984:517-18).

Dangers from *false brothers* concludes this grouping. The term *pseudadelphoi* is found elsewhere only in Galatians 2:4, where it is applied to those claiming the name of Christ who infiltrated the church at Antioch to spy on the believers' freedom in Christ and make them slaves. Judaizing issues are absent from 2 Corinthians, so Paul may be thinking here of so-called brothers and sisters who betrayed him to the local authorities (Héring 1967:86). Ralph P. Martin may be correct in speculating that *false brothers* is placed last to drive home to the Corinthians the enormity of their offer of hospitality to such people (1986:379).

These dangers are followed by a list of five types of deprivations: *labored and toiled, . . . often gone without sleep, . . . known hunger and thirst, . . . often gone without food* and *been cold and naked. Labored and toiled* is a phrase employed elsewhere for the hard life of the itinerant laborer (for example, in 1 Thess 2:9; 2 Thess 3:8). *Kopos* refers to manual labor that is physically exhausting (comparable to our expression "dead tired"), while *mochthos* stresses the hardship or pain involved in the work.

Gone without sleep (*agrypnia;* literally "sleeplessness," "wakeful-

---

11:27 *Agrypnia* ("gone without sleep") usually denotes sleeplessness or wakefulness of the voluntary sort. Eric Bishop speculates that in Paul's case it was due in large part to his habit of staying up late to talk about the Messiah (1965:31). He also thinks that "in famine and drought" is a more realistic, Eastern Mediterranean rendering for *en limē kai dipsei* than the usual "in hunger and thirst" (1966:169).

ness") could have been the involuntary result of illness or insomnia. But in Paul's case it was more likely self-inflicted. If 11:28-29 is any indication, it was the consequence of burning the midnight oil out of prayerful concern for his converts and his coworkers. It can also be an indication that he did his tentmaking during the day and engaged in missionary labors during the evening hours (as in Acts 20:7).

I have known hunger and thirst (en limō kai dipsei) is essentially a repetition of what Paul said in 6:5. Both terms bespeak involuntary actions. The pairing is most likely descriptive of the hard life of the itinerant, rather than a condition of poverty per se.

The next one in the list is voluntary in character: *I have often gone without food. Nēsteia,* unlike *limos,* refers to self-imposed abstinence. Fasting was a common practice among pious Jews and was often done as a means of focusing one's energies on the task of intercession. There may also have been times when Paul went hungry to avoid being a burden on anyone (2 Cor 11:7-10).

Last but not least, Paul had been *cold and naked*—that is, he had gone without adequate shelter and clothing. Since he mentions this as well in 1 Corinthians, it must have been a relatively common experience ("to this very hour . . . we are in rags"—1 Cor 4:11).

Pastoral Concerns (11:28-29) *Besides everything else,* Paul says, *I face daily the pressure of my concern for all the churches.* If the church at Corinth is in any way typical, Paul's pastoral lot must have been close to insufferable. In an age when we can pick up the phone and find out in seconds how someone is doing, or hop on a plane and be halfway around the world within twenty-four hours, it is hard to appreciate the weeks or months it would have taken Paul to get news of a colleague or church. This state of affairs quite clearly caused him some concern—a concern that he claims was a daily *pressure.* The Greek term *epistasis* denotes "that which comes upon" (KJV; for example, pressure, care, oversight) or "against" (such as hindrances). Because the word appears

11:28 *Chōris tōn parektos* can mean either "apart from these external things" (NEB, Phillips, KJV) or "skipping over those things that might have been mentioned" (TEV, JB, RSV). On the whole the latter reading is preferable. Paul could have mentioned many other dangers and deprivations. For example, bears, wolves and wild boar were known to populate the region between Thessalonica and Berea (Murphy-O'Connor 1985:45). But instead he moves on to pastoral concerns.

in only one other place in the New Testament (Acts 24:12), it is difficult to determine whether Paul is referring to daily pressures (NASB, TEV, NIV, RSV, Phillips), concerns (NEB, JB) or obstacles that he faced in the ministry.

It is equally difficult to define the term *merimna (concern)*. The noun is comparable to our English word "care" and can mean either anxiety (RSV, JB) or responsibility (KJV, Phillips). Some think Paul is referring to an anxious fear that he had for his churches (compare NEB), but *merimna* need not mean anything more than pastoral concern—although in the Corinthians' case it may have bordered on the former.

Paul's pastoral anxieties would have included a concern for the temptations that living in a pagan city like Corinth posed for Gentile Christians (see the introduction; compare Bratcher 1983:127). Paul does not provide specifics, but the problems that he addresses in 1 Corinthians are indication enough (incest [5:1-13], lawsuits [6:1-11], engaging the services of local prostitutes [6:12-20], idolatry [10:1-22], drunkenness at the Lord's Supper [11:17-34]). He does, however, give two examples: *Who is weak, and I do not feel weak? Who is led into sin, and I do not inwardly burn?* (v. 29). The term *weak* is susceptible to a variety of interpretations. Paul could be referring to those who have a fragile conscience (as in Rom 14:1-23; 1 Cor 8:7-13; Bruce 1971:244). Alternatively, he may have in mind the powerless in society (Murphy-O'Connor 1991:116). Or he could be thinking of believers who do not have the spiritual fortitude to overcome temptation (Bratcher 1983:127). Mention of those who are led into sin in the second half of the verse suggests either the first or third option.

Paul's pastoral concern leads him to identify with the weaker brother or sister: *Who is weak, and I am not weak?* If *weak* refers to the brother or sister with scruples, then Paul would be saying that he refrains from doing anything that would cause that brother or sister to stumble (as in

---

11:29 *Led into sin* is literally "who is made to stumble." The image is that of laying of a trap or snare (Liddell, Scott and Jones 1978). If *weak* is to be connected with 1 Corinthians 8, then the situation would be a mature Christian's example prompting a brother or sister to do something that their conscience tells them is still wrong. For example, mature Christians would feel free to eat meat sacrificed to an idol because they know that an idol is nothing. Immature Christians are encouraged to follow their example even though their conscience tells them that the idol is indeed something and that the activity is wrong. In

JB's "when any man has had scruples, I have had scruples with him"). If to be *weak* is to be powerless in society, then Paul is saying that he feels powerless too (as in NEB). On the whole, the former option provides the most consistent reading.

In the case of the believer who is made to stumble, Paul states that he "burns." What, though, is meant by *burn?* Ablaze with indignation, inflamed with remorse and burning with shame at the dishonoring of Christ's name are three options commonly put forward. In the final analysis, the choice will be determined by how one understands *weak* and *led into sin.*

Daring Escapades (11:30-33) Paul turns next to daring escapades (vv. 30-33). Consistent with his determination to play the fool, Paul chooses an incident that demonstrates weakness rather than strength. *If I must boast,* he states, *I will boast of the things that show my weakness* (v. 30). The form of the conditional denotes fact: "since I must boast" (*ei* + indicative). Paul has been forced to become a braggart by the exigencies of the Corinthian situation. The church is being led down the garden path by some smooth-talking con artists. Paul will do whatever it takes to help the church to see this—even to the extent of boasting as his rivals do.

When asked to provide a vita, we tend to pick things that make us look good in the eyes of others. Paul turns instead to what makes him look bad. He also chooses an episode that caused him no little personal humiliation—a quick exit from the city of Damascus under cover of darkness. His account is prefaced with an oath. The veracity of what he is about to say is at stake: *The God and Father of the Lord Jesus, who is to be praised forever, knows that I am not lying* (v. 31). Oaths are used twice earlier in this chapter (11:10, 11; also see 1:18). In fact, Paul tends to use them whenever he suspects that the truthfulness of his claims might be questioned (as in "I assure you before God," Gal 1:20; "God

---

the process, the conscience's ability to distinguish between right and wrong is destroyed.

11:30 Some take verse 30 with what precedes rather than with what follows (as in KJV, NEB, REB). There is support for this in the plural *ta (the things that show my weakness).* But then verses 32-33 are left to stand on their own as a kind of afterthought. Alternatively, verses 30-31 serve as an admirable introduction to Paul's humiliating experience in Damascus and his heavenly rapture fourteen years prior.

is our witness," 1 Thess 2:5). Paul's oath in 2 Corinthians 11:31 is made even more weighty by the additions *the God and Father of the Lord Jesus* and *who is to be praised forever*. The former phrase occurs elsewhere only in 2 Corinthians 1:3 (see the commentary) and Ephesians 1:3. The latter phrase is a Jewish expression of reverence and adoration (Bratcher 1983:128).

Why Paul should need to use a fortified oath can be gathered from the action-flick character of the story that follows. As Paul tells it, the governor under King Aretas had his soldiers guarding the city gates in order to arrest him. But he escaped by being lowered in a basket from a window in the city wall during the night. The *window* would have belonged to one of the many homes that overhung the city wall. The *basket* in question would have been a bag of braided rope, suitable for carrying hay, straw or bales of wool (Bauer, Arndt and Gingrich 1979). This episode, which Luke also recounts, came about three years after Paul's encounter with the risen Christ on the road to Damascus (Acts 9:1-22; compare Gal 1:17). Damascus was the capital city of Syria, located on a plain at about a twenty-two-thousand-foot elevation east of the Anti-Lebanon Mountains and west of the Syrian-Arabian desert.

The political status of the city at the time of Paul's stay is not certain. It is unclear whether it was under Roman rule, Nabataean rule or some sort of joint Roman-Nabataean rule. Part of the difficulty is that the Greek term "ethnarch" *(ethnarchēs)* could refer to the governor of the city or to the ruler of a major ethnic group within the city. Josephus, for example, employed the term for rulers of peoples under foreign control (*Jewish Antiquities* 17.11.4; *Jewish Wars* 2.6.3), and Strabo tells of how an ethnarch was granted to the Jews in Alexandria because of their large numbers (17.798; see Hughes 1962:424-25). A reasonable conjecture is that "ethnarch" refers to the leader of a semi-autonomous colony of Nabataeans during the reign of Gaius (A.D. 37-41)—a time when the policy of client kingdoms on the eastern frontier was in force (Murphy-

---

11:32-33 Philip Hughes resolves the seeming discrepancy between Luke's "Jews" and Paul's "ethnarch" by postulating that the ethnarch was himself a Jew and that the guard appointed by him was composed entirely of Jews (1962:424). But that Luke would mention only the Jews is not surprising. It illustrates his point that the former persecutor of the church now finds himself in the position of the persecuted. It makes sense that Paul, on the other hand, would focus on his escape from the clutches of King Aretas as a fitting

O'Connor 1991:117; Bruce 1971:245).

Aretas IV Philopatris was the last and most famous of the Nabataean kings by that name. He reigned through his deputy at Petra from 9 B.C. to A.D. 40. Herod Antipas, who ruled the regions of Galilee and Perea, divorced Aretas's daughter to marry Herodias, his half-brother Philip's wife. Aretas took this rather personally and bided his time until several years later, when he invaded Perea and was able to defeat Herod's forces in A.D. 36. It is thought that his rule at that time included Damascus, which would explain his ability to guard the city gates continually (imperfect tense). The absence of Roman coinage between A.D. 34 and 62 suggests this as well (Hemer 1982).

Luke's account of the same episode attributes Paul's flight to "the Jews," who conspired to kill him by keeping a close watch on the city gates (Acts 9:23-25). Rather than postulate two different episodes—which, given Paul's track record with municipal authorities, is altogether feasible—we can assume it is likely that the Jews and the Arabs teamed up in their attack on Paul. Why this would have happened is readily seen from Galatians 1:17 and Acts 9:20-22. After Paul's commissioning in the city of Damascus, Luke tells us that he immediately began to preach in the synagogues that Jesus is the Son of God (Acts 9:20). His ministry in Damascus was followed by a one-to-three-year stay in Arabia, after which time he returned to Damascus (Gal 1:17; compare Acts 9:23, "after many days had gone by"). That the Jewish authorities would plot to kill him is no surprise. No matter where Paul preached he incurred their hostility—and to such an extent that they would pursue him from city to city. The hostility of the Nabataean Arabs is also easily explained. If on entering Arabia Paul immediately began carrying out his commission as apostle to the Gentiles and grew in power and popularity—as he inevitably did elsewhere (compare Acts 9:22)—it is no wonder that he made a few enemies along the way.

Paul's flight from Damascus seems somewhat out of place in a vita

example of the daring escapade.

11:33 Luke adds that this occurred at night, that the Jews watched the city gates day and night, and that Paul was aided and abetted by his followers (Acts 9:23-25). William Barclay notes that city walls in Paul's day were wide enough to accommodate a carriage (1954:255).

that highlights an impeccable heritage, a sterling service record and examples of great personal sacrifice. So why is it included? Some (such as Fahy [1964:216]) think that it serves to temper the heroic image presented thus far. Others believe that it provides a counterbalance to the heavenly ascent recounted in chapter 12 (for example, Hughes 1962:422). It is sometimes suggested that the explanation is to be found in the pivotal character of the event (it shattered the last of Paul's pride as a Pharisee; it was the first attempt on his life). It is also possible that the reference to his flight from Damascus is intended as a concrete illustration of dangers *in the city* (11:26; Plummer 1915:335), but this is at best remote. It may simply be that his critics had used it to ridicule him.

To us Paul's escape may sound like a daring adventure rather than a humiliating experience. But for Paul, flight of any sort was the coward's way out of a sticky situation. Flogging or imprisonment was far preferable in his way of thinking. Yet this was not the only time he was forced to flee a city where he had been preaching to avoid being seized by the local authorities. On at least two other occasions he had had to make a quick exit—once from Jerusalem, after the Jews made an attempt on his life (Acts 9:29-30), and then again from Thessalonica at the insistence of the church leaders (Acts 17:10; 1 Thess 2:17). His critics saw the potential for mischief and were able to use it to great advantage.

Ecstatic Experiences (12:1-6) In the Western church we cultivate and value people with vision—those forward-looking, direction-setting individuals who can see where God would have the church move in

---

12:1 The JB translates the first part of verse 1 as a rhetorical question: "Must I go on boasting . . . ?"

Optasia occurs in the New Testament only in Luke 1:22 and 24:23, Acts 26:19 and 2 Corinthians 12:1, while the plural *apokalypseis* appears only in 2 Corinthians 12:1, 7. The combination is without parallel in the New Testament. This suggests that *visions and revelations* may be a slogan that Paul has taken over from the Corinthian intruders (Barrett 1973:306). If so, it would be appropriate to put the phrase in quotes: "I will go on to 'visions and revelations.' " Compare Paul's use of slogans in 1 Corinthians 6:12 and 10:23 ("Everything is permissible for me"), 6:13 ("Food for the stomach and the stomach for food") and 7:1 ("It is good for a man not to have sexual relations with a woman" [literally, "not to touch a woman"]).

Paul is no stranger to visions and revelations. Luke records a number of them (Acts 9:12; 16:9-10; 18:9-10; 22:17-21), and Paul himself states that his second postconversion trip to Jerusalem was undertaken *in response to a revelation* (Gal 2:2; compare 1:16).

the coming decades. Little place, however, is given to visions per se—that is, to something beheld in a God-given dream, trance or ecstasy. Yet visions were a regular means of divine communication in biblical times. In the Old Testament visions were a familiar medium by which God let it be known what he was going to do (Dahn 1978:514). They are also common in the New Testament. In fact, the outpouring of the Spirit in the latter days is associated with sons and daughters prophesying, young men seeing visions and old men dreaming dreams (Acts 2:17). Typical examples are the vision Peter had of heaven opening and something like a large sheet being let down by its four corners (Acts 10:9-15) and the vision Paul had of a man standing and begging him to come over to Macedonia (Acts 16:9). The value that the early church placed on such experiences can be seen from the fact that Paul in his boasting turns last to *visions and revelations* (12:1).

Paul cannot pass up an opportunity to reiterate that all this boasting serves no good purpose. *There is nothing to be gained* by going on to such experiences; but "it is necessary" (NIV *I must go on*, v. 1). This is the only time that Paul says he *must* boast. It can be fairly concluded that his rivals have laid claim to visionary and revelatory experiences. But this in and of itself was probably not enough to force his hand. The Corinthians must have looked on the ecstatic as the trump card in what was already thought to be a winning hand. So Paul feels compelled to match his rivals' boasting or lose the church to those he thinks are deceitful workers and Satan's henchmen (11:13-15, 20).

Still, even though he finds it necessary, he does not find it a "prof-

---

The *men . . . de* structure of verse 1 is to be noted. The force is most likely concessive: "*although* it profits nothing, I will go on to visions and revelations" (Bauer, Arndt and Gingrich 1979:no. 1a).

There are two textual variations in verse 1. Some early manuscripts have *de* ("but"; ℵ* D* Ψ) instead of *dei* ("it is necessary"; p[46] B D[2] F G L P). The dropping of the *i* could be accidental. On the other hand, it could also be a scribal attempt to harmonize *I must boast* with what Paul said earlier (as in 10:17: "Let him who boasts, boast in the Lord"). H, some itala and the Vulgate add *ei* ("*if* I must boast")—undoubtedly an attempt to soften the blow. A fair number of Byzantine uncials have *dē* ("now," "indeed") rather than *dei*—quite likely an accidental error due to similarity of sound. There are also some manuscripts that read *sympherei* (D*) or *sympherei moi* (D[1] H K L Ψ) instead of *sympheron men*. The neuter participle + *men* is quite clearly the more difficult construction. So a scribe could easily have been tempted to provide an easier grammatical construction.

itable" exercise (NIV *there is nothing to be gained*). The Greek term *sympheron* in Paul's writings typically refers to what is beneficial or helpful. Here it denotes that which is useful. What use are ecstatic experiences for ministry? Can they equip? Can they direct? Can they instruct? They cannot even be properly communicated (*things that man is not permitted to tell*, v. 4). So what good are they? If they possess no ministerial value, why then boast about them as his rivals are doing? And why are the Corinthians placing such importance on them? That the Corinthians would value ecstatic experiences is not surprising. They were highly prized in the Greco-Roman world and in Judaism. Even in rabbinic circles there is frequent mention of visions, fiery appearances and voices (Oepke 1964b:456).

Having cleared the air about the senselessness of such boasting, Paul finds it nonetheless necessary to proceed to *visions and revelations* (v. 1). The phrase is without parallel in the New Testament, so Paul may be picking up the language of the Corinthian intruders. The distinction between a vision and a revelation is not immediately obvious. The Greek term *optasia* denotes that which is seen (compare "optical"). *Apokalypsis* ("revelation"), on the other hand, is a broader term that applies to all forms of divine disclosure and can involve the whole range of senses (sight, hearing, smell, taste and touch). It is strange that Paul puts what he recounts in verses 1-10 in the category of *visions and revelations*. It is not actually a vision, since he *heard* inexpressible things rather than saw them (v. 4). Nor is it a revelatory event in any explicit sense. It comes closest to an ecstasy—that is, a transportation out of one's normal, mundane sphere of existence into the supramundane realm of the divine (v. 2, *heaven*). So perhaps it is best to understand *visions and revelations* as a catchall phrase for a wide range of supramundane experiences. Whatever Paul experienced, it was decidedly "of the Lord." The genitive could be objective: "visions and revelations of the Lord himself" (Phillips). Or, more probably, it is subjective: *visions and revelations from the Lord* (TEV, NIV, JB, NEB).

12:2 Paul's mention of *fourteen years* both here and in Galatians 2:1 is purely coincidental.

When one is narrating a remarkable event, it is natural to begin with the date. So the temporal marker at 2 Corinthians 12:2 is not unexpected. The Old Testament prophets and

In order to match his rivals boast for boast, Paul breaks a vow of silence and mentions an ecstatic experience that occurred fourteen years earlier (v. 2). This would place the event during the so-called silent years, when Paul was in the region of Syria and Cilicia (Acts 9:30; Gal 1:21). It happened well before his evangelistic foray in Corinth (c. A.D. 50-52), but not before his Damascus road encounter with the risen Christ (*I know a man in Christ*).

The story is narrated in the third-person singular: *I know a man. . . . He heard inexpressible things.* Paul's use of the third person is indeed puzzling. He cannot be telling about someone else's experience; otherwise there would be no grounds for personal boasting. Plus, all the details of the story point to its being a personal experience. Attempts to explain it are wide-ranging: it is symptomatic of his aversion to boasting (Bruce 1971:246); he did it to avoid suggesting that he was special because of his experiences (M. J. Harris 1976:395); the style reflects the sense of self-transcendence that such experiences seem to entail (Furnish 1984:544); he didn't allocate much importance to it (Loubser 1991:77); he will speak personally only of things that show weakness (Käsemann 1942:66-67); or he is distancing his apostolic self from the self in which he has been forced to boast (Baird 1985:654). But it may simply be that speaking of himself impersonally is the only way he can look at the experience with any kind of detachment (Barclay 1954:256; Murphy-O'Connor 1991:118). Paul is already a reluctant competitor. To boast of ecstatic experiences in a personal way may just have been beyond him.

Compared to other first-century accounts of heavenly journeys, Paul's is notably terse. Only two things are mentioned. One, he was *caught up to the third heaven* (v. 2), and two, he heard *inexpressible things* (v. 4). The NIV *caught up* might more accurately be translated "seized" or "snatched" *(harpazō)*. The verb means to "grasp" something forcibly ("plunder," "steal") and suddenly ("snatch"). Luke uses it of the Spirit's physically seizing Philip and transporting him to another geographical

---

pseudepigraphic seers regularly did this (for example, Amos 1:1: "two years before the earthquake"; *Testament of Abraham* 3:1: "In the thirtieth year after the destruction of our city, I, Salathiel . . ."). Paul's report is notably restrained in detail compared to the elaborate accounts of Enoch and others.

location (Acts 8:39-40), while in eschatological contexts it denotes a mighty operation of God (as in 1 Thess 4:17; Rev 12:5; Foerster 1964:472-73).

Paul says that he was snatched up to the *third heaven*. *Heaven* is the abode of God and of those closely associated with him (see "our Father in heaven," Mt 6:9; "the angels in heaven," Mk 13:32). A journey to heaven where revelations are received about things on the other side is a familiar idea in first-century apocalyptic and rabbinic materials (Bietenhard 1976:191-92). The notion of a multiplicity of heavens began to surface in the intertestamental period (2 Macc 15:23; 3 Macc 2:2, "king of the heavens"; Wisdom of Solomon 9:10, "the holy heavens"; Tobit 8:5, "the heavens"). Some Jewish materials speak of only one heaven (such as Philo; 2 Esdras 4:9), while others tell of three (*Testament of Levi* 2-3, "the uppermost heaven"), five (*3 Baruch* 11, "the angel led me to the fifth heaven") and even seven heavens (such as *Pesiqta Rabbati* 98a, "God opened seven heavens to Moses").

Paul is not sure whether he was *in the body* or *out of the body* when he made his heavenly journey (v. 2). Bodily translation is a distinctly Jewish notion (as in "he immediately became invisible and went up into heaven and stood before God," *Testament of Abraham* 8; compare *1 Enoch* 12:1). Even so, a Hellenistic Jew like Philo can state that it is contrary to holy law for what is mortal to dwell with what is immortal (*Who Is the Heir of Divine Things* 265; compare Josephus *Jewish Wars* 7.8.7). For the Greek and Gnostic alike it was the soul freed from the body that was able to soar to heaven. Ecstatic experiences of this sort often entailed a loss of sense perception and voluntary control, so that Paul may genuinely have not known whether he was physically transported to heaven or not. God alone holds this knowledge (*God knows*, vv. 2-3), and to Paul's way of thinking it mattered very little. What mattered was what he *heard*. *This man*, he says, *heard inexpressible things* (vv. 3-4). The phrase *arrēta rhēmata* can mean words that are either ineffable (too

---

12:4 Some think that in verses 1-6 Paul is describing one rapture that occurred in two stages. But the identification in Jewish literature of *third heaven* (v. 2) with *paradise* (v. 4) is against this.

Paradeisos ("paradise") occurs in only two other places in the New Testament. Luke uses it of the present abode of the righteous (Lk 23:43), while in Revelation 2:7 the right to eat of the tree of life in paradise is promised to the one who overcomes. Given the use

lofty to be spoken) or inexpressible (too difficult to verbalize). *Things that a man is not permitted to tell,* in the second half of verse 4, makes the former option the likelier one. The verb *exestin (permitted)* denotes that which is lawful or allowable (compare 1 Cor 6:12; 10:23). Paul has no right to share the details of his experience, and so he doesn't. His rivals, on the other hand, freely divulge and in so doing call into question the genuineness of their purported experiences.

Paul seems to start all over again in verses 3-4: *And I know that this man—whether in the body or apart from the body, I do not know* . . . Is he relating a *second* ecstatic experience? The opening *and* suggests this. But the virtually identical phraseology says otherwise. Paul's fumbling and restarting are merely symptomatic of great unease. Even though his hand is forced, he is having a hard time getting the words out.

This second time around, the third heaven is identified as *paradise.* *Paradeisos* is a Persian loanword for a circular enclosure and is generally used of a garden or park area (Bietenhard and Brown 1976:760-61). Myths from many nations speak of a land or a place of blessedness on the edge of the known world. Paradise for the first-century Jew, on the other hand, was located in heaven—or even in a third heaven (*2 Enoch* 8.1-8; *Adam and Eve* 40.1)—and was thought to be the abode of the righteous after death (*3 Baruch* 10.5, "the place where the souls of the righteous come when they assemble"). It was in this uppermost heaven of all that God dwelt, and with him the archangels (*Testament of Levi* 3). So the very fact that Paul was transported to God's abode meant that he could compete with anything his rivals boasted about. Jesus, it will be remembered, promised one of the men crucified with him that he would be with him in paradise that very day (Lk 23:40-43). So also in Revelation 2:7 the right to eat of the tree of life in paradise is promised to the one who overcomes.

About a man like that, Paul says, *I will boast;* on the other hand, *I will not boast about myself* (or, more accurately, "on behalf of a man . . .

---

of *paradeisos* in Genesis 2:8—3:24, it is not at all surprising to find in Jewish circles the expectation that paradise would be a garden much like that of Eden. Eden imagery is, to be sure, strongly present in the last chapters of Revelation ("the tree of life," "the river of the water of life," "twelve crops of fruit").

12:5 *Tou toioutou* could be neuter ("about such experiences") or, as is likely, masculine ("about such a man").

on behalf of myself" [*hyper* + the genitive]; v. 5). The distinction between the narrator and the individual in question is maintained. Why this is becomes clearer with the final phrase of verse 5: *I will not boast except about my weaknesses* (technically, "in my weaknesses" [*en* + the dative]). Paul can boast if he looks at himself dispassionately. But when he considers himself personally, he can commend only what his rivals would consider weaknesses (Bruce 1971:247).

An important qualifier is thrown in at this point. *If I should choose to boast, I would not be a fool* (v. 6). The term *fool* (*a* + *phrōn*, or "un-wise") denotes a lack of sense or reason. Although Paul plays the fool, what he says is by no means foolish. And if he chose to boast in something other than his weaknesses, he would not be making a fool of himself (as the Corinthian intruders were). Why not? Because, unlike his rivals, who had an exaggerated opinion of themselves that had little or no foundation in reality, he would be *speaking the truth*. So Paul could legitimately boast, but he refrains from doing so for two reasons. First, he would have *no one think more of [him] than is warranted by what he does or says* (v. 6). The word translated *warranted* (*logisētai*) means to "draw a logical conclusion" from a given set of facts (Eichler 1978:822-23). Paul wants the Corinthians' judgment of him to be based on what they themselves have witnessed and not pie-in-the-sky claims that he makes about himself. Second, he refrains because of the *surpassingly great revelations* that he experienced (v. 7). *Hyperbolē* has the force of a superlative (JB "extraordinary"; NEB "magnificent")

12:7 The inferential conjunction *dio* is absent from p[46] D K Ψ and the majority of Byzantine uncials. It should, nonetheless, be retained. It is the more difficult reading and has strong Alexandrian (ℵ A B 33 81 1739) and Western (G it[B]) support. Several important witnesses also omit the second occurrence of *hina mē hyperairōmai* (ℵ* A D F G 33, part of itala, vg). The repetition, however, is well supported (p[46] B Ψ K L P). Moreover, it is easier to imagine a scribe omitting the second occurrence as repetitious rather than adding it (see Metzger 1971:585).

Almost all English translations begin a new thought at verse 7. Yet the UBS and Nestlé-Aland editions of the Greek text take the first half of verse 7 *(because of these surpassingly great revelations)* as the conclusion of verse 6. (The NIV's *to keep me from becoming conceited* follows, rather than precedes, this phrase in the Greek text.) The UBS and Nestlé-Aland interpretation is supported by (1) the presence of the conjunction *kai* ("and") at verse 7 (which links it with what precedes) and (2) the disjunctive *dio* ("therefore") halfway through the verse. Following this punctuation of the text, *kai tē hyperbolē tōn apokalypseōn* would supply a second reason Paul refrains from boasting: because of the extraordinary character of his experience.

rather than a comparative (NIV *surpassing*). So extraordinary were the revelations that others would be tempted to think highly of him if he were to share the details. And so he refrains from saying any more. **Paul's Stake (12:7-10)** Extraordinary religious experiences often come at personal cost. When Jacob wrestled with God, he hobbled away lame (Gen 32:25). When Paul entered paradise, he came away with a *thorn in [his] flesh* (v. 7). Few remarks in Scripture have generated as much scholarly discussion as this one. What exactly happened to Paul is difficult to ascertain. The term *skolops* denoted something pointed and was used of everything from a stake or thorn to a surgical instrument or the point of a fishhook. Paul's mention of a *skolops in my flesh (tē sarki)* is commonly taken to be a physical (epilepsy, a speech impediment, malaria, an ophthalmic malady, leprosy, attacks of migraine) or emotional (hysteria, periodic depressions, inability to reach his own people) ailment of some kind. The difficulty is that *sarx* can also refer to what is mortal, flawed, worldly or even human (Bauer, Arndt and Gingrich 1979). So the list can legitimately be expanded to include such possibilities as persecution, troublesome people, spiritual snares and carnal temptations.

Even so, certain options are likelier than others. An attractive option is to identify the *skolops* with troublesome Jews. A troublesome person today is commonly referred to as a "pain in the neck." In antiquity such a person was called a "barb in the eye" or a "thorn in the side" (Num 33:55; Josh 23:13; Judg 2:3; Ezek 28:24). So Paul could be speaking

Tē sarki may be a local dative ("embedded *in* the flesh") or a dative of disadvantage ("*for* the flesh"; Blass, Debrunner and Funk 1961:no. 188). Tasker reads *sarx* in its peculiarly Pauline sense of "the lower nature" and the *skolops* as that which prevents *sarx* from becoming aggressive (1934-1935:174). This, however, is not a good fit with the overall context (*my weaknesses* are identified as *insults . . . hardships . . . persecutions* and *difficulties* in 12:10).

David Park convincingly argues that *skolops* should be translated "stake" rather than *thorn* (1980:179-83). The stake, as a first-century instrument of war and implement of torture, fits better the intensity of Paul's language in these verses. Injuries inflicted by thorns, although painful, were nonetheless superficial. The range of suggestions for the identity of the *skolops* is quite amazing. To note just a few: (1) Paul's adversaries (Barré 1980:216-27), (2) failing eyesight (Nisbet 1969:126), (3) the aftermath of Paul's stoning at Lystra (Fahy 1964:220-23), (4) physical illness (Baird 1985:660) and (5) the Corinthian church's rejection of Paul's apostleship (McCant 1988:550-72).

Speaking of an obstacle as *a messenger of Satan* is not unique to 2 Corinthians. A similar hindrance to ministry is mentioned in 1 Thessalonians 2:18: "Satan stopped us."

metaphorically of the Jews who constantly dogged his steps and hindered his ministry (compare the mention of insults, hardships, persecutions and difficulties in v. 10). But how likely would it be for him to pray that his ministry be free of opposition? Then too, he was beset by opponents even before his ecstatic experience (Acts 9:23-30).

A recurring physical ailment is a promising possibility. "A stake in the flesh" was a common figure of speech in Paul's day for excruciating physical pain (Delling 1971:409-11). Moreover, the most common use of *sarx* is with reference to what is material or physical. Can we get even more specific? Galatians 4:14 ("my illness was a trial to you") and 4:15 ("you would have torn out your eyes and given them to me") lend support to some sort of eye problem. In fact, Paul closes his letter to the Galatians with "See what large letters I use as I write to you with my own hand" (6:11)—a statement one is tempted to understand in terms of some sort of ophthalmic disability.

Whatever the *skolops* was, the net effect for Paul was *torment* (v. 7). The Greek term *(kolaphizō)* actually means to "strike with the fist," "beat" or "cuff" (compare "brutally treated" in 1 Cor 4:11). The present tense suggests frequent bouts. Paul's stake was not an isolated episode. It repeatedly came back to plague him—like the school bully who waits each day for his victim to round the corner.

Paul calls his *skolops* a *messenger of Satan (angelos Satana)*—a statement that has been widely misinterpreted in the church. The *angelos* in the Greek and Hellenistic world was the one who brought a message. This has led some to suppose that Paul is referring to opponents or even demons. But the term is also used of animate (such as birds of augury) and inanimate objects (such as beacons). By this Paul is not suggesting that illness or difficulties in the ministry are automatically the work of Satan. For one thing, the previous phrase, *there was given me,* implies some sort of divine action (*edothē* = a theological passive; see Zerwick 1963:no. 236 and Blass, Debrunner and Funk 1961:no. 130 [1]). And for another, the reason for the stake was to prevent him *from becoming*

12:8 *Hyper toutou* ("concerning this") may refer, if masculine, back to *angelos* or *skolops*, or, if neuter, to Paul's situation in general.

The fact that Paul typically includes the article with *kyrios* when referring to Christ and

conceited (hina mē hyperairōmai); that is, it had a beneficial purpose. Paul says this twice in verse 7. *Hyperairomai* means to "raise oneself up over others." It is found elsewhere in the New Testament only in 2 Thessalonians 2:4, where the man of lawlessness is described as exalting himself over even God himself. Here it is a clear statement of beneficent intent and not Satanic scheming.

So where does Satan fit into the picture? If he is not the prime mover, what exactly is his role? Elsewhere in 2 Corinthians Satan plays a fairly prominent role. He schemes against the church (2:11), is called the god of this age (4:4), is able to masquerade as an angel of light (11:14) and uses his servants to great effect in the church (11:15). Here he is portrayed as God's instrument in preparing Paul for effective service (Bruce 1971:248). This is not to say that he becomes a willing instrument for good. Satan intends the stake for Paul's undoing. But God, who has ultimate control over the situation, intends it for Paul's good.

The good is defined negatively: *to keep me from becoming conceited.* We have the saying "an ounce of prevention is worth a pound of cure." This is particularly true of human arrogance, which once provoked is very difficult to curb. Some people might be tempted to think quite highly of themselves as a result of such extraordinary experiences: "I must be a special person in God's sight that he would allow me to have such remarkable experiences." The stake was given to prevent this from happening to Paul. The Greek text is quite explicit. It was given "in order to" (*hina* + the subjunctive) prevent a loftier-than-thou attitude from developing from Paul's extraordinary experience.

Paul's positive assessment of his "stake" is from the vantage point of fourteen years of reflection. This was not initially the case. When he first received it, he was so troubled that *three times [he] pleaded with the Lord to take it away* (v. 8). The NIV *pleaded* does not accurately render the verb. *Parakaleō* is a term commonly used in Hellenistic Greek for a routine request, although it sometimes carries the sense of "urge" or "earnestly petition." *Three times* could mean that Paul made his request on three separate occasions or thrice in quick succession (compare Mk

drops it when referring to Yahweh would suggest that his request for the removal of his stake is made of Christ *(ton kyrion).*

14:32-42). Why Paul would pray *three* times is a puzzle. It may reflect the Jewish practice of praying three times daily. A threefold petition for assistance was also a common feature of Hellenistic accounts of divine healing (H. D. Betz 1969:292-93). It was to *the Lord (ton kyrion)* that Paul addressed his three petitions. The presence of the article with *kyrios* indicates that he directed his requests to Christ. This is theologically unusual. Paul routinely instructed his converts to pray to the Father (as in "through [Christ] we both have access to the Father by one Spirit"—Eph 2:18). But there are a few instances in the New Testament where prayers are offered directly to [Christ] (such as Acts 1:24; 7:59; see M. J. Harris 1976:396).

The request Paul makes is for the stake to be *taken away* (v. 8). The Greek is literally "to cause to stand away" *(aphistēmi)*. Paul wanted nothing more to do with it. He does not make his request for selfish reasons. Verses 9-10 make it clear that whatever this painful disability was, it hampered Paul's ministry and, to his way of thinking, the spread of the gospel. This is why he calls it a *messenger of Satan.*

The reply Paul received was undoubtedly not the one he was hoping for: *He said to me, "My grace is sufficient for you"* (v. 9). The verb *legei* is commonly used to introduce the edicts of emperors and magistrates (Moulton-Milligan 1930:372). The tense is perfect, denoting finality *(eirēken)*. What God *said* to Paul was not subject to change or revision. The first thing to observe is that Paul's request was not granted. The stake was not taken away. Instead he was provided the *grace* to bear it. The noun *charis* occurs eighteen times in 2 Corinthians but only once in chapters 10—13. Most frequently it refers to God's unmerited favor. Here it most likely denotes divine power. This grace, Paul is told, *is sufficient* for him. The verb *arkeō* means to "suffice for," "satisfy" with the idea of being enough (Kittel 1964:464). The promise is that whenever the messenger of Satan afflicts him, he will be given sufficient strength to bear up.

In certain circles within evangelicalism today, there is a belief that it is God's will that everyone should be healthy and happy and that if healing does not occur in answer to prayer it is because a person lacks

---

12:9 The force of the perfect tense, *eirēken*, is debated. Common suggestions are that it denotes an answer ringing in his ears, a recollection that stayed with him (M. J. Harris 1976:396), an abiding source of assurance and comfort (Bruce 1971:249) or a permanently valid decision (Murphy-O'Connor 1991:119; Barrett 1973:316).

faith (Smith 1959:415). This thinking clearly runs contrary to Paul's experience. Without a doubt Paul had great faith, but his request for the removal of the stake was not answered. This is not to say that he didn't receive an answer. He most assuredly did—*My grace is sufficient for you.* But it is not the answer the mindset focused on self and what God can do for me wants to hear. Yet hear we must, lest our witness to the world lack credibility and theological soundness.

God's grace is sufficient because his *power is made perfect in weakness* (v. 9). This aphoristic phrase is commonly taken as the theme of this letter—and not without cause. The fact that suffering is the typical lot of the gospel minister is a point that Paul tries repeatedly to drive home to the Corinthians (see the introduction). Those who preach the gospel "carry around . . . the [dying] of Jesus" and are "always being given over to death" (4:10-11).

There is a good reason for this. Where human strength abounds, the effects of divine power may be overlooked (Plummer 1915:354). But where human strength fails, the power is clearly seen to be God's. *Dynamis* ("power") denotes the inherent capacity of someone to carry out something (O. Betz 1976:601). The *dynamis* in question is identified at the end of verse 9 as "the power of Christ." Paul is probably thinking of the power that raised Christ from the dead (objective genitive) rather than *Christ's power* (possessive genitive; NIV). This divine strength, Paul says, *is made perfect in weakness. Weakness* (*astheneia* and cognates) is a word that crops up frequently in these last four chapters (10:10; 11:21, 29, 30; 12:5, 9, 10; 13:3, 4, 9). It does not signify timidity or lack of resolve. Nor does it refer to humility or self-abasement. It is, rather, Paul's term for the frailties of human existence and the adversities of the gospel ministry, as the reference to insults, hardships, persecutions and difficulties in verse 10 makes clear.

Paul's statement is a rather startling one: God's power neither displaces weakness nor overcomes it. On the contrary, it comes to its full strength *in* it *(en + astheneia).* At issue is how God manifests his

---

En + dative denotes the sphere in which God's power is displayed.

Mallon does not normally strengthen a superlative and should be taken with the verb *kauchēsomai* ("I will boast instead") rather than with *hēdista* ("even more gladly"; Plummer 1915:355).

power. Paul's opponents claimed that it is best seen in visions, ecstasies and the working of signs and wonders (12:1, 12). Paul, on the other hand, maintained that God's power is most effectively made known in and through weakness. Indeed, God's power is *made perfect* in weakness (*teleitai* = "to find consummation" or "to be accomplished"; v. 9). As one commentator notes, "There is a certain finishing and perfecting power in weakness" (Carpus 1876:178). Not that we are to cherish our infirmities. Weakness of itself will perfect nothing. But when the human vessel is weak, the divine power is especially evident, and the weakness proves to be a fine discipline (B. Hanson 1981:44).

So far from hindering the gospel, Paul's stake actually served to advance it. This is why he aims to boast only in his weaknesses (11:30; 12:5)—and he does it *all the more gladly* (v. 9). *Hēdista* (from *hēdys,* "pleasant to taste") means "with pleasure" or "merrily." Paul not only has accepted his weaknesses and learned to live with them, but he also takes pleasure in them. Why? Because these very weaknesses afford the opportunity for the power of Christ to *rest on* him (v. 9). The verb *episkēnoō,* found only here in the New Testament, actually means to "make one's quarters in" or "take up one's abode in." So God's power not merely "rested on" (KJV, NIV, NEB, RSV) or "over" (TEV, JB) Paul but took up residence in him.

This is why Paul can go on to say, "I am content with my weaknesses" (v. 10; not *I delight in* as in the NIV). This time he adds *for Christ's sake.* The phrase *hyper Christou* is oddly placed in the verse. It can go with the verb—"I am content for Christ's sake" (RSV, NIV, NEB)—or, as is more likely from its terminal position in the clause, it can conclude the list of hardships in verse 10—"the agonies I go through for Christ's sake" (JB, TEV, KJV, Phillips).

Paul proceeds to list four examples of the troubles that he has endured for Christ's sake. Three of the four appear in the earlier tribulation lists. All four are troubles that Paul faced on his missionary travels. The first one, *hybris,* denotes a wanton act of violence. Paul uses it in 1 Thessalonians 2:2 of the "insult" that he experienced at Philippi when he was publicly whipped and imprisoned without cause (Acts

---

12:10 The verb *eudokeō* means to "be content with," "find pleasure in." See Liddell, Scott and Jones 1978.

Furnish speculates that Paul added *insults* to the list of adversities to reflect the slander

16:22-24; compare 14:5). *Anankē* (compare 6:4, "hardships") refers to that which compels, forces or necessitates such adverse circumstances as calamity, torture and bodily pain. *Diōgmos* is commonly used of tracking a prey or enemy (compare 4:9, "persecutions"). Paul may well be thinking of how he was pursued from city to city by hostile Jews. *Stenochōria* (compare 6:4, "difficulties") refers to finding oneself in a tight corner or in narrow straits with no apparent way of escape—not unlike an army under attack in a long narrow pass with no space to maneuver or retreat (Barclay 1954:213).

Paul concludes with *for when I am weak, then I am strong* (v. 10). His statement has the character of a settled conviction rather than a rote repetition of God's answer. But what does it mean? How can one be weak and strong at the same time? The paradox is noted by all. It is sometimes suggested that Paul is saying that whenever God's servants humble themselves and acknowledge their weakness, Christ's power can flow through them (as in Martin 1986:423). But the point throughout has been that Christ's power is perfected *in*, not in spite of, weakness. It is likelier that Paul is asserting that the weaknesses themselves represent the effective working of Christ (Furnish 1984:552). How so? We often think that without human strength we are destined to fail and without personal courage we are bound to falter. Yet good as these are, such qualities tend to push us to self-sufficiency and away from God-dependency. Samson was superlatively endowed with strength, but in the end this very strength brought about his destruction (Judg 15:16; 16:18-30). Human strength is like the flower of the field that has its day in the sun but then shrivels up and dies. Enduring strength lies in God alone.

The Matter Is Summed Up (12:11-18) His boasting now concluded, Paul repeats that the Corinthians forced him to engage in this foolish exercise: *I have made a fool of myself, but you drove me to it* (v. 11). The verb "to drive" *(anankazō)* means to "cause" or "compel" someone with everything from a bit of friendly pressure to brute force (Grundmann 1964b:345). Paul's point is that only the strongest kind of pressure could

that he had to put up with from rival missionaries and certain members of the Corinthian church (1984:551).

have forced his hand. If it had been only his own reputation at stake, it would have mattered little. But it was his status as an apostle that was in jeopardy and, with it, the gospel itself. Plus, he should not have had to do his own boasting—especially since the Corinthians had witnessed firsthand God's power at work in his ministry (1 Cor 2:4-5). They should have been ready and willing to speak up on his behalf—in fact they were obligated to do so (imperfect tense, *ōpheilon;* see the note): *I ought to have been commended by you.*

Two reasons are given: one, Paul is *not in the least inferior to the "super-apostles"* (v. 11), and two, the Corinthians had witnessed *the things that mark an apostle* (v. 12). This is the second time in these chapters Paul has avowed that he is in no way inferior to the "super-apostles" (see 11:5). Some identify the "super-apostles" with the Twelve (see the commentary on 11:5). But Paul may simply be citing his opponents' own self-designation—or perhaps the Corinthians' estimate of the intruders. After all, his rivals claim to have the power of the Spirit at their disposal (11:4; 12:12) and extraordinary visions and revelations to their credit (12:1). Yet as Paul has shown in chapters 11:22—12:5, he in no way compares unfavorably with them. In fact, if truth be told, he is far superior—although he is careful to say merely that he does not "fall below" *(hysterēsa)* them.

Why Paul should feel the need at the end of verse 11 to tack on the statement *even though I am nothing (ei kai ouden eimi)* is puzzling. *Ei + indicative connotes fact in someone's eyes. So Paul could be saying

---

12:11 In expressions of obligation, the imperfect tense denotes something that needed to be done but did not take place (Blass, Debrunner and Funk 1961:no. 358 [1]). The Corinthians were obligated *(ōpheilon)* to support Paul but did not. *Egō* ("I") is added for stress, and *hyph' hymōn* ("by you") is in an emphatic position: "I, by you, ought to have been commended."

Paul employed the perfect tense in 11:5 *(hysterēkenai).* Now he uses the aorist *(hysterēsa,* "I lacked"). If this is taken in its historic sense, Paul is most likely referring to a previous visit that afforded the Corinthians an opportunity to compare him and his rivals. On the other hand, the aorist may be constative, summing up the substance of Paul's dealings with the church over the long haul (Barrett 1973:320).

12:12 Within Judaism, miracles were regarded as the confirmatory sign of a prophetic or messianic claim (as in Mt 16:1; Jn 6:30). This is why the Jews were constantly looking for a miracle from Jesus.

It is not entirely clear whether *signs, wonders and miracles* in verse 12 defines the content of the marks of apostleship or what accompanied them. The problem is the

that in the eyes of the world—and maybe even in the eyes of some of the Corinthians—he does not amount to much. The opposition has already alleged that he lacks formal letters of reference, his speaking amounts to nothing and in person he is unimpressive (3:1-3; 10:10). Or it may reflect his own personal estimate. While he was not the least bit inferior to the other apostles, he always attributed his success to the grace of God within him (1 Cor 15:10). In and of himself he was the "least apostle" and the "foremost of sinners," because he had persecuted the church of God (1 Cor 15:9; 1 Tim 1:15).

Not only had the Corinthians seen that he was not one whit inferior to the other apostles, but they had also witnessed in Paul's ministry the *things that mark an apostle* (v. 12). The Greek is literally "the signs of the apostle." The basic meaning of *sēmeia* is a mark or token by which a particular person or thing is recognized (Hofius 1976a:626). Paul undoubtedly is thinking of deeds that validated his preaching. What deeds would these be, though? The NIV, TEV, JB and Phillips understand them to be the *signs, wonders and miracles* that Paul says *were done among* the Corinthians *with great perseverance* (v. 12). This fits the biblical data. Jesus' own ministry—and that of his disciples—was accredited by "miracles, wonders and signs" (Mk 3:13-15 and parallels; Acts 2:22).

Signs and wonders also regularly accompanied the early church's proclamation of the gospel (Acts 2:43; 5:15-16; 8:6-8; 9:32-42; 15:12). In this respect Paul's ministry was no different. That word and mighty deed

---

repetition of *semeia* in the dative plural, which commonly defines instrument or accompaniment ("with signs, wonders and miracles"). Reference, however, to the "working" *(kateirgasthē)* of signs along with the frequency of this type of anacoluthon in Paul tips the balance in favor of the former (Blass, Debrunner and Funk 1961:no. 467). This would mean that Paul is using *semeia* in two different ways in verse 12. The first occurrence would refer more generally to the things that "mark" an apostle—that is, the deeds that validate an apostolic claim. The second occurrence, grouped as it is with "wonders" and "mighty deeds," would more specifically denote "miraculous signs" (see Acts 2:22; Rom 15:19; 2 Thess 2:9). Some would extend the apostolic marks to include such things as faithfulness to the kerygma, changed lives and conduct becoming an apostle (for example, M. J. Harris 1976:398; Martin 1986:434-35). It goes without saying that these would be essential to any apostolic claim. But *were done among you* is against their inclusion here.

The Corinthians placed great store in the miraculous. Paul himself did not. So *the things that mark an apostle—signs, wonders and miracles* may well be the Corinthians' words being quoted back to them.

were inextricably linked is clearly attested in Luke's account of the missionary journeys. Miracles were performed in virtually every city that Paul visited (Paphos [Acts 13:6-12]; Iconium [14:3]; Lystra [14:8-10]; Philippi [16:16-18]; Thessalonica [1 Thess 1:5]; Corinth [1 Cor 2:4]; Ephesus [Acts 19:11-12]; Troas [20:9-12]; Malta [28:1-10]). In fact, Paul in his letters says repeatedly that his preaching was not merely one of word but of "power and the Spirit" (for example, Rom 15:19; 1 Cor 2:4; Gal 3:5; 1 Thess 1:5).

The deeds that were worked among them are specified as *signs, wonders* and *miracles.* The differences, though slight, are to be noted. When grouped with spectacular phenomena, *sēmeion* ("sign") has the meaning "miraculous sign" and signifies an event that contradicts the natural order of things (Hofius 1976a:626). Healings and casting out of demons, presaging the messianic age, come readily to mind as examples of miraculous signs. In extrabiblical Greek *teras* ("wonder") is used of portents or wonders that elicit fear or horror (Hofius 1976b). The sun turning to darkness and the moon to blood fall into this category (Mt 28:45, 51; Acts 2:19-20). *Dynamis* ("miracle") refers to strength or ability and is generally used of the mighty acts of God—like the parting of the Red Sea (Ex 14:15-31) or the violent earthquake in Philippi that loosed the chains of Paul and Silas (Acts 16:26).

Paul states that these marks of an apostle *were done among* the Corinthians (v. 12). The verb is a Greek term that means to "achieve" or "work out" *(kateirgasthē).* The passive voice implies that this was God's doing and not Paul's (Zerwick 1963:no. 236; Blass, Debrunner and Funk 1961:no. 130 [1]). The aorist tense suggests a specific occasion—quite likely the founding visit, which lasted about eighteen months (Acts 18:1-18). Paul's rivals, in all probability, also claimed the working of miraculous signs, wonders and mighty deeds. What distinguished Paul from them is captured in the phrase *with great perseverance (en pasē hypomonē). Hypomonē* here, as in 6:4, means "to stand firm"

12:13 It appears from 1 Corinthians 9:12-18 that it was Paul's unwavering policy to support himself by tentmaking while engaged in outreach.

It is hard to know whether Paul's remark *Forgive me this wrong* is made sarcastically or playfully. The heavy sarcasm of the surrounding chapters suggests the former.

or "to hold one's ground" in the face of difficulties. The implication is that Paul faced serious opposition while preaching the gospel in Corinth. Luke records only the initial resistance from the Jewish leadership (Acts 18:6). He does, however, include the fact that one night Paul received a vision from the Lord, telling him to keep speaking and not be afraid (18:9-10). This would indicate that opposition was most definitely there—even though the details are not provided.

The only so-called *mark* that was missing at Corinth was Paul's acceptance of any kind of financial support from the church: *How were you inferior to the other churches, except that I was never a burden to you?* he asks (v. 13). The *other churches* could be all the Gentile congregations that Paul had founded (as in 11:28) or just the Macedonian churches (11:8-9). The only other churches that he mentions accepting support from are the latter ones (Phil 4:15-16).

Paul's persistent rejection of support must have really upset the Corinthians, given that it is mentioned twice in these chapters (11:7-12; 12:13-18; compare 1 Cor 9:1-18). One wonders if the church's real concern was Paul's credibility or their own. If the genuineness of Paul's apostolate were questioned, would it not impact them too? This would explain why Paul goes on to ask their pardon for this alleged injustice (Furnish 1984:556): *Forgive me this wrong!* The Greek term *adikia* commonly signifies a concrete wrong or an unjust action—like theft, incest or wrong treatment of parents (for example, Josephus *Antiquities* 3.274; 16.1; *Against Apion* 2.217)—although it can refer more generally to a harm or injury (as in *Testament of Solomon* 13:4). In any case, the Corinthians thought that by rejecting their support Paul had done them a personal injury.

Regardless of their feelings, Paul announces that during his forthcoming visit he will maintain his policy of financial independence. *Now I am ready to visit you for the third time, and I will not be a burden to you* (v. 14). *Now* is perhaps more accurately translated "Look!" (*idou;*

12:14 *Triton* ("third") can go with *elthein* ("to come a third time") or *betoimōs* ("ready a third time"). The former would mean that this will be Paul's third visit to Corinth. The latter would be saying that this is the third time he is preparing to come to Corinth. Some have argued for the second reading, but the wording of 13:1 ("This will be my third visit to you") demands the first.

"behold" in KJV; "here" in RSV, NEB)—a particle that aims to arouse the attention of the listener (compare 5:17; 6:2, 9; 7:11). Paul is trying to draw the Corinthians' attention to the fact that this will be his *third* visit. His first visit was an eighteen-month stay that saw the establishment of the Corinthian church (Acts 18:1-18). The second visit was a painful one for Paul. While he was there, someone in the congregation publicly insulted him and challenged his authority, demanding proof that Christ was speaking through him (13:3). The church, meanwhile, sat by and did nothing to support him (see the introduction). Now he will be making a third visit, and he promises that he will continue to *not be a burden* on them. *Burden* translates a verb that means to "grow numb" under a heavy weight *(katanarkaō)*. While the Corinthians looked on Paul's refusal of support as a personal injustice, he saw it as an opportunity to relieve his children of the undue weight of his daily needs.

Other itinerant preachers invoked the well-accepted tenet that laborers are worthy of their wages. Paul himself argues for this in 1 Corinthians 9. But his relationship to the Corinthian church is not merely that of a laborer to a boss. Paul is the Corinthians' spiritual father. And *children should not have to save up for their parents, but parents for their children* (v. 14). Philo calls it "the natural order of things" (*On the Life of Moses* 2.245).

In Paul's day, the father in particular was obliged to provide support for his children (Martin 1986:441). The Greek verb employed for this kind of support is to "store" or "lay up" as treasure *(thēsaurizō;* Hauck 1965:138). It implies something more than helping someone out financially. The idea is of setting aside money in an intentional way and for a specific purpose—much like a trust fund or savings account today. This set Paul apart from his rivals, who were only out to exploit the Corinthians for personal gain (11:20). It also distinguished him from itinerant preachers of the day who had an eye only for what would be financially profitable. What the Corinthians can't

---

12:15 Paul enjoys pairing words where the second intensifies the meaning of the first. Compare with 1:13 *(anaginōskete kai epiginōskete)*, 4:8 *(aporoumenoi all' ouk exaporoumenoi)* and 12:15 *(dapanēsō kai ekdapanēthēsomai)*.
The primary textual problem in verse 15 is whether to read the indicative *agapō* ("I

seem to grasp is that Paul is not like other itinerant preachers; he is not after their money but them. *What I want is not your possessions but you* (v. 14).

Does Paul's statement represent an inconsistency? After all, he accepted support from the Macedonian churches (Phil 4:15-16). In fact, it was a gift from the Macedonian churches that had allowed Paul to set aside his trade and devote himself completely to evangelism during his first stay in Corinth (Acts 18:5). The important thing to see, however, is that Paul is not articulating a guiding principle for his ministry in general. He is giving a rationale for why he refused to accept support from the Corinthians specifically. A rumor was circulating in Corinth that the Jerusalem collection was Paul's way of tricking them into supporting him (12:16). If he had taken their money, it likely would have been misunderstood. The Macedonian churches, on the other hand, were spiritually mature enough to equate giving with ministry (8:4). Then too, they had their priorities straight. They gave themselves first to God and only thereafter to Paul (8:5).

This, anyhow, is the bottom line for Paul. He, and he alone, is the Corinthians' spiritual father. So it is only right that they not have to support him. And like the responsible parent that he is, he will sacrifice for them (v. 15). The thought is even stronger. The opening *I* is emphatic: *I will very gladly spend for you everything I have and expend myself as well.* The human father stores up for his children. Paul not only does this *(spend)* but does it to the very limit of his capability *(expend)*. There is a play on words here that is difficult to capture in English. Both verbs are found only here in Paul's writings. The first verb, *dapanaō*, denotes spending money for or on something. The second verb is a compound of *ek* + *dapanaō* and means to "exhaust" or "wear out." *Spend* and *expend* nicely catch the sense (NIV; compare JB).

What Paul expends is not merely his finances but himself—that is, his time, energy, affection, reputation and, if need be, his health (Tasker

---

love") or the participle *agapōn* ("loving"). The participle has the better support (p[46] ℵ[2] B D F G K L P Ψ), but it is the indicative (ℵ* A) that produces a grammatically complete thought. The UBS places the final *n* in square brackets (Metzger 1971:586-87).

1958:182; Martin 1986:443). And he does it all *for you* (v. 15). The Greek is literally "on behalf of your souls." In the New Testament the "soul" is the seat of life and embraces all the earthly concerns that a person takes constant care over (see Mt 6:25, "Do not worry about your life [literally 'soul'], what you will eat or drink"; Harder 1978:682-83).

Paul takes pleasure in expending himself on their behalf, and he gives of himself to the Corinthians *very gladly.* The adverbial form of *hēdys* ("pleasant to taste") means "with pleasure" or "merrily." All he asks in return is a fair exchange for his efforts—the kind of exchange that parents expect from their children: *If I love you more, will you love me less?* (v. 15). And why shouldn't they love him? If he loves them even more than a parent loves his or her children, then how can they love him any less than children would love their parents (M. J. Harris 1976:399)? Paul has the younger child in view here. Adult children do indeed have a responsibility to support their parents. In fact, Paul says elsewhere that they are obligated to provide for any relative in need, and not just their parents (1 Tim 5:8, 16).

So what was standing in the way of a fair exchange between the Corinthians and Paul? From verses 16-17 it would appear that the rumor mill is to blame. Gossip is classified as one of the detestable sins in the Old Testament (Prov 6:19)—and rightfully so. It is like a weed that, once it takes root, is almost impossible to eradicate and if left untended will take over an entire lawn. The gossip may not even be true. But the mere suspicion of fiscal or moral blame can cause irreparable damage—like mud thrown against a clean wall, it may not stick but it always leaves a mark.

In this case, the perpetrators are the Corinthian intruders. When all other efforts to compromise Paul's financial integrity failed, it seems they resorted to innuendos and hearsay about misappropriation of collection funds. The gist of what they said is found in verse 16: *crafty fellow that I am, I caught you by trickery.* The Greek term for *crafty* means "capable

---

12:16 *Estō de* is literally "so be it." Paul is assuming that the Corinthians will grant him the point that he has not been a financial burden on anyone.

Barrett argues that the coincidence of language between 8:16-24 ("Titus . . . is coming. . . . We are sending along with them our brother") and 12:18 *(I urged Titus to go to you and I sent our brother with him)* is such that it is impossible not to conclude that chapter 12 was written later than chapters 8—9 (1969:12-13). The difficulty, though, is that in chapter

of anything" *(pan + ourgos)*. In the New Testament it is used of someone who uses his or her native ability unscrupulously, not unlike the con artist today. The insinuation is that Paul's collection effort was merely a sly way—or *trickery*—to get the churches to contribute to what in truth was a Paul-and-company fund. The word translated *trickery (dolos)* refers properly to bait used to catch a fish. The bait, in this case, was the story of how the believers in Judea were in desperate need of the Corinthians' help. And the Corinthians fell for it hook, line and sinker (*elabon*, "taken in")—at least initially.

The Corinthians must have wanted to think the worst of Paul to give credence to gossip such as this. They clearly turned a blind eye to all the precautions he had taken. For one, he had insisted that the collection occur prior to his coming so that he not be involved in the actual handling of the monies (1 Cor 16:2). Two, he had instructed the Corinthians to appoint their own representatives to accompany the collection, exempting him from any blame regarding the transportation of the funds (1 Cor 16:3). And three, he sent a trusted colleague to finish the collection effort, rather than going himself (2 Cor 8:6).

Paul's response to the rumor of foul play is twofold. First, he calls on the Corinthians to bring forward specific evidence: *Did I exploit you through any of the men I sent you?* (v. 17). *Pleonekteō (exploit)* means to "take advantage" of someone with the intent to cheat. The verb translated *I sent (apostellō)* is a technical term for the dispatching of an envoy on a particular mission or service. Here it is envoys in the plural: "those I sent you." Paul made a regular practice of using coworkers to represent him when he could not come himself. Those sent to Corinth include Timothy (1 Cor 4:17-18; 16:10-11), Titus (2 Cor 7:13-15; 8:16-17), "our brother" (12:18) and possibly Sosthenes (1 Cor 1:1). Paul's response is phrased in the form of a question that expects a negative response: "Surely *(mē)* none of those I sent took advantage of you?" His confidence is based on a shared understanding about the envoy in Greco-Roman

8 Paul sends not one but two brothers (8:18-22), while chapter 12 makes reference to a visit when only one brother had been sent. It is just as reasonable to think that Paul in chapter 12 is looking back to Titus's first, not second, visit to Corinth, when he made a beginning on collecting monies for the Jerusalem relief fund (see the commentary on 8:1-7). That Paul would have sent a companion with Titus makes sense, given the fiscal nature of the mission.

society. The envoy so closely represented the interests and actions of the sender that to see the envoy was, in effect, to see the one who sent him. And to judge the envoy was to judge the one who sent him. So if none of Paul's emissaries exploited the Corinthians, it is a sure thing that he is not out to exploit them either.

Paul's second response to the rumor of foul play is to recall a specific occasion when a trusted emissary had been sent: I urged Titus to go to you and I sent our brother with him (v. 18). The strategy is astute. The fact that Titus had to be urged to go suggests that he had ventured to Corinth with a certain amount of doubt regarding the outcome. Undoubtedly this was due to negative reports that he had heard about the church. Titus's visit, then, hardly smacks of a conspiracy to get through an agent what Paul declined to accept personally. Moreover, Titus had gained the Corinthians' respect and affection (7:13-15), and he had established a good working relationship with the church in the matter of giving (8:6). So if Titus, Paul's envoy, showed himself to be a person of integrity, then the Corinthians must credit the same to Paul. So sure is Paul that the Corinthians will agree with him that he uses the strengthened form of the negative (mhti): "No way did Titus exploit you, did he?"

Titus did not make this visit by himself. *Our brother* had been sent with him (v. 18). Who this brother was and why he is mentioned at this point is something of a mystery. This is the second time in the letter that Paul has refrained from naming an envoy (8:18-24). *Our* points to someone with whom the Corinthians were familiar, and *brother* to someone they considered family. The verb *sent (apesteila),* a technical term for the dispatch of an emissary, indicates that the individual in question was not a member of the Corinthian congregation and that he came representing Paul. But beyond this, we are left in the dark.

Which of Titus's visits is Paul referring to here? By most accounts Titus, up to this point, has made only one trip to Corinth, when he delivered the painful letter and enforced its dictates (2:12-13; 7:5-16). The difficulty is that no mention is made in 7:13-15 of a traveling companion. But there Paul focuses on the obedience that Titus was able

---

12:18 While the aorist could be epistolary ("I am sending Titus and our brother"), the broader context shows that it must be historic *(I sent).* Paul's case rests on demonstrating

to muster and not on the collection itself. He may well have held out the hope that once the Corinthians' obedience could be secured, the collection effort could go forward. In this case, another person on the scene would have served as an additional safeguard against any suspicions of mishandling of funds.

Some propose that the visit mentioned in 12:18 is to be identified with the one mentioned in 8:16-24, where Paul announced his plan to send Titus in advance of his own arrival to complete what he had started on the previous visit. This, of course, presumes that chapters 10—13 were written separately and subsequently to chapters 1—9. Even so, Titus was to be accompanied by two brothers on this visit, and not one (8:18-24). And the brothers are described as representing their respective churches, not Paul (8:23). Could it be that Paul is referring to a third, unrecorded visit beyond those mentioned in chapters 7 and 9? Some think so, but there is scarcely enough time between A.D. 54 and 56 to accommodate two visits by Paul, let alone three by Titus.

Having established what Titus did not do, Paul turns next to what Titus did do while at Corinth. He phrases his response in the form of a question that expects the answer yes: "Surely we acted in the same spirit, did we not? Surely we followed the same course?" (*ou . . . ou;* v. 18). "To act" is literally "to walk" *(peripateō),* a favorite word of Paul's for the Christian life. Paul dares the Corinthians to find evidence that he and Titus did not walk according to *the same spirit (pneuma). Pneuma* is sometimes used of the Holy Spirit, while at other times of the human spirit. R. V. G. Tasker, along with the LB, NEB and REB, capitalizes *spirit* and argues for the meaning "inspired and guided by the Holy Spirit" (1958:184). There is some support for this in Paul's assertion that his opponents proclaimed a "different" Spirit (11:4). But the parallel idea in the next clause of following the same course points to a human disposition. The TEV's "Did we not act from the same motives?" catches the idea. To phrase it another way, Paul asks, *Did we not . . . follow the same course [ichnesin]?* The image is graphic. *Ichnesin* refers to a set of footprints that mark a trail. Here it denotes the trail left by someone's

---

that none of those he sent to Corinth could be faulted with respect to their motives or conduct (v. 17).

conduct that others can mark and follow (Stumpff 1965:402). The idea is that Paul blazed a trail in matters of money that Titus then followed on his arrival at Corinth.

Paul Threatens Punishment on His Next Visit (12:19—13:4) The reality of the church is not seen in the splendor of its buildings, the size of its congregation, the number of its programs, the amount of its budget or the sophistication of its liturgy. It is seen in changed lives—and if there are no changed lives, there is no church. Paul, in rather blunt language, reminds the Corinthians of this truth in the final section of his letter: "Examine yourselves to see whether you are in the faith; test yourselves. Do you not realize that Christ Jesus is in you—unless, of course, you fail the test?" (13:5). The challenge is not an idle one. There is every possibility that the Corinthians—or any church, for that matter—will fail the test, if the vices listed in verses 20-21 are, to any extent, a reality in the life of the congregation (see Rev 2—3).

But before Paul can call the Corinthians to account, he must dispel any notion that he is the one on trial here. All this bragging that he has been doing could sound as if he were mounting a defense that the church, as judge and jury, was called to pass judgment on: *Have you been thinking all along that we have been defending ourselves to you?* (v. 19). In actuality the apostles' only judge is God, in whose sight they speak (v. 19). The Corinthian intruders cared a great deal about what people thought of them, and so they fashioned their preaching to appeal to their audience (11:4). But Paul cared only about God's opinion, which was wholly determined by whether he spoke *in Christ* (as Christ's representative) or "in himself" (as his own advocate).

The authority Paul received as Christ's representative was intended for constructive, not destructive purposes—although not everyone always saw it that way, especially where discipline was involved. Growth toward spiritual maturity is not always an easy process for the church. Just as correction is a necessary, if somewhat painful, part of growing up for children, so also it serves as a needful part of the maturing

---

12:19 Translators are evenly divided on whether verse 19 should be read as a statement—"All this time you have been thinking that our defense is addressed to you"

process for the church. Yet the church rarely looks on correction in this way. Too often we gravitate toward the pastor or teacher who flatters us and not the one who corrects us.

This is why Paul goes on to say that *everything* he does *is for* the church's *strengthening. Ta panta* (literally, "the whole") is placed first for emphasis. *Everything* without exception is done for their good—even correction. The good, in this case, is defined as that which "builds up" (NIV *strengthens). Oikodomē* is Paul's favorite term for the church's growth toward spiritual maturity (Rom 14:19; 15:2; 1 Cor 14:3, 5, 12, 26; 2 Cor 12:19; Eph 4:12, 16, 29). The image is of a building that is still under construction. In some cases the work involves laying the foundation of a new church (1 Cor 3:9); in other cases it is erecting the walls of a more established congregation (Eph 2:21). This is what ultimately distinguished Paul from his rivals. He did whatever it took to upbuild the church, while his rivals did whatever they could to upbuild themselves.

The average pastor does not enjoy rebuking a congregation. Paul is no different. For this reason he expresses two fears about his upcoming visit to Corinth. His first fear is that when he comes, he will not find the church as he wants them to be (v. 20). The Corinthian worst-case scenario is formidable: *quarreling, jealousy, outbursts of anger, factions, slander, gossip, arrogance and disorder* (v. 20)—not to mention *impurity, sexual sin and debauchery* (v. 21). The eight vices listed in verse 20 typify a community fractured by envy, conceit and selfish ambition. The initial four—*quarreling, jealousy, outbursts of anger, factions*—are found in the same order in Galatians 5:20.

Quarreling (or better, "rivalry," *eris*) heads the roster. The basic idea is fighting over pride of place. Jesus' disciples argued over who was the greatest (Mk 9:33-34) and who was to sit at Jesus' right and left hand (Mk 10:35-38). Pride of place also characterized the Corinthians from early on (1 Cor 1:11; 3:3). *Jealousy (zēlos)* should logically precede quarreling, since it is what often gives rise to it. With the exception of this reference, *zēlos* is a positive attribute in 2 Corinthians, denoting the

---

(JB; see also TEV, NEB, NASB)—or as a question—*Have you been thinking all along that we have been defending ourselves to you?* (NIV; see also KJV, RSV, Phillips).

capacity of passionate commitment to a person or cause ("zeal"; Stumpff 1964a:877). But when zeal is for the things another person possesses, it easily moves—as it does here—toward *jealousy*. *Thymos* is passion that wells up or boils over. The NIV's *outbursts of anger* catches the sense well.

The word translated *factions (eritheiai)* most likely refers to a self-seeking mindset that views everything from a what's-in-it-for-me perspective. In the New Testament it is commonly linked with envy for what others have (Gal 5:20; Jas 3:14, 16). The next two vices are closely related. *Slander* is something that is spoken publicly, while *gossip* (literally "whispering") is something that is whispered behind the back. Both can be (and often are) devastating to the life of the church.

The Greek word translated *arrogance (physiōsis)* means to be "inflated with a sense of one's own importance." It is a problem that crops up repeatedly in 1 Corinthians (4:6, 18, 19; 5:2; 8:1; 13:4). Finally, *disorder (akatastasia)* renders a term that normally denotes a public disturbance. It occurs in 2 Corinthians 6:5 in a list of troubles accompanying Paul's missionary labors. But here it likely refers to congregational disturbances of the sort implied in 1 Corinthians 14 and 1 Timothy 2. Along similar lines, James states that "where you have envy and selfish ambition, there you find disorder and every evil practice" (3:16).

Paul's second fear is that the Corinthians will not find him to their liking when he comes. He prefers to come to them in gentleness. But if his worst fears are realized, he will come to them with the rod that his rivals claimed he was too timid to wield (10:1; compare 1 Cor 4:21). This will especially be the case if he comes and finds *impurity, sexual sin and debauchery* still in evidence (v. 21). *Akatharsia* ("impurity") is a general term for uncleanness of any kind—anything that would make a person unfit to enter God's presence (Barclay 1954:265). *Porneia*, on the other hand, refers more specifically to "sexual sins," which includes adultery but goes beyond (such as prostitution and homosexual offenses [1 Cor 6:9; 1 Tim 1:10]). *Aselgeia* ("debauchery") denotes wanton defiance of public decency (Plummer 1915:370).

12:20 *Eritheia* occurs prior to the New Testament only in Aristotle, where it denotes a self-seeking pursuit of political office by unfair means. So its meaning in the New Testament is largely conjectural (see Rom 2:8; Gal 5:20; Phil 1:17; 2:3; Jas 3:14, 16). If Hermann Büchsel

The trio is startling, especially since concern for such gross sins does not surface earlier in the letter. Indeed, the perfect tense signifies an ongoing state of affairs *(proēmartēkotōn)*, and Paul anticipates that on visiting the Corinthians he will *be grieved over many who have sinned earlier and have not repented* (v. 21).

If Paul finds the sins listed in verses 20-21 present on his return, he will, in the first place, be humbled: *God will humble me before you* (v. 21). How exactly Paul expects to be humbled is not clear. He could be fearful that his third visit will be a repeat of the second one, when he was publicly humiliated and the Corinthians did nothing to support him (2:5-11; 7:8-13). Or he may be worried that on his return the Corinthians will show a preference for the false apostles over him, which would cause acute pain. The most likely possibility is that Paul will be humiliated by the Corinthians' lack of moral discipline. After all, like any good parent he took pride in his Gentile churches, and anything that disgraced them also disgraced him (Plummer 1915:369).

Paul has been bragging about the Corinthians to the Macedonian believers. If his pride in them proves to be false, he will experience no little embarrassment before the Macedonians who accompany him to Corinth. Moreover, such reports of sexual promiscuity would confirm the worst fears of the Jewish community about the Gentiles' ability to live a moral life apart from the Mosaic law. As apostle to the Gentiles and advocate of Christian freedom, Paul could well feel as if he were directly responsible for the Corinthians' lack of moral fortitude.

Continuing sin will cause Paul, in the second place, to *be grieved* on his return to Corinth (v. 21). *Pentheō* usually refers to sorrow that expresses itself in a demonstrative fashion (such as lament, wailing, tears). So Paul may fear that he will be overcome by sorrow at the shame brought on the community by the reprehensible activities of some of its members. Then too, if faced with the kinds of sins listed in verse 21—not to mention those found in verse 20—he would be reduced to using his authority in a punitive way, which would cause him great sadness.

It is startling to hear Paul give voice to such ethical misgivings at

is to be followed, "base self-seeking" is its New Testament meaning (1964b:661). Victor Furnish, on the other hand, thinks that it may denote factiousness more than selfishness (1984:561).

this point in the letter (Plummer 1915:370). Nothing in the earlier chapters prepares us for what we find here. How is it to be explained? The sins in verse 21 are of the libertine sort that Paul tackled in 1 Corinthians ("a man has his father's wife. And you are proud!" 5:2). Verse 20, on the other hand, catalogs some old and some new problems. *Quarreling, jealousy, factions* and *arrogance* are old. *Outbursts of anger, slander, gossip* and *disorder* are new.

The single ingredient that would account for both the new and the old concerns is the activity of the Corinthian intruders. The list in verse 20, in particular, is symptomatic of the schismatic influence of outsiders on congregational life. Many of these problems were undoubtedly there all along, but Paul had restrained himself in order to address the larger issue of his apostolic authority. After all, if he does not have the Corinthians' loyalty and is no longer confident of their ready obedience, how can he hope to effect a willing change in their behavior? What would be the point of reasoning with them as he did in 1 Corinthians?

Paul's response on finding such sins at Corinth will not stop at shame and grief. He will, third, be forced to act severely toward the Corinthians. If the church does not clean up its act by the time he comes, he assures them that punishment will not be spared them, as it was on his previous visit (1:23).

In the Roman legal system, punishment was meted out on the basis of a verdict reached by a magistrate (and sometimes his council) regarding a person's innocence or guilt. As in our Western legal system today, the process included the drawing up of charges, the formal act of accusation, the solicitation of witnesses, the hearing of evidence and

13:1 The Deuteronomic legal requirement of two or three witnesses (Deut 19:15) is also cited by Jesus as a normative principle in matters of church discipline (Mt 18:16) and by Paul regarding accusations brought against church elders (1 Tim 5:19). The identity of the witnesses in 2 Corinthians 13:1 has been debated. The two most common proposals are (1) the three warnings that occur in the Corinthian correspondence (1 Cor 4:21; 2 Cor 10:2-6; 13:2) and (2) Paul's three visits to Corinth (Acts 18:1-18; 2 Cor 1:23—2:1; 13:1). The emphatic position of *triton* (*third* visit) makes the latter option more probable. It is sometimes argued that Paul's founding visit would hardly constitute a witness against the congregation. But from the start the Corinthians had a difficult time distancing themselves from the immoral practices of their former pagan life (1 Cor 5:9-11; 6:9-11). Moreover, Paul spent sufficient time in Corinth during his founding visit to be able to identify those whose lifestyles showed no evidence of change (Acts 18—about eighteen months). Others object that to construe Paul's Corinthian visits as legal witnesses in a court of law is to presume the presentation of arguments for and against the accused (compare Jn 18:28—19:16). At 13:1 Paul turns the tables on the Corinthians and puts them in the position of the accused, while he takes up the role of the plaintiff. The expert witnesses become Paul's visits to Corinth: *This will be my third visit to you. "Every matter must be established by the testimony of two or three witnesses."*

It is legitimate to put the second half of verse 1 in quotation marks, as the NIV does. Paul is quoting Deuteronomy 19:15, which stipulates that one witness is not enough to convict a person accused of a crime; such matters must be established by the testimony of at least two witnesses. Paul had previously made two visits to Corinth—his founding visit in A.D. 50-52 (Acts 18:1-17) and his so-called painful visit a few years later, at which time he had been humiliated (2 Cor 11:21) and his apostolic authority publicly challenged by someone in the Corinthian congregation (12:3). This *third* visit will constitute the decisive witness, going beyond the minimum witnesses required by Jewish law.

For some infractions of Jewish and Roman law it was possible to merely give a *warning* (as in Acts 4:18). Paul's grace extends to giving the Corinthians not one, but two warnings. He had given the Corinthians a warning on his second visit, which he now repeats while still absent: *On my return I will not spare those who sinned earlier or any of the others. Those who sinned earlier* are most likely members of the Corinthian church who were still engaging in the illicit acts mentioned in 12:21 *(proēmartēkotōn)*. Who then are "all the rest" *(kai tois loipois pasin;* NIV's *any of the others)?* It is improbable that Paul is referring to those who had fallen into sin since his last visit (Bratcher 1983:143).

---

a too fanciful application of the Old Testament legal requirement (Hughes 1962:474). But this is not the first time Paul has solicited unconventional witnesses on his behalf (compare 1:12, "our conscience testifies," and 1:23, "God as my witness").

Some think that *every matter* refers to unsubstantiated accusations made by Paul's opponents against him (e.g., Tasker 1958:186). Yet the immediate context focuses on Corinthian wrongdoing, not on Paul's perceived faults (12:20-21; 13:5-10). Others believe Paul means that on his third visit he will set up judicial proceedings and, on the testimony of two or three witnesses, will convict and then punish the offenders (for example, Hughes 1962:475). This, however, is reading too much into Paul's use of Deuteronomy 19:15. The simplest explanation is that Paul is saying that this *third visit* to Corinth will constitute the decisive witness against the congregation, in accordance with the accepted standards of jurisprudence.

2 CORINTHIANS 12:19—13:4 □

More likely prospects are those who had come under the sway of the false apostles (M. J. Harris 1976:412) or those who were committing the divisive sins listed in 12:20—although in all probability the two groups are one and the same.

The disciplinary action Paul promises to carry out is not specified. Public censure would surely be a part of it (compare Mt 18:17). Excommunication was what Paul mandated in the case of the incestuous Corinthian Christian (1 Cor 5). Some suppose that supernatural infliction of bodily suffering would be included (for example, Plummer 1915:374). The Corinthians had experienced this early on as a punishment for their disdain of poorer brothers and sisters at the Lord's Supper (1 Cor 11:27-34).

Either way, they will have the *proof* they *are demanding.* Paul will clearly show them that *Christ is speaking through [him]* (v. 3). The Corinthians had apparently insisted that Paul give some convincing sign of his apostolic status. They may well have been looking for some display of miraculous power similar to what his rivals laid claim to. Paul states that he will indeed provide proof, but it may not be the proof that they are expecting. For one, it will not be his power but Christ's: *He is not weak in dealing with you, but is powerful among you* (v. 3). Two, the power Paul speaks of will not be a wonderworking display but a disciplinary rod used on members of the congregation who continue to sin in flagrant disobedience of Paul's authority.

Paul goes on to warn the Corinthians not to be fooled by his gentle demeanor. It may seem as if he operates out of weakness, but beware: this was the same mistaken estimate that Jesus' adversaries made of him. *For to be sure, he was crucified in weakness, yet he lives by God's power* (v. 4). What Paul means by *he was crucified in weakness* is debated. He

---

13:2 Additional suggestions for the identity of "all the rest" include (1) those Corinthians who were turning a blind eye to the immoral conduct of the other group (Furnish 1984:570) and (2) those guilty of both strife and sexual immorality but unknown as yet to Paul at the time of writing (Martin 1986:471).

Paul's use of *ean* + the subjunctive should not be taken as expressing doubt about his actually making a third visit. It is true that this form of the conditional is usually employed where the situation is hypothetical or uncertain. But there are exceptions (Blass, Debrunner and Funk 1961:no. 372 [1a]). See, for example, 1 Thessalonians 3:8 ("since you are standing firm"). As Martin observes, it makes little sense to threaten someone if the person issuing

could be speaking of an erroneous human perception, similar to his statement in 5:16: "we once regarded Christ [from a worldly point of view]." By the world's standards Jesus' ministry was a failure. He claimed to be the Messiah and asserted that he would usher in the kingdom of God. But in the end he succumbed to weakness and died a criminal's death.

Yet this reading of the text overlooks the aorist. Christ *was* crucified in weakness—not "seemed" to be or "was regarded" as such. The opening *kai* confirms this point: *to be sure* (NIV), "true" (NEB), "yes" (JB, Phillips). Paul is acknowledging that Christ did in fact die in weakness. The Greek is literally "out of weakness." *Ex astheneias* can specify the reason ("by reason of weakness," Bauer, Arndt and Gingrich 1979:3f) or the underlying rule or principle ("because of weakness," Bauer, Arndt and Gingrich 1979:3i). Either way, the point is the same: the crucifixion showed Christ's essential mortality. Weak and frail human being that he was, when he was subjected to physical trauma, he died just as we do.

Unlike us, however, Christ did not remain in weakness. Divine power prevailed over human weakness, and he came to life. The same idea is powerfully captured in the familiar lyric by Sandi Patti, "They Could Not":

So, finally upon a rugged cross
They killed the man who would not suffer loss
And when at last they took what willingly he gave
He died—but could they keep him in the grave?
They could not; they could not.
Praise God, they could not!

Not only did Christ come to life, but even more, he now *lives by God's*

the threat is unsure of returning to make good on it (1986:472).

13:3 *En emoi* could be local ("that Christ is speaking *in* me"; KJV, NKJV, RSV, NRSV, JB) or instrumental ("that Christ is speaking *through* me"; TEV, NIV, NEB). Contextually, the latter is to be preferred. The Corinthians seek some kind of outward display, validating Paul's claim to apostleship (that is, divine power manifested through Paul).

En hymin could be local ("powerful in you"; Phillips, RSV, NRSV, KJV, NKJV). But in light of parallelism with *eis hymas* ("in dealing with you"), it must mean either "toward you" or *among you* (TEV, NIV, JB, NEB, REB).

power (zē ek dynameōs theou, v. 4). The present tense emphasizes ongoing life. So we might translate this "he continues to live by the power of God." As Ralph P. Martin notes, Christ's weakness, as shown in the crucifixion, was not the result of a lack of power. When Christ chose the cross, he did so because he was acting in God's power (1986:475). And as Christ, so the apostle: *Likewise, we are weak in him, yet by God's power we will live with him to serve you* (v. 4). Paul places the pronoun *hēmeis* in an emphatic position and broadens the thought to include his associates: *we are weak*. He undoubtedly is referring to the frailty and hardship that typify the life of the itinerant preacher (11:23-27). His rivals thought otherwise—as did some of the Corinthians. But just as many were mistaken about Christ, so they are mistaken about the lot of the apostle.

Even so, his opponents were right on one point. There is a very real power at the disposal of the Christian. Not only does Paul share in Christ's sufferings and become like him in his death, but at the same time he also shares in the power of his resurrection: *By God's power we will live with him to serve you. We will live with him* has an eschatological ring to it. But *to serve you* snaps us back into the present order of things. So what is Paul talking about? How will he *live with Christ to serve* the Corinthians? *Eis hymas (to serve you)* is perhaps better translated "toward you" or "in our dealings with you." That is, the same power that raised Christ from the dead and sustains his life even now is the power that Paul will wield on his next visit to Corinth (that is, "by God's power we will live toward you").

Paul Calls for Congregational Self-Examination (13:5-11) Paul challenges the Corinthians, in preparation for his visit, to *examine [themselves] to see whether [they] are in the faith* (v. 5). In the Greek *yourselves* is placed first for emphasis: *"yourselves,* examine." *Examine* translates a verb that normally means "tempt" (*peirazō;* 1 Cor 7:5; Gal 6:1; 1 Thess 3:5). But here, as in 1 Corinthians 10:9, it denotes "test." The Corinthians have put Paul to the test. He has complied (11:16—

13:4 Rudolf Bultmann rightly observes that the *kai gar . . . kai gar* structure of verse 4 makes little sense in the immediate context (1976:243). Most translations drop the second *gar* (as in NIV's *for to be sure, he . . . likewise, we*). Jan Lambrecht's proposal that the first

12:6), and now it is their turn.

The kind of testing Paul envisions is that which proves the worth or genuineness of something (*dokimazō;* compare 2 Cor 2:9; 8:8, 22; 9:13). In this case it is the Corinthians' *faith* that is to be proven. *Pistis* in this context denotes profession. The Corinthians have professed a belief in Christ, but does their life match their profession? If the life of the congregation is not in conformity with the truths of the gospel, it negates any claim to standing firm in the faith (1 Cor 16:13). The challenge sounds foreboding. Yet true profession should issue in a life characterized by "love, joy, peace, patience, kindness, goodness, faithfulness, gentleness and self-control" (Gal 5:22). From all appearances, the Corinthians, on Paul's return, will be found wanting on virtually every count.

Of course, such testing requires that the Corinthians possess the wherewithal to recognize Christ's presence among them. Paul's sarcasm (which is lost in the NIV translation) comes to the fore: "Or can you not even recognize that Jesus Christ is in your midst?" (v. 5). The verb "to recognize" (NIV *realize*) means "to know fully enough to be able to act on that knowledge" *(epi + ginōskō).* Perhaps the Corinthians' perceptions have become so skewed that they no longer possess the ability to recognize Christ's presence in the community—in which case they stand the real possibility of *failing the test. Adokimos* denotes that which has been tested and found to be counterfeit. The very fact that the Corinthians are demanding proof that Christ is speaking through Paul would suggest that they are out of touch with genuine evidences of the Spirit's work in the community.

Yet if the Corinthians have their spiritual wits about them, they *will discover that* Paul "is not counterfeit" (NIV *have not failed the test)*—at least he *trust[s]* (or, better, "hopes" *[elpizō])* that this will be the case (v. 6). Paul gets a little ahead of himself. We would expect *unless, of course, you fail the test* (v. 5) to be followed by the hope and expectation that the Corinthians will indeed pass. Instead, his wish is that in their self-examination he will not be judged a fake. The verb is in the future

kai modifies the entire clause ("for indeed") and the second *kai* modifies *hēmeis* ("for we too") is a credible solution (1985:263-68). Paul's conviction would then be that out of Christ's death and resurrection life come both his own weakness and his apostolic power.

tense: *I trust that you will discover.* The idea is that as they examine themselves and find themselves to be genuine Christians, they will be led, in turn, to evaluate Paul and see that he also has passed the test.

Paul shifts at this point to the first-person plural and includes his associates *(that we have not failed)*. This is to remind the church that the work at Corinth was and continues to be a team effort. So to question Paul's authenticity is to question the authenticity of the team effort (that is, Paul, Silas, Timothy and Titus). And to question the authenticity of the team effort is to put the authenticity of the Corinthian community in jeopardy. Paul, however, has met and exceeded all the tests of a true apostle, and he hopes that the Corinthians will have enough integrity to admit that (Murphy-O'Connor 1991:134). This may be hard for them to do. If they affirm Paul's standing as an apostle (as they must, if they affirm their own Christian standing), then they must accept Paul and reject the intruders.

In the final analysis, however, what matters to Paul is that they *will do what is right*—even if it means that his work at Corinth *may seem to have failed* (v. 7). Not that Paul expected to fail the test. But such a price would be worth paying if it guaranteed that the Corinthians would do the *right* thing. The Greek term *kalos* denotes what is beautiful, noble and honorable. As Christians we are called to live in a way that commands the respect and esteem of those around us—and Paul asks no less of the Corinthians (Beyreuther 1976:102-3). In fact, he makes it his *prayer to God.* It would be far worse if they "do what is wrong" just so that Paul and his coworkers might appear approved. The NIV translation *do wrong* is somewhat weak. The Greek term actually means to "do what is evil" *(kakos)*—that is, what is morally reprehensible in the eyes of others. A somewhat similar thought is found in Sirach 4:21: "There is shame which brings sin and there is a shame which is glory and favor." Christians should not be afraid of offending others so long as they do what is right.

Even if Paul's work at Corinth should appear to be discredited, the fact of the matter is that he *cannot do anything against the truth, but*

13:7 It is possible from a grammatical standpoint to construe *hymas* in verse 7 as the object of *poiēsai.* Paul would then be praying that neither God nor he himself would have to hurt the Corinthians ("we pray that we may not have to hurt you"). However, since

only for the truth (v. 8). Verse 8 has the ring of a familiar saying—somewhat like our "truth marches on." The idea of fighting or striving for truth was a traditional theme in the wisdom literature of Paul's day. "Never speak against the truth but be mindful of your ignorance," stated the noted teacher Jesus ben Sirach (Sirach 5:25). He also told his students to "strive even to death for the truth and the Lord God will fight for you" (v. 28). Not to speak against the truth implies choice. Paul, however, has no choice; he says that he *cannot do anything against the truth.* The *truth* here is undoubtedly the gospel or the truths that the gospel embodies. Just as Christ's sacrificial love compels Paul to preach the gospel (5:14), so too his commissioning as Christ's apostle hems him in to doing only what advances the gospel.

Paul concludes by restating that his task at Corinth is to produce strength: *We are glad whenever we are weak but you are strong* (v. 9). The claim *you are strong* is made somewhat tongue in cheek. The Corinthians would certainly think of themselves as strong. They have been enriched in speech and knowledge (1 Cor 1:5); they do not lack any spiritual gift (1 Cor 1:7); they are already kings (1 Cor 4:8); they already are so wise in Christ (1 Cor 4:10). But Paul means something different by the term *strong.* For the Corinthians to be strong means that they are firm in faith (v. 5) and of one mind and heart (v. 11). And if their strength can be achieved only through his weakness, then Paul will gladly bear the label "timid" (10:1); for this means that he will not have to assert the strength of his apostolic authority against them when he returns (Bruce 1971:254).

Paul prays not only that they will do no wrong (v. 7) but also for their *perfection* (v. 9). The basic meaning of the noun *katartisis* is to "make suitable or fitting" for a particular task, not to "make perfect" as the NIV, TEV and JB translate (Schippers 1978:350). "That all may be put right with you" (NEB) or "be put in order" (Liddell, Scott and Jones 1978) catches the sense. The Corinthians have a great deal to put in order before they can set about the task of serving God.

This is why I write these things when I am absent, Paul says (v. 10).

---

hymeis is the subject in the second half of verse 7, *hymas* in the first part of verse 7 should be understood similarly: "We pray that *you* not do what is evil but that *you* do what is honorable" (virtually all modern translations).

A reference to writing signaled to the reader in Paul's day that the writer was drawing matters to a close. It also provided a final opportunity to state the purpose of writing. His purpose, Paul reminds the Corinthians, is *that when I come I may not have to be harsh in my use of authority*—that is, his motivation is essentially pastoral. Paul was not one to show his authority for the sake of showing it (Barclay 1954:267)—a temptation that leaders in any organization constantly face. The exercise of authority in the church must have as its aim *building up*, not *tearing down;* otherwise it is power in its most abusive form.

This is the third time Paul has made this point in chapters 10—13 (10:8; 12:19). No doubt he wants the Corinthians to be very clear that he is not out to take advantage of them or slap them around, as his rivals are prone to do (11:20). But there is also a veiled warning in his statement. Although he is not in the business of tearing down, sometimes demolition is a necessary prelude to rebuilding. And demolish Paul will do, if it is the only way to ensure a sound structure.

Paul follows the reminder of his purpose in writing with a last word of exhortation (v. 11)—a typical feature of the closing section of the letter body. *Finally, brothers, good-by. Aim for perfection, listen to my appeal, be of one mind, live in peace.* This is the only time Paul addresses the Corinthians as "dear friends" in these four chapters (*adelphoi* is the generic term in Greek for "people" or "friends" and should not be translated *brothers* as in the NIV). To do so now is to acknowledge his solidarity with them (Furnish 1984:581).

The series of five exhortations in this verse focuses on congregational unity and harmony—the very thing that the Corinthians are lacking. At first glance, the imperative *chairete* would look to the Greek reader like the typical form of greeting given at the close of a letter: *good-by* (NIV, TEV), "farewell" (KJV, NEB, RSV). Paul, however, uses the term more often than not with the sense "rejoice" or "be glad" (as in Phil 4:4; 1 Thess 5:16). Coming at the head of what quite obviously is a series of exhortations, "be happy" (JB, LB) or "cheer up" (Phillips) is the better fit.

13:11 A concluding exhortation is common in the body-closing materials of Paul's letters. See, for example, "be on your guard; stand firm in the faith; be men of courage; be strong" (1 Cor 16:13).

The basic meaning of the noun *katartizō* is to "make suitable or fitting" for a particular

Paul's second command is "mend your ways" (RSV, NEB), not the NIV *aim for perfection* (*katartizesthe;* see the commentary on v. 9). He has already said he is praying that they will be able to set matters in order at Corinth. Now he puts it in the form of a command.

It is difficult to pin down Paul's third command. The verb *parakaleō* can mean to encourage or to exhort, and the voice can be passive ("be exhorted" [that is, listen to my appeal], "be encouraged") or middle ("encourage one another"; "exhort one another"). Paul stresses throughout the chapter that he expects the Corinthians to take action prior to his return; thus the middle is preferable and the meaning "exhort" is the logical one in the context. Paul may be thinking of persistent sins at Corinth and how the task of correction is not the sole prerogative of the apostle or pastor. It is a responsibility that we have toward one another as members of Christ's body—a truth that the Corinthians have been loath to acknowledge (as in 1 Cor 5:1-2, "a man has his father's wife. And you are proud!").

Paul's fourth command is literally "Think the same thing" *(to auto phroneite)*. One suspects this would be a tall order for the Corinthian congregation.

The final exhortation, *live in peace,* can be carried out only if the other four are in place. Only one other time does Paul exhort a church to pursue that which leads to peace (Rom 14:19)—although he does pass along a wish for peace to the Galatian (Gal 6:16) and Ephesian (Eph 6:23) churches.

If they do these things, Paul states, *the God of love and peace will be with you* (v. 11). A peace benediction is the way Paul normally closes the body of his letters (see Rom 15:33; 16:20; Eph 6:23; Phil 4:9; 1 Thess 5:23; 2 Thess 3:16). Quite often the wish for peace comes, as here, after a series of exhortations (as in Rom 16:17-19; Phil 4:8; 1 Thess 5:12-22; 2 Thess 3:14-15). What is unusual about this peace wish is the addition of love *(the God of love and peace will be with you)*. Ephesians is the only other letter where Paul closes in this

---

task, not to *aim for perfection* as the NIV translates (see the commentary on v. 9). "Mend your ways" (RSV, NEB) catches the sense. *Katartizesthe* could be passive ("be mended"), but the middle ("mend your ways") fits the context better.

fashion. Both love and peace are fruits of the Holy Spirit (Gal 5:22). Paul probably includes them at this juncture to point the Corinthians to the divine resources available to help them fulfill the previous commands (compare "May God himself, the God of peace, sanctify you through and through," 1 Thess 5:23). To be sure, love and peace are two resources most needed in a fractured congregation like that at Corinth.

Paul usually includes mention of an upcoming visit—either his own or that of a coworker—in the closing section of the body of his letters. It is also typical for him to express confidence that his readers will do as they have been asked (for example, "confident of your obedience," Philem 21). Yet the omission of both elements at the close of 2 Corinthians is not surprising (Doty 1973:36-37). Paul has informed the Corinthians twice in chapters 10—13 (12:14; 13:1) that he is ready to visit them for the third time. Then too, an expression of confidence would hardly be appropriate after the challenge Paul has put before them in the earlier verses (12:19—13:9).

☐ **Closing Exhortation and Greetings (13:12-13)**
"Give my greetings to so and so" is a typical way we close our letters today. It was the same in Paul's day. The greeting had a twofold purpose in the Hellenistic letter. It was used to mark the transition from the body of the letter to its close, and it served to strengthen the relationship between the writer and the reader.

The greetings in 2 Corinthians are quite brief. First, Paul asks the Corinthians to *greet one another with a holy kiss*—a familiar request, although the origin of the custom escapes us (see also Rom 16:16; 1 Cor 16:20; 1 Thess 5:26; 1 Pet 5:14). *Kiss (philēma)* comes from the Greek word for "friend" *(philos)*—a person to whom one is under a basic

---

13:12 Paul's standard closing conventions include greetings and a benediction. Other common conventions are a greeting written in his own hand (1 Cor 16:21; Gal 6:11; Col 4:18; 2 Thess 3:17), mention of the secretary's name (Rom 16:22), identification of the carrier (Eph 6:21; Col 4:7-9), a command to pass along the letter to another church (Col 4:16) and a charge to have the letter read (1 Thess 5:27).
13:13(14) There is a discrepancy in versification among translations. In some chapter 13 has a total of fourteen verses, while in others it has only thirteen verses. The UBS and Nestlé-Aland Greek editions have thirteen verses. The difference comes at verse 12, where *Greet one another with a holy kiss. All the saints send their greetings* is either kept as a single

obligation. It was both a friendly sign of greeting and a token of farewell (Günther 1976:547-49). Friends in the early church gave one another a kiss as a sign of the bond they shared in Christ. It was not the intimate caress that we think of today. A public kiss of this sort was not given on the mouth but on the cheek, forehead, eyes, shoulders, foot or, especially, on the hand (Stählin 1974:120-21). In the second place, *all the saints* send their greetings. From earlier verses in the letter it is clear that Paul is somewhere in the province of Macedonia (9:1-5). But he does not tell his readers exactly where.

We want to be careful not to read too much into the fact that Paul does not give further greetings. In letters to churches that he knew well, he tended to conclude with the most general of greetings. It was to churches that he did not know personally, like the churches at Rome and Colossae, that he sent and solicited detailed greetings (Rom 16:1-23; Col 4:7-15). The reason for this is easy to see. There would be a tendency to keep greetings to a familiar church brief and general so as not to give offense to anyone whose name might be accidentally left off the list. When Paul was writing to an unfamiliar church, however, specific greetings would be an important bridging device.

All of Paul's letters, in common with Hellenistic letters of the day, conclude with a wish for the well-being of his readers—somewhat like our "take care." In the Hellenistic letter, "fare thee well," which combined a goodby and a wish for good health, was pretty much standard. Paul's closing wish, on the other hand, has a decidedly spiritual focus, and he concludes virtually every letter in the same fashion: "The grace of our Lord Jesus Christ be with you all." Second Corinthians, however, is distinctive in two respects. The usual benediction is expanded to include all three members of the Trinity, and the *grace* wish is coupled with an

verse (as in TEV, JB, NJB, RSV) or divided into two verses (as in KJV, RV, ASV, RSV, NIV, NEB, REB). Furnish notes that a fourteen-verse chapter appears to have originated with the second folio edition of the Bishops' Bible (the basic version for the King James translation), published in 1572 (1984:583).

The role of the Spirit in bringing about unity in the body of Christ is a familiar idea in Paul's writings. For example, it is the central thought of 1 Corinthians 12:13, "For we were all baptized by one Spirit into one body—whether Jews or Greeks, slave or free—and we were all given the one Spirit to drink," and of Ephesians 4:3, "Do your best to preserve the unity which the Spirit gives, by the peace that binds you together" (TEV).

additional wish for *love* and *fellowship*—a triad that is unique in Paul's letters. The result is a series of three genitive constructions without parallel in the New Testament: *The grace of the Lord Jesus Christ, and the love of God, and the fellowship of the Holy Spirit be with you all. The grace* of Christ has already been defined: "Though he was rich, yet for your sakes he became poor, so that you through his poverty might become rich" (8:9). *The love of God* is a phrase that is strangely absent from Paul's other letters. Coming after *the grace of the Lord Jesus Christ,* it recalls the concrete demonstration of God's love in sending his Son so that he might redeem and reconcile us to himself. Coming before *the fellowship of the Holy Spirit,* it leads us to think of the love that "God has poured . . . into our hearts by the Holy Spirit, whom he has given us" (Rom 5:5).

The main difficulty in verse 13 is in deciphering the final genitive construction, *the fellowship of the Holy Spirit.* Is Paul thinking of our participation in or partnership with the Spirit (objective genitive)? Or does he have in mind the fellowship we have with one another that the Spirit brings about (subjective genitive)? Most modern translations maintain the ambiguity: *the fellowship of the Holy Spirit.* The others are equally divided (as in "the fellowship that is ours in the Holy Spirit," Phillips; "fellowship in the Holy Spirit," NEB). Since Corinthian reconciliation with one another (12:20) and with Paul (6:1—7:2) is the foremost concern of this letter, the subjective genitive provides the best fit. Moreover, it is the activity of the Spirit, rather than our participation in the Spirit, that is highlighted throughout 2 Corinthians.

What better way to end the letter than by pointing to the perfect model of "congregational" unity—the unity of Father, Son and Holy Spirit! So Paul's concluding benediction is more than a theological flourish. The order "Christ's grace," "God's love" and "the Holy Spirit's fellowship" is eminently practical. Through Christ's gift of himself we experience, in the most concrete terms, God's love for us and the Spirit's power to fashion us into a oneness that serves as a beacon of hope in a fragmented and broken world.

Bibliography

Allo, Ernest-
Bernard
1956   *Seconde epître aux Corinthiens.* Paris: J. Gabalda.

Bain, John A.
1906-1907 "2 Cor 4:3-4." *Expository Times* 18:380.

Baird, William
1985   "Visions, Revelation and Ministry: Reflections on 2 Cor
      12:1-5 and Gal 1:11-17." *Journal of Biblical Literature*
      10:651-62.

Balz, Horst, and
Gerhard Schneider,
eds.
1990   *Exegetical Dictionary of the New Testament.* Grand Rapids,
      Mich.: Eerdmans.

Barclay, William
1954   *The Letters to the Corinthians.* Philadelphia: Westminster
      Press.

Barnett, Paul W.
1988   *The Message of 2 Corinthians: Power in Weakness.* The
      Bible Speaks Today. Leicester, U.K./Downers Grove, Ill.:
      InterVarsity Press.

Barré, Michael L.
1980   "Qumran and the 'Weakness' of Paul." *Catholic Biblical
      Quarterly* 42:216-27.

Barrett, C. K.
1969   "Titus." In *Neotestamentica et Semitica,* pp. 1-14. Edin-
      burgh: T & T Clark.

1970   " Ὁ ᾿ΑΔΙΚΗΣΑΣ (2. Cor 7,12)." In *Verborum Veritas,* pp.
      149-57. Wuppertal, Germany: Brockhaus.

1973   *The Second Epistle to the Corinthians.* New York: Harper
      & Row.

Batey, Richard
1963   "Paul's Bride Image." *Interpretation* 17:176-82.

Bauckham, Richard
1982   "Weakness: Paul's and Ours." *Themelios* 7:4-6.

Bauder, Wolfgang
1976   "πραΰς." In *New International Dictionary of New Testament Theology*, 2:256-59. Edited by Colin Brown. 3 vols. Grand Rapids, Mich.: Zondervan.

1978   "παράπτωμα." In *New International Dictionary of New Testament Theology*, 3:585-86. Edited by Colin Brown. 3 vols. Grand Rapids, Mich.: Zondervan.

Bauer, Walter,
William F. Arndt
and F. William
Gingrich
1979   *A Greek-English Lexicon of the New Testament and Other Early Christian Literature*. Revised ed. Translated by Frederick W. Danker. Chicago: University of Chicago Press.

Bauernfeind, Otto
1964   "ἁπλοῦς, ἁπλότης." In *Theological Dictionary of the New Testament*, 1:386-87. Edited by Gerhard Kittel and Gerhard Friedrich. 10 vols. Grand Rapids, Mich.: Eerdmans.

1967   "μάχομαι κτλ." In *Theological Dictionary of the New Testament*, 4:527-28. Edited by Gerhard Kittel and Gerhard Friedrich. 10 vols. Grand Rapids, Mich.: Eerdmans.

Beale, Gregory K.
1989   "The Old Testament Background of Reconciliation in 2 Corinthians 5—7 and Its Bearing on the Literary Problem of 2 Corinthians 6.14—7.1." *New Testament Studies* 35:550-81.

Becker, Oswald
1975   "πείθομαι." In *New International Dictionary of New Testament Theology*, 1:588-93. Edited by Colin Brown. 3 vols. Grand Rapids, Mich.: Zondervan.

Behm, Johannes
1965   "κυρόω κτλ." In *Theological Dictionary of the New Testament*, 3:1098-1100. Edited by Gerhard Kittel and Gerhard Friedrich. 10 vols. Grand Rapids, Mich.: Eerdmans.

Belleville, Linda L.
1986   " 'Under Law': Structural Analysis and the Pauline Concept of Law in Galatians 3:21—4:11." *Journal for the Study of*

the New Testament 26:53-78.

1987　　　　　"Continuity or Discontinuity? A Fresh Look at 1 Corinthians in the Light of First-Century Epistolary Forms and Conventions." *Evangelical Quarterly* 59:15-37.

1989　　　　　"A Letter of Apologetic Self-Commendation: 2 Cor. 1:8—7:16." *Novum Testamentum* 31, no. 2: 142-64.

1991　　　　　*Reflections of Glory: Paul's Polemical Use of the Moses-Doxa Tradition in 2 Corinthians 3. Journal for the Study of the New Testament* Supplement 52. Sheffield, U.K.: Sheffield Academic Press.

1993a　　　　"Authority." In *Dictionary of Paul and His Letters,* pp. 54-59. Edited by Gerald Hawthorne, Ralph P. Martin and Daniel Reid. Downers Grove, Ill.: InterVarsity Press.

1993b　　　　"Tradition or Creation? Paul's Use of the Exodus 34 Tradition in 2 Corinthians 3:7-18." In *Paul and the Scriptures of Israel.* Edited by Craig A. Evans and James A. Sanders. *Journal for the Study of the New Testament* Supplement 83; Studies in Scripture and Early Judaism Series 1. Sheffield, U.K.: Sheffield Academic Press.

1994　　　　　"Canon of the New Testament." In *Foundations for Biblical Interpretation,* pp. 374-95. Edited by David S. Dockery, K. A. Mathews and R. B. Sloan. Nashville: Broadman & Holman, 1994.

1995　　　　　"Paul's Polemic and Theology of the Spirit in 2 Corinthians." *Catholic Biblical Quarterly* (forthcoming).

Bertram, Georg
1972　　　　　"ὕψος κτλ." In *Theological Dictionary of the New Testament,* 8:602-20. Edited by Gerhard Kittel and Gerhard Friedrich. 10 vols. Grand Rapids, Mich.: Eerdmans.

Best, Ernest
1986　　　　　"II Corinthians 4:7-15: Life Through Death." *Irish Biblical Studies* 8:2-7.

Betz, Hans Dieter
1969　　　　　"Eine Christus-Aretalogie bei Paulus (2 Cor 12,7-10)." *Zeitschrift für Theologie und Kirche* 66:288-305.

1985　　　　　*2 Corinthians 8—9.* Hermeneia. Philadelphia: Fortress.

Betz, Otto

1976   "δύναμις." In *New International Dictionary of New Testament Theology*, 2:601-6. Edited by Colin Brown. 3 vols. Grand Rapids, Mich.: Zondervan.

Beyreuther, Erich

1976   "καλός." In *New International Dictionary of New Testament Theology*, 2:102-5. Edited by Colin Brown. 3 vols. Grand Rapids, Mich.: Zondervan.

Bietenhard, Hans

1976   "οὐρανός." In *New International Dictionary of New Testament Theology*, 2:188-96. Edited by Colin Brown. 3 vols. Grand Rapids, Mich.: Zondervan.

Bietenhard, Hans,
   and Colin Brown

1976   "παράδεισος." In *New International Dictionary of New Testament Theology*, 2:760-64. Edited by Colin Brown. 3 vols. Grand Rapids, Mich.: Zondervan.

Bishop, Eric F. F.

1965   "The 'Why' of Sleepless Nights." *Evangelical Quarterly* 37:29-31.

1966   "In Famine and Drought." *Evangelical Quarterly* 38:169-71.

Blass, F.,
A. Debrunner and
Robert W. Funk

1961   *A Greek Grammar of the New Testament*. Chicago: University of Chicago Press.

Böcher, Otto

1990   "Beliar." In *Exegetical Dictionary of the New Testament*, 1:212. Edited by Horst Balz and Gerhard Schneider. Grand Rapids, Mich: Eerdmans.

Bornkamm,
   Günther

1961-1962   "The History of the Origin of the So-Called Second Letter to the Corinthians." *New Testament Studies* 8:258-64.

Bratcher,
   Robert G.

1983   *A Translator's Guide to Paul's Second Letter to the Corinthians*. New York: United Bible Societies.

Brown, F.,
S. R. Driver and
C. A. Briggs
1953   *Hebrew and English Lexicon of the Old Testament.* Oxford:
              Clarendon.

Bruce, F. F.
1971   *I and II Corinthians.* Grand Rapids, Mich.: Eerdmans.

Büchsel, Hermann
1964a   "γνήσιος." In *Theological Dictionary of the New Testament,*
              1:727. Edited by Gerhard Kittel and Gerhard Friedrich.
              10 vols. Grand Rapids, Mich.: Eerdmans.

1964b   "ἐριθεία." In *Theological Dictionary of the New Testament,*
              2:660-61. Edited by Gerhard Kittel and Gerhard
              Friedrich. 10 vols. Grand Rapids, Mich.: Eerdmans.

1965   "κρίνω κτλ." In *Theological Dictionary of the New Testa-
              ment,* 3:921-23, 933-54. Edited by Gerhard Kittel and
              Gerhard Friedrich. 10 vols. Grand Rapids, Mich.: Eerdmans.

Bultmann, Rudolf
1985   *The Second Letter to the Corinthians.* Minneapolis: Augs-
              burg.

Carpus
[Samuel Cox]
1876   "The Strength of Weakness." *Expositor's,* 1st ser., 3:161-84.

Carrez, Maurice
1986   *La deuxième epître de saint Paul aux Corinthiens.* Geneva:
              Labor et Fides.

Carson, D. A.
1984   *From Triumphalism to Maturity.* Grand Rapids, Mich:
              Baker Book House.

Cassidy, R.
1971   "Paul's Attitude to Death in II Corinthians 5:1-10." *Evangel-
              ical Quarterly* 43:210-17.

Collange, J. F.
1972   *Enigmes de la deuxième epître de Paul aux Corinthiens:
              Études exégetique de 2 Cor 2.14-7.4.* Society for New
              Testament Studies Monograph Series 18. Cambridge:
              Cambridge University Press.

Colson, Charles,
  and Ellen Santilli
  Vaughn
1992   "Welcome to McChurch." *Christianity Today* 36:28-32.

Craddock, Fred B.
1968   "The Poverty of Christ: An Investigation of II Corinthians
                 8:9." *Interpretation* 22:158-70.
Cranfield, C. E. B.
1965   "Minister and Congregation in the Light of II Corinthians
                 4:5-7: An Exposition." *Interpretation* 19:163-67.

1989   "The Grace of Our Lord Jesus Christ." *Communio
                 Viatorum* 32:105-9.
Dahl, Nils A.
1977   *Studies in Paul: Theology for the Early Christian Mission.*
                 Minneapolis: Augsburg.
Dahn, Karl
1978   "ὁράω." In *New International Dictionary of New Testa-
                 ment Theology,* 3:511-18. Edited by Colin Brown. 3 vols.
                 Grand Rapids, Mich.: Zondervan.
Danker, Frederick
1989   *II Corinthians.* Minneapolis: Augsburg.

Davies, Samuel
1868   "Remarks on the Second Epistle to the Corinthians 4:3-4."
                 Bibliotheca Sacra 25:23-30.
Deissmann, Adolf
1923   *Bible Studies.* Reprint ed. Winona Lake, Ind.: Alpha.

Delling, Gerhard
1971   "σκόλοψ." In *Theological Dictionary of the New Testament,*
                 7:409-13. Edited by Gerhard Kittel and Gerhard Friedrich.
                 10 vols. Grand Rapids, Mich.: Eerdmans.

1972   "τέλος κτλ." In *Theological Dictionary of the New Testa-
                 ment,* 8:49-87. Edited by Gerhard Kittel and Gerhard
                 Friedrich. 10 vols. Grand Rapids, Mich.: Eerdmans.
Denney, James
1900   *The Second Epistle to the Corinthians.* 2nd ed. New York:
                 A. C. Armstrong & Son.
Derrett, J. D. M.
1978   "2 Cor 6,14ff.: A Midrash on Dt 22,10." *Biblica* 59:231-50.

Doty, William G.
1973   *Letters in Primitive Christianity*. Philadelphia: Fortress.

Douglas, J. D., ed.
1982   *New Bible Dictionary*. 2nd ed. Downers Grove, Ill: Inter-
               Varsity Press.
Duff, P. B.
1991a   "Apostolic Suffering and the Language of Processions in
               2 Corinthians 4:7-10." *Biblical Theology Bulletin* 2:158-65.

1991b   "Metaphor, Motif and Meaning: The Rhetorical Strategy
               Behind the Image 'Led in Triumph' in 2 Corinthians 2:14."
               Catholic Biblical Quarterly 53:79-92.
Egan, R. B.
1977   "Lexical Evidence on Two Pauline Passages." *Novum Testa-
               mentum* 19:34-62.
Eichler, Johannes
1978   "λογίζομαι." In *New International Dictionary of New Testa-
               ment Theology*, 3:822-26. Edited by Colin Brown. 3 vols.
               Grand Rapids, Mich.: Zondervan.
Fahy, Thomas
1964   "St. Paul's 'Boasting' and 'Weakness.' " *Irish Theological
               Quarterly* 31:214-27.
Fallon, Francis T.
1980   *2 Corinthians*. Wilmington, Del.: Michael Glazier.

Feinberg,
   Charles L.
1976   "Tithe." In *Zondervan Pictorial Encyclopedia of the Bible*,
               5:756-58. Edited by Merrill C. Tenney. Grand Rapids, Mich.:
               Zondervan.
Fischer, Fred
1975   *Commentary on 1 and 2 Corinthians*. Waco, Tex.: Word.

Foerster, Werner
1964   "ἁρπάζω, ἁρπαγμός." In *Theological Dictionary of the
               New Testament*, 1:472-74. Edited by Gerhard Kittel and
               Gerhard Friedrich. 10 vols. Grand Rapids, Mich.: Eerd-
               mans.
Foreman,
   Kenneth J.
1961   *The Second Letter of Paul to the Corinthians*. Richmond,
               Va.: John Knox.

Fuchs, Ernst
1971 "σκοπός κτλ." In *Theological Dictionary of the New Testament*, 7:413-16. Edited by Gerhard Kittel and Gerhard Friedrich. 10 vols. Grand Rapids, Mich.: Eerdmans.

Furnish,
Victor Paul
1984 *II Corinthians*. New York: Doubleday.

Georgi, Dieter
1986 *The Opponents of Paul in Second Corinthians*. Philadelphia: Fortress.

Glasson, T. F.
1990 "2 Corinthians v.1-10 Versus Platonism." *Scottish Journal of Theology* 43:145-55.

Goetzmann, Jürgen
1975 "μετάνοια." In *New International Dictionary of New Testament Theology*, 1:357-59. Edited by Colin Brown. 3 vols. Grand Rapids, Mich.: Zondervan.

Goppelt, Leonhard
1968 "πίνω κτλ." In *Theological Dictionary of the New Testament*, 6:135-60. Edited by Gerhard Kittel and Gerhard Friedrich. 10 vols. Grand Rapids, Mich.: Eerdmans.

Goudge, Henry L.
1927 *The Second Epistle to the Corinthians*. London: Methuen.

Grundmann,
Walter
1964a "δέχομαι κτλ." In *Theological Dictionary of the New Testament*, 2:50-59. Edited by Gerhard Kittel and Gerhard Friedrich. 10 vols. Grand Rapids, Mich.: Eerdmans.

1964b "ἀναγκάζω κτλ." In *Theological Dictionary of the New Testament*, 1:344-47. Edited by Gerhard Kittel and Gerhard Friedrich. 10 vols. Grand Rapids, Mich.: Eerdmans.

1964c "δῆμος κτλ." In *Theological Dictionary of the New Testament*, 2:63-65. Edited by Gerhard Kittel and Gerhard Friedrich. 10 vols. Grand Rapids, Mich.: Eerdmans.

Guhrt, Joachim
1975 "διαθήκη." In *New International Dictionary of New Testament Theology*, 1:365-72. Edited by Colin Brown. 3 vols. Grand Rapids, Mich.: Zondervan.

Günther, Walther
1976   "φιλέω." In *New International Dictionary of New Testament
                Theology, 2:547-49. Edited by Colin Brown. 3 vols. Grand
                Rapids, Mich.: Zondervan.
1978   "ἀδικία." In *New International Dictionary of New Testa-
                ment Theology*, 3:573-76. Edited by Colin Brown. 3 vols.
                Grand Rapids, Mich.: Zondervan.
Gutbrod, Walter
1965   " Ἰουδαῖος κτλ." In *Theological Dictionary of the New Testa-
                ment*, 3:369-91. Edited by Gerhard Kittel and Gerhard
                Friedrich. 10 vols. Grand Rapids, Mich.: Eerdmans.

Haarbeck, Hermann,
Hans-Georg Link
and Colin Brown
1976   "καινός." In *New International Dictionary of New Testa-
                ment Theology*, 2:670-73. Edited by Colin Brown. 3 vols.
                Grand Rapids, Mich.: Zondervan.
Hafemann, Scott
1989   "The Comfort and Power of the Gospel: The Argument of
                2 Corinthians 1—3." *Review and Expositor* 86:325-44.

1990   *Suffering and Ministry in the Spirit*. Grand Rapids, Mich.:
                Eerdmans.
Hahn, Hans-
Christoph
1975   "συνείδησις." In *New International Dictionary of New
                Testament Theology*, 1:348-51. Edited by Colin Brown. 3
                vols. Grand Rapids, Mich.: Zondervan.

1976   "φῶς." In *New International Dictionary of New Testament
                Theology, 2:490-95. Edited by Colin Brown. 3 vols. Grand
                Rapids, Mich.: Zondervan.

1978a   "ἐργάζομαι." In *New International Dictionary of New
                Testament Theology*, 3:1147-52. Edited by Colin Brown. 3
                vols. Grand Rapids, Mich.: Zondervan.

1978b   "ζῆλος." In *New International Dictionary of New Testa-
                ment Theology*, 3:1166-68. Edited by Colin Brown. 3 vols.
                Grand Rapids, Mich.: Zondervan.
Hanson, Bradley
1981   "School of Suffering." *Dialog* 20:39-45.

Hanson, P. C.
1962   *The Second Epistle to the Corinthians.* London: SCM Press.

Harder, Gunther
1978   "ψυχή." In *New International Dictionary of New Testa-
                ment Theology,* 3:676-86. Edited by Colin Brown. 3 vols.
                Grand Rapids, Mich.: Zondervan.
Harris, Murray J.
1976   *2 Corinthians.* Vol. 10 of *The Expositor's Bible Commen-
                tary.* Edited by Frank E. Gaebelein. Grand Rapids, Mich.:
                Zondervan.

1978a   "*dia.*" In *New International Dictionary of New Testament
                Theology,* 3:1181-84. Edited by Colin Brown. 3 vols. Grand
                Rapids, Mich.: Zondervan.

1978b   "*en.*" In *New International Dictionary of New Testament
                Theology,* 3:1190-93. Edited by Colin Brown. 3 vols. Grand
                Rapids, Mich.: Zondervan.

1978c   "*pros.*" In *New International Dictionary of New Testa-
                ment Theology,* 3:1204-6. Edited by Colin Brown. 3 vols.
                Grand Rapids, Mich.: Zondervan.
Harris, R. L., ed.
1980   *Theological Wordbook of the Old Testament.* 2 vols.
                Chicago: Moody Press.
Hauck, Friedrich
1965   "θησαυρός, θησαυρίζω." In *Theological Dictionary of the
                New Testament,* 3:136-38. Edited by Gerhard Kittel and
                Gerhard Friedrich. 10 vols. Grand Rapids, Mich.: Eerdmans.

1967   "(ὀδύρομαι), ὀδυρμός." In *Theological Dictionary of the
                New Testament,* 5:116. Edited by Gerhard Kittel and Ger-
                hard Friedrich. 10 vols. Grand Rapids, Mich.: Eerdmans.
Hauck, Freidrich,
and Siegfried Schulz
1968   "πραΰς, πραΰτης." In *Theological Dictionary of the New
                Testament,* 6:645-51. Edited by Gerhard Kittel and Gerhard
                Friedrich. 10 vols. Grand Rapids, Mich.: Eerdmans.

Heidland, Hans
Wolfgang
1967a   "λογίζομαι, λογισμός." In *Theological Dictionary of the
                New Testament,* 4:284-92. Edited by Gerhard Kittel and

Gerhard Friedrich. 10 vols. Grand Rapids, Mich.: Eerdmans.

1967b   "ὀχύρωμα." In *Theological Dictionary of the New Testament*, 5:590-91. Edited by Gerhard Kittel and Gerhard Friedrich. 10 vols. Grand Rapids, Mich.: Eerdmans.

1967c   "ὀψώνιον." In *Theological Dictionary of the New Testament*, 5:591-92. Edited by Gerhard Kittel and Gerhard Friedrich. 10 vols. Grand Rapids, Mich.: Eerdmans.

Hemer, Colin
1972   "A Note on 2 Corinthians 1:9." *Tyndale Bulletin* 23:103-7.

1975   "Alexandria Troas." *Tyndale Bulletin* 26:79-112.
1982   "Aretas." In *New Bible Dictionary*, p. 81. Edited by J. D. Douglas. 2nd ed. Downers Grove, Ill: InterVarsity Press.

Héring, Jean
1967   *The Second Epistle of Saint Paul to the Corinthians.* Translated by A. W. Heathcote and P. J. Allcock. London: Epworth.

Hess, Klaus
1978   "λατρεύω." In *New International Dictionary of New Testament Theology*, 3:549-51. Edited by Colin Brown. 3 vols. Grand Rapids, Mich.: Zondervan.

Hofius, Otfried
1976a   "σημεῖον." In *New International Dictionary of New Testament Theology*, 2:626-27. Edited by Colin Brown. 3 vols. Grand Rapids, Mich.: Zondervan.

1976b   "τέρας." In *New International Dictionary of New Testament Theology*, 2:633. Edited by Colin Brown. 3 vols. Grand Rapids, Mich.: Zondervan.

Horst, Johannes
1967   "μακροθυμία κτλ." In *Theological Dictionary of the New Testament*, 4:374-87. Edited by Gerhard Kittel and Gerhard Friedrich. 10 vols. Grand Rapids, Mich.: Eerdmans.

Hughes, Philip E.
1962   *Paul's Second Epistle to the Corinthians.* Grand Rapids, Mich.: Eerdmans.

Judge, Edwin A.
1980   "The Social Identity of the First Christians: A Question of Method in Religious History." *Journal of Religious History* 11:201-17.

1982   "Macedonia." In *New Bible Dictionary*, p. 721. Edited by

Kaiser, Walter
1980

Käsemann, Ernst
1942

Kittel, Gerhard
1964a

1964b

Köster, Helmut
1971

Kruse, Colin G.
1988

Lambrecht, Jan
1985

1989

Lampe, G. W. H.
1967

Laubach, Fritz
1975

Leivestad, R.
1966

J. D. Douglas. 2nd ed. Downers Grove, Ill: InterVarsity Press.

"*bᵉlîya'al.* Worthlessness." In *Theological Wordbook of the Old Testament,* 1:111. Edited by R. L. Harris, Gleason L. Archer and Bruce K. Waltke. Chicago: Moody Press.

"Die Legitimität des Apostels: Eine Untersuchung zu II Korinther 10—13." *Zeitschrift für die neutestamentliche Wissenschaft* 41:33-71.

"αἰχμάλωτος κτλ." In *Theological Dictionary of the New Testament,* 1:195-97. Edited by Gerhard Kittel and Gerhard Friedrich. 10 vols. Grand Rapids, Mich.: Eerdmans.

"ἀρκέω κτλ." In *Theological Dictionary of the New Testament,* 1:464-67. Edited by Gerhard Kittel and Gerhard Friedrich. 10 vols. Grand Rapids, Mich.: Eerdmans.

"συνέχω, συνοχή." In *Theological Dictionary of the New Testament,* 7:877-87. Edited by Gerhard Kittel and Gerhard Friedrich. 10 vols. Grand Rapids, Mich.: Eerdmans.

"The Offender and the Offence in 2 Corinthians 2:5 and 7:12." *Evangelical Quarterly* 88:129-39.

"Philological and Exegetical Notes on 2 Cor 13,4." *Bijdragen* 46:261-69.

"The Favorable Time: A Study of 2 Cor 6,2a in Its Context." In *Vom Urchristentum zu Jesus,* pp. 377-91. Edited by Hubert Frankemölle and Karl Kertelge. Freiburg: Herder.

"Church Discipline and the Interpretation of the Epistles to the Corinthians." In *Christian History and Interpretation,* pp. 337-61. Edited by William R. Farmer, C. F. D. Moule and Richard R. Niebuhr. Cambridge: Cambridge University Press.

"ἐπιστρέφω." In *New International Dictionary of New Testament Theology,* 1:354-55. Edited by Colin Brown. 3 vols. Grand Rapids, Mich.: Zondervan.

" 'The Meekness and Gentleness of Christ': II Cor X.1." *New Testament Studies* 12:156-64.

Lewis, C. S.
1956   *Christian Reflections.* San Diego, Calif.: Harcourt Brace.

Liddell, Henry G.,
Robert Scott and
Henry S. Jones
1978   *A Greek-English Lexicon.* Oxford: Clarendon.

Link, Hans-Georg
1978   "αἰσχύνη." In *New International Dictionary of New Testament Theology,* 3:562-64. Edited by Colin Brown. 3 vols. Grand Rapids, Mich.: Zondervan.

Link, Hans-Georg,
and Johannes
Schattenmann
1978   "καθαρίζω." In *New International Dictionary of New Testament Theology,* 3:102-8. Edited by Colin Brown. 3 vols. Grand Rapids, Mich.: Zondervan.

Lohse, Eduard
1974   "χείρ κτλ." In *Theological Dictionary of the New Testament,* 9:424-37. Edited by Gerhard Kittel and Gerhard Friedrich. 10 vols. Grand Rapids, Mich.: Eerdmans.

Loubser, J. A.
1991   "Exegesis and Proclamation: Winning the Struggle (Or, How to Treat Heretics) (2 Corinthians 12:1-10)." *Journal of Theology for Southern Africa* 75:75-83.

Louw, Johannes P.,
and Eugene
A. Nida
1988-1989   *Greek-English Lexicon of the New Testament.* New York: United Bible Societies.

Macdonald, Donald
1986   "The Price of Poverty." *Review for Religious* 45:3-14.

Malherbe,
Abraham J.
1983   "Antisthenes and Odysseus and Paul at War." *Harvard Theological Review* 76:143-73.

1986   *Moral Exhortation: A Greco-Roman Sourcebook.* Philadelphia: Westminster Press.

Marshal, P.
1983   "A Metaphor of Social Shame: *Thriambeuein* in 2 Cor.

2:14." *Novum Testamentum* 24:302-17.

Martin, Ralph P.
1986   *Second Corinthians*. Word Biblical Commentary. Waco,
            Tex.: Word.

1988   "The Spirit in 2 Corinthians in Light of the 'Fellowship of
            the Holy Spirit' in 2 Corinthians 13:14." In *Eschatology
            and the New Testament*, pp. 113-28. Edited by W. H. Gloer.
            Peabody, Mass.: Hendrickson.

Maurer, Christian
1971   "σκεῦος." In *Theological Dictionary of the New Testament*,
            7:358-67. Edited by Gerhard Kittel and Gerhard Friedrich.
            10 vols. Grand Rapids, Mich.: Eerdmans.

1972   "τίθημι κτλ." In *Theological Dictionary of the New Testa-
            ment*, 8:152-68. Edited by Gerhard Kittel and Gerhard
            Friedrich. 10 vols. Grand Rapids, Mich.: Eerdmans.

McCant, Jerry W.
1988   "Paul's Thorn of Rejected Apostleship." *New Testament
            Studies* 34:550-72.

McClelland,
  Scott E.
1982   " 'Super-Apostles, Servants of Christ, Servants of Satan': A
            Response." *Journal for the Study of the New Testament*
            14:82-87.

McComiskey,
Thomas
1976   "βῆμα." In *New International Dictionary of New Testament
            Theology*, 2:369-70. Edited by Colin Brown. 3 vols. Grand
            Rapids, Mich.: Zondervan.

McGrath, Alister
1995   "Why Evangelicalism Is the Future of Protestantism."
            Christianity Today 39:18-23.

Menzies, Allan
1912   *The Second Epistle of the Apostle Paul to the Corinthians*.
            London: Macmillan.

Merkel,
  Friedemann
1975   "φθείρω." In *New International Dictionary of New Testa-
            ment Theology*, 1:467-70. Edited by Colin Brown. 3 vols.
            Grand Rapids, Mich.: Zondervan.

Metzger, Bruce
1971   *A Textual Commentary on the Greek New Testament*.
            Stuttgart: United Bible Societies.

Michel, Otto
1967   "ὁμολογέω κτλ." In *Theological Dictionary of the New Testament*, 5:199-220. Edited by Gerhard Kittel and Gerhard Friedrich. 10 vols. Grand Rapids, Mich.: Eerdmans.

Mitton, C. Leslie
1958   "Paul's Certainties, Part V: The Gift of the Spirit and Life Beyond Death—2 Corinthians v.1-5." *Expository Times* 69:260-63.

Motyer, J. A.
1975   "Courage, Boldness." In *New International Dictionary of New Testament Theology*, 1:364-65. Edited by Colin Brown. 3 vols. Grand Rapids, Mich.: Zondervan.

Moule, C. F. D.
1959   *An Idiom-Book of New Testament Greek*. Cambridge: Cambridge University Press.

Moulton, Harold K.
1968   "Of." *Bible Translator* 19:18-25.

Moulton, James H., and George Milligan
1930   *The Vocabulary of the Greek Testament*. Reprint ed. Grand Rapids, Mich.: Eerdmans.

Mozley, J. P.
1930-1931   "2 Corinthians 11:12." *Expository Times* 42:212-14.

Muller, Richard A.
1985   *Dictionary of Latin and Greek Theological Terms*. Grand Rapids, Mich.: Baker Book House.

Murphy-O'Connor, Jerome
1985   "Traveling Conditions in the First Century: On the Road and on the Sea with St. Paul." *Bible Review* 1:38-47.

1991   *The Theology of the Second Letter to the Corinthians*. Cambridge: Cambridge University Press.

Nickle, Keith F.
1966   *The Collection*. Naperville, Ill.: Alec R. Allenson.

Nisbet, Patricia
1969   "The Thorn in the Flesh." *Expository Times* 80:126.

Oepke, Albrecht
1964a   "γυμνός κτλ." In *Theological Dictionary of the New Testament*, 1:773-76. Edited by Gerhard Kittel and Gerhard Friedrich. 10 vols. Grand Rapids, Mich.: Eerdmans.

1964b   "ἔκστασις, ἐξίστημι." In *Theological Dictionary of the New Testament*, 2:449-60. Edited by Gerhard Kittel and Gerhard Friedrich. 10 vols. Grand Rapids, Mich.: Eerdmans.

Osei-Bonsu, J.
1986   "Does 2 Cor. 5:1-10 Teach the Reception of the Resurrection Body at the Moment of Death?" *Journal for the Study of the New Testament* 28:81-101.

Packer, J. I.
1973   *Knowing God*. Downers Grove, Ill.: InterVarsity Press.

Park, David M.
1980   "Paul's ΣΚΟΛΟΨ ΤΗ ΣΑΡΚΙ:Thorn or Stake? (2 Cor. XII.7)." *Novum Testamentum* 22:179-83.

Perriman, Andrew
1989   "Between Troas and Macedonia." *Expository Times* 101:39-41.

Plummer, Alfred
1915   *The Second Epistle of St. Paul to the Corinthians*. Edinburgh: T & T Clark.

Rengstorf, Karl Heinrich
1964   "δοῦλος κτλ." In *Theological Dictionary of the New Testament*, 2:261-80. Edited by Gerhard Kittel and Gerhard Friedrich. 10 vols. Grand Rapids, Mich.: Eerdmans.

Robertson, E. H.
1973   *Corinthians 1 and 2*. New York: Macmillan.

Schippers, Reinier
1976   "τέλος." In *New International Dictionary of New Testament Theology*, 2:59-65. Edited by Colin Brown. 3 vols. Grand Rapids, Mich.: Zondervan.

1978   "ἄρτιος." In *New International Dictionary of New Testament Theology*, 3:349-51. Edited by Colin Brown. 3 vols. Grand Rapids, Mich.: Zondervan.

Schlier, Heinrich
1965   "θλίβω, θλῖψις." In *Theological Dictionary of the New Testament*, 3:139-48. Edited by Gerhard Kittel and Gerhard Friedrich. 10 vols. Grand Rapids, Mich.: Eerdmans.

Schönweiss, Hans
1975   "ἐπιθυμία." In *New International Dictionary of New Testament Theology*, 1:456-58. Edited by Colin Brown. 3 vols. Grand Rapids, Mich.: Zondervan.

Sherwin-White,
A. N.
1963   *Roman Society and Roman Law in the New Testament.* Oxford: Oxford University Press.

Siede, Burghard
1978   "ἀρκέω." In *New International Dictionary of New Testament Theology*, 3:726-28. Edited by Colin Brown. 3 vols. Grand Rapids, Mich.: Zondervan.

Smith, Neil G.
1959   "The Thorn That Stayed." *Interpretation* 13:409-16.

Sorg, Theo
1976   "Heart." In *New International Dictionary of New Testament Theology*, 2:180-84. Edited by Colin Brown. 3 vols. Grand Rapids, Mich.: Zondervan.

Stählin, Gustav
1974   "φιλέω κτλ." In *Theological Dictionary of the New Testament*, 9:113-71. Edited by Gerhard Kittel and Gerhard Friedrich. 10 vols. Grand Rapids, Mich.: Eerdmans.

Stambaugh,
John E., and
David L. Balch
1986   *The New Testament in Its Social Environment.* Philadelphia: Westminster Press.

Stern, Ephraim
1976   "War, Warfare." In *Zondervan Pictorial Encyclopedia of the Bible*, 5:898-900. Grand Rapids, Mich: Zondervan.

Stowers, Stanley K.
1990   *"Peri men gar* and the Integrity of 2 Cor. 8 and 9." *Novum Testamentum* 32:340-48.

Stumpff, Otto
1964a   "ζῆλος κτλ." In *Theological Dictionary of the New Testament*, 2:877-88. Edited by Gerhard Kittel and Gerhard Friedrich. 10 vols. Grand Rapids, Mich.: Eerdmans.

1964b   "ζημία, ζημιόω." In *Theological Dictionary of the New Testament*, 2:888-92. Edited by Gerhard Kittel and Gerhard Friedrich. 10 vols. Grand Rapids, Mich.: Eerdmans.

1965   "ἴχνος." In *Theological Dictionary of the New Testament*,
                       3:402-6. Edited by Gerhard Kittel and Gerhard Friedrich.
                       10 vols. Grand Rapids, Mich.: Eerdmans.
Tasker, R. V. G.
1934-1935   "St. Paul and the Earthly Life of Jesus." *Expository Times*
                       46:557-62.

1958   *The Second Epistle of Paul to the Corinthians*. Grand Rap-
                       ids, Mich.: Eerdmans.
Theissen, Gerd
1982   *The Social Setting of Pauline Christianity*. Philadelphia:
                       Fortress.
Thompson, R. J.
1982   "Tithes." In *New Bible Dictionary*, p. 1205. Edited by J. D.
                       Douglas. 2nd ed. Downers Grove, Ill: InterVarsity Press.
Thrall, Margaret E.
1965   *The First and Second Letters of Paul to the Corinthians*.
                       Cambridge: Cambridge University Press.

1994   *The Second Epistle of St. Paul to the Corinthians*, vol. 1.
                       Edinburgh: T & T Clark.
Tolbert, Malcolm
1983   "Theology and Ministry: 2 Corinthians 5:11-21." *Faith and
                       Mission* 1:63-70.
Tozer, A. W.
1961   *The Knowledge of the Holy*. New York: Harper & Row.

Turner, Nigel
1963   *Syntax*. Vol. 3 of *A Grammar of New Testament Greek*.
                       Edited by J. H. Moulton. Edinburgh: T & T Clark.

1976   *Style*. Vol. 4 of *A Grammar of New Testament Greek*.
                       Edited by J. H. Moulton. Edinburgh: T & T Clark.
Von Hodgson,
  Robert
1983   "Paul the Apostle and First Century Tribulation Lists."
                       Zeitschrift für die neutestamentliche Wissenschaft 74:59-80.
Vorländer, Herwart,
  and Colin Brown
1978   "καταλλάσσω." In *New International Dictionary of New
                       Testament Theology*, 3:166-74. Edited by Colin Brown. 3
                       vols. Grand Rapids, Mich.: Zondervan.
Wagner, Guy
1981   "The Tabernacle and Life 'in Christ': Exegesis of 2 Corin-

thians 5.1-10." *Irish Biblical Studies* 3:145-65.

Waldrop, William
1984   "Who Is Responsible and What Is Enough?" In *Supporting World Missions in an Age of Change*, pp. 35-45. Edited by Gail C. Bennett. Wheaton, Ill.: Association of Church Missions Commitees.

Weiss, Johannes
1970   *Earliest Christianity: A History of the Period A.D. 30-150.* Translated by F. C. Grant and P. S. Kramer. 2 vols. Gloucester, Mass.: Peter Smith.

Wells, David
1993   *No Place for Truth.* Grand Rapids, Mich.: Eerdmans.

White, John L.
1972   *The Body of the Greek Letter.* SBL Dissertation Series 2. Missoula, Mont.: Scholars Press.

Wicks, Henry J.
1917-1918   "St. Paul's Teaching as to the Rewards of Liberality." *Expository Times* 29:424-25.

Williams,, David J. W.
1985   *Acts.* San Francisco: Harper & Row.

Willimon, William H.
1993   "I Was Wrong About Christian Schools." *Christianity Today* 37:30-32.

Wright, J. S.
1982   "Marriage." In *New Bible Dictionary,* pp. 742-46. Edited by J. D. Douglas. 2nd ed. Downers Grove, Ill: InterVarsity Press.

Zerwick, Maximilian
1963   *Biblical Greek.* Rome: Pontifical Institute.
1993   *A Grammatical Analysis of the Greek New Testament.* 4th rev. ed. Rome: Biblical Institute Press.